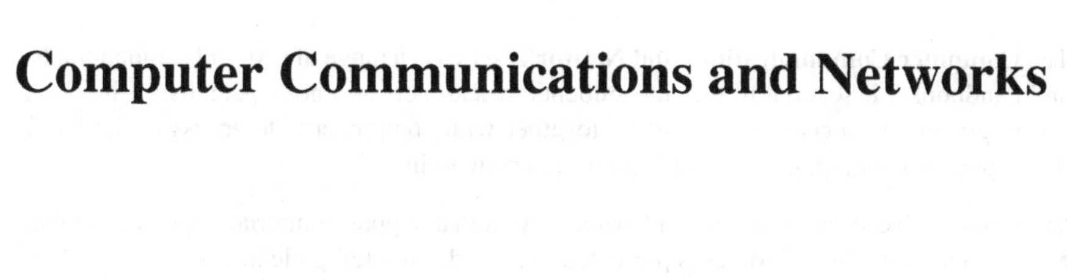

Computer Communications and Networks

For further volumes:
http://www.springer.com/series/4198

The **Computer Communications and Networks** series is a range of textbooks, monographs and handbooks. It sets out to provide students, researchers and non-specialists alike with a sure grounding in current knowledge, together with comprehensible access to the latest developments in computer communications and networking.

Emphasis is placed on clear and explanatory styles that support a tutorial approach, so that even the most complex of topics is presented in a lucid and intelligible manner.

Zaigham Mahmood • Saqib Saeed
Editors

Software Engineering Frameworks for the Cloud Computing Paradigm

Editors
Zaigham Mahmood
School of Computing and Mathematics
University of Derby
Derby, UK

Saqib Saeed
Department of Computer Sciences
Bahria University
Islamabad, Pakistan

Series Editor
A.J. Sammes
Centre for Forensic Computing
Cranfield University
Shrivenham Campus, Swindon, UK

ISSN 1617-7975
ISBN 978-1-4471-6026-7 ISBN 978-1-4471-5031-2 (eBook)
DOI 10.1007/978-1-4471-5031-2
Springer London Heidelberg New York Dordrecht

Printed on acid-free paper

Springer is part of Springer Science+Business Media (www.springer.com)

To
Rehana, Zoya, Imran, Hanya and Ozair
For their love and support

Editors

Dr Zaigham Mahmood

Dr Mahmood is a researcher and author. He has an M.Sc. in Mathematics, M.Sc. in Computer Science and Ph.D. in Modelling of Phase Equilibria. Dr Mahmood is a Senior Technology Consultant at Debesis Education UK, a researcher at the University of Derby UK and Professor Extraordinaire at the North West University in South Africa. He is, currently, also a Foreign Professor at NUST Islamabad Pakistan.

Professor Mahmood has published over 100 articles in international journals and conference proceedings in addition to two reference texts on *e-government* and three books on *cloud computing* viz *Cloud Computing: Concepts, Technology and Design; Cloud Computing for Enterprise Architectures* and *Cloud Computing: Methods and Practical Approaches*. He is also the Editor-in-Chief of the *Journal of E-Government Studies and Best Practices*.

Dr Mahmood is an active researcher; he also serves as editorial board member of several journals, books and conferences; guest editor for journal special issues; organiser and chair of conference tracks and workshops; and keynote speaker at conferences. His research interests encompass subject areas including software engineering, project management, enterprise computing, e-government studies and cloud computing.

Professor Mahmood can be reached at *z.mahmood@debesis.co.uk*. He welcomes your views and comments.

Dr Saqib Saeed

Dr Saqib Saeed is an Assistant Professor in the Computer Science department at Bahria University, Islamabad, Pakistan. He holds a Ph.D. in Information Systems from the University of Siegen, Germany, and a master's degree in Software Technology from Stuttgart University of Applied Sciences, Germany.

Dr Saeed is also a certified Software Quality Engineer from American Society for Quality. He is a member of advisory boards of several international journals besides being guest editor or co-editor of several special issues. Dr Saeed's research interests lie in the areas of software engineering, human-centred computing and computer-supported cooperative work.

Preface

Overview

Software engineering is a well-established discipline for the design and development of large-scale software systems. It is a staged process that follows a software development life cycle (SDLC) consisting of requirements, design and development phases. Many methodologies and frameworks also exist for such developments, and, depending on the application domain, there are proven function-oriented, object-oriented and component-based methodologies as well as service-oriented and agile frameworks. With the emergence of cloud computing, however, there is a need for the traditional approaches to software construction to be adapted to take full advantage of the cloud technologies.

Cloud computing is an attractive paradigm for business organisations due to the enormous benefits it promises, including savings on capital expenditure and availability of cloud-based services on demand and in real time. Organisations can self-provision software development platforms, together with infrastructure if so required, to develop and deploy applications much more speedily. Since the cloud environment is dynamic, virtualised, distributed and multi-tenant, necessary characteristics that cloud-enabled software must exhibit need to be inherently built into the software systems. This is especially so if the software is to be deployed in the cloud environment or made available for access by multiple cloud consumers. In this context, it is imperative to recognise that cloud SDLC is an accelerated process and that software development needs to be more iterative and incremental. Also, the application architecture must provide characteristics to leverage cloud infrastructure capabilities such as storage connectivity and communications. It is important that the chosen frameworks are suitable for fast cycle deployments. Methodologies must also ensure satisfaction of consumer demands of performance, availability, security, privacy, reliability and, above all, scalability and multi-tenancy. All this suggests that software architects require a shift in mindset and need to adapt to new approaches to design and deployment so that software systems are appropriate for cloud environments.

This book, *Software Engineering Frameworks for Cloud Computing Paradigm*, aims to capture the state of the art in this context and present discussion and guidance on the relevant software engineering approaches and frameworks. Twenty-six researchers and practitioners from around the world have presented their works, case studies and suggestions for engineering software suitable for deployment in the cloud environment.

Objectives

The aim of this book is to present current research and development in the field of software engineering as relevant to the cloud paradigm. The key objectives for this book include:

- Capturing the state of the art in software engineering approaches for developing cloud-suitable applications
- Providing relevant theoretical frameworks, practical approaches and current and future research directions
- Providing guidance and best practices for students and practitioners of cloud-based application architecture
- Advancing the understanding of the field of software engineering as relevant to the emerging new paradigm of cloud computing

Organisation

There are 15 chapters in *Software Engineering Frameworks for Cloud Computing Paradigm*. These are organised in four parts:

- Part I: Impact of Cloud Paradigm on Software Engineering. This section focuses on cloud computing paradigm as relevant to the discipline of software engineering. There are three chapters that look at the impact of Semantic web, discuss cloud-induced transformation and highlight issues and challenges inherent in cloud-based software development.
- Part II: Software Development Life Cycle for Cloud Platform. This comprises five chapters that consider stages of software development life cycle, in particular the requirements in engineering and testing of cloud-based applications. The chapters also discuss the design and development of software with virtualisation and multi-tenant distributed environment in mind.
- Part III: Software Design Strategies for Cloud Adoption. There are five chapters in this part that focus on feature-driven and cloud-aided software design and present strategies for cloud adoption and migration. Development of applications in the hybrid cloud environment and architectural patterns for migration of legacy systems are also discussed.

- Part IV: Performance of Cloud Based Software Applications. This section consists of two chapters that focus on efficiency and performance of cloud-based applications. One chapter discusses the effective practices for cloud-based software engineering, and the other chapter presents a framework for identifying relationships between application performance factors.

Target Audience

Software Engineering Frameworks for Cloud Computing Paradigm has been developed to support a number of potential audiences, including the following:

- *Software engineers and application developers* who wish to adapt to newer approaches to building software that is more suitable for virtualised and multi-tenant distributed environments
- *IT infrastructure managers and project leaders* who need to clearly understand the requirement for newer methodologies in the context of cloud paradigm and appreciate the issues of developing cloud-based applications
- *Students and university lecturers* of software engineering who have an interest in further developing their expertise and enhancing their knowledge of the cloud-relevant tools and techniques to architect cloud-friendly software
- *Researchers* in the fields of software engineering and cloud computing who wish to further increase their understanding of the current practices, methodologies and frameworks

Suggested Uses

Software Engineering Frameworks for Cloud Computing Paradigm can be used as a primer and textbook on university courses on cloud computing and software engineering. It can also be used as a reference text by practitioners in the field of software engineering.

For adoption as a course text, we suggest the following programme of study for a 12-week teaching semester format:

- Weeks 1–3: Part I
- Weeks 3–7: Part II
- Weeks 7–11: Part III
- Weeks 11–12: Part IV

Acknowledgements

The editors acknowledge the help and support of the following colleagues during the review and editing phases of this book:

- Dr Wasif Afzal, Bahria University, Islamabad, Pakistan
- Dr Daniel Crichton, Jet Propulsion Laboratory, California Inst Tech, USA
- Dr Ashraf Darwish, Helwan University, Cairo, Egypt
- Dr Shehzad Khalid, Bahria University, Islamabad, Pakistan
- Prof Francisco Milton Mendes, Rural Federal University of the Semi-Arid, Brazil
- Prof Mahmood Niazi, King Fahd University of Petroleum and Minerals, Dhahran
- Dr S. Parthasarathy, Thiagarajar College of Engineering, Madurai, India
- Dr Pethuru Raj, Wipro Technologies, Bangalore, India
- Dr Muthu Ramachandran, Leeds Metropolitan University, Leeds, UK
- Dr C. R. Rene Robin, Jerusalem College of Engineering, Chennai, India
- Dr Lucio Agostinho Rocha, State University of Campinas, Brazil
- Dr Lloyd G. Waller, University of the West Indies, Kingston, Jamaica
- Dr Fareeha Zafar, GC University, Lahore, Pakistan

The editors would also like to thank the contributors of this book; the 26 authors and co-authors, from academia as well as the industry from around the world, who collectively submitted 15 chapters. Without their efforts in developing quality contributions, conforming to the guidelines and meeting often the strict deadlines, this text would not have been possible.

Grateful thanks are also due to our family members for their support and understanding.

University of Derby, UK
January 2013

Zaigham Mahmood

Contents

Part III Software Design Strategies for Cloud Adoption

Part IV Performance of Cloud Based Software Applications

Contributors

Alain Abran Department of Software Engineering and Information Technology, ETS – University of Quebec, Montreal, Canada

Olumide Akerele School of Computing and Creative Technologies, Faculty of Arts, Environment and Technology, Leeds Metropolitan University, Leeds, UK

Rengarajan Amirtharajan School of Electrical and Electronics Engineering, SASTRA University, Thanjavur, Tamil Nadu, India

Alain April Department of Software Engineering and Information Technology, ETS – University of Quebec, Montreal, Canada

Colin Atkinson Software Engineering Group, University of Mannheim, Mannheim, Germany

Suchitra Ravi Balasubramanyam Education and Research Unit, Infosys Limited, Mysore, India

Rahul Bandopadhyaya Infosys Labs, Infosys Limited, Bangalore, India

Inderveer Chana Computer Science and Engineering Department, Thapar University, Patiala, India

Priyanka Chawla Computer Science and Engineering Department, Thapar University, Patiala, India

Mark Dixon School of Computing and Creative Technologies, Faculty of Arts, Environment and Technology, Leeds Metropolitan University, Leeds, UK

Dirk Draheim IT Service Management Division, University of Innsbruck, Innsbruck, Austria

Sidharth Subhash Ghag Infosys Labs, Infosys Limited, Pune, India

Radha Guha ECE Department, PESIT, Bangalore, India

R. Jayakrishnan Infosys Ltd., Bangalore, India

Sowmya Karunakaran Department of Management Studies, Indian Institute of Technology (IIT), Madras, India

Radha Krishna Infosys Ltd., Bangalore, India

Anil Kumar Muppalla High Performance Computing Laboratory, Department of Computer Science and Engineering, M S Ramaiah Institute of Technology, Bangalore, India

Karahan Öztürk British Sky Broadcasting, London, UK

N. Pramod High Performance Computing Laboratory, Department of Computer Science and Engineering, M S Ramaiah Institute of Technology, Bangalore, India

Pethuru Raj Wipro Technologies, Bangalore, India

Muthu Ramachandran School of Computing and Creative Technologies, Faculty of Arts, Environment and Technology, Leeds Metropolitan University, Leeds, UK

Lucio Agostinho Rocha Department of Computer Engineering and Industrial Automation (DCA) at the School of Electrical and Computer Engineering (FEEC), State University of Campinas, São Paulo, Brazil

K.G. Srinivasa High Performance Computing Laboratory, Department of Computer Science and Engineering, M S Ramaiah Institute of Technology, Bangalore, India

Bedir Tekinerdogan Department of Computer Engineering, Bilkent University, Ankara, Turkey

Veeramuthu Venkatesh School of Electrical and Electronics Engineering, SASTRA University, Thanjavur, Tamil Nadu, India

Luis Eduardo Bautista Villalpando Department of Electronic Systems, Autonomous University of Aguascalientes, Aguascalientes, Mexico

Department of Software Engineering and Information Technology, ETS – University of Quebec, Montreal, Canada

Part I
Impact of Cloud Paradigm on Software Engineering

Chapter 1
Impact of Semantic Web and Cloud Computing Platform on Software Engineering

Radha Guha

Abstract Tim Berners-Lee's vision of the Semantic Web or Web 3.0 is to transform the World Wide Web into an intelligent Web system of structured, linked data which can be queried and inferred as a whole by the computers themselves. This grand vision of the Web is materializing many innovative uses of the Web. New business models like interoperable applications hosted on the Web as services are getting implemented. These Web services are designed to be automatically discovered by software agents and exchange data among themselves. Another business model is the cloud computing platform, where hardware, software, tools, and applications will be leased out as services to tenants across the globe over the Internet. There are many advantages of this business model, like no capital expenditure, speed of application deployment, shorter time to market, lower cost of operation, and easier maintenance of resources, for the tenants. Because of these advantages, cloud computing may be the prevalent computing platform of the future. To realize all the advantages of these new business models of distributed, shared, and self-provisioning environment of Web services and cloud computing resources, the traditional way of software engineering has to change as well. This chapter analyzes how cloud computing, on the background of Semantic Web, is going to impact on the software engineering processes to develop quality software. The need for changes in the software development and deployment framework activities is also analyzed to facilitate adoption of cloud computing platform.

Keywords Software engineering • Semantic Web • Cloud computing platform • Agile process model • Extreme Cloud Programming

---

R. Guha (✉)
ECE Department, PESIT, Feet Ring Road, BSK III Stage,
560085, Bangalore, India
e-mail: radhaguha@pes.edu

Z. Mahmood and S. Saeed (eds.), *Software Engineering Frameworks for the Cloud Computing Paradigm*, Computer Communications and Networks,
DOI 10.1007/978-1-4471-5031-2_1, © Springer-Verlag London 2013

1.1 Introduction

Since the inception of the World Wide Web (WWW) in 1990 by Tim Berners-Lee, there has been a large warehouse of documents on the WWW, and the number of documents is growing very rapidly. But, unless the information from these documents can be aggregated and inferred quickly, they do not have much use. Human readers cannot read and make decisions quickly from large number of mostly irrelevant documents retrieved by the old search engines based on keyword searches. Thus, Tim Berners-Lee's vision is to transform this World Wide Web into an intelligent Web system or Semantic Web [1–8] which will allow concept searches rather than keyword searches. First, Semantic Web or Web 3.0 technologies will transform disconnected text documents on the Web into a global database of structured, linked data. These large volumes of linked data in global databases will no longer be only for human consumption but for quick machine processing. Just like a relational database system can answer a query by filtering out unnecessary data, Semantic Web technologies will similarly filter out information from the global database. This capability requires assigning globally accepted explicitly defined semantics to the data in the Web for linking. Then these linked data in the global database will collectively produce intelligent information by software agents on behalf of the human users, and the full potential of the Web can be realized.

Anticipating this transition of the Web where data integration, inference, and data exchange between heterogeneous applications will be possible, new business models of application deployment and delivery over the Internet have been conceptualized. Applications can be hosted on the Web and accessed via the Internet by geographically dispersed clients. These XML (eXtensible Markup Language)-based, interoperable applications are called Web services which can publish their location, functions, messages containing the parameter list to execute the functions, and communication protocols for accessing the service using it correctly by all. As the same service will be catered to multiple clients, they can even be customized according to clients' likes. Application architecture and delivery architecture will be two separate layers for these Web applications for providing this flexibility. XML-based Web 2.0 and Web 3.0 protocols like Service-Oriented Architecture (SOA), Simple Object Access Protocol (SOAP), Web Service Description Language (WSDL), and Universal Description, Discovery and Integration (UDDI) registry are designed to discover Web services on the fly and to integrate applications developed on heterogeneous computing platforms, operating systems, and with varieties of programming languages. Applications like Hadoop and Mashup [9, 10] can combine data and functionalities from multiple external sources hosted as Web services and are producing valuable aggregate new information and creating new Web services. Hadoop and Mashup can support high-performance computing involving distributed file system with petabytes of data and parallel processing on more than hundreds to thousands of computers.

In another business model, the application development infrastructure like processors, storage, memory, operating system, and application development tools and software can all be delivered as utility to the clients over the Internet. This is what is dubbed as cloud computing where a huge pool of physical resources hosted on the Web will be shared by multiple clients as and when required. Because of the many benefits of this business model like no capital expenditure, speed of application deployment, shorter time to market, lower cost of operation, and easier maintenance of resources for the clients, cloud computing may be the prevalent computing platform of the future.

On the other hand, economies of all developed countries depend on quality software, and software cost is more than hardware cost. Moreover, because of the involvement of many parties, software development is inherently a complex process, and most of the software projects fail because of lack of communication and coordination between all the parties involved. Knowledge management in software engineering has always been an issue which affects better software development and its maintenance. There is always some gap in understanding about what the business partners and stakeholders want, how software designers and managers design the modules, and how software developers implement the design. As the time passes, this gap in understanding increases due to the increased complexity of the involvement of many parties and continuously changing requirements of the software. This is more so at the later stage when the software has to be maintained and no one has the comprehensive knowledge about the whole system.

Now, with the inclusion of the Free/Libre/Open Source Software (FLOSS) [11] pieces, Web services, and cloud computing platform, software development complexity is going to increase manifold because of the synchronization needs with third-party software and the increased communication and coordination complexity with the cloud providers. The main thesis of this chapter is that the prevalent software process models should involve the cloud providers in every step of decision-making of software development life cycle to make the software project a success. Also, the software developers need to change their software artifacts from plain text documents to machine-readable structured linked data, to make them Semantic Web ready. With this semantic transformation knowledge, management in software engineering will be much easier, and compliance checking of various requirements during project planning, design, development, testing, and verification can be automated. Semantic artifacts will also give their product a competitive edge for automatic discovery and integration with other applications and efficient maintenance of their artifacts.

This chapter explores how Semantic Web can reduce software development work with automatic discovery of distributed open source software components. Also, Semantic Web techniques are explored that need to be incorporated in software development artifacts to make them Semantic Web ready. Then, to realize the many advantages of the cloud computing business model, how the well-established software engineering process models have to adapt is analyzed. As the cloud provider is an external entity or third party, how difficult will be the interactions with them? How to separate the roles of software engineers and cloud providers? As a whole, cloud computing paradigm on Semantic Web background makes software development project more complex.

In Sect. 1.2, background literatures on transformation to Semantic Web, cloud computing platform, and software engineering are surveyed. In Sect. 1.3, first emphasis is given on the need for producing software artifacts for the Semantic Web. Secondly, how the software developers are coping with the changing trend of application development on cloud platform with Web 2.0 and Web 3.0 protocols and application deployment over the Web is reported. Thirdly, challenges of cloud computing platform for software engineering are analyzed. In Sect. 1.4, an agile process model which incorporates interaction with cloud provider is proposed and analyzed. Section 1.5 concludes the chapter.

1.2 Literature Survey

1.2.1 Transformation to Semantic Web

World Wide Web was invented in 1990 by Tim Barners-Lee. Since then, the transformation of the Web has been marked with Web 1.0, Web 2.0, and Web 3.0 technologies. In Web 1.0, the HTML (hypertext markup language) tags were added to plain text documents for displaying the documents in a specific way on Web browsers. Each document on the Web is a source of knowledge or a resource. In the World Wide Web, with the hypertext transport protocol (HTTP), if the URL (Universal Resource Locator) of any Web site (document) is known, then that resource can be accessed or browsed over the Internet. Domain name service (DNS) registry was developed to discover a machine on the Internet which hosts a Web page URL. This capability of Web 1.0 published information pages which were static and read only. HTML's <href> tag (a form of metadata) links two documents for human readers to navigate to related topics. In Web 1.0, for quick search and retrieval, metadata (data about data) that describes the contents of electronic documents or resources are added in the document itself, which has the same purpose as indexes in a book or catalogues in a library. Search engines like Google and Yahoo create metadata databases out of those metadata in Web documents to find the documents quickly. In Web 1.0, the contents of the Web pages are static and the meanings of the Web pages are deciphered by the people who read them. Web contents are developed by HTML and user input is captured in Web forms in the client machine and sent to remote server via a common gateway interface (CGI) for further processing.

In Web 2.0, XML (eXtensible Markup Language) was designed to give hierarchical structure to the document content, to transform it into data, and to transport the document as data. Where HTML tags prescribe how to display the Web content in client computer, the XML tags add another layer of metadata to query the Web document for specific data. XML documents can be read and processed by computers (by a parser) automatically and can be exchanged between applications developed on heterogeneous computing platforms, operating systems, and varieties of programming languages once they all know the XML tags used in the documents. As for example, in order to use text generated by a Word Processor and data from spreadsheets and relational databases together, they all need to be transformed into a common XML format first. This collaboration of applications is possible in a closed community when all the applications are aware of the common XML tags. Web 2.0 technologies also enabled pervasive or ubiquitous Web browsing involving personal computers, mobile phones, and PDA (Personal Digital Assistant) running different operating systems like Windows, Macintosh, or Linux, connected to the Internet via wired or wireless connections. Web 2.0 technologies like XML, DHTML, and AJAX (Asynchronous Java Script and XML) allowed two-way communications with dynamic Web contents and created social communities like Facebook, MySpace, and Twitter. Web 2.0 has also seen the revolution of using the Web as the practical medium for conducting businesses. An increasing number of Web-enabled e-commerce applications like e-Bay and Amazon have emerged in this trend to buy and sell products online.

But, for collaboration in the open, ever-expanding World Wide Web by all, everybody on the Web has to agree on the meaning of the Web contents. XML alone does not add semantics to the Web content. Thus, in Web 3.0, Resource Description Framework (RDF) protocol is designed to add another layer of metadata to add meaning or semantics to the data (text, images, audio, or video) inside the document with RDF vocabularies understood by machines. As computer memory is not expensive anymore, this metadata can be verbose even for human understanding instead of being only for machine understanding. Authors, publishers, and users all can add metadata about a Web resource in a standardized format. This self-describing data inside the document can be individually addressed by HTTP URI (Universal Resource Identifier) mechanism, processed and linked to other data from other documents, and inferred by machine automatically. URI is an expansion on the concept of Universal Resource Locator or URL and can both be a name and location. Search engines or crawlers will navigate the links and generate query response over the aggregated linked data. This linked data will encourage reuse of information, reduce redundancy, and produce more powerful aggregate information.

To this end, we need a standardized knowledge representation system [12, 13]. Modeling a knowledge domain using standard, shared vocabularies will facilitate interoperability between different applications. Ontology is a formal representation of knowledge as a set of concepts in a domain. Ontology components are classes, their attributes, relations, restrictions, rules, and axioms. DublinCore, GFO (General Formal Ontology), OpenCyc/SUMO (Suggested Upper Merged Ontology), DOLCE (Descriptive Ontology for Linguistic and Cognitive Engineering), WordNet, FOAF (Friend of a Friend), SIOC (Semantically Interlinked Online Communities), SKOS (Simple Knowledge Organization System), DOAP (Description of a Project), vCard, etc., are the much used well-known ontology libraries of RDF vocabularies. For example, implementation of DublinCore makes use of XML and a Resource Description Framework (RDF).

RDF triples describe any data in the form of subject, predicate, and object. Subject, predicate, and object all are URIs which can be individually addressed in

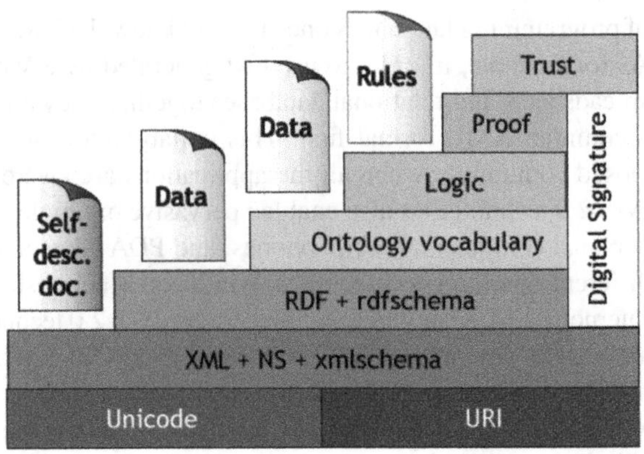

Fig. 1.1 Semantic Web Wedding Cake [8]

the Web by the HTTP URI mechanism. Subject and object can be URIs from the same document or from two separate documents or independent data sources linked by the predicate URI. Object can also be just a string literal or a value. RDF creates a graph-based data model spanning the entire Web which can be navigated or crawled following the links by software agents. RDF schema (RDFS), Web ontology language (OWL), and Simple Knowledge Organization System (SKOS) are developed to write rules and express hierarchical relations, inference between Web resources. They vary in their expressiveness, logical thinking, and hierarchical knowledge organization from being more limited to more powerful in RDFS to SKOS. For querying the RDF data written in RDFS, OWL, or SKOS, RDF query language named SPARQL has been developed.

RDF tags can be added automatically or semiautomatically by tools like RDFizers [7], D2R (Database to RDF), JPEG → RDF, and Email → RDF. Linked data browsers like Disco, Tabulator, and Marbles are getting designed to browse linked data Semantic Web. Linked data search engines like Falcon and SWSE (Semantic Web search engine) are getting designed for human navigation, and Swoogle and Sindice are getting designed for applications.

Figure 1.1 shows the Semantic Web protocol stacks (Wedding Cake) proposed by Tim Barners-Lee in 2000. The bottom of the Wedding Cake shows standards that are well defined and widely accepted, whereas the other protocols are yet to be implemented in most of the Web sites. Unicode is a 16-bit code word which is large enough (2^{16}) for representing any characters in any languages in the world. URI (Universal Resource Identifier) is the W3C's codification for addressing any objects over the Web. XML is for structuring the documents into data, and RDF is the mechanism for describing data which can be understood by machines. Ontologies are vocabularies from specific knowledge domain. Logic refers to making logical inferences from associated linked data. Proof is keeping track of the steps of logical inferences. Trust refers to the origin and quality of the data sources. This entire protocol stack will transform the Web into a Semantic Web global database of linked data for realizing the full potential of the Web.

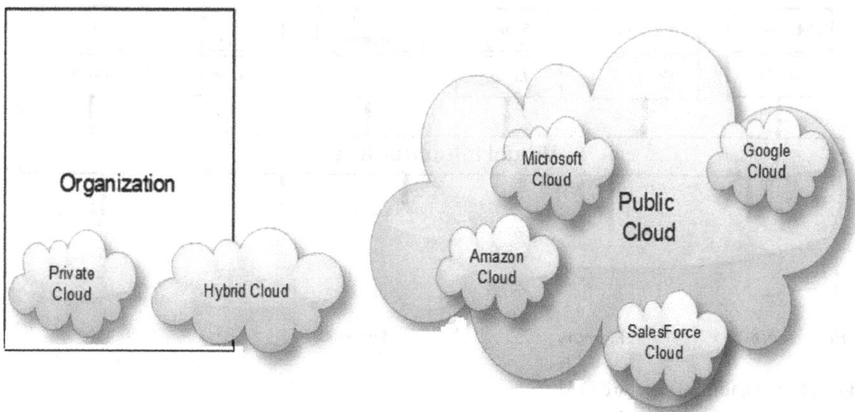

Fig. 1.2 Cloud computing platform

1.2.2 Cloud Computing Platform

Cloud computing [14–16] is the most anticipated future trend of computing. Cloud computing is the idea of renting out server, storage, network, software technologies, tools, and applications as utility or service over the Internet as and when required in contrast to owning them permanently. Depending on what resources are shared and delivered to the customers, there are four types of cloud computing. In cloud computing terminology, when hardware such as processors, storage, and network are delivered as a service, it is called infrastructure as a service (IaaS). Examples of IaaS are Amazon's Elastic Cloud (EC2) and Simple Storage Service (S3). When programming platforms and tools like Java, Python, .Net, MySQL, and APIs are delivered as a service, it is called platform as a service (PaaS). When applications are delivered as a service, it is called software as a service (SaaS).

Depending on the amount of self-governance or control on resources by the tenant, there are three types of cloud like internal or private cloud, external or public cloud, and hybrid cloud (Fig. 1.2). In private cloud, an enterprise owns all the resources on-site and shares them between multiple applications. In public cloud, the enterprise will rent the resources from an off-site cloud provider, and these resources will be shared between multiple tenants. Hybrid cloud is in the middle where an enterprise owns some resources and rents some other resources from a third party.

Cloud computing is based on Service-Oriented Architecture (SOA) of Web 2.0 and Web 3.0 and virtualization [16–18] of hardware and software resources (Fig. 1.3). Because of the virtualization technique, physical resources can be linked dynamically to different applications running on different operating systems. Because of the virtualization technique, physical resources can be shared among all users, and there is efficient resource management which can provide higher resource utilization and on-demand scalability. Increased resource utilization brings down

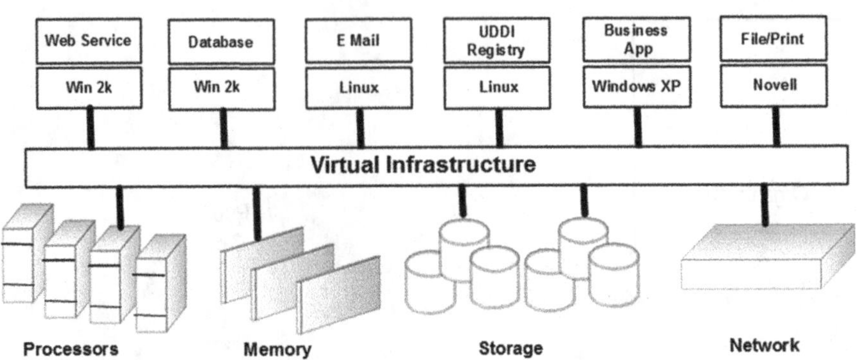

Fig. 1.3 Virtual infrastructure [13]

the cost of floor space, power, and cooling. Power savings is the most attractive feature of cloud computing and is the renewed initiative of environment-friendly green computing or green IT movement of today. Cloud computing not only reduces cost of usage of resources but also reduces maintenance cost of resources for the user.

Cloud computing can support on-demand scalability. An application with occasional demand for higher resources will pay for the higher resources only the time it is used instead of leasing all the resources from the very beginning in anticipation of future need. This fine-grained (hourly) pay-by-use model of cloud computing is going to be very attractive to the customers. There are many other benefits of cloud computing. Cloud infrastructure can support multiple protocols and change in business model for applications more rapidly. It can also handle increased performance requirements like service scaling, response time, and availability of the application, as the cloud infrastructure is a huge pool of resources like servers, storage, and network and provides elasticity of growth to the end users.

With this business model of catering multiple clients with shared resources, world's leading IT companies like Microsoft, Google, IBM, SalesForce, HP, and Amazon are deploying clouds (Fig. 1.2). Web services and applications like Hadoop and Mashup can run on these clouds. Though there are many advantages of cloud computing platform, there are few challenges regarding safety and privacy of tenant's information in cloud platform which can threaten the adoption of cloud computing platform by the masses. If these few challenges can be overcome, because of many of its advantages, this cloud computing model may be the prevalent computing model of the future.

1.2.2.1 Safety and Privacy Issues in Cloud Computing Platform

All the resources of the cloud computing platform are shared by multiple tenants (Fig. 1.4) over the Internet across the globe. In this shared environment, having trust of data safety and privacy is of utmost importance to customers. Safety of data means no loss of data pertaining to the owner of the data, and privacy of data means

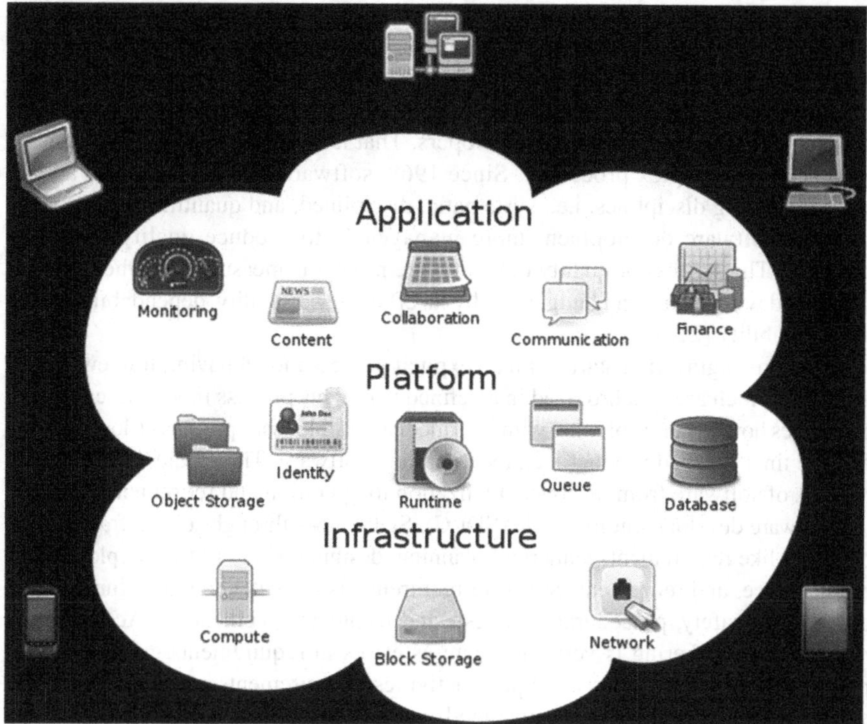

Fig. 1.4 Shared resources in cloud computing

no unauthorized use of the sensitive data by others. As cloud provider has greater resource pool, they can easily keep copies of data and ensure safety of user data. Privacy of data is of more concern in public cloud than in private cloud. In public cloud environment as data is stored in off-premise machines, users have less control over the use of their data, and this mistrust can threaten the adoption of cloud computing platform by the masses. Technology and law enforcement both should protect privacy concerns of cloud customers [19, 20]. Software engineer must build their applications as Web services which can guarantee to lessen this risk of exposure of sensitive data of cloud customers.

Next, we look into the preexisting software development methodologies to develop quality software products in traditional environment not involving Web services and cloud computing platform.

1.2.3 Traditional Software Engineering Process

Here, we delve into preexisting software development methodologies first to develop quality software products in traditional environment not involving Web services and cloud computing platform. Over the last half-century, rapid advances of hardware technology such as computers, memory, storage, communication networks, mobile devices, and embedded systems are pushing the need for larger and more complex software. Software development not only involves many different hardware technologies, it also involves many different parties like customers, stakeholders, end users, and software developers. That is why software development is an inherently complex procedure. Since 1968, software developers had to adopt the engineering disciplines, i.e., systematic, disciplined, and quantifiable approach to make software development more manageable to produce quality software products. The success or quality of a software project is measured by whether it is developed within time and budget and by its efficiency, usability, dependability, and maintainability [21, 22].

Software engineering starts with an explicit process model having framework of activities which are synchronized in a defined way. This process model describes or prescribes how to build software with intermediate visible work products (documents) and the final finished product, i.e., the operating software. The whole development process of software from its conceptualization to operation and retirement is called the software development life cycle (SDLC). SDLC goes through several framework activities like requirements gathering, planning, design, coding, testing, deployment, maintenance, and retirement. Software requirements are categorized as functional, contractual, safety, procedural, business, and technical specification. Accuracy of requirements gathering is very important as errors in requirements gathering will propagate through all other subsequent activities. Requirements arising from different sectors need to be well documented, verified to be in compliance with each other, optimized, linked, and traced. All software engineering process activities are synchronized in accordance to the process model adopted for a particular software development. There are many process models to choose from like water fall model, rapid application development (RAD) model, and spiral model depending on the size of the project, delivery time requirement, and type of the project. As an example, development of an avionic embedded system will adopt a different process model than development of a Web application. Another criterion for choosing a suitable process model is its ability to arrest errors in requirements gathering.

Even though software engineering takes engineering approach, success of software product is more difficult than products from other engineering domain like mechanical engineering or civil engineering. This is because software is intangible during its development. Software project managers use a number of umbrella activities to monitor software framework activities in a more visible way. These umbrella activities are software project tracking and control, risk management, quality assurance, measurements, configuration management, work-product or documents generation, review, and reusability management. CMMI (Capability Maturity Model Integration) is a software process improvement model for software development companies by comparing their process maturity with the best practices in the industry to deliver quality software products.

Even after taking all these measures for sticking to the plan and giving much importance to document generation for project tracking and control, many software projects failed. Oftentimes volume of paper documents is too large for aggregating information by humans. More than 50 % of software projects fail due to various

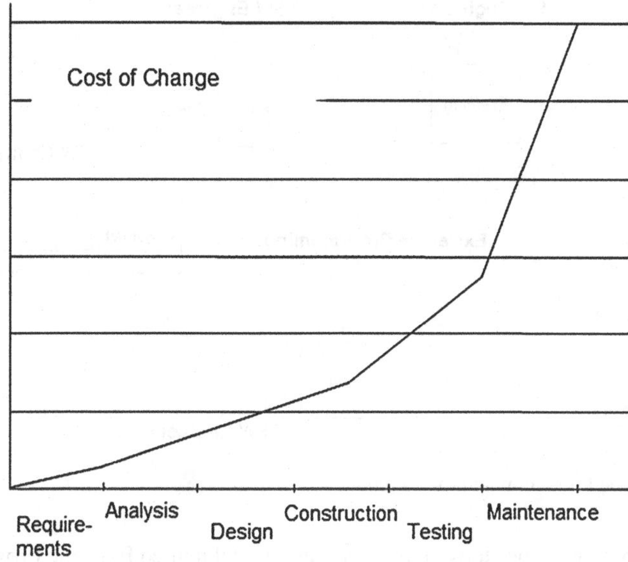

Fig. 1.5 Economics of software development

reasons like schedule and budget slippage, non-user-friendly interface of the software, and non-flexibility for maintenance and change of the software. And the reasons for all these problems are lack of communication and coordination between all the parties involved.

Requirement changes of a software are the major cause of increased complexity, schedule, and budget slippage. Incorporating changes at a later stage of SDLC increases the cost of the project exponentially (Fig. 1.5). Adding more number of programmers at a later stage does not solve the schedule problem as increased coordination requirement slows down the project further. It is very important that requirements gathering, planning, and design of the software are done involving all the parties from the beginning.

That is the reason why several agile process models like Extreme Programming (XP) (Fig. 1.6), Scrum, Crystal, and Adaptive have been introduced in mid-1990s to accommodate continuous changes in requirements during the development of the software. These agile process models have shorter development cycles where small pieces of work are "time-boxed," developed, and released for customer feedback, verification, and validation iteratively. One time-box takes a few weeks to maximum a month of time. Agile process model is communication intensive as customer satisfaction is given the utmost importance. Agile software development is possible only when the software developers are talented, motivated, and self-organized. Agile process model eliminates the exponential increase of cost to incorporate changes as in the waterfall model by keeping the customer involved throughout and validating small pieces of work by them iteratively. These agile process models work better for most of the software projects as changes are inevitable, and responding to the changes is the key to the success of a project.

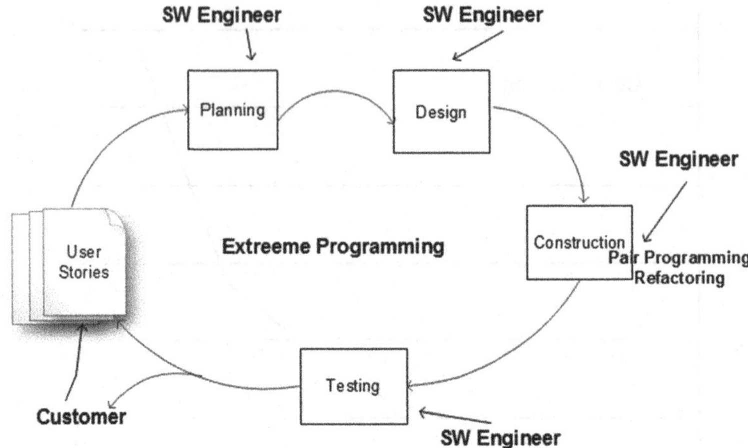

Fig. 1.6 Extreme Programming process model

Figure 1.6 depicts the steps of agile process model named Extreme Programming (XP) for a traditional software development where the customer owns the developing platform or software developers develop in-house and deploy the software to the customer after it is built. XP has many characteristics like user story card and CRC (class, responsibility, collaboration) card narrated during the requirements gathering stage jointly by the customer and the software engineers. Customer decides the priority of each story card, and the highest priority card is only considered or "time-boxed" for the current iteration of software development. Construction of code is performed by two engineers sitting at the same machine so that there is less scope of errors in the code. This is called pair programming. Code is continuously refactored or improved to make it more efficient.

In the following sections, analysis for the need for producing software development artifacts for the Semantic Web and the challenges of the current business model of application development and deployment involving Web 2.0 and Web 3.0 technologies and cloud computing platform are reported. Finally, methodologies to develop quality software that will push forward the advances of the cloud computing platform have been suggested.

1.3 Need for Modification of Software Engineering: Analysis

1.3.1 Need for Semantic Web-Enabled Software Artifacts

Semantic Web effort has just started and not all are aware of it, even the IT professionals. The linked data initiative [7] that was taken in 2007 by a small group of academic researchers from universities now has participants of few large companies like BBC, Thompson Reuters, and Library of Congress who have transformed their

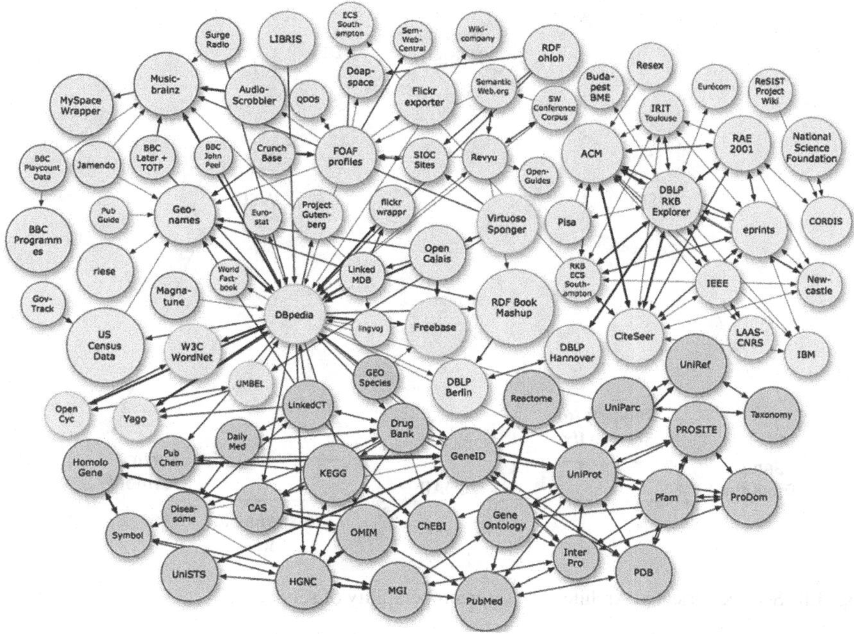

Fig. 1.7 Linking open data cloud diagram giving an overview of published data sets and their interlinkage relationships [7]

data for the Semantic Web. DBpedia is another community effort to transform the Wikipedia documents for Semantic Web. Sophisticated queries can be run on DBpedia data and link to other Semantic Web data. Friend of a Friend (FOAF) is another project to link social Web sites and their people and describe what they create or do. Federal and State governments are also taking initiatives to publish public data online. US Census data is one such semantic data source which can be queried and linked with other semantic data sources. Unless all government public data can be transformed for the Semantic Web, they will not be suitable for interoperable Web applications.

Figure 1.7 shows the current size of the linked data Web as of March 2009. Today there are 4.7 billion RDF triples which are interlinked by 142 million RDF links. Anybody can transform their data in linked data standards and can link to the existing linked data Web. In Fig. 1.7, the circles are nodes of independent data sources or Web sites, and the arcs are their relationship with other data sources. The thicker links specify more connections between the two data sources, and bidirectional links mean both data sources are linked to each other.

Once the software engineers grasp the Semantic Web technologies and understand their capabilities and their many advantages like interoperability, adaptability, integration ability of open and distributed software components with other applications, they will make their software artifacts Semantic Web ready. Once the software artifacts are transformed into semantic artifacts software, maintainability will be

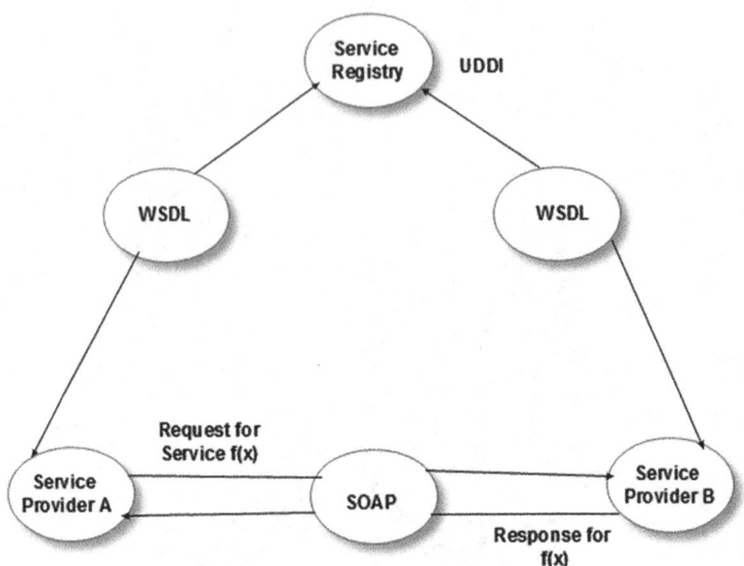

Fig. 1.8 Service-Oriented Architecture for interoperability of services

much more efficient and cheaper. All requirements can be optimized, linked, and traced. Aggregating of information from requirements document will be easy, and impact analysis before actual changes are made can be done more accurately. Increased maintainability of software will also increase reliability of the software. Semantic Web services will be easy to discover on the Web, and that will give a competitive edge to their products. Semantic Web services which can be linked with other Web services will create new and more powerful software applications, encourage reuse, and reduce redundancy.

1.3.2 Creating a Web Service

Benefits of Web services [23–26] are code reuse and speedy development of software projects. But in order to use Web services from the Web, the application must create a Web client which can interface with the Web services and request for services and receive services. In Fig. 1.8, the Service-Oriented Architecture (SOA) that has emerged to deliver software as a service (SaaS) business model is illustrated.

An application programming interface (API) of Web service is first created as WSDL document using XML tags, for advertising to the world over the Internet. WSDL documents have five major parts. It describes data types, messages, port, operation (class and methods), binding (SOAP message), and location (URL). WSDL documents need not be manually created. There are automatic tools like Apache Axis [25], which will create the API from a Java programming code. Apache Axis is an open source, XML-based Web service framework.

After creating the WSDL document, a Web client to consume the Web service is needed. Web client is created using SOAP to communicate request and response messages between the two applications. SOAP is an XML messaging format for exchanging structured data (XML documents) over HTTP transport protocol and can be used for remote procedure call (RPC). SOAP structure has three parts: (1) envelop, (2) header, and (3) body. Body defines the message and how to process it.

Software engineers have to master XML language and other Web technologies like WSDL and SOAP in addition to knowing a programming language like Java or C++ in order to use or create a Web service.

1.3.3 How SW Engineers Are Coping in Cloud Platform

This section surveys how software development industry is trying to survive in the era of Web 2.0 and Web 3.0 with Web services and cloud computing. In reference [27], the authors present framework activities for designing applications based on discovery of Semantic Web service using software engineering methodologies. They propose generating semiautomatic semantic description of applications exploiting the existing methodologies and tools of Web engineering. This increases design efficiency and reduces manual effort of semantically annotating the new application composed from Web services of multiple enterprises.

In Reference [28], Salesforce.com finds that agile process model works better on cloud computing platform. Before cloud computing, release of the software to the user took time and getting feedback from the customer took more time which thwarted the very concept of agile development. Whereas now, new releases of the software can be uploaded on the server and used by the users immediately. Basically in this chapter, what they have described is the benefits of software as a service hosted on the Internet and how it complements agile computing methodology. They have not considered the challenges of cloud computing in developing new business software.

Cloud computing being the newest hype of the IT industry, the challenges of software engineering on cloud computing platform have not been studied yet, and no software development process model for cloud computing platform has been suggested yet. We analyze the challenges of the cloud computing platform on software development process and suggest extending the existing agile process model, named Extreme Programming, to mitigate all the challenges in Sect. 1.3.4.

1.3.4 Impact of Cloud Computing on Software Engineering

In the rapidly changing computing environment with Web services and cloud platform, software development is going to be very challenging. Software development process will involve heterogeneous platforms, distributed Web services, and multiple enterprises geographically dispersed all over the world. Existing software process models and framework activities are not going to be adequate unless interaction with cloud providers is included.

Requirements gathering phase so far included customers, users, and software engineers. Now it has to include the cloud providers as well, as they will be supplying the computing infrastructure and maintain them too. As the cloud providers only will know the size, architectural details, virtualization strategy, and resource utilization percentage of the infrastructure, planning and design phases of software development also have to include the cloud providers. The cloud providers can help in answering these questions about (1) how many developers are needed, (2) component reuse, (3) cost estimation, (4) schedule estimation, (5) risk management, (6) configuration management, (7) change management, and (8) quality assurance.

Because of the component reuse of Web services, the size of the software in number of kilo lines of code (KLOC) or number of function points (FP) to be newly developed by the software engineer will reduce, but complexity of the project will increase manyfold because of lack of documentations of implementation details of Web services and their integration requirements. Only description that will be available online is the metadata information of the Web services to be processed by the computers automatically.

Only coding and testing phases can be done independently by the software engineers. Coding and testing can be done on the cloud platform which is a huge benefit as everybody will have easy access to the software being built. This will reduce the cost and time for testing and validation.

However, software developers need to use the Web services and open source software freely available from the cloud instead of procuring them. Software developers should have more expertise in building software from readily available components than writing it all and building a monolithic application. Refactoring of existing application is required to best utilize the cloud infrastructure architecture in a cost-effective way. In the latest hardware technology, the computers are multi-core and networked, and the software engineers should train themselves in parallel and distributed computing to complement these advances of hardware and network technology. Software engineers should train themselves in Internet protocols, XML, Web service standards and layered separation of concerns of SOA architecture of Internet, and Semantic Web technologies to leverage all the benefits of Web 2.0. Cloud providers will insist that software should be as modular as possible for occasional migration from one server to another for load balancing as required by the cloud provider [16].

Maintenance phase should also include the cloud providers. There is a complete shift of responsibility of maintenance of the infrastructure from software developers to cloud providers. Now because of the involvement of the cloud provider, the customer has to sign a contract with them as well so that the "Software Engineering code of ethics" is not violated by the cloud provider. In addition, protection and security of the data is of utmost importance which is under the jurisdiction of the cloud provider now.

Also, occasional demand of higher resource usage of CPU time or network from applications may thwart the pay-by-use model of cloud computing into jeopardy

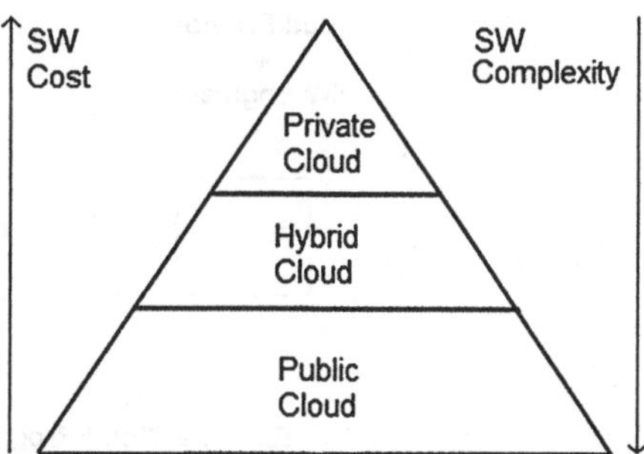

Fig. 1.9 Economics vs. complexity of software

as multiple applications may need higher resource usage all at the same time not anticipated by the cloud provider in the beginning. Especially when applications are deployed as "software as a service" or "SaaS" model, they may have occasional workload surge not anticipated in advance.

Cloud provider uses virtualization of resource technique to cater many customers on demand in an efficient way. For higher resource utilization, occasional migration of application from one server to another or from one storage to another may be required by the cloud provider. This may be a conflict of interest with the customer as they want dedicated resources with high availability and reliability of their applications. To avoid this conflict, cloud providers need to introduce quality of service provisions for higher-priority tenants.

Now we analyze how difficult will be the interaction between cloud providers and the software engineers. The amount of interactions between software engineers and cloud providers will depend on the type of cloud like public, private, or hybrid cloud involvements. In private cloud, there is more control or self-governance by the customer than in public cloud. Customer should also consider using private cloud instead of using public cloud to assure availability and reliability of their high-priority applications. Benefits of private cloud will be less interaction with cloud provider, self-governance, high security, reliability, and availability of data (Fig. 1.9). But cheaper computing on public cloud will always outweigh the benefits of less complexity of SW development on private cloud platform and is going to be more attractive.

1.4 Proposed SW Process Model for Cloud Platform

Innovative software engineering is required to leverage all the benefits of cloud computing and mitigate its challenges strategically to push forward its advances. Here an extended version of Extreme Programming (XP), an agile process model for cloud computing platform named Extreme Cloud Programming (Fig. 1.10), is proposed. All the phases like requirements gathering, planning, design, construction, testing, and deployment need interaction with the representatives from cloud provider.

The roles or activities by the cloud provider and SW developers are separated and listed in Table 1.1. Resource accounting on cloud platform will be done by the cloud

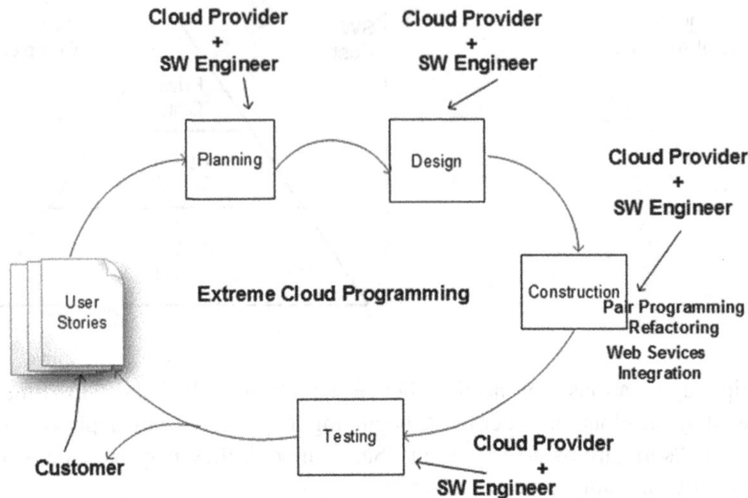

Fig. 1.10 Extreme Cloud Programming development on cloud computing [29]

Table 1.1 Software engineering-role separation [29]

	Roles	
Activity	Software developer	Cloud provider
Requirements gathering	Elicitation	Resource accounting Virtual machine
Analysis	SW modules	SW/HW architecture
Design	Interface design Data types Cost estimation Schedule estimation	Component reuse
Construction	Coding Integration of Web services	Implementation details
Testing	Unit test Integration test	Integration test
Deployment		Operation and maintenance

provider in the requirements gathering phase. Software architecture, software architecture to hardware architecture mapping, interface design, data types design, cost estimation, and schedule estimation of the project all should be done in collaboration with the cloud provider. During the construction phase of the application, if Web services are integrated where many different enterprises are involved, then error should be mitigated with the mediation of the cloud provider. Maintenance contract with cloud provider will be according to the Quality of Service agreement.

A software metric is required for effort estimation of SW development using the new Extreme Cloud Programming process model. This metric is required as American consultant Tom DeMarco aptly stated in 1997 in his book [30] about

Table 1.2 COCOMO [29]

Software proj.	*a*	*b*	*c*	*d*
Organic	2.4	1.05	2.5	.38
Semidetached	3.0	1.12	2.5	.35
Embedded	3.6	1.2	2.5	.32
Cloud comp.	4	1.2	2.5	.3

managing risk in software projects that "You cannot control what you cannot measure." Constructive cost estimation model (COCOMO) is mostly used model for cost estimation of various software development projects. In COCOMO model (Table 1.2), three classes of software projects have been considered so far. These software projects are classified as (1) Organic, (2) Semidetached, (3) Embedded according to the software team size, their experiences, and development (HW, SW, and operations) constraints. We extend [29] this cost estimation model with a new class of software project for cloud computing platform. In basic COCOMO model effort (man month), development time (months) and number of people required are given by the following equations.

$$\text{Effort Applied} = a(\text{KLOC})^b\,[\text{man} - \text{months}]$$

$$\text{Development Time} = c\left(\text{Effort Applied}\right)^d\,[\text{months}]$$

$$\text{No. of People} = \text{Effort Applied} / \text{Development Time}[\text{no.}]$$

The typical values of the coefficients *a*, *b*, *c*, *d* for different classes of software projects are listed in Table 1.2. In anticipation of additional interaction complexity with the cloud providers, coefficient *a* is increased to 4 for cloud computing platform. Coefficients *a*, *b* for cloud computing are determined so that the effort curve is steeper than the other three classes but is linear like the other three classes. Similarly, coefficients *c*, *d* for cloud computing are determined so that the development time curve is less steeper than the other three classes but is linear like the other three classes. The coefficients *a*, *b*, *c*, *d* in cloud computing are readjusted to new values of 4, 1.2, 2.5, and .3.

Because of component reuse, software development with cloud computing will reduce KLOC (kilo lines of code) significantly. We deduce new $\text{KLOC} = i * C +$ $(\text{KLOC}) * C$, where C is the % of component reuse and i is the coefficient adjustment for new interface design effort.

Figure 1.11 plots software effort estimation for project size varying from 10 to 50 KLOC for all four classes of projects. We assumed 30 % component reuse in cloud computing case. If more percentage of component reuse is possible, it will mitigate the higher interaction complexity in coefficient *a* and will be beneficial for cloud computing platform. Figure 1.12 plots the corresponding software development time estimation for all four classes of software projects. With 30 % component reuse possibility, software development on cloud computing platform will take least amount of time.

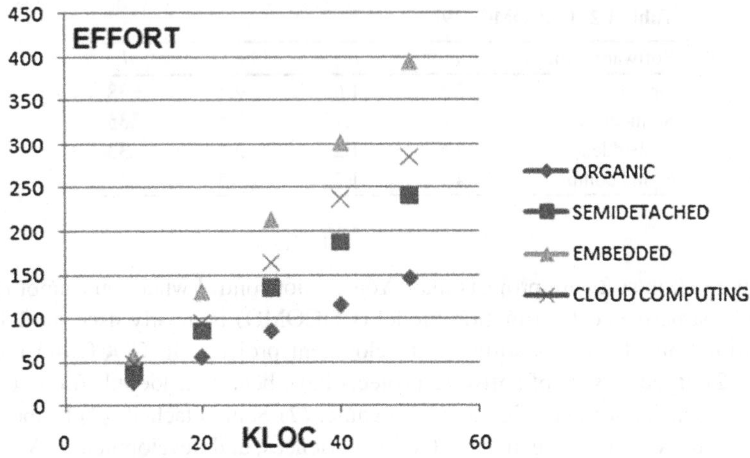

Fig. 1.11 Extended COCOMO for SW effort estimation [29]

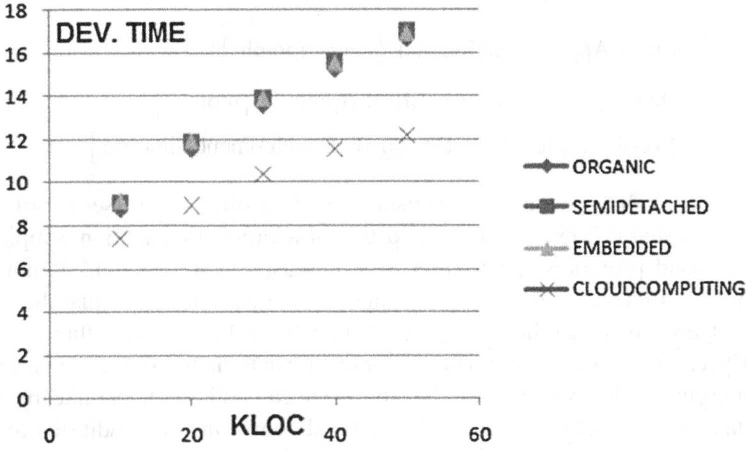

Fig. 1.12 Extended COCOMO for SW dev. time [29]

1.5 Conclusion

The development of Semantic Web or Web 3.0 can transform the World Wide Web into an intelligent Web system of structured, linked data which can be queried and inferred as a whole by the computers themselves. This Semantic Web capability is materializing many innovative use of the Web such as hosting Web services and cloud computing platform. Web services and cloud computing are paradigm shifts over traditional way of developing and deploying of software. This will make software engineering more difficult as software engineers have to master the Semantic Web skills for using open source software on distributed computing platform and they have to interact with a third party called the "cloud provider" in all stages of software processes. Automatic discovery and integration with Web services will reduce the amount of work in terms of line of code (LOC) or function points (FP) required for developing software on cloud platform but there will be added semantic skill requirements and communication and coordination requirements with the cloud providers which makes software development project more complex.

First, the Semantic Web techniques are explored on what the software developers need to incorporate in their artifacts in order to be discovered easily on the Web to give their product a competitive edge and for efficient software integration and maintenance purposes. Then, the need for changes in the prevalent software process models is analyzed to suggest that they should incorporate the new dimension of interactions with the cloud providers and separate roles of software engineers and cloud providers. A new agile process model is proposed in this chapter which includes the anticipated interactions requirement with the cloud provider which will mitigate all the challenges of software development on cloud computing platform and make it more advantageous to develop and deploy software on the cloud computing platform.

Cloud computing being the anticipated future computing platform, more software engineering process models need to be researched which can mitigate all its challenges and reap all its benefits. Also, safety and privacy issues of data in cloud computing platform need to be considered seriously so that cloud computing is truly accepted by all.

References

1. Barners-Lee, T.: Future of the web. http://dig.csail.mit.edu/2007/03/01 (2007)
2. Guha, R.: Toward the intelligent web systems. In: Proceedings of IEEE CS, First International Conference on Computational Intelligence, Communication Systems and Network, pp. 459–463. IEEE, Los Alamitos (2009)
3. Handler, J., Shadbolt, N., Hall, W., Berners-Lee, T., Weitzner, D.: Web science: an interdisciplinary approach to understanding the web. Commun. ACM **51**(7), 60–69 (2008)
4. Chong, F., Carraro, G.: Architecture Strategies for Catching the Long Tail. Microsoft Corporation, Redmond (2006)
5. Banerjee, J., Aziz, S.: SOA: the missing link between enterprise architecture and solution architecture. SETLabs Brief. **5**(2), 69–80 (2007)
6. Barners-Lee, T.: Linked data. http://www.w3.org/DesignIssues/LinkedData.html (2012)
7. Bizer, C., Heath, T., Berners-Lee, T.: Linked data – the story so far. Special issue on linked data. Int. J. Semant. Web Inf. Syst. (IJSWIS). http://tomheath.com/papers/bizer-heath-berners-lee-ijswis-linked-data.pdf (2012)
8. Niemann, B., et al.: Introducing Semantic Technologies and the Vision of the Semantic Web, SICoP White Paper (2005)
9. HADOOP: http://en.wikipedia.org/wiki/Hadoop (2010)
10. Taft, D.: IBM's M2 Project Taps Hadoop for Massive Mashups. www.eweek.com (2010)
11. Wikipedia: Free and open source software. http://en.wikipedia.org/wiki/Free_and_open-source_software. Accessed July 2012

12. Wikipedia: Web Ontology Language. http://en.wikipedia.org/wiki/Web_Ontology_Language. Accessed July 2012
13. Code{4}lib: Library Ontology. http://wiki.code4lib.org/index.php/Library_Ontology Accessed July 2012
14. Sun Microsystem: Introduction to Cloud Computing Architecture, White Paper, 1st edn. (2009)
15. Sun Microsystem: Open Source & Cloud Computing: On-Demand, Innovative IT on a Massive Scale (2012)
16. Singh, A., Korupolu, M., Mahapatra, D.: Server-storage virtualization: integration and load balancing in data centers. In: IEEE/ACM Supercomputing (SC) Conference. IEEE Press, Piscataway (2008)
17. VMWARE: Virtualization overview. www.vmware.com (2012)
18. Reservoir Consortium: Resources and Services Virtualization Without Barriers. Scientific Report (2009)
19. Pearson, S.: Taking Account of Privacy when Designing Cloud Computing Services. HP Labs, Bristol (2009)
20. Jansen, W.A.: Cloud Hooks: Security and Privacy Issues in Cloud Computing. NIST
21. Pressman, R.: Software Engineering: A Practitioner's Approach, 7th edn. McGraw-Hill Higher Education, New York (2009)
22. Sommerville, I.: Software Engineering, 8th edn. Pearson Education, Harlow (2006)
23. Cavanaugh, E.: Web services: benefits, challenges, and a unique, visual development solution. www.altova.com (2006)
24. Nickull, D., et al.: Service Oriented Architecture (SOA) and Specialized Messaging Patterns (2007)
25. Web services-Axis: axis.apache.org/axis (2012)
26. W3C: Web services Description Language (WSDL) Version 2.0 (2012)
27. Brambilla, M. et al.: A Software Engineering Approach to Design and Development of Semantic Web Service Applications (2006)
28. Salesforce.com: Agile Development Meets Cloud Computing for Extraordinary Results. www.salesforce.com (2009)
29. Guha, R., Al-Dabass, D.: Impact of Web 2.0 and cloud computing platform on software engineering. In: Proceedings of 1st International Symposium on Electronic System Design (ISED) (2010)
30. DeMarco, T., Lister, T.: Waltzing with Bears: Managing Risk on Software Projects. Dorset House Publishing Company, Incorporated, New York (2003)

Chapter 2
Envisioning the Cloud-Induced Transformations in the Software Engineering Discipline

Pethuru Raj, Veeramuthu Venkatesh, and Rengarajan Amirtharajan

Abstract The software engineering field is on the move. The contributions of software solutions for IT-inspired business automation, acceleration, and augmentation are enormous. The business values are also rapidly growing with the constant and consistent maturity and stability of software technologies, processes, infrastructures, frameworks, architectural patterns, and tools. On the other hand, the uncertainty in the global economy has a direct bearing on the IT budgets of worldwide organizations. That is, they are expecting greater flexibility, responsiveness, and accountability from their IT division, which is being chronically touted as the cost center. This insists on shorter delivery cycles and on delivering low-cost yet high-quality solutions. Cloud computing prescribes a distinguished delivery model that helps IT organizations to provide quality solutions efficiently in a manner that suits to evolving business needs. In this chapter, we are to focus how software-development tasks can get greatly simplified and streamlined with cloud-centric development processes, practices, platforms, and patterns.

Keywords Cloud computing • Software engineering • Global software development • Model-driven architecture • MDA • Lean methodology • Distributed computing

2.1 Introduction

The number of pioneering discoveries in the Internet space is quite large. In the recent past, the availability of devices and tools to access online and on-demand professional and personal services has increased dramatically. Software has been

---

P. Raj (✉)
Wipro Technologies, Bangalore 560035, India
e-mail: peterindia@gmail.com

V. Venkatesh • R. Amirtharajan
School of Electrical and Electronics Engineering, SASTRA University,
Thanjavur, Tamil Nadu, India

Z. Mahmood and S. Saeed (eds.), *Software Engineering Frameworks for the Cloud Computing Paradigm*, Computer Communications and Networks,
DOI 10.1007/978-1-4471-5031-2_2,

pervasive and persuasive. It runs on almost all kinds of everyday devices that are increasingly interconnected as well as Internet-connected. This deeper and extreme connectivity opens up fresh possibilities and opportunities for students, scholars, and scientists. The devices at the ground level are seamlessly integrated with cyber applications at remote, online, on-demand cloud servers. The hardware and software infrastructure solutions need to be extremely scalable, nimble, available, high-performing, dynamic, modifiable, real-time, and completely secure. Cloud computing is changing the total IT landscape by presenting every single and tangible IT resource as a service over any network. This strategically sound service enablement decimates all kinds of dependencies, portability, interoperability issues, etc.

Cloud services and applications are becoming very popular and penetrative these days. Increasingly, both business and IT applications are being modernized appropriately and moved to clouds to be subsequently subscribed and consumed by global user programs and people directly anytime anywhere for free or a fee. The aspect of software delivery is henceforth for a paradigm shift with the smart leverage of cloud concepts and competencies. Now there is a noteworthy trend emerging fast to inspire professionals and professors to pronounce the role and responsibility of clouds in software engineering. That is, not only cloud-based software delivery but also cloud-based software development and debugging are insisted as the need of the hour. On carefully considering the happenings, it is no exaggeration to say that the end-to-end software production, provision, protection, and preservation are to happen in virtualized IT environments in a cost-effective, compact, and cognitive fashion. Another interesting and strategic pointer is that the number and the type of input/output devices interacting with remote, online, and on-demand cloud are on the climb. Besides fixed and portable computing machines, there are slim and sleek mobile, implantable, and wearable devices emerging to access, use, and orchestrate a wider variety of disparate and distributed professional as well as personal cloud services. The urgent thing is to embark on modernizing and refining the currently used application development processes and practices in order to make cloud-based software engineering simpler, successful, and sustainable.

In this chapter, we discuss cloud-sponsored transformations for IT and leveraging clouds for global software development and present a reflection on software engineering. The combination of agility and cloud infrastructure for next-generation software engineering, the convergence of service and cloud paradigms, the amalgamation of model-driven architecture, and the cloud and various mechanisms for assisting cloud software development are also discussed. At the end, cloud platform solutions for software engineering are discussed, and software engineering challenges with respect to cloud environments are also presented.

2.2 Cloud-Sponsored Transformations for IT

The popularity of the cloud paradigm is surging, and it is overwhelmingly accepted as the disruptive, transformative, and innovative technology for the entire IT field. The direct benefits include IT agility through rationalization, simplification, higher utilization, and optimization. This section explores the tectonic and seismic shifts of IT through the cloud concepts.

- *Adaptive IT* – There are a number of cloud-inspired innovations in the form of promising, potential, and powerful deployment; delivery; pricing; and consumption models in order to sustain the IT value for businesses. With IT agility setting in seamlessly, business agility, autonomy, and adaptivity are being guaranteed with the adoption and adaption of cloud idea.
- *People IT* – Clouds support centralized yet federated working model. It operates at a global level. For example, today there are hundreds of thousands of smartphone applications and services accumulated and delivered via mobile clouds. With ultrahigh broadband communication infrastructures and advanced to compute clouds in place, the vision of the Internet of devices, services, and things is to see a neat and nice reality. Self-, surroundings-, and situation-aware services will become common, plentiful, and cheap; thereby, IT promptly deals with peoples' needs precisely and delivers on them directly.
- *Green IT* – The whole world is becoming conscious about the power energy consumption and the heat getting dissipated into our living environment. There are calculated campaigns at different levels for arresting climate change and for sustainable environment through less greenhouse-gas emission. IT is being approached for arriving at competent green solutions. Grid and cloud computing concepts are the leading concepts for green environment. Especially the smart energy grid and the Internet of Energy (IoE) disciplines are gaining a lot of ground in order to contribute decisively for the global goal of sustainability. The much-published and proclaimed cloud paradigm leads to lean compute, communication, and storage infrastructures, which significantly reduce the electricity consumption.
- *Optimal IT* – There are a number of worthwhile optimizations happening in the business-enabling IT space. "More with less" has become the buzzword for both business and IT managers. Cloud enablement has become the mandatory thing for IT divisions as there are several distinct benefits getting accrued out of this empowerment. Cloud certainly has the wherewithal for the goals behind the IT optimization drive.
- *Next-Generation IT* – With a number of delectable advancements in wireless and wired broadband communication space, the future Internet is being positioned as the central figure in conceiving and concretizing people-centric discoveries and inventions. With cloud emerging as the new-generation compute infrastructure, we will have connected, simplified, and smart IT that offers more influential and inferential capability to humans.
- *Converged, Collaborative, and Shared IT* – The cloud idea is fast penetrating into every tangible domain. Cloud's platforms are famous for not only software deployment and delivery but also for service design, development, debugging, and management. Further on, clouds, being the consolidated, converged, and centralized infrastructure, are being prescribed and presented as the best bet for enabling seamless and spontaneous service integration, orchestration, and

collaboration. With everything (application, platform, and infrastructure) are termed and touted as publicly discoverable, network-accessible, self-describing, autonomous, and multitenant services, clouds will soon become the collaboration hub. Especially business-aware, process-centric, and service-oriented composites can be easily realized with the cloud-based collaboration platform.

- *Real-Time IT* – Data's variety, volume, and velocity are on the climb. The current IT infrastructures are insufficient in order to extract actionable insights out of pouring data. Hence, the emergence of big data computing and analysis technologies are given due diligence and attention. These fast-maturing technologies are able to accomplish real-time transition from data to information and to knowledge. Cloud is the optimized, automated, and virtualized infrastructure for big data computing and analytics. That is, with the infrastructure support from clouds, big data computing model is to see a lot of improvements in the days ahead so that the ultimate goal of real-time analytics can be realized very fluently and flawlessly.

2.3 Leveraging Clouds for Global Software Development (GSD)

Globalization and distribution are the two key concepts in the IT field. Software development goes off nations' boundaries and tends toward places wherein quality software engineers and project managers are available in plenty. On-site, off-shoring, near-shoring, etc., are some of the recent buzzwords in IT circles due to these developments. That is, even a software project gets developed in different locations as the project team gets distributed across the globe. With the sharp turnarounds in a communication field, a kind of tighter coordination and collaboration among team members are possible in order to make project implementation successful and sustainable. In-sourcing has paved the way for outsourcing with the maturity of appropriate technologies. As widely known, software sharply enhances the competitive advantage and edge for businesses. Hence, global software development (GSD) has become a mandatory thing for the world organizations. Nevertheless, when embarking on GSD, organizations continue to face challenges in adhering to the development life cycle. The advent of the Internet has supported GSD by bringing new concepts and opportunities resulting in benefits such as scalability, flexibility, independence, reduced cost, resource pools, and usage tracking. It has also caused the emergence of new challenges in the way software is being delivered to stakeholders. Application software and data on the cloud are accessed through services, which follow SOA principles.

GSD is actually the software-development process incorporating teams spread across the globe in different locations, countries, and even continents. The driver for this sort of arrangement is by the fact that conducting software projects in multiple geographical locations is likely to result in benefits such as cost reduction and reduced time to market, access to a larger skill pool, proximity to customer, and 24-h development by following the sun. But, at the same time, GSD brings challenges to distributed software-development activities due to geographic, cultural, linguistic, and temporal distance between the project development teams.

Because of the distance between the software-development teams, GSD encounters certain challenges in terms of collaboration, communication, coordination, culture, management, organizational, outsourcing, development process, development teams, and tools. The real motive for using the cloud for supporting GSD is that the cloud idea thrives as it is closely related to the service paradigm. That is, services are created, provisioned, and delivered from cloud-based service platforms. Since SOA runs a mechanism for development and management of distributed dynamic systems, and it evolved from the distributed-component-based approach, it is argued that cloud has the innate potential and strength to successfully cater for the challenges of GSD where a project is developed across different geographical locations. GSD challenges can be overcome through SOA. This will contribute to increased interoperability, diversification, and business and technology alignment. Cloud as the next-generation centralized and service-oriented infrastructure is capable of decimating all the internal as well as externally imposed challenges.

- Global Software Development (GSD) in Cloud Platforms [1] – Clouds offer instant resource provisioning, flexibility, on-the-fly scaling, and high availability for continuously evolving GSD-related activities. Some of the use cases include.
- Development Environments – With clouds, the ability to acquire, deploy, configure, and host development environments become "on-demand." The development environments are always on and always available to the implementation teams with fine-grained access control mechanisms. In addition, the development environments can be purpose-built with support for application-level tools, source code repositories, and programming tools. After the project is done, these can also be archived or destroyed. The other key element of these "on-demand" hosting environments is the flexibility through its quick "prototyping" support. Prototyping becomes flexible, in that as new code and ideas can be quickly turned into workable proof of concepts (PoCs) and tested.
- Developer Tools – Hosting developer tools such as IDEs and simple code editors in the cloud eliminates the need for developers to have local IDEs and other associated development tools, which are made available across time zones and places.
- Content Collaboration Spaces – Clouds make collaboration and coordination practical, intuitive, and flexible through easy enabling of content collaboration spaces, modeled after the social software domain tools like Facebook, but centering on project-related information like invoices, statements, RFPs, requirement documents, images, and data sets. These content spaces can automate many project-related tasks such as automatically creating MS Word versions of all imported text documents or as complex as running work flows to collate information from several different organizations working in collaboration. Each content space can be unique, created by composing a set of project requirements. Users can invite

internal and external collaborators into this customized environment, assigning appropriate roles and responsibilities. After the group's work is "complete," their content space can be archived or destroyed. These spaces can be designed to support distributed version control systems enabling social platform conversations and other content management features.

- Continuous Code Integration – Compute clouds let "compile-test-change" software cycle on the fly do continuous builds and integration checks to meet strict quality checks and development guidelines. They can also enforce policies for customized builds.
- APIs and Programming Frameworks – Clouds force developers to embrace standard programming model APIs where ever possible and adhere to style guides, conventions, and coding standards in meeting the specific project requirements. They also force developers to embrace new programming models and abstractions such as .NET Framework, GWT, Django, Rails, and Spring Framework for significantly increasing the overall productivity. One more feature of using clouds is that they enforce constraints, which push developers to address the critical next-generation programming challenges of multicore computing, parallel programming, and virtualization. As explained earlier in the chapter, global software development is picking up fast, and the emergence of clouds is to boost the GSD activities further.

2.4 A Reflection on Software Engineering

Radha Guha writes in [2] that over the last half-century, there have been robust and resilient advancements in the hardware engineering domain. That is, there are radical and rapid improvisations in computers, memory, storage, communication networks, mobile devices, and embedded systems. This has been incessantly pushing the need for larger and more complex software. Software development not only involves many different hardware elements, it also involves many different parties like end users and software engineers. That is why software development has become such an inherently complicated task. Software developers are analyzing, articulating, and adopting the proven and prescribed engineering disciplines. That is, leveraging systematic, disciplined, and quantifiable approach to make software development more manageable to produce quality software products. The success or quality of a software project is measured by whether it is developed within the stipulated time and agreed budget and by its throughput, user-friendliness, consumability, dependability, and modifiability.

Typically, a software engineering engagement starts off with an explicit and elegant process model comprising several formally defined and synchronized phases. The whole development process of software from its conceptualization to implementation to operation and retirement is called the software-development life cycle (SDLC). SDLC goes through several sub-activities like requirement's gathering, planning, design, coding, testing, deployment, maintenance, and retirement.

These activities are well synchronized in accordance to the process model adopted for a particular software development. There are many process models to choose from like water fall model, rapid application development (RAD) model, and spiral model depending on the size of the project, delivery time requirement, and type of the project. The development of an avionic embedded system will adopt a different process model from development of a Web application.

Even though software engineering [3] takes the engineering approach, the success of software products is more difficult than products from other engineering domains like mechanical engineering or civil engineering. This is because software is intangible during its development. Software project managers use a number of techniques and tools to monitor the software building activities in a more visible way. These activities include software project tracking and control, risk management, quality assurance, measurements, configuration management, work product or document's generation, review, and reusability management.

Even after taking all these measures for sticking to the plan and giving much importance to document generation for project tracking and control, many software projects failed. More than 50 % of software projects fail due to various reasons like schedule and budget slippage, non-user-friendly interface of the software, and non-flexibility for maintenance and change of the software. Therefore, there is a continued and consistent focus on simplifying and streamlining software implementation. In this chapter, we are to see some of the critical and crucial improvements in software engineering process with the availability of cloud infrastructures.

The Evolutions and Revolutions in the Software Engineering Field – There are a number of desirable and delectable advancements in the field of software engineering in order to make the tough task of software construction easier and quicker. This section describes the different levels and layers in which the software engineering discipline and domain evolve.

At the *building-block level*, data, procedures, classes, components, agents, aspects, events, and services are the key abstraction and encapsulation units for building and orchestrating software modules into various types of specific and generic software. Services especially contribute in legacy modernization and migration to open service-oriented platforms (SOPs) besides facilitating the integration of disparate, distributed, and decentralized applications. In short, building blocks are the key ingredient enabling software elegance, excellence, and evolution. In the recent past, formal models in digital format and service composites are evolving fast in order to further simplify and streamline the tough task of software assembly and implementation. As software complexity is on the rise, the need for fresh thoughts and techniques is too on the climb.

On the *language level*, a bevy of programming languages (open source as well as proprietary) were produced and promoted by individuals, innovators, and institutions. Even, there are efforts underway in order to leverage fit-for-purpose languages to build different parts and portions of software applications. Software libraries are growing in number, and the ideas of software factory and industrialization are picking up fast lately. Service registry and repository are an interesting phenomenon for speeding up software realization and maintenance. Programming languages and approaches thrive as there are different programming paradigms such as object orientation, event- and model-driven concepts, componentization, and service orientation. Further on, there are script languages in the recent past generating and getting a lot of attention due to their unique ability of achieving more with less code. Formal models in digitalized format and service composites are turning out to be a blessing in disguise for the success and survival of software engineering. There are domain-specific languages (DSLs) that could cater to the specific demands of domains quite easily and quickly.

As far as *development environments* are concerned, there are a number of diverse application building platforms for halving the software developmental complexity and cost. That is, there are a slew of integrated development environments (IDEs), rapid application development (RAD) tools, code generators and cartridges, enabling CASE tools, compilers, debuggers, profilers, purpose-specific engines, generic and specific frameworks, best practices, key guidelines, etc. Plug and play mechanism has gained a lot with the overwhelming adoption of eclipse IDE for inserting and instantiating different language compilers and interpreters. The long-standing objectives of platform portability (Java) and language portability (.NET Framework) are being achieved at a middleware level. There are standards-compliant toolkits for process modeling, simulation, improvement, investigation, and mapping. Services as the well-qualified process elements are being discovered, compared, and orchestrated for partial or full process automation.

At the *process level*, waterfall is the earliest one, and thereafter there came a number of delicious variations in software-development methodology with each one having both pros and cons. Iterations, increments, and integrations are being touted as the fundamental characteristics for swifter software production. Agile programming is gaining a lot of ground as business changes are more frequent than ever before and software complexity is also growing. Agility and authenticity in software building are graciously achieved with improved and constant interactions with customers and with the enhanced visibility and controllability on software implementation procedures. Agility, being a well-known horizontal technique, matches, mixes, and merges with other paradigms such as service-oriented programming and model-driven software development to considerably assist in lessening the workload of software developers and coders. Another noteworthy trend is that rather than code-based implementation, configuration-based software production catches up fast.

At the *infrastructural level,* the cloud idea has brought in innumerable transformations. The target of IT agility is seeing a neat and nice reality and this in turn could lead to business agility. Technically, cloud-inspired infrastructures are virtualized, elastic, self-servicing, automated, and shared. Due to the unique capabilities and competencies of cloud IT infrastructures (in short, clouds), all kinds of enterprise IT platforms (development, execution, management, governance, and delivery) are being accordingly manipulated and migrated to be hosted in clouds, which are extremely converged, optimized, dynamic, lean, and green. Such meteoric movement decisively empowers application platforms to be multitenant, unified, and centralized catering to multiple customers and users with all the enhanced productivity, extensibility, and effectiveness. In other words, cloud platforms are set to rule and reign the IT world in the days to unfold. In other words, platforms are getting service-enabled so that any service (application, platform, and infrastructure) can discover and use them without any barriers. Service enablement actually expresses and exposes every IT resource as a service so that all kinds of the resource's incompatibilities are decimated completely. That is, resources readily connect, concur, compose, and collaborate with one another without any externally or internally imposed constrictions, contradictions, and confusions. In a nutshell, the unassailable service science has come as a unifying factor for the dilapidated and divergent IT world.

In summary, the deeply dissected, discoursed, and deliberated software-development discipline is going through a number of pioneering and positive changes as described above.

2.5 Combination of Agility and Cloud Infrastructure for Next-Generation Software Engineering

As indicated previously, there have been many turns and twists in the hot field of software engineering. It is an unquestionable fact that the cloud paradigm, without an iota of doubt, has impacted the entire IT elegantly and exceedingly. Besides presenting a bright future on the aspect of centralized deployment, delivery, and management of IT resources, the cloud idea has opened up fresh opportunities and possibilities for cloud-based software design, development, and debugging in a simplified and systematic fashion. That is, with the overwhelming adoption and adaption of cloud infrastructures (private, public, community, and hybrid), producing and preserving enterprise-scale, mission-critical, and value-added software are going to be definitely distinct. There are four key drivers that unanimously elevate the software development to be advanced to an accomplished in a cloud. These are:

- *Time, Cost, and Productivity* – The developer community is being mandated to do more, quicker, and with fewer resources.
- *Distributed Complex Sourcing* – Due to various reasons, IT project team members are geographically dispersed.
- *Faster Delivery of Innovation* – The focus is on enabling architects and developers to think ingeniously in order to deliver business value.
- *Increasing Complexity* – In today's world, an enterprise-scale project easily consumes several million lines resulting in more complexity.

In order to reduce complexity, resources, cost, and time considerably, professionals and professors are vigorously and rigorously striving and searching for incredibly inventive solutions. Newer concepts, process optimization, best practices, fresh programming models, state-of-the-art platforms, design patterns and metrics, and advanced tools are being increasingly unearthed and utilized for lessening the software development workload. Researchers are continuously at work in order to discover competent and compact methods and mechanisms for simplifying and streamlining the increasingly multifaceted tasks of constructing and conserving next-generation software systems. The major benefits of agile methodology over the traditional methods are:

- Faster time to market
- Quick return on investment
- Shorter release cycles
- Better adaptability and responsiveness to business changing requirements
- Early detection of failure and immediate correction

There are several agile development methods such as Scrum, extreme programming, test-driven development, and lean software development [4]. With agile models, business houses expect that services and solutions are being delivered incrementally earlier rather than later, and delivery cycle time period comes down sharply. That is, one delivery cycle takes up from 2 to 4 weeks. However, in the midst of these turnarounds, there arise a number of critical challenges, as mentioned below:

- High effort and cost involved in setting up infrastructures
- Lack of skilled resources
- Lack of ability to build applications from multiple places across the globe

There are a few popular cloud platforms available in order to enable software development in cloud environments. Google App Engine, salesforce.com, cloudfoundry.org, cloudbees.com, corenttech.com, heroku.com, windowsazure.com, etc., are the leading platforms for cloud-based application development, scaling, and sustainability.

Collabnet (http://www.collab.net/), a product firm for enabling software development in cloud-based platforms, expounds and enlightens on the seamless convergence of the agile programming models, application lifecycle management (ALM) product, and clouds for a precise and decisive answer for the perpetual software engineering challenges, changes, and concerns. It convincingly argues that cloud technologies reduce development barriers by providing benefits in the following critical areas:

- *Availability* – Code is centralized and infrastructure is scalable and available on demand.
- *Access* – Ensures flexible access to test environments and transparency to project data for the entire team.
- *Overhead* – Reduced support overhead, no upgrade latency – teams use an on-demand model to get what they need, quickly and easily.

Agile processes set the strong and stimulating foundation for distributed teams to work closely together with all the right and relevant stakeholders to better anticipate and respond to user expectations. Agile teams today are empowered to clearly communicate with users to act and react expediently to their feedback. That is, they are able to collaboratively and cleverly iterate toward the desired state and user satisfaction. Cloud intrinsically facilitates open collaboration across geographies and time zones with little investment or risk. With more and more development and test activities moving toward clouds, organizations are able to save time and money using virtual and shared resources on need basis. Developers could save time by leaving configuration, upgrades, and maintenance to cloud providers, who usually employ highly educated and experienced people. Anytime anywhere access is facilitated for those with proper authentication and authorization, and assets are completely centralized and controlled.

Agile and cloud are being positioned together and prescribed as a powerful and pathbreaking combination for the software-development community. This might seem counterintuitive to those entrenched in waterfall processes or those comfortable with the idea of a daily stand-up and colocated teams. The reality is altogether different. That is, there are a number of technical and business cases emerging for using the agile methods in the cloud. The agility concepts make development teams responsive to the changing needs of businesses and empower them to be adaptable and flexible. Further on, proven agile processes help to break down all sorts of barriers and blockages between development and production, allowing teams to work together to concentrate on meeting stakeholder expectations. The synchronization of agile and cloud paradigms fully free up developers from all kinds of difficulties to achieve more with less, to innovate fast, and to ultimately bring value to the business.

2.6 Convergence of Service and Cloud Paradigms

The service idea has matured and stabilized as the dominant approach for designing, developing, and delivering open, sustainable, and interoperable service-oriented systems for enterprise, Web, embedded, and cloud spaces. Even many of the modules of packaged business software solutions are modified and presented as services. Services are publicly discoverable and accessible, reusable, and composable modules for building distinct and specific applications through configuration and customization, runtime matching, selection and usage of distributed, disparate and decentralized services, replacement of existing service components through the substitution of new advanced service components, and service orchestration. Services as process elements are supporting and sustaining process-oriented systems, which are generally more flexible. That is, operation and controlling of software solutions at process level considerably reduce the software development, management, and maintenance tasks.

Thus, the process propensity of the service paradigm and cloud-centric service-oriented infrastructures and platforms bring a number of distinct advantages for software engineering. Services and cloud computing have garnered much attention from both industry and academia because they enable the rapid and radical development of enterprise-scale, mission-critical, high-performance, dynamic, and distributed applications. Agility, adaptivity, and affordability, the prime characteristics of next-generation software systems, can be realized with the smart leverage of processes, services, and cloud platforms. Precisely speaking, the service paradigm is to energize futuristic software design, whereas cloud platforms are being tipped and touted as the next-generation service-centric platforms for service development, deployment, management, and delivery.

Service-Oriented Software Development – It is to see a lot of delectable and decisive shifts with the adoption of cloud platforms. The smooth and seamless convergence of services and clouds promises shining days for software-development community. Of course, there are a few challenges that need utmost attention from scholars, scientists, and students. Security, visibility, controllability, performance, availability, usability, etc., need to be obviated in order to fast-track service-based software implementation in clouds.

As widely pronounced, services are being positioned as the most flexible and fertile component for software production. That is, software solutions are made of interoperable services. It is all about the dynamic discovery and purposeful interactions among a variety of services that are local or remote, business or IT-centric, and owned or subscribed from third-party service providers. Services are standards-compliant, self-describing, and autonomous entities in order to decimate all kinds of dependencies and incompatibilities, to promote seamless and spontaneous collaborations, and to share each of their capability and competency with others over networks. Process and workflow-based service compositions result in dynamic applications that are highly portable. XML is the key data representation, exchange, and persistence mechanism facilitating service interoperability. Policies are being framed and encouraged in order to achieve automated service finding, binding, usage, monitoring, and governance. The essence of service governance is to explicitly establish pragmatic policies and enforce them stringently. With a consistent rise in automation, there is a possibility for deviation and distraction, and hence the service governance discipline is gaining a lot of ground these days.

As there is a clear distinction between service users and providers, service-level agreement (SLA) and even operation-level agreement (OLA) are becoming vital for service-centric business success and survival. Furthermore, there are geographically distributed several providers providing identical or similar services and hence SLA, which unambiguously describes runtime requirements that govern a service's interactions with different users, has come as a deciding factor for service selection and utilization. A service contract describes its interface and the associated contractual obligations. Using standard protocols and respective interfaces, application developers can dynamically search, discover, compose, test, verify, and execute services in their applications at runtime. In a nutshell, SOA-based application development is through service registration, discovery, assessment, and composition, which primarily involves three stakeholders:

- A service provider is one who develops and hosts the service in cloud platforms.
- A service consumer is a person or program that finds and uses a service to build an application.
- A service broker mediates between service providers and consumers. It is a program or professional in helping out providers publishing their unique services and guiding consumers to identify ideal services.

The service science is on the growth trajectory. There are service-oriented platforms, patterns, procedures, practices, products, and packages. Service management has become a niche area of study and research. The knowledge-driven service era is to dawn with the availability of competent service-centric technologies, infrastructures and processes, toolsets, architectures, and frameworks. Service engineering is picking up fast with the sufficient tweaking and tuning of software engineering principles, techniques, and tips. Everything related to IT is being conscientiously manipulated and presented as a service for the outside world setting the context and case for IT as a service (ITaaS). In other words, any service can connect and cooperate with other services individually or collectively to make bigger and better things for the total humanity.

The Synchronization Between Service and Cloud Ideas – As explained and elucidated above, the service and cloud computing models together signal a sunny and shining days ahead for software building. A combined framework comprising the service and the cloud concepts goes a long way in halving the application development drudgery. Cloud-centric application development gets a consolidated, centralized, virtualized, and shared IT infrastructure for efficiently constructing and preserving applications. Multitenancy, auto-provisioning, and elasticity features are the strong business and technical cases for embracing the cloud idea.

Now with the concepts of the Inter-cloud that are fast emerging and evolving, cloud integration and federation aspects are bound to grow significantly. That is, connected and federated clouds will become the common, casual, and cheap thing for next-generation enterprise IT. The federation of multiple types of clouds (mobile, device, sensor, knowledge, information cloud, high-performance cloud, etc.) is to enable distributed, global, and collaborative software development [5]. The open and industry-strength interoperability standards of SOA empower service-sponsored cloud integration and, on the other hand, cloud-hosted service integration. In short, the cloud grid is not an option but a necessity considering the growing complexity of IT toward sustaining the business dynamism.

The concept of designing and developing applications using SOA and delivery through cloud is to explode. Cloud brokerage firms could maintain cloud-hosted service registry and repository that works out as a single point of contact for global application developers. The service metadata offers the exact location, interface, and contract of services being probed for use. Service developers could host their services in service platforms of worldwide cloud providers, and this enables application developers to search and choose right and relevant services based on the business requirements. Service providers could also host integrated development environments and rapid application development tools, code generators and cartridges, debuggers, simulators, emulators, etc., in their own clouds or in third-party cloud infrastructures. Furthermore, they could publish software artifacts such as modifiable and extendible business processes, workflows, application templates, user interfaces, data schema, and policies to facilitate software development and generation. Developers can find viable and value-added services from multiple service providers and leverage these artifacts in order to come out with service-oriented applications. The fast-maturing federation science is to dictate the future of software engineering. In short, there are cloud-based components such as:

- Application development artifacts such as templates, processes, and workflows
- Service development environments and tools
- Service registry repository
- SCA-compliant application implementation platforms with service discovery, integration, and orchestration features and facilities leveraging the application artifacts
- Application delivery as a service via the Internet as the cheap and open communication infrastructure

Service-Based Software Design and Development – Development of service systems remains a quiet big challenge because services are being developed by different entities and deposited in geographically distributed locations. For an application to fructify, diverse services need to be smartly collected and consolidated. Different services are covered up with disparate policies. Varying capabilities decorate services. Also application development process is increasingly diversified because application developers, service brokers, and application service providers are distributed. The coordination here is very important for the SOA-based IT and business successes. Standardized protocols, messaging mechanisms, and interfaces are very essential services to be linked remotely and resiliently.

Software engineering revolves around two main activities: decomposition and composition. As business problem evolves and enlarges, the act of decomposition of business problem is required as our mental capability is limited. Once an appropriate solution for the business problem is designed, then identify those solution building blocks and compose them to develop the solution.

Similar to other development methodologies, service-oriented software development starts with requirements extraction, elucidation, and engineering. During this phase, the application developer develops a business model; works with the customer to articulate, analyze, authenticate, and refine requirements; designs a workflow for the business model; and finally decomposes the requirements into smaller and manageable modules. Then the application developer sends each of the disintegrated and disengaged requirements to a service brokerage to find suitable services that satisfy the enshrined requirements. Once the right services are identified for each of the requirement parts, the application developer simply composes them into an application. Service component architecture (SCA) is a recent architectural style enabling application componentization into service modules that in turn get assembled to form a single entity. There are SCA-compliant IDEs from different product vendors. In some cases, correct services might not be available and hence one has to develop those services from the scratch.

Cloud-Based Software Delivery – Software engineering encompasses not only the software-development processes but also the effective delivery of the developed software to users, which includes software deployment and maintenance. However, SOA does not prescribe any specific methods for software deployment, management, governance, and enhancement. These can be decided and activated by software service organizations differently. Clouds as the standardized and smart infrastructure come to the rescue here by ensuring effective application delivery. Applications can be affordably deployed and maintained in advanced cloud platforms. Application capabilities can be provided as a service. All kinds of non-functional (quality of service (QoS)) attributes are effortlessly accomplished with clouds. Anytime anywhere resource access is being facilitated. Centralized monitoring and management are remarkably simplified here. That is, clouds as the next-generation service-oriented infrastructures (SOIs) have emerged in correct time in order to take the service idea to greater heights. It is therefore no exaggeration to proclaim that the software engineering field is greatly and grandiosely empowered by evolving cloud concepts.

Agile Service Networks (ASNs) [6, 7] – Cloud computing's high flexibility needs novel software engineering approaches and technologies to deliver agile, flexible, scalable, yet secure software solutions with full technical and business gains. One way is to allow applications to do the computing in cloud, and the other is to allow users to integrate with the applications. Agile service networks (ASNs) are themselves an emerging paradigm envisioning collaborative and dynamic service interactions (network edges) among global service-oriented applications (network nodes). ASNs can be used as a paradigm for software engineering in the cloud, since they are indeed able to deliver solutions which are both compliant to the cloud's needs and able to harness it, bringing about its full potential.

Context adaptation is used in ASNs to achieve agility. The concept of ASN is defined as a consequence of "late service binding." In the context of services' dynamism, which is achieved through late service binding, ASNs become a perfect example of how agility can be achieved in SOA systems. Adaptation is presented as one of the main tenets of SOA. This paradigm regards highly dynamic systems within a rapidly changing context to which applications must adapt. In this sense, ASNs are used to exemplify industrial needs for adaptive, context-aware systems.

ASN Key Features – ASNs are dynamic entities. Dynamism is seen as an essential part of the service interactions within collaborative industries (i.e., industrial value networks). Dynamism in ASNs is the trigger to service rearrangement and application adaptation. For example, an ASN made of collaborative resource brokering such as distributed stock markets is dynamic in the sense that different partners may participate actively, others may be dynamically added while brokering is ongoing, others may retire from the brokering process, and others may dynamically change their business goals and hence their brokering strategy. ASNs are business-oriented: ASNs are borne out of business corporative collaborations and represent complex service applications interacting in a networked business scenario involving multiple corporations or partners in different sites (i.e., different geo-locations). Within ASNs, business value can be computed, analyzed, and maximized.

Cloud-Induced Software Engineering Challenges – As widely reported, there are some important concerns with public clouds. Security, controllability, visibility, performance, and availability are the major issues. Virtualization, the central technology for the massive uptake and incontestable success of the cloud idea, has introduced new security holes. Typically, public clouds are more or less accommodating several customers to be economical, and there are real dangers and risks in a shared environment. If a cloud is not available for a few minutes, the resulting loss would be very enormous necessitating the sharp increment in guaranteeing cloud availability. Cloud reliability is another central and crucial factor not to be sidestepped easily. The security of data in rest or in transit has to be infallibly secure, and cryptography is the major source of inspiration for data security in a cloud environment. Identity and access management solutions are being conceived and concretized for the more open and risky cloud systems. Besides, application and service security and network and physical security aspects are also critical in a cloud environment.

Smartphone applications are becoming very popular and very large in the number with the massive production and release of slim and sleek, handy and trendy, yet multifaceted mobile phones. As there are literally more mobile devices compared to desktop and other powerful compute machines, application development for the fastest-growing mobile space is gaining unprecedented importance. Mobile technologies, application architectures and frameworks, toolsets, service delivery platforms, hypervisors for mobile devices, unified and integrated application development environments, etc., are being produced in plenty by competing parties in order to score over others in the mind and market shares. There are specific cloud infrastructures for securely storing a variety of mobile data, content, mails, services, and applications. Besides cell phones and smartphones, other mobile and portable devices incessantly capturing the imagination of people are the powerful tablets. Thus, there are several dimensions and directions in which the nifty and niche content and application development activities for the mobile landscape are proceeding.

With cloud emerging as the centralized place for mobile services, the days of anywhere anytime information and service access and upkeep are bright. Especially form builder applications for smartphones are being made available so that users could creatively produce their own forms in order to indulge in commercial and financial activities on the move. Hundreds of thousands of smartphone applications are being built, hosted, and subscribed by various smartphone vendors. Games are the other prominent and dominant entities for the mobile world. Precisely speaking, mobiles and clouds are increasingly coming closer for context-aware, customer-centric, and cognitive applications.

In summary, the penetration of cloud idea is simply mesmerizing and momentous. The cloud-based platforms are being positioned as the dynamic, converged, and fit-for-purpose ones for application engineering not only for enterprise IT but also for embedded IT, which incidentally includes mobile, wearable, portable, fixed, nomadic, wireless, implantable, and invisible devices. Extremely and deeply connected applications and services are bound to rule the IT in the coming days, and the cloud paradigm is the definite and decisive contributor for the future IT.

Although, the service and cloud concepts have greater affinity in strengthening software development and delivery, there are some serious issues to be addressed urgently in order to eliminate all kinds of doubts of in the minds of enterprise executives in order to reach into the promised land of cloud-sponsored service era.

2.7 Amalgamation of Model-Driven Architecture and the Cloud Paradigms

Modeling has been a fundamental and foundational activity for ages. Before a complex system gets formed, a model of the system is created as it could throw some light about the system's final structure and behavior. Models could extract and expose any kind of hidden risks and lacunae in system functioning and give a bit of confidence for designers and developers to plan and proceed obviating all kinds of barriers. Models give an overall understanding about the system to be built. In short, models decompose the system into a collection of smaller and manageable chunks in order to empower engineers to have a firm grip and grasp of the system under implementation. Modeling is one of the prominent and dominant complexity-mitigation techniques as systems across domains are fast-growing in complexity.

As IT systems are growing complexity, formal models are presented as the next-generation abstraction and encapsulation unit for them. In the recent past, models have been used as building blocks for having portable, sustainable, and flexible IT systems. Models are created digitally, stored, refined, and revitalized as per the changing needs. There are formats such as XML Metadata Interchange (XMI) for exporting models over the network or any other media to other systems as inputs for further processing. There are unified and visual languages and standardized notations emerging and energizing compact and formal model representation, persistence, manipulation, and exchange. Product vendors and open source software developers have come out with innumerable software tools for facilitating model creation, transformation, verification, validation, and exporting. For object orientation, unified modeling language (UML) has been the standard one for defining and describing models for various constructs and activities. For component-based assembly and service-orientation programming, UML profiles have been created in order to keep UML as the modeling language for software engineering. Further on, there are processing modeling and execution languages such as BPML and BPEL and notations such as BPMN in order to develop process-centric applications. That is, process models act as the building blocks for system engineering.

Model-driven architecture (MDA) is the associated application architecture. Model-driven software engineering (MDSE) is being presented as the most dynamic and drastic method for application engineering. Emerging and evolving MDSE techniques can automate the development of new cloud applications programmatically. Typically, cloud applications are a seamless union of several unique services running on different IT platforms. That is, for producing competent cloud applications, all the right and relevant services from diverse and geographically distributed servers have to be meticulously found, bound, and linked up in order to build and sustain modular (loosely coupled and highly cohesive) cloud applications. Precisely speaking, services have been overwhelmingly accepted as the most productive and pliable building block for realizing adaptive, mission-critical, and enterprise-scale applications.

For building service-oriented cloud applications, there is a need for modernizing all the legacy software modules into services. Model-driven reverse engineering techniques are capable of discovering and generating standardized models out of legacy software modules. The overall idea is to use such techniques and enabling frameworks such as MoDisco framework to speed up the task of model creation from legacy modules. These formal models can be subjected to further transformation to derive corresponding services that in collaborate with other cloud-based services in order to craft fresh cloud applications quickly. That is, just as software as a service (SaaS) paradigm, the notion of modeling as a service (MaaS) is to see brighter days ahead especially in assisting the formation of cloud applications out of existing non-cloud applications. As there are billions of legacy code still contributing extensively for fortune corporations across the globe, MaaS is to grow exponentially. There will be processes to be defined, frameworks to be produced, cloud platforms to be immensely utilized, etc. Reverse engineering of application modules into a PIM and then into one or more PSMs to automate the service realization out of old software components is the cleverest and clear-cut approach for the forthcoming cloud era. It is keenly anticipated that similar to SaaS, MaaS will become a pioneering initiative. Here are some possible applications of MaaS [8]:

- Creation of collaborative and distributed modeling tools to allow the specification and sharing of software models among team members in real time.
- Definition of modeling mash-ups as a combination of MDSE services from different vendors.
- Availability of model transformation engines in the cloud to provide platform-independent model management services.
- Improving Scalability of MDSE – Models of real-life applications (especially those obtained by reverse engineering of running systems) are usually very large. Modeling services in the cloud would ensure the scalability of MDSE techniques in those scenarios.
- Facilitating Model Execution and Evolution – Moving code-generation and simulation services to cloud would facilitate the deployment and evolution of software applications (regardless of whether those applications were implemented as SaaS) and substantially reduce the time to market. The cloud service providers (CSPs) with their infrastructure administration experts could set up the relevant infrastructures to compile and deploy the applications quickly.
- Solving Tool Interoperability Problems – Exchanging data (and metadata) among MDSE tools is one of the major challenges nowadays. So far, the problem is being addressed by defining bridges among the tools, but MaaS is to offer a more transparent and global solution to this problem. For instance, bridges could be defined as services and executed on demand automatically by other services when incompatibility issues surface.
- Distributed Global Model Management – Complex MDSE projects involve several models (possibly conforming to different metamodels), model transformations, model injectors and projectors, etc. The MaaS paradigm is to facilitate the manipulation of all these modeling artifacts in a distributed environment.

Model-Driven and Cloud-Sponsored Legacy Enablement Toward Mainstream Computing – Long-living software systems [9] constantly undergo a number of changes during their lifetime. These are triggered by a changing system context (system usage and technology stacks) and/or changing system requirements. The changes include functional and/or non-functional attributes, for example, the capability and capacity of the system to deal with increasing system workload. The latter is often a direct consequence of providing the access to existing systems over the Internet, for example, for the integration of the systems into novel service compositions.

Cloud computing brings a new ray of hope of addressing this issue very deftly by providing almost unlimited amount of compute or storage resources. In order to utilize this new offer, long-living software systems have to be migrated to cloud. Often this implies major changes (invasive) to the system structure for which no systematic engineering process is available today. This vacuum can lead to high risks or even project failures. There has to be a bridge between the conventional and classic computing and the cloud computing architectures. That is, the age-old architectural styles and patterns such as three-tier client/server architecture do help in building business applications. With cloud's emergence, new-generation architectural styles emerge for the efficient use of the almost unlimited computational resources in the cloud. There is a new architectural style (the so-called SPOSAD style: Shared, Polymorphic, Scalable Application and Data) allowing massive replication of the business logic, which is enabled by a smart physical data distribution. This evolution in different directions and dimensions has to be bridged through a systematic engineering support for facilitating the movement from the old to new architecture. The authors have focused on supporting performance and scalability predictions.

They have proposed a formal process. First, existing systems have to be reverse-engineered to obtain a performance prediction model. These models contain both static as well as dynamic aspects such as contributing components and their interactions. Second, the software architect has to select a set of potential target architecture styles or patterns, which have to be appropriately formalized. For example, the architect plans to evaluate the impact of the classical system architecture movement to MapReduce or to the SPOSAD style, and, thus, he/she automatically adapts the reverse-engineered performance prediction models by the selected architectural styles.

Third, the performance of the target architectures is evaluated to get a final ranking and to come to a recommendation for the migration. Finally, based on the analyzed target architecture, the system's implementation has to be adapted. The major foundations for the sketched process are already in place (software architectural patterns, software performance engineering, architecture evolution, and model transformations).

2.8 Mechanisms for Assisting Cloud Software Development

Today, not only development processes but also environments have to be very agile [10] and anticipative as software development becomes more sophisticated. Cloud-induced agile IT environments are being presented as the viable and valuable resources for new-generation software construction. The unique capabilities of clouds are being succinctly indicated below:

- On-demand provisioning and de-provisioning of resources in minutes through a self-service access.
- Non-function requirements of servers, storages, and network products are being ensured.
- Implicit support for virtual development environments and multi-tier application architectures.
- Easier migration of the existing virtual-server images and workloads into the cloud.

Clouds can accelerate the development cycle by creating multiple development environments that enable several software activities to be carried out simultaneously. Testing can be accomplished along with development. The unique on-demand resource provisioning capability of clouds makes this parallelization possible. Cloud supports different levels of quality of service (QoS). Developers could choose the appropriate QoS level as per the applications. This means that a higher level of performance, security, and availability needs to be assigned to a development environment for performance and scalability testing. In exchange, the hourly cost of such environment goes up. The QA process will also benefit from on-demand up and down scaling of cloud resources, as this finally solves the problem of testing performance and scalability of applications at a large scale, but without indefinitely reserving and paying for resources when they are unused.

Cloud virtual machines (VMs) support multi-tier application development and testing. That is, presentation tier, business logic tier, and data tier are being deployed in different VMs. When the development in a virtual cloud environment is finished, the images of virtual servers can be easily transferred to the production environment.

The advantage is to avoid problems related to configuring a new application for transfer from the development to the production environment, which again affects the speed of the application time to market.

The Lean Thinking Principles for Cloud Software Development – There are lean approaches and principles being sincerely and seriously examined and expounded by professionals and pundits for optimally implementing a variety of industrial systems. Software engineers are also vigorously following the same line of thinking for producing high-quality software solutions for a variety of business and societal problems. The core elements of the lean principle are "eliminate waste, build quality in, create knowledge, defer commitment, deliver fast, respect people and optimize the whole." This set of well-intended tasks definitely creates a sound case for contemporary cloud enterprises. As corporates are planning and assimilating cloud technologies as a part of their business transformation initiative, there are other mandatory things to be accomplished in parallel in order to reap the envisioned advantages.

Here is what a few software companies have achieved by applying lean principles to their development process [11]:

- *Salesforce.com* has improved time to market of major software releases by 61 % and boosted productivity across their R&D organization by 38 % since adopting agile development.

- *BT Adastral,* the largest telecommunications company in the UK, completed its first major lean software project 50 % sooner than expected and incorporated many product changes along the way. The product yielded 80 % ROI in the first year.
- *PatientKeeper,* specializing in software for the healthcare industry, puts out weekly maintenance releases, monthly new feature releases, and quarterly new application releases. This company completes 45 development cycles in the time it takes their competitors to do 1 cycle.
- *Timberline Software* (now part of The Sage Group), serving the construction and real estate market, estimates that improvements in quality, costs, and time to market were all greater than 25 % as a result of switching to lean software development.

Lean thinking is important for scaling agile in several ways [12]:

- Lean provides an explanation for why many of the agile practices work. For example, Agile Modeling's practices of lightweight, initial requirements envisioning followed by iteration modeling and just-in-time (JIT) model storming work because they reflect deferment of commitment regarding what needs to be built until it is actually needed, and the practices help eliminate waste because we are only modeling what needs to be built.
- Lean offers insight into strategies for improving our software process. For example, by understanding the source of waste in IT, we can begin to identify it and then eliminate it.
- Lean principles provide a philosophical foundation for scaling agile approaches.
- It provides techniques for identifying waste. Value stream mapping, a technique common within the lean community, whereby we model a process and then identify how much time is spent on value-added work versus wait time, helps calculate overall time efficiency of what we are doing. Value stream maps are a straightforward way to illuminate our IT processes, providing insight into where significant problems exist.

The lean manufacturing with its emphasis on eliminating waste and empowering employees shook up the automotive industry. Lean principles are revolutionizing software development industry as well. Lean developers can build software faster, better, and cheaper than competitors using traditional bulky and bulging methods. By adopting agile practices and test-driven development, a software firm can go a long way toward leaning out its operations and serving its customers better.

Lean Agile Methodologies Accentuate Benefits of Cloud Computing [13] – Lean and agile are two different production methodologies that are used extensively in business. The lean approach is derived from the production processes adopted by Toyota, Japan. It focuses on a demand-driven approach with an emphasis on:

- Building only what is needed
- Eliminating anything that does not add value
- Stopping production if something goes wrong

The agile approach is focused on the notion that software should be developed in small iterations with frequent releases, because neither the end-user requirements nor the exact amount of efforts can be accurately finalized upfront. Even the end users themselves cannot fully articulate what they need. Hence, the requirements must be collaboratively discovered, analyzed, and finalized. Agile processes [14] involve building software in small segments, testing those segments, and then getting end-user feedback. The aim is to create a rapid feedback loop between the developers and the actual users.

Lean agile development methodologies and the cloud model complement each other very well. Cloud services take pride in meeting user requirements rapidly, delivering applications whenever and to whatever extent they are needed. Agile methods give high credence to user collaboration in requirements discovery. The lean agile system of software development aims to break down project requirements into small and achievable segments. This approach guarantees user feedback on every task of the project. Segments can be planned, developed, and tested individually to maintain high-quality standards without any major bottlenecks. The development stage of every component thus becomes a single "iteration" process. Moreover, lean agile software methods place huge emphasis on developing a collaborative relationship between application developers and end users. The entire development process is transparent to the end user and feedback is sought at all stages of development, and the needy changes are made accordingly then and there.

Using lean agile development in conjunction with the cloud paradigm provides a highly interactive and collaborative environment. The moment developers finalize a feature, they can push it as a cloud service; users can review it instantly and provide valuable feedback. Thus, a lengthy feedback cycle can be eliminated thereby reducing the probability of misstated or misunderstood requirements. This considerably curtails the time and efforts for the software development organization while increasing end-user satisfaction. Following the lean agile approach of demand-driven production, end users' needs are integrated in a more cohesive and efficient manner with software delivery as cloud services. This approach stimulates and sustains a good amount of innovation, requirement discovery, and validation in cloud computing.

2.9 Cloud Platform Solutions for Software Engineering

Compared to on-premise applications, cloud-based software as a service (SaaS) application are delivered through the Web, billed on a subscription basis, and service providers themselves are responsible for delivering the application at acceptable service levels. As a consequence, the economics of delivering SaaS is different from traditional software applications. Companies delivering SaaS/Cloud applications need to realize economies of scale and keep the application delivery costs low. These issues have a significant impact on how SaaS applications are architected, developed, and delivered. For the paradigm of SaaS to succeed, issues like application scalability, cost of delivery, and application availability had to be resolved comprehensively. A new set of architectural, development, and delivery principles have emerged and strengthened the spread of the SaaS model.

In order to achieve the acceptable levels of maturity, companies need to address issues in three core areas [15]:

- They need to build applications that support a multitenant architecture that enables a single instance of the application to be shared among multiple customers. Multitenancy has a significant impact on all layers of the application stack and is challenging to achieve. This architectural principle is a significant contributing factor in reducing application delivery costs.
- SaaS vendors need to address a significant number of non-functional application concerns that are essential for the success of the service. For example, traditional software vendors were not concerned with issues like metadata management, tenant customization and configuration, scalability, fault tolerance to meet SLAs, metering, monitoring, robust security in distributed environments, and a host of other concerns.
- As applications grow and scale, companies need to address automation of operations and application management. Automation of operations and application management is among the primary contributing factors in reducing application delivery costs. Despite emerging automation in areas like the infrastructure cloud, 75–80 % of the issues arising in operations are best solved at the application design and development level. Furthermore, it is difficult and expensive to achieve operational and administrative automation once the service is designed and developed. SaaS providers can achieve significant benefits if application architecture takes automation of operations into account early in the application life cycle.

The cloud idea is everywhere and engineers, executives, exponents, and evangelists are trying different ways and means of adopting and adapting the cloud concepts as per their organizational needs. Data centers are being pruned and tuned to be cloud centers, traditional applications are getting modernized and migrated to local as well as remote cloud environments, centralized delivery and management of IT resources are being insisted and illustrated, innovative and disruptive ideas get quickly concretized by renting needed compute and storage servers from public cloud providers, server systems exclusively for backup and disaster recovery to guarantee business continuity are being subscribed out of cost-effective cloud servers, all kinds of customer-centric applications such as collaboration software are unhesitatingly moved to cloud systems in order to reap their distinct advantages (technical as well as business), etc. In the recent past, cloud is being prescribed as the most productive solution for software coding and testing. That is, platform as a service (PaaS), which has been dormant and dumb for quite a long time, gets a fresh life with the realization across the globe that cloud-based platforms are much more effective, simpler, and quicker for software building.

How Azure Helps Cloud Software Development to Be Agile? – Microsoft Azure is an application platform on the cloud that provides a wide range of core infrastructure services such as compute and storage along with building blocks that can be consumed for developing high-quality business applications. Azure provides platform as a service (PaaS) capabilities for assisting application development, hosting, execution, and management within Microsoft cloud centers. Windows Azure is an open cloud platform that enables to quickly build applications in any language, tool, or framework. The advantages of Azure cloud are:

- Azure provides staging and production environments on the cloud which provide resource elasticity on demand, and this agility factor helps a lot for any Windows application development team.
- Only the development and unit testing is carried out on-premise systems.
- Cloud staging environment can be used to create different test environments on cloud such as integration, system, and UAT.
- Application source code can be maintained in Azure cloud storage.
- Developers test their application with a production-like environment as setting up a real production environment for testing involves more investment, planning, time, and resources. That is, all kinds of infrastructure-intensive software testing can be accomplished in Azure cloud with high dependability cost-effectively due to the inherent elastic nature of Azure. This enables application providers to ensure the SLA to their customers and consumers.
- A couple of integrated development environments such as Visual Studio.NET are provided by Microsoft in order to simplify and speed up cloud application development activities.
- Source code can be promoted from one environment to another rather seamlessly without developers having to write verbose deployment scripts or instruction manuals to set up the application in the target environments.

How Azure Helps Software Delivery to Be Agile? – Delivery is also facilitated by Azure cloud. By providing flexible infrastructures just in time, cloud software delivery is made agile. All kinds of fluctuations of infrastructure needs are being automatically taken care of Azure cloud. All kinds of plumping works are being delegated to cloud center experts so that designers, developers, and testers can focus on their core activities.

As Visual Studio IDE is tightly integrated with the cloud environment, application development and deployment happen faster and are hugely simplified. The cloud provides all the libraries and APIs upfront in order to lessen the developmental cost and complexity. Further on, in the Azure cloud, deployment and upgrade processes are completely automated to minimize or eliminate some of the lengthy and tedious steps while planning and executing the traditionally accomplished deployment process. Working prototypes built by geographically dispersed developers and centrally deployed in Azure can be made available and accessible immediately to prospective customers in order to elicit and extract their feelings and feedbacks as this arrangement sharply reduces time especially for contemplating any major or minor corrections to take the products to market quickly.

The Alice Platform [15] – In order to help companies with the challenges of building and delivering successful SaaS services, the authors have developed the first open SaaS platform called Alice. As a company focused on developing cloud-based SaaS services, it became quite evident that traditional JEE, .NET, and Ruby on Rails platforms were not designed to address base level architectural

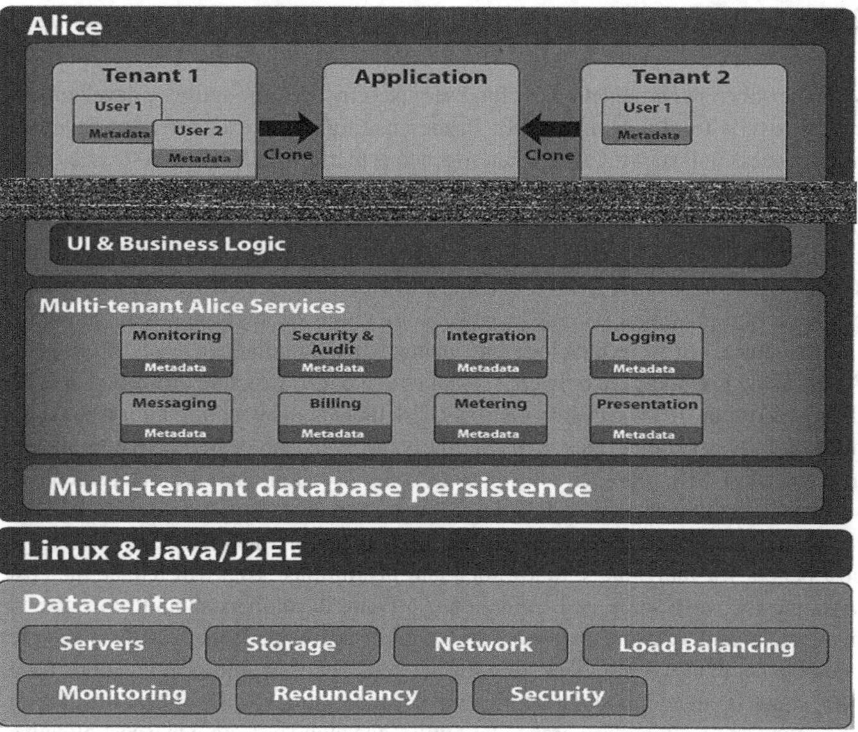

Fig. 2.1 The architectural diagram of the Alice platform

concerns of large and scalable SaaS applications. While building applications for our clients, developers had to address multitenancy, data management, security, scalability, caching, and many other features. Many of the most successful SaaS companies had themselves built their own platforms and frameworks to address their specific applications and cost needs. Companies like Salesforce and NetSuite, first and foremost, built platforms to meet their application needs and lower delivery costs, rather than building them to be sold as a platform as a service (PaaS).

Release of SaaS application platforms by companies like Salesforce has not made a significant difference in the development and delivery of commercial SaaS applications. Currently, many PaaS/SaaS platforms on the market are suitable for development of only small situational applications, rather than commercial business applications that are of interest to startups, independent software vendors (ISVs), and enterprises. These platforms use proprietary languages, are tied to a specific hardware/software infrastructures, and do not provide the right abstractions for developers. Alice was developed to address the above concerns and provide a robust and open platform for the rapid development of scalable cloud services applications. Figure 2.1 illustrates the reference architecture of the Alice Platform for SaaS application development and delivery.

2.10 Software Engineering Challenges in Cloud Environments

With the coherent participation of cloud service providers, the software development complexity is to climb further [3]. In the ensuing cloud era, software development process will start to involve heterogeneous platforms, distributed services, and multiple enterprises geographically dispersed all over the world. Existing software process models are simply insufficient unless the remote interaction with cloud providers is a part and parcel of the whole process. Requirements gathering phase so far included customers, end users, and software engineers. Now it has to include cloud service providers (CSPs) as well, as they will be supplying the computing infrastructure, software development, management, maintenance platforms, etc. As the cloud providers are only conversant with the infrastructure utilization details, their experts can do the capacity planning, risk management, configuration management, quality assurance, etc., well. Similarly, analysis and design activities should also include CSPs, who can chip in with some decision-enabling details such as software-development cost, schedule, resource, and time.

Development and debugging can be done on cloud platforms. There is a huge cost benefit for individuals, innovators, and institutions. This will reduce the cost and time for verification and validation. Software developers should have gained more right and relevant expertise in building software from readily available components than writing them from the scratch. The monolithic applications have been shunted out and modular application has the future. Revisiting and refactoring of existing application is required to best utilize the cloud paradigm in a cost-effective manner. In the recent past, computers are fit with multicore processors. Another trend is computers are interconnected as well as with the Web. Computers are becoming communicators and vice versa. Computers are multifaceted, networked, and shrinking in size, whereas the scope of computing is growing. Therefore, software engineers should train themselves in parallel and distributed computing to complement the unprecedented and inescapable advances in hardware and networking. Software engineers should train themselves in Web protocols, XML, service orientation, etc. Web is on the growing trajectory as it started with a simple Web (Web 1.0). Today it is the social Web (Web 2.0) and semantic Web (Web 3.0) attracting the attention of professionals as well as people. Tomorrow definitely it will be the smart Web (Web 4.0). The cloud proposition is on the fast track and thereby there will be a scintillating synchronization between the enlarging Web concepts and the cloud idea.

Cloud providers also have the appropriate infrastructure and methods in hand in order for application maintenance [14]. There is a service-level agreement (SLA) being established as a contract between cloud users (in this case, software engineers) and cloud providers. Especially the advanced cloud infrastructure ensures non-functional (scalability, availability, security, sustainability, etc.) requirements. Other serious challenges confronting the cloud-based software development include the following. As we see, the development of software is multilateral in a cloud environment unlike the collocated and conventional application software development.

The difference between these two radical approaches presents some of the noticeable challenges to software engineering:

- *Software Composition* – Traditionally, application software engineers develop a set of coherent and cohesive modules and assemble them to form an application, whereas in the fast-expanding cloud landscape, finding and composing third-party software components is a real challenge.
- *Query-Oriented Versus API-Oriented Programming* – MapReduce, streaming, and complex event processing require developers to adopt a more functional query-oriented style of processing to derive information. Rather than a large surface area of OO APIs, these systems use an extension of SQL-like operations where clients pass in application specific functions which are executed against associated data sources. Doing complex join queries or function composition such as MapReduce is a difficult proposition.
- *Availability of Source Code* – In the current scene, full source of the code is available. However, in the multilateral software development, there is no source code available because of third-party components. Therefore, the challenge for software engineers is the complete comprehension of the system.
- *Execution Model* – The application software developed generally is executed on single machine, whereas the multilateral software developed for cloud environment is often distributed between multiple machines. Therefore, the challenge for software engineers is the traceability of state of executing entity and debugging.
- *Application Management* – The challenges are there as usual when there is an attempt to embrace newer technologies. Application lifecycle management (ALM) is quiet straightforward in the traditional setting, whereas globally, collaborative and cloud-based application management is beset with definite concerns and challenges.

The need of the hour to make the cloud concepts more beneficial to all sections of the world is to activate the innovation culture; thereby, a stream of inventive approaches can be unearthed to reinvigorate the sagging and struggling software engineering domain. Here is one. Radha Guha [2] has come out with an improved cost estimation model for the cloud-based software development.

2.11 Conclusion

Nowadays, for most business systems, software is a key enabler of their business processes. The software availability and stability directly impact the company's revenue and customer satisfaction. Software development is therefore a critical activity. Software development is undergoing a series of key changes. A growing number of independent software vendors (ISVs) and system integrators (SIs) transform themselves into service providers delivering their customers' and partners' applications in the form of services hosted in the cloud.

The cloud technology could reduce the time needed for the development of business services and to take them to the market. Each additional month or quarter in which the cloud services are accessible to users has a direct impact on increasing revenues, which affects the final financial statements. The speed at which software applications can be developed, tested, and brought into production is definitely one of the critical success factors for many companies. Therefore, any solution accelerating the application time to market has an immediate and measurable impact on return on investment (ROI).

Application developers are regularly confronted with a request to establish special environments for developing, debugging, and compiling appropriate software libraries for making software solutions. Typically, these environments are established for a limited period of time. Accessing appropriately configured development environments with an adequate processing power and storage space on demand is very crucial for software engineering. To perform their tasks, the programmers should be able to quickly configure servers, storage, and network connections. Here comes the significance of cloud environments for taking software to market quickly. In this chapter, we primarily discussed the pathbreaking contributions of cloud infrastructures for realizing sophisticated and smart services and applications.

References

1. Yara, P., Ramachandran, R., Balasubramanian, G., Muthuswamy, K., Chandrasekar, D.: Global software development with cloud platforms. In: Software Engineering Approaches for Offshore and Outsourced Development. Lecture Notes in Business Information Processing. http://link.springer.com/chapter/10.1007/978-3-642-02987-5_10. vol. 35, pp. 81–95 (2009)
2. Guha, R.: Software engineering on semantic web and cloud computing platform. http://www.cs.pitt.edu/~chang/231/y11/papers/cloudSE (2011). Accessed 24 Oct 2012
3. Chhabra, B., Verma, D., Taneja, B.: Software engineering issues from the cloud application perspective. Int. J. Inf. Technol. Knowl. Manage. **2**(2), 669–673 (2010)
4. Kuusela, R., Huomo, T., Korkala, M.: Lean Thinking Principles for Cloud Software Development. VTT www.vtt.fi. A Research Summary of VTT Technical Research Centre of Finland (2010)
5. Hashmi, S.I.: Using the cloud to facilitate global software development challenges. In: Sixth IEEE International Conference on Global Software Engineering Workshops, 15–18 Aug 2011, pp. 70–77. IEEE XPlore Digital Library, IEEE, Piscataway (2011)
6. Tamburri, D.A., Lago, P.: Satisfying cloud computing requirements with agile service networks. In: IEEE World Congress on Services, 4–9 July 2011, pp. 501–506. IEEE XPlore Digital Library, IEEE, Los Alamitos (2011)
7. Carroll, N., et al.: The discovery of agile service networks through the use of social network analysis. In: International Conference on Service Sciences. IEEE Computer Society, IEEE, Washington, DC (2010)
8. Bruneli'ere, H., Cabot, J., Jouault, F.: Combining model-driven engineering and cloud computing. http://jordicabot.com/papers/MDE4Service10.pdf (2010). Accessed 24 Oct 2012
9. Becker, S., Tichy, M.: Towards model-driven evolution of performance critical business information systems to cloud computing architectures. In: MMSM. http://www.cse.chalmers.se/~tichy/2012/MMSM2012.pdf (2012). Accessed 24 Oct 2012

10. Dumbre, A., Senthil, S.P., Ghag, S.S.: Practicing Agile Software Development on the Windows Azure Platform. White paper by Infosys Ltd., Bangalore. http://www.infosys.com/cloud/resource-center/documents/practicing-agile-software-development.pdf (2011) Accessed 24 Oct 2012
11. Lean Software Development – Cutting Fat Out of Your Diet. A White Paper by Architech solutions. http://www.architech.ca/wp-content/uploads/2010/07/Lean-Software-Development-Cutting-Fat-Out-of-Your-Diet.pdf. Accessed 24 Oct 2012
12. Tripathi, N.: Practices of lean software development. http://cswf.wikispaces.com/file/view/Practices+in+Lean+Software+Development.pdf (2011). Accessed 24 Oct 2012
13. Talreja, Y.: Lean Agile methodologies accentuate benefits of cloud computing. http://www.the-technology-gurus.com/yahoo_site_admin/assets/docs/LACC_white_paper_ed_v5.320180428.pdf (2010). Accessed 24 Oct 2012
14. Das, D., Vaidya, K.: An Agile Process Framework for Cloud Application. A White Paper by CSC. http://assets1.csc.com/lef/downloads/CSC_Papers_2011_Agile_Process_Framework.pdf (2011). Accessed 24 Oct 2012
15. Alice Software as a Service(SaaS) Delivery Platform. A Whitepaper by Ekartha, Inc. http://www.ekartha.com/resources/Alice_saas_delivery_platform.pdf. Accessed 24 Oct 2012

Chapter 3
Limitations and Challenges in Cloud-Based Applications Development

N. Pramod, Anil Kumar Muppalla, and K.G. Srinivasa

Abstract Organisations and enterprise firms, from banks to social Web, are considering developing and deploying applications on the cloud due to the benefits offered by them. These benefits include cost effectiveness, scalability and theoretically unlimited computing resources. Many predictions by experts have indicated that centralising the computation and storage by renting them from third-party provider is the way to the future. However, before jumping into conclusions, engineers and technology officers must assess and weigh the advantages of cloud applications over concerns, challenges and limitations of cloud-based applications. Decisions must also involve choosing the right service model and knowing the disadvantages and limitations pertaining to that particular service model. Although cloud applications have benefits a galore, organisations and developers have raised concerns over the security and reliability issues. The idea of handing important data over to another company certainly has security and confidentiality worries. The implication does not infer that cloud applications are insecure and flawed but conveys that they require more attention to cloud-related issues than the conventional on-premise approaches. The objective of this chapter is to introduce the reader to the challenges of cloud application development and to present ways in which these challenges can be overcome. The chapter also discusses the issues with respect to different service models and extends the challenges with reference to application developer's perspective.

Keywords Challenges in the cloud • Vendor lock-in • Security in the cloud • SLA • Cost limitation • Traceability issue • Transparency in the cloud

---

N. Pramod • A.K. Muppalla • K.G. Srinivasa (✉)
High Performance Computing Laboratory, Department of Computer Science and Engineering, M S Ramaiah Institute of Technology,
Bangalore 560054, India
e-mail: npramod05@gmail.com; anil.kumar.848@gmail.com; srinivasa.kg@gmail.com

Z. Mahmood and S. Saeed (eds.), *Software Engineering Frameworks for the Cloud Computing Paradigm*, Computer Communications and Networks,
DOI 10.1007/978-1-4471-5031-2_3, © Springer-Verlag London 2013

3.1 Introduction

The paradigm of cloud computing introduces a change in visualisation of system and data owned by an organisation. It is no longer a group of computing devices present at one physical location and executing a particular (and only that program, unless mentioned otherwise) software program with all the required data and resources present at a static physical location but instead is a system which is geographically distributed with respect to both application and data. Researchers and engineers working in the field of cloud computing define it in many ways. These definitions are usually based on the application's perspective, that is, the way one is trying to employ cloud services for a particular application. A few definitions of cloud computing are as shown below:

> Cloud computing is a model for enabling convenient, on-demand network access to a shared pool of configurable computing resources (e.g., networks, servers, Storage, applications, and services) that can be rapidly provisioned and released with minimal management effort or service provider interaction. [1]
>
> A Cloud is a type of parallel and distributed system consisting of a collection of interconnected and virtualized computers that are dynamically provisioned and presented as one or more unified computing resources based on service-level agreements established through negotiation between the service provider and consumers. [2]

The desired properties of cloud computing can be characterised as technical, economic and user experience as in [3].

3.1.1 Characteristics of Cloud Systems

General characteristics of cloud computing are as follows [1]:

On-demand self-service: A consumer can unilaterally provision computing capabilities, such as server time and network storage, as needed automatically without requiring human interaction with each service provider.

Broad network access: Capabilities are available over the network and accessed through standard mechanisms that promote use by heterogeneous thin or thick client platforms (e.g. mobile phones, tablets, laptops and workstations).

Resource pooling: The provider's computing resources are pooled to serve multiple consumers using a multi-tenant model, with different physical and virtual resources dynamically assigned and reassigned according to consumer demand. There is a sense of location independence in that the customer generally has no control or knowledge over the exact location of the provided resources but may be able to specify location at a higher level of abstraction (e.g. country, state or data centre). Examples of resources include storage, processing, memory and network bandwidth.

Rapid elasticity: Capabilities can be elastically provisioned and released, in some cases automatically, to scale rapidly outward and inward commensurate with demand. To the consumer, the capabilities available for provisioning often appear to be unlimited and can be appropriated in any quantity at any time.

Measured service: Cloud systems automatically control and optimise resource usage by leveraging a metering capability at some level of abstraction that is appropriate to the type of service used (e.g. storage, processing, bandwidth and active user accounts). Resource usage can be monitored, controlled and reported, providing transparency for both the provider and consumer of the utilised service.

3.1.2 Cloud Service Models

There are three generally agreed cloud service delivery models [4]:

- SaaS – software as a service: Refers to providing on-demand applications over the Internet.
- PaaS – platform as a service: Refers to providing platform layer resources, including operating system support and software development frameworks.
- IaaS – infrastructure as a service: Refers to on-demand provisioning of infrastructural resources, usually in terms of VMs. A cloud owner that offers IaaS is called an IaaS provider [5].

Newer terminologies such as DaaS (Data as a Service) [6] have also emerged, but their applicability and use cases still remain a key question. In case of traditional IT deployment, all the resources are under the control of a particular organisation. This is not true anymore in case of cloud-based development. Cloud providers of each of the cloud service models offer control over various resources. Figure 3.1 depicts a generic view of the accessibility and control of resources with respect to IaaS, PaaS and SaaS service models.

3.2 Challenges

Cloud computing influences an adopting organisation in a variety of ways. Cost reduction capability in terms of savings on hardware resources, which increases with increase in horsepower of computation and are unused most of the times but are very much critical for crunch time usage. This flexibility in the availability of hardware resources implies that the application can be highly scalable and dynamic in nature in terms of utilisation of hardware resources. Amidst all the advantages, the following are the challenges that restrict an organisation to migrate to cloud applications (Fig. 3.2).

3.2.1 Security and Confidentiality

All Web service architectures have issues relating to security. On a similar note, cloud application can be viewed as a different Web service model that has similar security loopholes in them. Organisations which are keen on moving the in-house

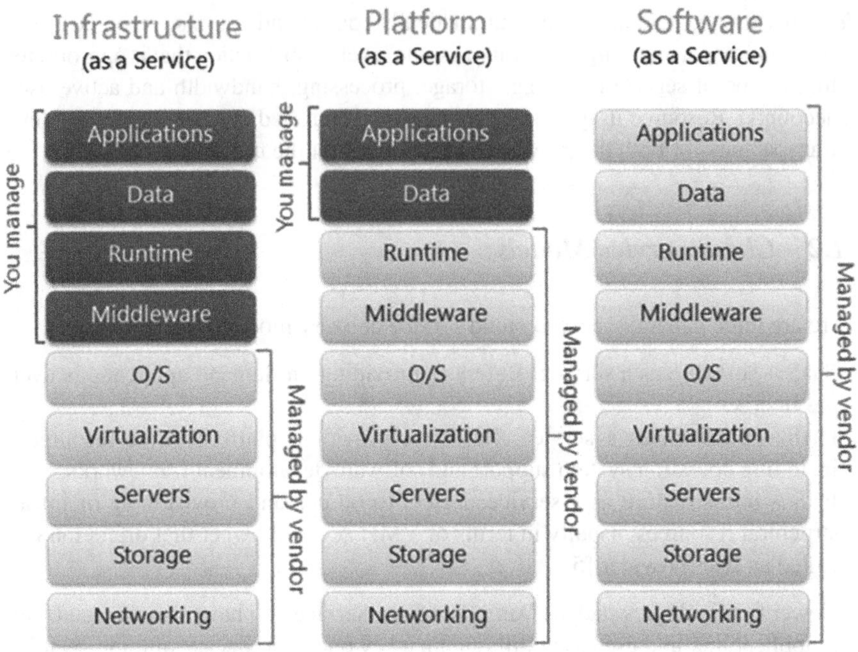

Fig. 3.1 Consumer and vendor controls in cloud service models [24]

Fig. 3.2 Technology in charge and security engineers of an organisation must consider the inherent issues before migrating to cloud

applications to cloud must consider the way in which the application security behaves in a cloud environment. Well-known security issues such as data loss and phishing pose serious threats to organisation's data and software. In addition to those, there are other security issues which arise due to the third-party dependency for services pertaining to cloud application development and deployment. From a very naive point of view, it looks daunting to put an organisation's critical and confidential data and its software into a third person's CPU and storage. The multi-tenancy model and the pooled computing resources in cloud computing have introduced new security challenges that require novel techniques to tackle with [7].

One of the top cloud application security issues is lack of control over the computing infrastructure. An enterprise moving a legacy application to a cloud computing environment gives up control over the networking infrastructure, including servers, access to logs and incident response. Most applications are built to be run in the context of an enterprise data centre, so the way they store and the way they transmit data to other systems is assumed to be trusted or secure. This is no more true in case of cloud environment. All the components that have traditionally been very trusted and assume to be running in a safe environment now are running in an untrusted environment. Many more issues such as the Web interface, data storage and data transfer have to be considered whilst making security assessments. The flexibility, openness and public availability of cloud computing infrastructures challenge many fundamental assumptions about application security. The lack of physical control over the networking infrastructure might mandate the use of encryption in the communication between servers of an application that processes sensitive data to ensure its confidentiality. Risks that a company may have accepted when the application was in-house must be reconsidered when moving to a cloud environment.

Ex. 1

If an application is logging sensitive data in a file on the on-premise server and not encrypting it, a company might accept that risk because it owns the hardware. This will not be a safe acceptance anymore on the cloud environment as there exists no static file system where the application log will reside due to the reason that the application is executed in different virtual machines which may be on different physical machines depending on the scale. The logging thus takes place onto some shared storage array and hence the need to encrypt it arises. The security threat model takes a different dimension on the cloud, and, hence, a lot of vulnerabilities which were low are now high and they must be fixed.

Ex. 2

A company hosting an application in its own data centre might ward off a denial-of-service attack with certain infrastructure or could take actions such as blocking the attacking IP addresses. In case of cloud, if the provider handles the mitigation of attacks, then the consumer or the organisation hosting application needs to re-account for how the risk or attack can be mitigated as there is no control or visibility.

3.2.1.1 Overcoming the Challenge

It is important to understand the base security solutions provided by the service provider, for example, firewalls and intrusion detection systems, which are built into to the cloud architecture. Also, it is important to note assurances the provider is willing to offer in the case of breaches or loss. These details will help an organisation in making security-related decisions and answering some important questions such as 'Are these solutions and assurances sufficient for the data which is being put into the cloud?' Employing a strong user authentication scheme for cloud service will reduce many of the security breaches and data loss. In the end, an enterprise should ensure that the cloud workloads will have at least the same level of protection as their sensitive on-premise workloads, but for less sensitive workloads, they should avoid paying for excessive security.

3.2.2 Control

Introduction of third-party service provider decreases an organisation's control over its software and data. This holds good especially in case of SaaS where the SaaS cloud provider may choose to run software from various clients on a single machine and storage at a given point of time. There is no control over the decision pertaining to the above issue. Furthermore, the actual control over the software and service is limited to the condition mentioned in the policy and user agreement and only via certain service provider defined API (and keys).

As an example, code snippet for authentication in a Rackspace [8] cloud service (sent as JSON) is as shown below:

```
curl -i \
-H "Content-Type: application/json" \
-H "Accept: application/json" \
-d \
'{
"credentials": {
"username": "my_Rackspace_username",
"key": "12005700-0300-0010-1000-654000008923"}
}' \
https://auth.api.rackspacecloud.com/v1.1/auth
```

where:

username – is the assigned username for which the authentication request is being sent
key – the API key provided to access the cloud service

If, for instance, the consumer wishes to introduce another layer of authentication, then the cloud provider does not allow for this facility as the API is not designed to provide such facility. This can be extended not only to authentication but to the entire APIs used for various purposes during cloud application development. This hinders access and limits any tweaking which can enable the application function better or help the organisation in curbing cost [9]. Also, as a security concern, the ability to limit access to certain confidential data will eventually go in vain as the data is still available in some form or the other at the service provider and poses a serious threat to confidentiality.

3.2.2.1 Overcoming the Challenge

Agreements and standardisation is one way to overcome the problem of control in a cloud environment. Also, the paradigm of cloud does not make it feasible for a provider to give access control beyond a certain limit.

3.2.3 Reliability

For the cloud, reliability is broadly a function of the reliability of three individual components:

- The hardware and software facilities offered by providers: The hardware (applicable to SaaS, PaaS, IaaS models) and software (applicable to SaaS, PaaS models) provided by the service provider, though not completely in the consumer's control, are a major reliability factor as low-performing and low-quality setup could lead to failure. This also is decisive about the availability of the application. The less hardware failure and faster recovery from failure will ensure that the cloud application is more reliable.
- The provider's personnel and the consumer's personnel: The personnel interacting with the cloud service and the application may also cause reliability issues. For example, if an employee is accessing resources for purposes other than the assigned, then during crunch time it could lead to failure. Also, if the maintenance of the systems is not undertaken regularly or is ignored, then this could cause failure.
- Connectivity to subscribed services: Network resources connecting the cloud service provider and the organisation are also accountable for the reliability of the system.

Many suggestions on how to adopt trust models have been proposed, and one of such can be found tabulated in Table 3.1: "Summary of cloud service providers, properties, resource access and key challenges over different cloud service models" [10].

Table 3.1 Summary of cloud service providers, properties, resource access and key challenges over different cloud service models

	Providers	Properties	Access to resources	Key challenges
SaaS	NetSuite – enterprise resource planning (ERP) SaaS	Web interface	SaaS consumers have only access to the software which is provided as a service. No control over tuning the software, operating system and hardware resources	Credential management on cloud
	Taleo – human resource SaaS	No installation required		Usage and accountability
	SalesForce – customer relationship management SaaS (CRM)	Shared software, i.e. used by many organisation		Traceability of data
	Google – Google Docs, online office suite	Ownership is only on data		Data security
	Microsoft – Office Live, Dynamics Live CRM	Pay as you use		Protection of API keys
PaaS	Google App Engine	Platform for developing scalable applications	PaaS consumers have access to the application development environment, e.g. the operating system. Tools and libraries can be used to build application over the given platform. No control over hardware resources and control over choice of platform, i.e. the choice of tuning and changing the operating system	Privacy control
	Microsoft Windows Azure	Test, deploy, host and maintain in the same environment		Traceability of both application and data
	Force.com	Easy integration with Web services and databases		Maintenance of audit trail
	AT&T Synaptic			Protecting API keys
				Application Security
IaaS	Amazon EC2	Virtual machines are offered to consumers	IaaS consumers have access to the virtual machine instance which can be configured in a way to suit the operating system instance or image and application running over it. No control over the hardware resources, i.e. the physical resources such as the choice of processor on each machine, size and capacity of memory on each machine	Governance
	IBM	Freedom of choice on operating system		Data encryption, especially in case of storage service
	HP			API Key Protection
	Rackspace			
	Eucalyptus			
	Cisco			
	Joyent			

3.2.3.1 Overcoming the Challenge

In cloud, the control of physical resources is under the cloud provider, and, hence, the responsibility for workload management, uptime and persistence also falls on him. Therefore, it is important to understand provider's infrastructure, architecture and the policies and processes governing them. The assurances of uptime and availability properties must be considered whilst choosing a provider. Also, the compensation and backup measure which will be in place in case of failure of any kind must be part of the agreement, thus taking into account the reliability factors.

3.2.4 Transparency

As discussed earlier, security issues due to third-party involvement give rise to another subsidiary issue of trust and transparency. The problem of transparency relates to the accountability of data usage, traceability of files and services on the cloud, maintenance of audit trail, etc. on both the cloud provider and the cloud consumer ends. According to Cloud Security Alliance (CSA), secrecy is not the only way to build effective security measure. Their emphasis is on adopting and adhering best practices and standards that create a more transparent and secure environment. CSA is trying to get across to the purveyors of cloud services with STAR [11], which is open to all cloud providers, and allows them to submit self-assessment reports that document compliance to CSA published best practices. The searchable registry will allow potential cloud customers to review the security practices of providers, accelerating their due diligence and leading to higher quality procurement experiences. CSA STAR represents a major leap forward in industry transparency, encouraging providers to make security capabilities a market differentiator.

The software used to monitor the audit trail and to track the files on cloud must be capable of tracking all the activities irrespective of the type of architecture, that is, multi-tenant or single tenant. This software can be used by both the consumer and the provider and tally the same as a test for common audit trail. Transparency in case of multi-tenant SaaS provider becomes a challenging task as the application data is present in multiple machines along with other application (which may or may not contain vulnerability).

The transparency issue arises mainly due to the paradigm change in cloud. It is a shift from a focus on systems to a focus on data. Due to the inability of the current logging and other mechanism to cope with the tracing issues, researchers explored newer methods which worked accordingly on a cloud set up. The existing logging mechanisms were mainly system-centric and built for debugging or monitoring system health. They were not built for tracing data created within and across machines. Furthermore, current logging mechanisms only monitor the virtual machines layer, without paying attention to the physical machines hosting them. Additionally, whilst file-intrusion detection and prevention tools such as *TripWire* [12, 13] existed, they merely compared key signature changes and did not record and track the history and evolution of data in the cloud. Research personnel at HP are working on *TrustCloud* [14], a project launched to increase trust in cloud computing via detective, file-centric approaches that increase data traceability, accountability and transparency in the cloud. With accurate audit trail and a transparent view of data flow and history on cloud, the cloud services are bound to become more reliable and the consumer has fairly more control over things which overcomes a lot of potential challenges that hinders growth and migration towards cloud.

3.2.4.1 Overcoming the Challenge

Trust and following the best practices are one way to overcome this challenge. Trust is developed over time by the provider by maintaining a clean track record in terms of the characteristics of a particular cloud service. An organisation must look for the following aspects before choosing a service provider:

- The history of the service provider
- The operational aspects apart from the ones mentioned in the service brochure, for example, 'Where are the data centres located?' 'Is the hardware maintenance outsourced?'
- Additional tools, services and freedom offered to improve visibility and traceability in the cloud environment

For example, users of IBM's cloud services can use Tivoli management system to manage their cloud and data centre services. *TrustCloud* can be another example of a tool which can be used to increase transparency.

3.2.5 Latency

In a stand-alone system, it matters a lot where the data and other resources are situated for computation. In conventional client server architecture, the application server is made to be located as close to the client as possible via the means of data centres and CDNs (content delivery network). On a similar note it matters a lot where the cloud is situated and that a cloud provider may have plenty of Web bandwidth from a given data centre, but if that data centre is thousands of miles away, then developers will need to accommodate and program for significant latency. Latency is generally measured as the round-trip time it takes for a packet to reach a given destination and come back, usually measured using the standard Linux program, "ping". As an example, if the cloud application is an email server, it is better to have the cloud situated nearby. The multimedia content present in the application can be handled by the services provided by CDNs which invisibly brings this content closer to the client.

Irrespective of the type of cloud service deployed, all cloud computing initiatives have one thing in common, that is, data is centralised, whilst users are distributed.

This means that if deployment is not planned carefully, there can be significant issues due to the increased latency between the end users and their application servers. All cloud services inherently use shared WANs, making packet delivery – specifically dropped or out of order IP packets during peak congestion – a constant problem in these environments. This results in packet retransmissions which, particularly when compounded by increased latency, lower effective throughput and perceived application performance.

Fortunately, in parallel with the cloud trend, WAN optimisation technology has been evolving to overcome these challenges. WAN optimisation helps "clean up" the cloud in real time by rebuilding lost packets and ensuring they are delivered in the correct order, prioritising traffic whilst guaranteeing the necessary bandwidth, using network acceleration to mitigate latency in long-distance environments and de-duplicating data to avoid repetition. So with WAN optimisation, it is possible to move the vast majority of applications into the cloud without having to worry about geographic considerations [15].

3.2.5.1 Overcoming the Challenge

Organisations moving their latency-sensitive applications should consider negotiating with the service provider for possible support to reduce it and increase end-to-end performance. At times, few service providers provide such facilities but mostly are customised and configured for a specific consumer's needs usually combining with custom network configurations and private cloud. Also, care should be taken in order to maintain the quality of normal services amidst all the tweaks to reduce latency.

3.2.6 Costing Model

It becomes important to differentiate between the cloud provider, consumer and the actual customer who uses the application. The consumer is a person or an organisation that has access to cloud resources (depending on the service model, agreement and the application type). Now this organisation must analyse and consider the trade-offs amongst the computation, communication and integration. Cloud applications can significantly reduce the infrastructure cost, but it uses more network resources (data usage, bandwidth) and hence raises the cost of data communication. The cost per unit of computing resource used is likely to be higher as more resources are used during the data exchange between the cloud service and the organisation. This problem is particularly prominent if the consumer uses the hybrid cloud deployment model where the organisation's data is distributed amongst a number of public/private (in-house IT infrastructure)/community clouds. Notable and commonly used pricing models in thirdparty systems are pay as you go and subscription pricing. In the former, the billing is based on usage stats, and it is based on fixed, agreed-upon prices in the latter case.

3.2.6.1 Overcoming the Challenge

Developers and architects should analyse the cloud provider's costing model and make an appropriate decision of choosing the most suitable model according to the requirements. This decision includes understanding the trade-offs which the costing model will result into; for example, in case of an IaaS model adoption scenario, consideration towards a hybrid infrastructure wherein the sensitive and frequently used large data or application can be part of a private cloud and the rest could be a thirdparty service. Every approach has pros and cons, and the decision on costing must exploit the market options and the requirements and at the same time should also note this pro-con trade-off. Pay as you go could be useful if the requirements are not well defined and the budget is limited, and the subscription pricing is useful when the requirements are long term and are well defined.

3.2.7 Charging Model

The data usage charges in case of conventional models are fairly straightforward and are with respect to bandwidth and online space consumption. But in case of the cloud, the same does not hold good as the resources used is different at different point in time due to the scalable nature of the application. Hence, due to the pool of resources available, the cost analysis is a lot more complicated. The cost estimate is now in terms of the number of instantiated virtual machines rather than the physical server; that is, the instantiated VM has become the unit of cost. This resource pool and its usage vary from service model to service model. For SaaS cloud providers, the cost of developing scalability or multi-tenancy within their offering can be very substantial. These include alteration or redesign and development of a software under consideration which was initially developed for a conventional model, performance and security enhancement for concurrent user access (similar to synchronisation and read and write problem) and dealing with complexities induced by the above changes. On the other hand, SaaS providers need to consider the trade-off between the provision of multi-tenancy and the cost savings yielded by multi-tenancy such as reduced overhead through amortisation and reduced number of on-site software licences. Therefore, the charging model must be tailored strategically for SaaS provider in order to increase profitability and sustainability of SaaS cloud providers [7].

3.2.7.1 Overcoming the Challenge

A provider with better billing models and frameworks which determine usage of a cloud service appropriately and accurately should be given preference over the rest. For example, Rackspace has a billing model which is efficient and at the same time well represented and easy to understand with a well-defined set of information on the cloud admin dashboard. The cloud infrastructure has become more efficient and mature over the years and quite a lot of measures have been taken to overcome these problems which include better tracking softwares and billing systems.

3.2.8 Service-Level Agreement (SLA)

Although cloud consumers do not have control over the underlying computing resources, they do need to ensure the quality, availability, reliability and performance of these resources when consumers have moved their core business functions onto their entrusted cloud. In other words, it is vital for consumers to obtain guarantees from providers on service delivery. Typically, these are provided through service-level agreements (SLAs) negotiated between the providers and consumers. The very first issue is the definition of SLA specifications in such a way that has an appropriate level of granularity, namely, the trade-offs between expressiveness and complicatedness, so that they can cover most of the consumer expectations and is relatively simple to be weighted, verified, evaluated and enforced by the resource allocation mechanism on the cloud. In addition, different cloud offerings (IaaS, PaaS and SaaS) will need to define different SLA meta-specifications. This also raises a number of implementation problems for the cloud providers. Furthermore, advanced SLA mechanisms need to constantly incorporate user feedback and customisation features into the SLA evaluation framework [16].

3.2.9 Vendor Lock-In

The issue of *vendor lock-in* is a rising concern due to the rapid development of cloud technology. Currently, each cloud offering has its own way on how cloud consumers/applications/users interact with the cloud. This severely hinders the development of cloud ecosystems by forcing vendor locking, which prohibits the ability of cloud consumers to choose from alternative vendors/offering simultaneously or more from one vendor to another (migration) in order to optimise resources at different levels within an organisation. More importantly, proprietary or vendor-specific cloud APIs make it very difficult to integrate cloud services with an organisation's own existing legacy systems. The primary goal of interoperability is to realise the seamless fluid data across clouds and between cloud and local applications. Interoperability is essential due to various reasons. Many of the IT components of a company are routine and static applications which need to handle numbers and for which cloud service can be adopted. These applications vary from being storage based to computation based. An organisation would prefer two different vendors to achieve cost efficiency and performance enhancement via respective

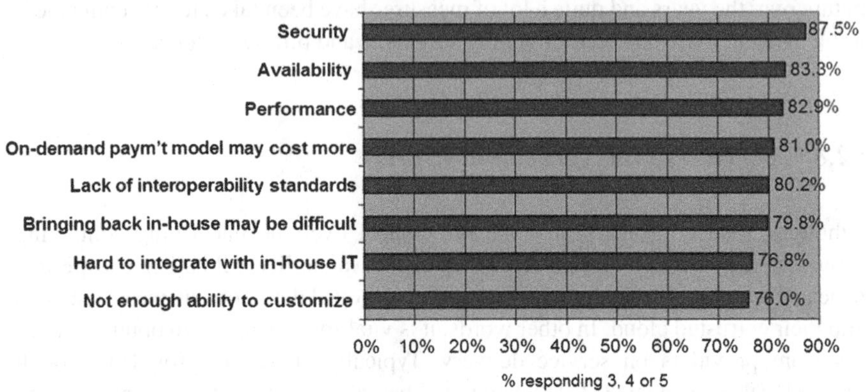

Fig. 3.3 The result of survey conducted by CSA

service. But eventually these separate applications need to interact with the core IT assets of the company, and, hence, there must exist some common way to interact with these various cloud applications spread over different vendors. Standardisation appears to be a good solution to address the interoperability issue. However, as cloud computing is still a spreading wild fire, the interoperability problem has not appeared on the pressing agenda of major industry cloud vendors [7].

3.2.9.1 Overcoming the Challenge

Wise choice in choosing a vendor is the only way to overcome this issue. Currently, there are no standards governing cloud application platforms and services and hence is a significant challenge to overcome in the coming years. However, steps have been taken recently to manage this problem. The Federal Risk and Authorization Management Program (FedRAMP) [17] is a government-wide program that provides a standardised approach to security assessment, authorisation and continuous monitoring for cloud products and services. Cloud service providers are now required to follow this standard, and hopefully it could be extended to a lot of migration and interoperability issues.

Amongst these generic issues, few are of serious concern than the rest and few have not seen the broad daylight due to the infancy of cloud computing. A survey conducted by CSA involving over 240 organisations found that security is one of the biggest issues with 87.5 % of the people voting for it followed by performance, cost, etc. Figure 3.3 represents the survey statistics for the same question (i.e. rate challenges/issues of the cloud/on-demand model) over various issues.

3.3 Security Challenges in Cloud Application Development

In a cloud environment, an enterprise cannot necessarily use the same tools and services they deployed internally for security, such as a Web application firewall. For example, a company that has deployed a Web application firewall (WAF) as another level of security for a legacy app when exposing it to the Web no longer has that option as the ownership and control of infrastructure at various levels changes in case of cloud. The CSA's cloud application security guidance noted that IaaS vendors have started to offer cloud application security tools and services, including WAFs, Web application security scanning and source code analysis. The tools are specific to either the provider or third party, the report noted. It will be wise to explore all possible APIs that might provide strong logging which in turn help as leverage for security-related activity [18].

Having seen various issues in general, it is time now to look at security in particular with the service model point of view, that is, the issues which are inherent and affect across various service models.

3.3.1 Challenges in Case of PaaS

3.3.1.1 Privacy Control

This is the first step in securing private data before sending it to the cloud. Cyber laws and policies currently exist which disallow and impose relevant restrictions on sending of private data onto third-party systems. A cloud service provider is just another example of a third-party system, and organisations must apply the same rules of handling third-party systems in this case. It is already clear that organisations are concerned at the prospect of private data going to the cloud. The cloud service providers themselves recommend that if private data is sent onto their systems, it must be encrypted, removed or redacted. The question then arises "How can the private data be automatically encrypted, removed, or redacted before sending it up to the cloud service provider?"; that is, "How can the whole process be automated?". It is known that encryption, in particular, is a CPU-intensive process which threatens to add significant latency to the process.

Any solution implemented should broker the connection to the cloud service and automatically encrypt any information an organisation does not want to share via a third party. For example, this could include private or sensitive employee or customer data such as home addresses or social security numbers, or patient data in a medical context. Security engineers should look to provide for on-the-fly data protection by detecting private or sensitive data within the message being sent up to the cloud service provider and encrypting it such that only the originating organisation can decrypt it later. Depending on the policy, the private data could also be removed or redacted from the originating data but then reinserted when the data is requested back from the cloud service provider.

3.3.1.2 Traceability and Audit

As an organisational requirement, in order to monitor the financial consumption of a rented or a paid for technology or service, the financial department needs to keep track of the units of usage and audit trail. The cloud service providers themselves provide this information on most occasions, but in the case of a dispute, it is important to have an independent audit trail. Audit trails provide valuable information about how an organisation's employees are interacting with specific cloud services, legitimately or otherwise.

The end-user organisation could consider a cloud service broker (CSB) solution (such as CloudKick, CloudSwitch, Eucalyptus), as a means to create an independent audit trail of its cloud service consumption. Once armed with his/her own records of cloud service activity, the security engineer can confidently address any concerns over billing or to verify employee activity. A CSB should provide reporting tools to allow organisations to actively monitor how services are being used. There are multiple reasons why an organisation may want a record of cloud activity, which leads us to discuss the issue of governance [19].

3.3.2 Challenges in Case of SaaS

3.3.2.1 Governance: Applying Restrictions and Exit Strategy

Being a third-party service, cloud resources need to have controlled and accounted access. Governance in cloud computing is when an organisation wants to prevent rogue (or unauthorised) employees from misusing a service. For example, the organisation may want to ensure that a user working in marketing part of the application can only access specific leads and does not have access to other restricted areas. Another example is that an organisation may wish to control how many virtual machines can be spun up by employees, and, indeed, that those same machines are spun down later when they are no longer needed. So-called rogue cloud usage must also be detected, so that the employees setting up their own accounts for using a cloud service are detected and brought under an appropriate governance umbrella.

Whilst cloud service providers offer varying degrees of cloud service monitoring, an organisation should consider implementing its own cloud service governance framework. The need for this independent control is of particular benefit when an organisation is using multiple SaaS providers, that is, HR services, ERP and CRM systems. However, in such a scenario, the security engineers also need to be aware that different cloud providers have different methods of accessing information. They also have different security models on top of that.

That points to the solution provided by a cloud broker, which brokers the different connections and essentially smoothes over the differences between them. This means organisations can use various services together but only have to interact with a perfectly configured CSB application. In situations where there is something relatively commoditised like storage as a service, they can be used interchangeably. This solves the issue of what to do if a cloud provider becomes unreliable or goes down and means the organisation can spread the usage across different providers. In fact, organisations should not have to get into the technical weeds of being able to understand or mitigate between different interfaces. They should be able to move up a level where they are using the cloud for the benefits of saving money.

3.3.2.2 Data Encryption

As discussed earlier, when moving data onto a third-party infrastructure, secrecy can be one of the factors for security. This applies to storage infrastructure service as well. Most of the companies are now moving for a cloud-based storage solution, and this calls for an important aspect of secrecy, encryption. Encryption can be handled in many ways. It must also be noted that encrypting data is a CPU-intense process. Many organisations prefer to handle encryption in-house; that is, they prefer to generate own keys and decide on a particular encryption algorithm to further increase confidentiality. Cloud storage provider also provides the encryption facility at the consumer end with unique and dynamically generated consumer-specific encryption keys. The latest trends suggest that organisations are making use of CSBs to accomplish this task. It is interesting to note that many organisations prefer providers whose data centres are accessible and have better traceability than others where it is difficult to track the data being sent onto cloud.

3.3.3 Challenges Relating to SaaS, PaaS, IaaS

3.3.3.1 Using API Keys

Many cloud services are accessed using simple REST [20] Web services interfaces. These are commonly called "APIs", since they are similar in concept to the more heavyweight C++ or Java APIs used by programmers, though they are much easier to leverage from a Web page or from a mobile phone, hence their increasing ubiquity. In order to access these services, an API key is used. These are similar in some ways to passwords. They allow organisations to access the cloud provider. For example, if an organisation is using a SaaS offering, it will often be provided with an API key. This is one security measure employed by the provider to increase accountability; that is, if in case something goes wrong, then that can be easily tracked as every application instance running would have a unique API key (which is associated with a particular user credential) and the source application for the cause of the mistake would also bear an API key. Hence, the misuse of a correct application can be only through misuse of API keys, and it becomes important to protect them.

Consider the example of Google Apps. If an organisation wishes to enable single sign-on to their Google Apps (so that their users can access their email without having to log in a second time), then this access is via API keys. If these keys were to be stolen, then an attacker would have access to the email of every person in that organisation.

The casual use and sharing of API keys is an accident waiting to happen. Protection of API keys can be performed by encrypting them when they are stored on the file system, by storing them within a hardware security module (HSM) or by employing more sophisticated security systems such as Kerberos [21] to monitor single sign-on.

3.4 Challenges for Application Developers

An application developer comes into picture in service models where the organisation has control over applications and computing resources. Hence, this perspective is mainly applicable to PaaS where application development is on a particular third-party cloud platform and to IaaS where the choice of platform is with the organisation, and over the chosen platform the developer writes applications. The following are a few challenges currently faced by programmers and application developers in developing applications on cloud platforms:

3.4.1 Lack of Standardisation

Cloud is still in its very early stages of development. There has been a surge in enterprises adopting cloud technologies, but on the other hand, the technology has not emerged enough to handle issues with this surge. The growth in different industries has been very self-centred, that is, the cloud providers have developed their own APIs, virtualisation techniques, management techniques, etc. From a developer's perspective, every cloud provider supports different programming language and syntax requirement, though most of them expose hash-based data interfaces or more commonly JSON or Xml. This needs immediate attention, and steps must be taken to standardise interfaces and programming methods. In case of conventional counterpart, an application developed in PERL or PHP works fine when the application is moved from one host to another or when there is a change in operations system. Considerable developmental efforts are required in order to move from one cloud provider to another which in turn implies that the cost of migration is significantly high. History has shown us that languages like SQL and C were standardised to stop undesired versions and proliferation.

3.4.2 Lack of Additional Programming Support

One of the key characteristics of good Web applications is that they are highly available. In order for this to be possible in a cloud application, it must be made to dynamically replicate and mirror on machines across cloud with ease. Once this is done, the load balancing servers can serve these applications on demand, hence increasing availability and without delays, that is, decrease in latency. As most of the cloud platform providers employ multi-tenancy model, servicing hundreds of application forces them to automate the task of mirroring and replication. In order to achieve this seamlessly, the application must use very little or no state information. The state variables include transactional or server variables, static variables and variables which are present in the framework of the whole application. These variables are always available in case of traditional environment as there is a static application server and memory where they can be stored and accessed, but these are very hard to find in a cloud environment. One of the ways of handling this situation is to make use of a datastore or the cache store. Restriction on installing third-party libraries, limited or no access with write permission to file systems hinders the capability of an application to store state information and hence forces an organisation to use the providers' datastore service which comes at a price.

3.4.3 *Metrics and Best Practices*

Cloud follows a pay-as-you-use policy, and, hence, consumers pay for almost every bit of CPU usage. This necessitates the provider to present appropriate metrics on processor usage and memory. A profile of the application with the skeleton of classes or functions and their corresponding execution time, memory used and processing power utilised, etc. will help the developer tune the code to optimise the use of available processing power by choosing e.g. a different data structure or algorithm with lesser time and space complexity

One of the solutions to this concern can be provided by the cloud host by abstracting the common code patterns which are frequently used into optimal default libraries as the cloud provider could easily employ optimisation techniques which would suit the hardware underneath and the operating system used. This helps the developer to be assured that a piece of code is employing optimal techniques to produce the desired effect. As an example, Apache PIG [22] gives a scripting-like interface to Apache Hadoop's [23] HDFS for analysing large-scale datasets.

In the end, the summary of cloud service models and their providers, properties, access to resources and key challenges can be tabulated as in Table 3.1.

3.5 Conclusion

Cloud applications certainly have taken the IT industry to a new high, but like every other technology, they have come short of a few things. In the search of exploiting benefits of cloud applications, the inevitable trail of challenges has followed them all along. The challenges in employing cloud services are discussed in this chapter. The security challenges which are more specific to a type of service, that is, the type of service model, are also described. With emerging trends in cloud-based applications development, the time has come to actually take a look at the pitfalls and address them. The chapter has given an insight into how these challenges can be overcome.

The major of all the concern turns out to be security that needs serious attention. The overall conclusion is that cloud computing is in general prepared to successfully host most typical Web applications with added benefits such as cost savings, but applications with the following properties need more careful study before their deployment:

- Have strict latency or other network performance requirements.
- Require working with large datasets.
- Needs for availability are critical.

As a developer, one would like to see much advancement in terms of the developmental tool kit and the standardisation of APIs across various cloud development platforms in the near future. This would also help in the transition from traditional application to cloud-based environment as the intellectual investment required to bring about this transition is less, and more developers can move from traditional application development to cloud.

References

1. Mell, P., Grance, T.: The NIST Definition of Cloud Computing. Special Publication 800–145, September 2001
2. Buyya, R., Yeo, C.S., Venugopal, S.: Market-oriented cloud computing: vision, hype, and reality for delivering it services as computing utilities. In: High Performance Computing and Communications, 2008, HPCC '08, Dalian, China. 10th IEEE International Conference, pp. 5–13 (2008)
3. Gong, C., et al.: The characteristics of cloud computing. In: 2010 39th International Conference on Parallel Processing Workshops, San Diego
4. Zhang, Q., Cheng, L., Boutaba, R.: Cloud computing: State-of-the-art and research challenges. J. Internet Serv. Appl. **1**(1), 7–18 (2010)
5. Cloud Computing: What is infrastructure as a service. http://technet.microsoft.com/en-us/magazine/hh509051.aspx
6. Wang, L., Tao, J., Kunze, M., Castellanos, A.C., Kramer, D., Karl, W.: Scientific cloud computing: early definition and experience. 10th IEEE Int. Conf. High Perform. Comput. Commun. **9**(3), 825–830 (2008)
7. Ramgovind, S., Eloff, M.M., Smith, E.: The management of security in cloud computing. In: PROC 2010 I.E. International Conference on Cloud Computing, Indianapolis, USA (2010)
8. API and usage documentation for developer using Rackspace service. http://docs.rackspace.com
9. Wu, R., Ahn, G., Hongxin Hu, Singhal M.: Information flow control in cloud computing. In: Collaborative Computing: Networking, Applications and Worksharing (CollaborateCom), 2010 6th International Conference, Brisbane, Australia, pp. 17. IEEE (2010)
10. Shimba, F.: Cloud computing: strategies for cloud computing adoption. Masters Dissertation, Dublin Institute of Technology (2010)
11. About STAR: https://cloudsecurityalliance.org/star/faq/
12. Description of standard service by TripWire. http://www.tripwire.com/services/standard/
13. Description of Custom service by TripWire. http://www.tripwire.com/services/custom/

14. Ko, R.K.L., Jagadpramana, P., Mowbray, M., Pearson, S., Kirchberg, M., Liang, Lee, B.S., HP Laboratories: TrustCloud: a framework for accountability and trust in cloud computing. http://www.hpl.hp.com/techreports/2011/HPL-2011-38.pdf
15. Minnear, R.: Latency: The Achilles Heel of cloud computing, 9 March 2011. Cloud Expo: Article, Cloud Comput. J. http://cloudcomputing.sys-con.com/node/1745523 (2011)
16. Kuyoro, S.O., Ibikunle, F., Awodele, O.: Cloud computing security issues and challenges. Int. J. Comput. Netw. **3**(5) (2011)
17. FedRAMP: U.S General Services Administration Initiative. http://www.gsa.gov/portal/category/102371
18. Security Guidance for Critical Areas of Focus in Cloud Computing V2.1, Prepared by CSA 2009. https://cloudsecurityalliance.org/csaguide.pdf
19. Weixiang, S., et al.: Cloud service broker, March 2012. http://tools.ietf.org/pdf/draft-shao-opsawg-cloud-service-broker-03.pdf (2012)
20. Tyagi, S.: RESTful web service, August 2006. http://www.oracle.com/technetwork/articles/javase/index-137171.html (2006)
21. Kerberos in the Cloud: Use Case Scenarios. https://www.oasis-open.org/committees/download.php/38245/Kerberos-Cloud-use-cases-11june2010.pdf
22. Apache PIG: http://pig.apache.org/
23. Apache Hadoop: http://hadoop.apache.org/
24. SAAS, PAAS and IAAS – Making Cloud Computing Less Cloudy. http://cioresearchcenter.com/2010/12/107/

Part II
Software Development Life Cycle for Cloud Platform

Chapter 4
Impact of Cloud Services on Software Development Life Cycle

Radha Krishna and R. Jayakrishnan

Abstract Cloud computing provides a natural extension to service-oriented architecture (SOA) and the World Wide Web. It leads to a complete paradigm shift in a number of areas such as software development, deployment, IT usage, and software services industry. Among these areas, the impact on software development life cycle needs special attention as they form a pivotal part in the cloud assessment and migration. In this context, some key aspects include (a) implications of cloud-based (public cloud based) solution on the privacy requirements, (b) implications of cloud-based solution on testing services and project testing methodology, and (c) implications of cloud-based solution of configuration management. In this chapter, we propose to address the impacts, strategies, and best practices to minimize the negative effects of these implications. The chapter discusses variations to software development life cycle and related processes with respect to private cloud, public cloud, and hybrid cloud models. These variations are analyzed based on the usage pattern of each cloud-based solution, especially with respect to requirement analysis, architecture and design, software construction, testing, and rollout. Relevant processes such as project management, configuration management, and release management are also discussed. The chapter concludes with a summary of various cloud usage patterns and their impact on each of the software development life cycle stages. These usage patterns and the impacts are generalized and can form the backbone of an enterprise cloud application development methodology.

Keywords Software development life cycle • Usage patterns • Design for failure • Design for parallelism • Information architecture • Private cloud • Public cloud

---

R. Krishna (✉) • R. Jayakrishnan
Infosys Ltd., 4252, 65th Cross, Kumaraswamy Layout II Stage, Bangalore 560078, India
e-mail: radha@gmail.com; jkramdas@infosys.com

Z. Mahmood and S. Saeed (eds.), *Software Engineering Frameworks for the Cloud Computing Paradigm*, Computer Communications and Networks,
DOI 10.1007/978-1-4471-5031-2_4, © Springer-Verlag London 2013

4.1 Introduction

It is generally agreed that evolution of a new paradigm requires adaptation in usage patterns and associated functional areas to fully benefit from the paradigm shift [1]. Likewise, to leverage the benefit of cloud paradigm shift in software segment, software development life cycle (SDLC) must continuously adopt new changes to be the guideline for development/implementation of cloud-based projects. The user communities, such as management professionals, academicians/researchers, or software engineers, are very much keen in understanding and adopting the current state and new changes in SDLC while adapting to the paradigm changes. This chapter mainly describes the changes that are required in SDLC (part of software engineering process) while adopting the cloud computing environment. An SDLC typically comprises the following phases:

- Requirements
- Architecture
- Design
- Implementation
- Testing
- Production
- Support and Maintenance

To truly benefit from cloud environment, software development teams should look at the cloud computing environment as a new development paradigm and leverage it to lead to differentiated value. The rest of the chapter explains positioning of the application development process to enable to take the advantage of the distributed nature of cloud environment.

4.2 Requirement Analysis

The industry, in general, tends to think of cloud as an enabler or rather a solution and hence believes that it has no bearing on requirements. The truth is that cloud is more of a choice at enterprise level. Hence, the fitment of the choice is an important aspect of the analysis phase. Along with the choice, the guidelines and checklists that aid in requirement analysis are also required for applications moving to cloud to be successful. The requirement analysis needs to address this assessment. These relevant requirements are mostly non-functional in nature.

This implies the following additional tasks that need to be planned as part of requirement analysis:

- Cloud assessment
- Cloud usage pattern identification and capturing data points to support requirement analysis based on usage patterns

4.3 Cloud Assessment

Cloud readiness assessment will help to evaluate the cloud readiness and applicability for an enterprise. The assessment also helps to determine the business case and return on investment. Typical assessment questions are listed below for reference. Note that this list is not exhaustive:

- Does cloud architecture fit the requirements for the application?
- How interconnected is this application with other application in the enterprise—for public cloud, can these interfaces be exposed for access from external networks?
- Is the enterprise comfortable with public cloud, or should the enterprise focus only on private cloud option among other options?
- Identifying suitable cloud service provider (IAAS/PAAS [2]—and the specific vendor under the category)
- Defining the strategy in adopting cloud for future projects
- Assessing the cost of using cloud (private or public cloud) (compare—capital expense of hosted option vs. running cost of cloud option)
- How would applications be monitored after they are hosted on public cloud?

It is important to note that cloud assessment guidelines are defined at enterprise level. The enterprise can optionally create tools to aid the projects and new initiatives to perform cloud assessment.

4.4 Usage Patterns and Requirements Capture

Below we present a list of common usage patterns [3] and corresponding requirement capturing questionnaire that helps to arrive at workload of an application and decide on its readiness for cloud-based architecture.

4.4.1 Constant Usage of Cloud Resources over Time

This pattern is applicable to both internal and external (e.g., Web sites) applications that are constantly used by enterprise users/external users, and there is little variance in load and usage of these applications. Requirement analysis should detail out the following information:

- Availability of applications at regular intervals.
- Defining the strategy for application downtime and uptime.
- More requirement analysis is required in designing the respective scripts to make the application available at a required point of time.
- Defining limits of data loss in case of application crash.

4.4.2 Cyclic Internal Load

This pattern applies to recurrent business functionalities like batch jobs that execute at end of day and data processing applications.

- Detail out the I/O volume required to satisfy the business process (costing of the cloud solution is very I/O sensitive).

4.4.3 Cyclic External Load

This pattern includes applications that are developed to serve a particular demand, like publishing examination results/election campaign and sites related to entertainment.

- Detail out level of concurrency required across time periods and hence amount of parallelism that can be applied to improve the performance of the system.

4.4.4 Spiked Internal Load

This pattern applies to executing one-time jobs for processing at a given point in time.

- Detail out requirements on identifying number of concurrent users accessing the system.
- Identify volume of data that is required to process the business functionality.
- Detail out the network bandwidth and expected delay in response while processing heavy load business functionality.
- Analyze variety of data that is used in day-to-day business.
- Define set of business functionalities and business components that can execute side by side.
- Identify reusability of components.
- Identify different failure scenarios and respective handling mechanisms.

4.4.5 Spiked External Load

This pattern applies to applications that should be able to handle a sudden load which may come from an external source example: customers, vendors, or public users.

- Define the limit of independence to access the application.
- Identify and analyze country-level regulations to handle the load.
- Identify industry-specific regulations while handling the load.
- Identify institutional specific fragility and capacity challenges.

4.4.6 *Steady Growth over Time*

This pattern usually applies to a mature application or Web site, wherein as additional users are added, growth and resources are tracked.

- Cost of maintaining application on cloud

4.5 Architecture

In general, software that is to be deployed in cloud environments should be architected differently than on-premise hosted/deployed applications. Cloud computing as a development environment for distributed model has led to emergence of varieties of design and architecture principles. The new architecture paradigm requires improving the thought process for horizontally scaling out the architectures by developing and designing large number of smaller components that are loosely coupled and easy to deploy in distributed environments.

Cloud computing solutions should operate on a network which is capable of handling massive data transactions. The software development teams should be aware that apart from general architecture and design principles, one needs special skills to handle solutions with high I/O volume/velocity, and architects should come up with a strategic and competitive skills to leverage the service provided by distributed environment vendors.

With every increase in demand of quality software from clients, enterprises must produce the software that can be adapted to new environments without degrading the existing parameters of quality of service for the application. To take the advantage of distributed environment while developing cloud-based applications, there are couple of changes and additions identified that are critical in determining the scalability of the architecture to take the advantage of scalable infrastructure available in distributed environment. For example, architects should start thinking of architecting and designing applications that support multi-tenancy, concurrency management, denormalized partitioned and shared-nothing data, asynchronous and parallel processing, service-oriented composition supporting restful services [15], etc.

4.6 Information Architecture

As the world is growing and becoming more connected every day, data plays a vital role in software application. The key in building the information architecture is to closely align information to business process by availing the features available in cloud environment. This process enables all stakeholders like business leaders, vendors, consumers, service providers, users, and all other stakeholders in evaluating, reconciling, and prioritizing on the information vision and related road map. The information architecture should provide great care that should be taken in defining strategy on development approach ensuring right decisions in development and execution of an application.

Understanding the key considerations of data architecture in distributed environment and trade-offs for decisions made related to technology and architecture choices in cloud environments is essential for good information architecture. For example, decisions like data sharing is very crucial while defining the data services. This topic mainly describes different varieties of data (relational, geospatial, unstructured data, etc.) and different classifications and compliance of data (internal and external).

The information architecture provides information for relevant concepts, frameworks, and services to access information in unique, consistent, and integrated way by adopting new cutting-edge technology and guarantees responsiveness and trustworthy information. Following are core decision points of information architecture:

- *Access Information:* Information services should provide unconstrained access to the right users at the right time.
- *Reusable Services:* Facilitate discovery, selection, and reuse of services and encourage uniformity of services.
- *Information Governance:* Provide proper utilities to support efficiency of information governance strategy.
- *Standards:* Define set of standards to information where technology will support process simplification.

4.7 Information Security

Security is one of the important nonfunctional requirements demanded by clients. Information security plays a vital role in distributed environments while defining information architecture. The level of security applied depends on the type of information (Fig. 4.1).

In general, information is classified into four main categories as defined in Table 4.1.

Authentication, authorization, and data protection are different mechanisms of implementing security that every system should adopt. These security mechanisms need to be applied to information which may be available in different formats and dates like:

- Information at Rest
- Information in Transit
- Transient Information
- Information CRUD

Table 4.2 provides information on strategies for various information categorization and security options.

Information architecture should help the system in segregating information into the above-mentioned categories, and each category will have challenging information classification for different security mechanisms as defined in Table 4.3.

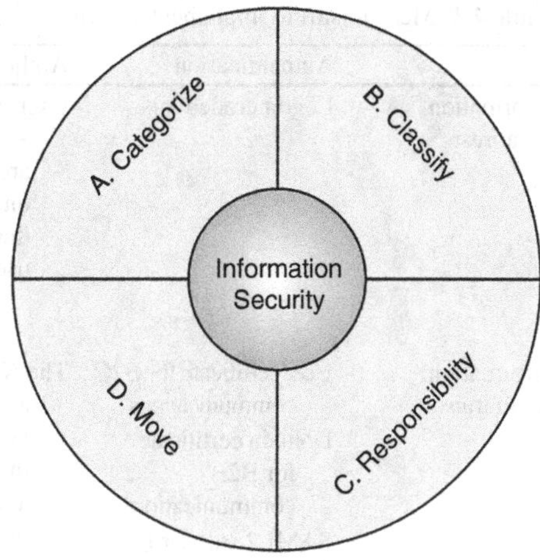

Fig. 4.1 Levels of information security

Table 4.1 Information categories

Public	Private	Confidential	Secret
Data available for general public	Data private to organization	Data to be disclosed on need-to-know basis after approval from the owner	Data never disclosed and can be seen only by the owner of the data
	For Ex:	For Ex:	For Ex:
	Intranet information	Customer information	Password
	Org chart	Organization policy and would-be changes	Pin number
	List of employees	Source code for business critical modules	SSN
	Source code for in-house/ utility modules		Credit card number, authorization code, and expiry data combination
For Ex:			Account number, last 4 digits of SSN, birth date combination
Annual reports			Source code for decryption
Share price			

Table 4.3 should be understood with the following in mind:

- Authenticating the access to public information is optional.
- Authenticating the access to information that is private to the organization is mandatory, and the same is applicable for the information that is classified under confidential and secret categories.
- Authorizing the access to public/private information is optional.
- Authorizing the access to confidential and secret information is mandatory.
- Protecting the access to public/private information is optional.
- Protecting the access to confidential and secret information is mandatory.

Table 4.2 Mechanisms to implement security

	Authentication	Authorization	Protection
Information at rest	Logon credentials	User group-based access. User groups are created based on department and thus represent users' entitlements	Encryption at two levels: encryption at storage and encryption at individual record or fields XKMS can be used instead of PKI for key management services
Information in transit	User certificate for B2C communications Domain certificate for B2B communications SAML2 standards for user token-based authentication	The XACML standards and policy generated through that provide authorization for publish and subscribe as well as B2C Web services	4 levels of protection Domain authentication via SSL (2-way) SAML2 attributes encrypted using a different key, verification of token or attributes on federation DB, and finally any message level encryption for the SOAP message
Transient or temporary information	All the above options	All the above options	All the above options
CRUD operation on information	Logon credentials	Role-based access	

Table 4.3 Security mechanisms vs. information categories

	Public	Private	Confidential	Secret
Authentication	O	M	M	M
Authorization	O	O	M	M
Protection	O	O	M	M

M mandatory, *O* optional

Information security [10] defines responsibility of different stakeholders (consumer/vendor) based on the different cloud environments. Table 4.4 provides details about the responsibilities of different stakeholders.

As we move lower down the stack, consumer should be responsible in implementing security features:

- Vendor—the organization who provides cloud environments
- Consumer—the organization who uses cloud environment provided vendor

Table 4.5 defines different kind of information that may be moved to cloud environment based on the responsibility the vendor takes with respect to security of the data.

Table 4.4 Security with respect to cloud services

	IaaS	PaaS	SaaS	BPaaS
Physical security (hardware/infrastructure)	Vendor	Vendor	Vendor	Vendor
Network security (data over wire)	Consumer	Consumer	Vendor	Vendor
System security (operating systems, Web servers, message servers, etc.)	Consumer	Vendor	Vendor	Vendor
Application security (custom applications)	Consumer	Consumer	Vendor	Vendor

Table 4.5 Data security with respect to information categories

	Public	Private	Confidential	Secret
Data at rest	Yes	Yes	Responsibility on vendor	No
Transient or temporary data	Yes	Yes	Responsibility on vendor and consumer	No
Data in transit	Yes	Yes	Responsibility on consumer	No

This implies that confidential data can be in cloud but needs encryption and token-based authentication supported by cloud provider given that organization policy allows it.

4.8 Non-functional Information Details

The following non-functional information requirements need to be analyzed as part of information architecture.

4.8.1 Volume

As the world is growing day by day being more connected, sizing the data volume is mandatory non-functional information to be captured.

- More connected human resources = more data
- More connected with devices (phones, tablets, etc.) = more data
- How much data need to be required in a day?
- What is the expected data that can be added at a given point in time?

4.8.2 Variety

There are many varieties of data used in day-to-day business. The very first that comes to mind is relational and transactional data, but other sets of data include:

- Relational
- Configuration
- Graphs

- Geospatial
- Documents
- Unstructured data (videos, audio, text)

4.8.3 Internal and External

Internal requirements include:

- High impact
- Medium impact
- Low impact
- External requirements include:
- Regulations (country level/region level)
- Industry specific (SWIFT/HIPAA)

4.8.4 Ability to Query

The relevant requirements are:

- The ability to query or search the data stored in a distributed environment
- Level of querying demanded
  - Single field, multiple fields in a table, fully relational data
- Scope of query
  - Single logical partition or data distributed across multiple logical partitions
- Real-time data need
  - Query intervals and responsiveness
  - Data freshness

4.9 Partitioning Strategy

Partitioning data involves a trade-off between scalability, consistency, and flexibility. The main needs that influence data partitions are:

- Data size that is stored on a single server
- Transaction volume that needs to be processed on a single server
- Data variety that is stored in different places

In highly elastic scenarios of distributed environments, partitions may be needed for just few hours or days. As part of just-in-time partitioning strategy, if load is predictable, then:

- Partition before load commences
- Un-partition after load moderates

4.10 Information Processing

While processing information in distributed environment, sometimes it is mandatory to process large set of information. It is always a good practice to implement parallel data processing that is simple in concept as explained below.

- Take large problem.
- Break it into smaller parts.
- Distribute parts into multiple nodes for solving.
- Aggregate all smaller solutions into complete solution.

Architecture should identify all independent processes and implement parallelism wherever applicable.

4.11 Information Backup Strategy

In distributed cloud environment, backups can be on-premise to cloud, cloud to on-premise, or cloud to cloud. Architecture should define proper service-level agreements between cloud vendor and cloud consumer and should come up with appropriate backup strategy.

4.12 Cost as Non-functional Requirement

As cloud computing is methodology of using tools and accessing applications from the Internet, cloud computing always reduces IT cost is a general misconception everyone has. The success of cloud computing vendors also depends on pricing. In general, while cloud computing provides cost savings for enterprises when setting up initial infrastructure, running costs and other operational costs may negate the initial savings enterprises make. But it is always suggestible to compare the initial cost of setup with an on-premise option with the cost per month cloud option and then evaluate the cloud migration strategy.

Costing on cloud is of type of pay-per-use model. The service providers charge separately on multiple factors like number of instances, bandwidth, load balancing, transaction volume, and other factors.

There are four models [4] currently being used across various cloud providers in order to cost out their cloud solutions. Architects should identify the most cost-effective costing model for a given set of requirements. Also, sensitivity analysis for the costing model should be done based on the growth projections for the system.

4.12.1 *Weighted Cloud Costing*

This is perhaps the most indirect method of dividing up the cloud service costs. It looks at each business unit as a part of the whole company. That might be looked at from a budgetary perspective, or it might take into account headcount. You then divide up the cost of your cloud solutions to each business unit, based on this weighted percentage. This is the easiest and least accurate way to divide costs.

4.12.2 *Tiered Cloud Costing*

Another approach is to break up business units or other groups into tiers. Each tier requires greater resources than the tier below it. You charge a lower rate to the business units and groups who use the most resources, reflecting a discount based on demand. You then offer other discounts, for example, to those groups that are able to do their own server provisioning or management.

4.12.3 *Costing That Differentiates Service and Infrastructure*

This type of costing accounts for your infrastructure costs separately from your application costs. Thus, your data center expenses come in a different direction from your cloud computing solutions. This means that you can still charge a baseline per-head infrastructure charge while recovering either a tiered or consumption-based cost for your cloud solutions.

4.12.4 *Consumption Cloud Costing*

Consumption is the costing method that is most accurate and that requires the most resources. It looks at the actual amounts of service time that each unit requires and charges them accordingly.

4.13 Usage Patterns and Architecture

The previous sections explained how cloud has made an impact to architectural decisions at a high level. With this high-level overview in mind, let us analyze the cloud usage patterns explained in the Requirements section. Just as cloud usage patterns impact requirements in a standard way, their impacts on other life cycle stages are also in a standard manner.

4.13.1 Constant Usage of Cloud Resources over Time

This pattern is typically utilized to save cost and share many non-frequent and non-critical applications across the same virtual machine.

- Uses consumption cloud costing
- Calculates cost based on predictive usage
- Isolated applications that do not typically need real-time data and only update master tables

4.13.2 Cyclic Internal Load

This pattern is used to improve availability. Since it is internal load, private cloud can be an option. Cloud bursting can be thought of where data need not be real time.

4.13.3 Cyclic External Load

This pattern is for brand new public cloud application. Here cloud characteristics like multi-tenancy and parallelism become important.

4.13.4 Spiked Internal Load

This pattern is typical to cloud bursting scenario.

4.13.5 Spiked External Load

This pattern is typically an auto-scaling scenario.

4.13.6 Steady Growth over Time

This pattern applies usually for a mature application or Web site; as additional users are added, growth and resources track accordingly.

4.14 Design

The design patterns guide the composition of modules into complete systems. In addition to existing design patterns and number of other common patterns, applications developed for distributed environments need to work in B2C services and use respective credentials while accessing. Application designers should start thinking of designing applications for failure analysis and parallelism [5] to avail the cloud infrastructure.

4.15 Design for Parallelism [9]

Designing and programming to leverage multiple cores and multiple processors is called parallel programming. Nowadays, CPU manufacturers are shifting their focus on increasing the CPU core, and speeding up CPU is stagnated; especially this is happening in distributed environments like cloud. This is a major setback for programmer community because standard threading concept will not automatically run faster as expected because of those extra cores.

All server-based applications in distributed environment should leverage the multiple cores, where each thread can independently handle a separate request. Parallel programming in distributed environment should leverage multi-core processors to speed up computationally intensive applications. To leverage parallelism in distributed environment, the design should:

- Partition computationally intensive code into multiple chunks
- Execute those chunks in parallel implementing multithreading and asynchronous communications between these independent threads
- Collate the results once execution is completed in a thread-safe mode

Parallelism [5] can be applied at both data level (data parallelism) and task level (task parallelism).

4.15.1 Data Parallelism

When multiple tasks need to be performed on many data values, parallelism can be implemented by spawning threads that perform similar set of tasks on a subset of data [13]. Data is partitioned across threads in this scenario (Fig. 4.2).

4.15.2 Task Parallelism

Each processor executes a different thread on the same or different data. The tasks that need to implement such functionality are partitioned into multiple units to execute on multiple processors in parallel. The tasks execute simultaneously on multiple cores processing many different functions across data. Communication between threads takes place as part of workflow defined for the context. This is also called function parallelism or control parallelism (Fig. 4.3).

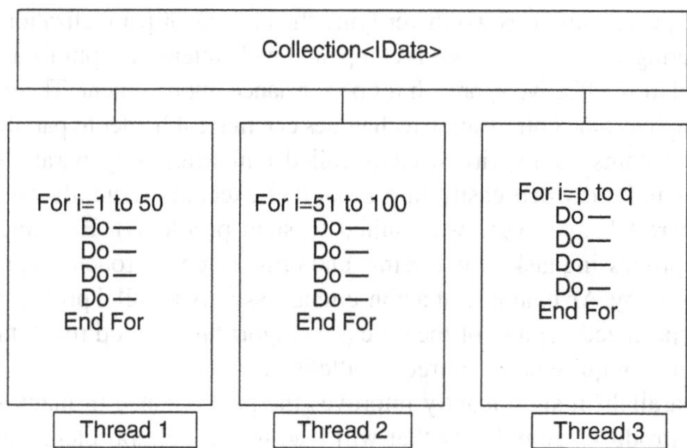

Fig. 4.2 Implementing data parallelism

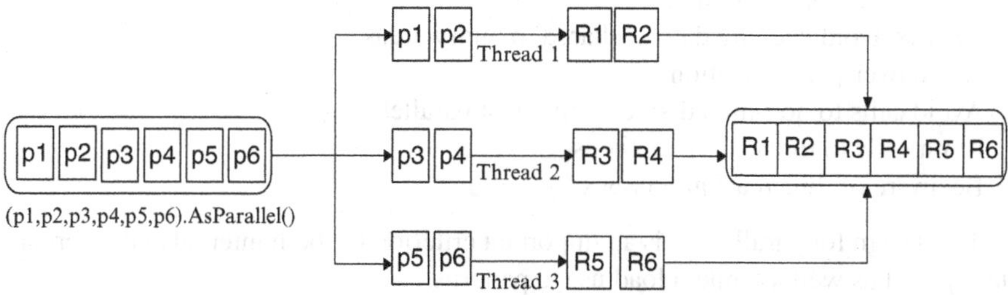

Fig. 4.3 Implementing task parallelism: [Tasks (p1,p2,p3,p4,p5,p6).ParallelExecute()=Result (R1,R2,R3,R4,R5,R6)]

Data parallelism is easier and scales better on highly parallel hardware, because it reduces or eliminates shared data (thereby reducing contention and thread-safety issues). Also, data parallelism leverages the fact that there are often more data values than discrete tasks, increasing the parallelism potential.

Data parallelism is also conducive to structured parallelism, which means that parallel work units start and finish in the same place in program. In contrast, task parallelism tends to be unstructured, meaning that parallel work units may start and finish in places scattered across your program. Structured parallelism is simpler and less error-prone and allows you to farm the difficult job of partitioning and thread coordination (and even result collation) out to libraries.

A challenge in leveraging multi-cores is Amdahl's law, which states that the maximum performance improvement from parallelization is governed by the portion of the code that must execute sequentially. For instance, if only two-thirds of an algorithm's execution time is parallelizable, you can never exceed a threefold performance gain even with an infinite number of cores.

So, before proceeding, it is worth verifying the process of parallelization. It is also worth considering whether your code is computationally intensive; optimization is often the easiest and most effective approach for performance improvement. There is a trade-off, though, in that some optimization techniques can make it harder to parallelize code.

The easiest gains come with what is called embarrassingly parallel problem, where a job can be divided easily into tasks that execute efficiently on their own (structured parallelism is very well suited to such problems). Examples include many image processing tasks, ray tracing, and brute force approaches in mathematics or cryptography. An example of a non-embarrassingly parallel problem is implementing an optimized version of the quicksort algorithm; a good result takes some thought and may require unstructured parallelism.

Though parallelism significantly improves the performance in many scenarios, parallelism introduces complexity that will lead to multiple problems that are not common or have not been encountered at all. Following are some of the best practices that must be taken into account before designing the systems for parallelism:

- Do not assume parallelism is always faster, and do not assume all iterations always execute in parallel.
- Always avoid keeping data in shared memory areas.
- Avoid over-parallelization.
- Avoid calls to non-thread-safe methods in parallel.
- Limit calls to thread-safe methods.
- Be aware of thread affinity issues.

The design for parallelism is an important criterion for both internal and external steady load as well as spiked load usage patterns.

4.16 Design for Failure

Failure analysis is a key pattern in deciding the behavior of application in failure scenarios. Design for failure [6] mainly improves application availability and ensures that application behaves as expected in a given environment. Design for failure [7] is essential to avoid disruptions in cloud applications in outage scenarios. Design for failure is imperative to take advantage of cost saving and agility offered by cloud service providers.

Following are some steps to be considered while designing applications for failure:

- Each application component must be deployed across redundant cloud components, ideally with minimal or no common points of failure.
- Each application component must make no assumptions about the underlying infrastructure—it must be able to adapt to changes in the infrastructure without downtime.
- Each application component should be partition tolerant—in other words, it should be able to survive network latency (or loss of communication) among the nodes that support that component.

- Automation tools must be in place to orchestrate application responses to failures or other changes in the infrastructure.

Architects and designers should consider following key factors as part of enterprise application development:

- Do not look for alternatives to design for failure.
- Application should be decoupled into isolated workable components.
- Consider partitioning data into multiple relevant chunks and deploy across multiple geographically distinct partitions; this could be well possible in case of NOSQL databases. It would be little difficult in case of RDBMS databases because of data consistency nature of RDBMS systems.
- Application software should quickly identify failures and retry requests in case of failure. This can be possible by running multiple redundant copies of service; one can retry to route around failed or unreachable services.
- Make sure that the services are idempotent in nature. Idempotent services will provide same results if executed once or multiple times.
- Define a fault tree analysis for services. Fault tree analysis is a graphical representation of the major faults or critical failures associated with a product, the causes for the faults, and potential countermeasures.

Design for failure is an important criterion for both internal and external steady load usage patterns.

4.17 Build

The additional impacts during build phase are typically centered on the organizations' effort to reduce cost. The impacts are more in terms of planning and prioritization rather than software build. The key questions are:

- How often the continuous integration should deploy on cloud?
- Provisioning of development and testing environment, which the organization decides the host as a cloud service.

4.18 Testing

Software testing has undergone significant progress in automation in recent years. Global market pressures are pushing enterprises to deliver more for less. Testing of applications deployed in cloud environment will be a little cumbersome due to the availability of resources and diversity in cloud environment [14]. Network latency is unpredictable when applications are distributed across different homogenous and heterogeneous cloud environments. Applications should be tested for checking compatibility with different services and environments on which the application is distributed [12]. The design of a system should emphasize decoupling, and each decoupled component should be implemented to allow independent testing. Modularization of a system will reduce testing effort. Implementing test automation process will be a little tricky in cloud environment. This topic explains different patterns to be considered while testing an application in cloud environment. Testing applications hosted on a distributed environment should follow the guidelines below.

4.18.1 Diversity of Deployment Environments

Cloud being a distributed environment, applications will be architected and designed as smaller components that can exist on their own and that can be hosted on different cloud and non-cloud environments and compatible for testing the functionality implemented. There are three different kinds of deployment environments for cloud-based applications [8]:

- A part of application is migrated to cloud, remaining part is available on-premise.
- Complete application is moved to cloud.
- Building the application in cloud itself.

The testing paradigm should be changed from testing entire cycle of an application to independently testing individual components. Integration testing and quality testing should happen at component level and not at application level that generally happens in non-cloud environments. Testing methodology should ensure virtualization of cloud infrastructure, network latency, business logic of an application, and the user experience.

Data migration and security-level testing is required in scenarios for partial migration to cloud.

4.18.2 Configuration and Network-Level Challenges

Cloud environment offers huge memory, storage [11], and processor power for computing when compared to traditional in-house built applications. At the same time, network landscape of cloud environment will have so many firewalls and need to connect to different heterogeneous environments and data centers.

Testing paradigm should ensure optimum memory usage and performance for all desired set of configuration and network bandwidth.

Application should be tested for different access rights as application should be connected to multiple components and storage areas to be accessed and should test compatibility of different services that can be accessed through SOAP and REST in both secured and non-secured way.

4.18.3 Changes in Application Development Methodologies

In order to deliver the benefits of faster time to market, the application implementation process will be changed from traditional software development models to newer ones. Application will be componentized and build will be available for smaller components instead of delivering a complete life cycle of functionality. Therefore, builds will be available much earlier and that imposes higher demand on testing team to reduce the testing life cycle without compromising on quality and coverage.

4.18.4 Application Limitations

There will be some limitations at data level for both hybrid and public cloud environments. As enterprises do not agree to have confidential and secret data in cloud environment, testing should ensure that no data other than public is allowed to access by publicly hosted applications directly.

4.18.5 Data Synchronization

As applications on cloud use data synchronization process to move the data across different applications/environments, testing process should ensure that data synchronization happens on time as expected. This testing should ensure data availability in heterogeneous environments.

4.18.6 Involved Extra Costing

Application testing over cloud always includes extra I/O costs, bandwidth cost, and other usage costs. Testing designers should segregate application testing into in-house testing and cloud testing that will reduce extra cloud usage cost.

4.19 Impact on Version Control and Configuration Management

The configuration management and version control tools available today are rigid and effort intensive in handling complex and dynamics of modern software. There is a lack of analytics required to handle uncontrolled frequent changes to critical decision-supportive information. There is no control on different kinds of artifacts and monitoring different environments for different kind of deployments like partial deployment, patch releases, and full and complete deployment, and creating respective rollback scenarios is very difficult to achieve using the currently available tools.

As cloud applications are distributed in nature, the changes in software also will be distributed. The new configuration management system should ensure the changes happening across environments and should provide a consolidated view of application stack. This facilitates delivery managers to monitor and control configuration changes across various layers and environments of application software that includes Web and application servers, databases, different third-party components, sharewares, operating systems, and hardware.

4.20 Conclusion

With this chapter, we have tried to visualize the different changes at each life cycle stage due to cloud development and bucket them into different cloud usage patterns. Just as the cloud solutions can have generalized standards and guidelines (which organizations like BIAN are trying to address), the impact of cloud solutions on software development methodology can also be standardized.

Another point to highlight is the fact that cloud impact on SDLC is often neglected as on surface; it seems as if there are not many differences. However, as explained in this chapter, from privacy laws of different countries that can impact requirements to consideration of cost of deployment on testing and implementation processes, the impacts need to be fully analyzed and thought through.

References

1. Musings from David Chou: Architect, Microsoft, Cloud computing as a new development paradigm, 20 July 2010. http://blogs.msdn.com/b/dachou/archive/2010/07/20/cloud-computing-as-a-new-development-paradigm.aspx (2010)
2. XOrient: Cloud computing services in a typical cloud ecosystem. http://www.xoriant.com/Cloud-Computing-Services-SaaS-PaaS-IaaS-models.html (2012)
3. Barr, J.: Amazon, six cloud usage patterns, 1 August 2011. http://cloudspring.com/cloud-usage-patterns/ (2011)
4. Nichols, C.: Top 4 cloud costing models, Wed, 28 March 2012. http://www.unitiv.com/it-solutions-blog/bid/84527/Top-4-Cloud-Costing-Models (2012)
5. Massingill, B.L., Mattson, T.G., Sanders, B.A.: Re-engineering for parallelism: an entry point into PLPP (Pattern Language for Parallel Programming) for legacy applications. http://parlab.eecs.berkeley.edu/wiki/_media/patterns/plpp.pdf (2006)
6. Varia, J.: Architecture for the cloud: best practices. Amazon Web Services http://media.amazonwebservices.com/AWS_Cloud_Best_Practices.pdf (2011)
7. Reese, G.: The AWS outage: the cloud's shining moment, 23 April 2011. http://broadcast.oreilly.com/2011/04/the-aws-outage-the-clouds-shining-moment.html (2011)
8. Naganathan, V.: Infosys, how is testing cloud based applications different from testing on premise applications in QA clouds, 8 November 2011. http://www.infosysblogs.com/testing-services/2011/11/how_is_testing_cloud_based_app.html (2011)

9. Ramdas, J (Senior Technology Architect, Infosys LTD)., Srinivas, J (Principal Architect, Infosys LTD).: Extend Java EE containers with cloud characteristics, 12 May 2011. www.ibm.com/developerworks/cloud/library/cl-jeecontainercloud/ (2011)
10. Godinez, M., Hechler, E., Koenig, K., Lockwood, S., Oberhofer, M., Schroeck, M.: The art of enterprise architecture. http://www.amazon.com/Art-Enterprise-Information-Architecture-Systems-Based/dp/0137035713 (2010)
11. Arista, C.: Cloud networking: design patterns for "Cloud-Centric" application environments. http://www.techrepublic.com/whitepapers/cloud-networking-design-patterns-for-cloud-centric-application-environments/2393983 (2009)
12. Kothandaraman, H.: Testing Applications n Cloud. LEF Grant Briefing. http://assets1.csc.com/lef/downloads/LEFBriefing_TestingApplicationsCloud_021011.pdf (2011)
13. Flynn, M.J.: Computer Architecture: Pipelined and Parallel Processor Design. http://public.callutheran.edu/~reinhart/CSC521MSCS/Week5/FlynnTaxonomies.pdf (1996)
14. Roodenrijs, E.: Testing on the cloud, A sogeti point of view on the potential of software testing using cloud computing. http://www.sogeti.com/upload/COM/Curious%20about%20us/Documents/PoV%20-%20A%20Sogeti%20Test%20Cloud_v1%200.pdf (2010)
15. Williams, B.J., Carver, J.C.: Characterizing software architecture changes: an initial study. In: ESEM 2007, pp. 410–419 http://www.google.co.in/url?sa=t&rct=j&q=characterizing%20software%20architecture%20changes%3A%20an%20initial%20study&source=web&cd=1&cad=rja&ved=0CC4QFjAA&url=http%3A%2F%2Fciteseerx.ist.psu.edu%2Fviewdoc%2Fdownload%3Fdoi%3D10.1.1.123.6396%26rep%3Drep1%26type%3Dpdf&ei=n3pJUbfSMY6zrAet64GYDQ&usg=AFQjCNHlS847JhguLPP23LfMh9Nonz1Fbw&bvm=bv.44011176,d.bmk (2007)

Chapter 5
Cloud-Based Development Using Classic Life Cycle Model

Suchitra Ravi Balasubramanyam

Abstract Information technology (IT) today has evolved into a rapidly changing and dynamic science. Timelines have shrunk drastically for technology from being termed cutting edge to becoming obsolete. In such a fast-changing and dynamic world needing customised solutions, cloud computing offers a viable alternative. Cloud can overcome the redundancy factor and evolve over time to suit user needs. It is characterised by a wide array of deployment models and services that are very promising. While the concept of cloud computing has been around for some time now, industry adoption has been rather slow. Due to the sheer possibilities on offer, one remains optimistic of wider acceptance of this technology in future. This chapter takes us through the steps needed to validate the choice of public cloud via risk-based feasibility analysis. The chosen option can be built into needed IT systems based on cloud variants of the classic life cycle model. This chapter discusses the phases and activities of this development. The Wrapper model discussed here will enable better understanding of system control determinants for services opted on the cloud. A case study is discussed to help provide a better insight and understanding of the life cycle model.

Keywords Software life cycle • Cloud provision • Wrapper model

5.1 Introduction

Rapid adoption of the World Wide Web has brought a paradigm shift in business computing. This transformation can be attributed to the robust client-server architecture of the Web and its request-response operation model. The days of using

S.R. Balasubramanyam (✉)
Education and Research Unit, Infosys Limited,
No 350, Hebbal Electronics City, Hootagalli, Mysore 570027, India
e-mail: suchitraravi_b@infosys.com

Z. Mahmood and S. Saeed (eds.), *Software Engineering Frameworks for the Cloud Computing Paradigm*, Computer Communications and Networks,
DOI 10.1007/978-1-4471-5031-2_5,

HTML only for information presentation are past. Web-based applications that augment the computing capabilities using Java, XML and Web Services are the current trend. Such Web-based applications provide both partial and complete business solutions, with the user interfaces being accessible anytime online through the Web. For any business, presence on the Internet implies availability of computing facilities on demand.

But there are costs involved for such anytime access. In addition to computational infrastructure, the software installation, configuration and updates, along with the operating system and upgrades, add to the costs. Involving third-party service providers of such services helps reduce such costs, which cloud computing is best suited for. Cloud offers flexibility in software, platform and infrastructure on the Web that are optimal for individual business needs. The pay-per-use model makes it even more attractive to potential customers.

Cloud computing evolved out of grid computing, which is a collection of distributed computers intended to provide computing power and storage on demand [1]. Grid computing clubbed with virtualisation techniques help to achieve dynamically scalable computing power, storage, platforms and services. In such an environment, a distributed operating system that produces a single system appearance for resources that exist and is available is solicited most [2]. In other words, one can say that cloud computing is a specialised distributed computing paradigm. Cloud differs with its on-demand abilities like scalable computing power – up or down, service levels and dynamic configuration of services (via approaches like virtualisation). It offers resources and services in an abstract fashion that are charged like any other utility, thus bringing in a utility business model for computing. Though virtualisation is not mandatory for cloud, its features like partitioning, isolation and encapsulation [3] and benefits like reduced cost, relatively easy administration, manageability and faster development [4] have made it an essential technique for resource sharing. Virtualisation helps to abstract underlying raw resources like computation, storage and network as one, or encapsulating multiple application environments on one single set or multiple sets of raw resources. Resources being both physical and virtual, distributed computing calls for dynamic load balancing of resources for better utilisation and optimisation [5]. Like any other traditional computing environment, a virtualised environment must be secure and backed up for it to be a cost saving technique [3]. Cloud computing is a transformation of computing by way of service orientation, distributed manageability and economies of scale from virtualisation [3].

The National Institute of Standards and Technology (NIST) defines cloud computing [6] as "Cloud Computing is a model for enabling ubiquitous, convenient, on-demand network access to a shared pool of configurable computing resources (e.g. networks, servers, storage, applications and services) that can be rapidly provisioned and released with minimal management effort or service provider interaction". According to NIST [6], the essential characteristics of cloud computing are on-demand self-service, broad network access, resource pooling, rapid elasticity and measured service. We are seeing a paradigm shift in business IT due to these characteristics.

5.1.1 Cloud for Business

The environment, the businesses operate in today, is increasingly getting complex, with rapid changes in markets, products, customers and regulatory demands. Growing businesses in these environments generate vast amounts of data for analysis, which means scaling up of IT infrastructure adding up to huge business costs.

Here, cloud offers a viable, sustainable and scalable alternative to businesses that are both resource and cost-effective. Thus, managing business growth while controlling costs on IT infrastructure is perfectly balanced. For example, resource pooling controls costs while addressing scalability. It also allows for mobility of operations, helping control businesses spread across locations.

With green technology and sustainable business practices gaining ground worldwide, the pooled IT resources under cloud models have an added advantage for businesses. It helps businesses significantly reduce their carbon footprint as they scale up.

Businesses have a choice when deciding on cloud deployment – public, private, hybrid or community based. Public cloud is deployed on the Internet externally. Private cloud resides on an intranet or private network, hybrid models are a combination of public and private cloud, while community cloud is shared by several organisations supporting a specific community. All the options offer software, platform and infrastructure as services. Regardless of the type of cloud deployed, it impacts the entire computational ecosystem. Be it a casual user, software developer, IT manager or hardware manufacturer, all levels of participants experience the impact in varying degrees [7]. The different cloud services, if chosen correctly, support business and its IT needs. The NIST definitions of cloud services, their benefits and the limitations are now given along with case scenarios to better understand their applicability.

Software as a Service (SaaS) offers software with or without customisation and allows changes only to the user-specific configuration settings. NIST definition of SaaS [6] is "The capability provided to the consumer is to use the provider's applications running on a cloud infrastructure. The applications are accessible from various client devices through either a thin client interface such as a web browser (e.g. web-based e-mail) or a program interface. The consumer does not manage or control the underlying cloud infrastructure including network, servers, operating systems, storage, or even individual application capabilities, with the possible exception of limited user-specific application configuration settings".

Some examples of software offered on cloud are productivity applications like word processor, spreadsheet, slide creators and image manipulators. Major enterprise applications like customer relationship management (CRM) are also part of the cloud offerings. They are largely ready-to-use and users pay per use. Users can access the software through a Web browser instead of installing them on individual computers. Sometimes, software like CRM may require limited customisation but still are very cost-effective tools. Benefits of SaaS include reduced cycle times to market, anywhere access, no licence requirements and automatic version updates, lower operating and maintenance costs and pay as you consume.

Platform as a Service (*PaaS*) offers environment to develop "cloud-ready" applications and deploy them with required configuration settings. The scalability of the application at run time is administered by the service provider as per the deployment settings. NIST definition [6] of PaaS is "The capability provided to the consumer to deploy onto the cloud infrastructure consumer created or acquired applications created using programming languages, libraries, services, and tools supported by the provider. The consumer does not manage or control the underlying cloud infrastructure including network, servers, operating systems, or storage, but has control over the deployed applications and possibly configuration settings for the application hosting environment".

Enterprise applications need an enabling technology termed as platform (also called application infrastructure or middleware). Operating systems, application servers, databases, business process management (BPM) tools and application integrators are a few examples. Platform services like Google App Engine provide run time environments for Java and Python Web applications. Once deployed, scaling up the application to handle increased traffic and enhance data storage will be handled by the service provider. Heroku, another cloud platform built on an open standard, is a polyglot. It supports several languages like Java and Ruby, multiple frameworks and databases. Other facilities on offer include HTTP caching, logging, memcache and instant scaling.

The above platforms are examples of ready-to-use, on demand services where the user is charged a fee depending on the computational infrastructure used. In many cases, the application development, testing and deployment are constrained by the platform provider specifications, application programming interfaces (API), among other parameters. However, platform services that leverage existing skill sets of developers are more appealing to customers. While recommending PaaS offerings, Gartner Analyst Yefim Natis [8] says "PaaS is still emerging. It is neither mature nor standardised". Among the positives, PaaS has the benefits of inherent dynamic scaling and perfect bundled environment for development, testing and production.

Infrastructure as a Service (*IaaS*) offers hardware like servers, processors and memory obtained on rental. The user has control over the rented resources, configure any operating system on them, install any software and host or run any application on them. NIST definition [6] of IaaS is "The capability provided to the consumer to provision processing, storage, network, and other fundamental computing resources where the consumer is able to deploy and run arbitrary software, which can include operating systems and applications. The consumer does not manage or control the underlying cloud infrastructure but has control over operating systems, storage, and deployed applications; and possibly limited control of select networking components (e.g. host firewalls)".

In the case of start-up enterprises, short-term business campaigns and seasonal businesses, investing on data storage centre may not be the right strategic choice. So would the case be with businesses needing growing infrastructure. In such conditions, outsourcing the building and maintenance of data centre appears more prudent. With an IaaS service, it is possible to reduce costs, space and management overheads. At the same time, the user can avail on-demand computing capability. Currently, infrastructure services are chosen mostly for non-critical applications. Principal Research Analyst Kyle Hilgendorf at Gartner states in his article titled "Evaluation Criteria for Public Cloud IaaS Providers" [8] that "IaaS is at the crossroads. To host mission critical business applications, IaaS should offer capabilities that convince the user, and it is yet to mature in this direction". However, key benefits include effective utilisation of infrastructure, resource provision on demand and reduced operating costs.

The key benefits of cloud services can be broadly summarised as enhanced business mobility, operating cost reduction, agility, flexibility and enabling green IT. However, key challenges still remain on cloud. These include among others security, data privacy, compliance and absence of standards, performance and availability issues. With these limiting factors, businesses need to make certain compromises when choosing cloud services. A risk analysis-based approach to decision making on availing cloud services will be of immense help, and the methodology is detailed in the following section.

5.2 Cloud-Based Development

5.2.1 Risk-Based Approach for Feasibility Analysis

The current business environment is characterised by only two constants – change and uncertainty. Business applications need to be agile to adapt to such fluidity, but constant changes to software and IT infrastructure is expensive. It is here that the characteristics and capabilities of the cloud, like the distributed model, high network availability and scalability can enable large Web-based applications to cope with constantly changing business demands. For businesses to select a cloud-based deployment, it is these benefits that are the decisive factors.

But, challenges like security, data privacy, regulatory issues and compliance are among the road blocks. The critical factor is security, as the user has no ownership or control over the cloud [3]. A related issue is the integrity of information in the hands of a third party, with current international laws and regulations governing such data misuse hazy. Other issues like governmental enforcement of IT laws and regulations, vendor lock-in that prevent federation of services from different providers, performance consistency and scalability also impact user decisions.

All stakeholders need to relook at all these issues holistically for wider and faster adoption of cloud services. One way to enhance user trust could be to consider international protocols and standards available, to certify cloud applications and Internet security. Certification is a proven technique to help establish identity and trust. Establishing trust is critical for cloud applications as the boundaries are more logical than physical. In the virtual world, access policies and privileges need to change dynamically depending on the user and workload [9]. Further, user location and device used to access the service are equally important. Standards will allow consistency, portability and interoperability [10]. However, expecting international standards to govern cloud security is quite impossible as of now. Among existing standards, some of them – federated identity across multiple systems and providers, interoperability between different services and context-based protection – would be appropriate, based on the nature of request, data criticality and risk profile of service provider. Establishing a federated credential management system involves a repository of heterogeneous credentials, transfer and translation of those credentials [11].

Businesses need to consider the following factors when decisions are made to move to cloud-based services:

- What data and applications to move to the cloud
- The services that are needed on cloud, based on gathered business requirements
- The risks of service provider integrity, security breach and privacy violations

Presently, there is no single international standard or specification existing that guarantees safeguards to cloud applications and protection against these risks. Service providers can enhance user trust by integrating with currently available international certifications and standards. These steps in combination with the following suggested best practices [12] establish a three-step approach for feasibility analysis. This approach inherently suggests how to choose service providers and the right cloud services.

Step 1: Conduct risk assessment – to minimise risks, assess and choose service providers based on parameters like interoperability, portability and legal compliance. Assess the providers risk profile, ecosystem, supply chain and the quality of their infrastructure and operations.

Step 2: Assessment of one's own security capability in a cloud environment – in any cloud environment, the higher the support from a provider, the narrower the scope and control for the consumer. From SaaS to IaaS, responsibility for security varies for the consumer from least to highest. This increases flexibility for the consumer in implementing security controls. Data and users' interactions with the system can be controlled by encryption, authentication and secure access points. These are achievable irrespective of service provider.

Step 3: Implementation of a governance network – consumers should ensure from the providers logging of event observation and notifications. User should opt for remote monitoring where possible. Contracts and SLAs help establish a robust governance framework [10].

This three-step approach will help potential users evaluate and adopt cloud, capitalise on emerging technologies and be a part of evolving cloud standards. Any cloud-based development must ensure such analysis as part of overall requirements gathering. Next, software system life cycle is presented before exploring classic life cycle model to help better understand cloud in the development context.

5.2.2 *Software System Life Cycle*

Information systems help organisation to capture and manage data to produce information useful for its employees, customers, partners and suppliers. Each information system has a life of its own. Engineering such a software system involves process, methods and tools that facilitate systematic, disciplined and quantifiable approach to the overall software development. Process is the foundation layer and comprises a framework of activities to be carried out regardless of domain, size and complexity, methods indicate how-to of each activity and tools support process and methods. The generic process framework for software engineering comprises communication phase, planning phase, modelling phase, construction phase and deployment phase. Typical set of activities carried out in each of these phases are listed below [13]:

- Communication phase: Requirements gathering, focus on what requirements, specify the requirements and project initiation.
- Planning phase: Prepare project schedule, estimate of efforts and task duration. Tracking of the schedule happens in parallel with the rest of the subsequent phases.
- Modelling phase: Contains analysis phase and design phase. Activities of analysis phase are model the requirements, build prototype and evaluate alternate options. Similarly design phase activities are translate the requirements into a blueprint for software construction and iterate to a fine grain level details needed for the coding.
- Construction phase: Construct the code, in other words implement the design, test unit wise, after code integration and finally the system.
- Deployment phase: Deliver, support and maintain the deployed software.

5.2.3 *Classic Life Cycle Model*

The classic life cycle model is also called waterfall model. In this model, the workflow is linear in nature from communication phase to deployment phase and the outputs of each phase act as inputs for the next phase. It is a theoretical and sequential model, not adaptable directly. But other process models in use today are basically iterative in nature, which is more practical. Customer requirements evolve over time resulting in extension of life cycle phases. In particular, the design phase needs to evolve to be in line with these requirements [14]. However, in an ideal scenario the classic model is the simplest to understand and implement and so is used as the reference model in this chapter.

The life cycle of a cloud-based development is discussed by referring to this model. However, different services of cloud result in variants of this model, which are discussed in subsequent sections. Before exploring the variants, it is to be noted that system controls vary depending on the service and is depicted in the Wrapper model that follows.

Fig. 5.1 Wrapper model

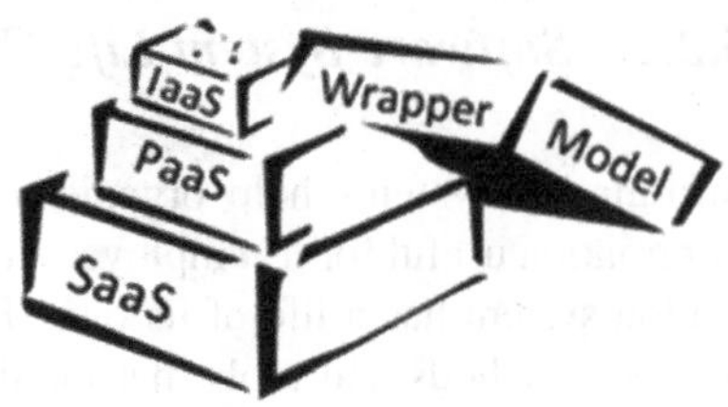

5.2.4 Cloud Services Wrapper Model

Consider any application software being used. The software needs a platform, which is resident on suitable infrastructure. The functional aspects of the application are dealt with at the software level, with the non-functional aspects spread beyond, reaching up to infrastructure including the platform. Cloud services follow the same pattern. SaaS is existent because it wraps a PaaS, which further wraps an IaaS. At each service level of the cloud, the non-functional facets are dependent on the underlying support. The scope of controls that can be exercised follows the same path and varies from low to high from outermost wrap to innermost. This wrapping of services can be shown as an abstract Wrapper model, represented as in Fig. 5.1. This model would help understand the variants of the classic life cycle phases better.

The model shows an IaaS wrapped inside a PaaS that in turn is wrapped inside SaaS. SaaS alone cannot exist without PaaS; similar is the case with PaaS. It is evident from the figure that IaaS and PaaS are hidden inside SaaS, and SaaS gets it support from PaaS which in turn depends on IaaS. Just dealing with outer wraps ignoring the inner ones will not help understand cloud relationships holistically.

5.2.5 Variants of Classic Life Cycle Model

The discussion in this section is based on the premise that software development is an outsourced activity and is for the public cloud. We also need to understand the relationships between the various stakeholders on the cloud. Given under Fig. 5.2 is the relationship between the customer, service provider and solutions provider in the cloud paradigm.

This model depicts the triangular relationship among Cloud Customer, Cloud Solutions Provider and Cloud Service Provider. The smaller triangles indicate the purpose of interaction between these stakeholders, like the customer interactions with solutions provider are for their IT needs. The Solutions provider offers solution catering to those needs by developing applications for the service provider's cloud. Now the service provider offers customised services to the customer on its cloud.

The customer needs a cloud-based IT system, which is developed by the solutions provider and deployed on the service providers cloud. The solutions provider may or may not utilise the public cloud for development and testing of the solution.

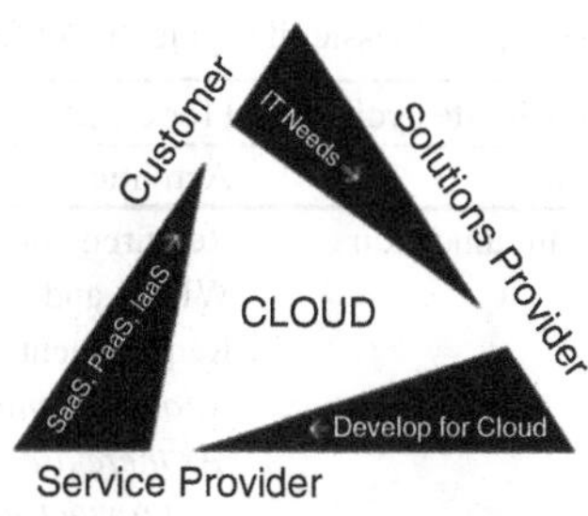

Fig. 5.2 Cloud stakeholders relationship

The focus here is only on the life cycle from the solution providers' perspective. It is assumed that the system may use any one, all or a combination of cloud services. In all the cases, the emphasis is only on the system under development and the activities are mentioned accordingly.

Following are the activities of cloud-based development with reference to classic life cycle model. There are generic activities involved in each of the phases, as well as different activities for each of the cloud services. Table 5.1 gives a general listing of activities irrespective of cloud services. Tables 5.2, 5.3, 5.4, 5.5 and 5.6 sum up phase-wise activities for SaaS, PaaS and IaaS.

The table highlights the common activities that are exclusively carried out for cloud-based development.

One of the important activities of the communication phase is requirements gathering and analysis. For large systems, requirements analysis is the most difficult and uncompromising activity [15]. Whether the system to be built is small or big, there are cases where the requirements have to be visualised and produced. With cloud this becomes more challenging as the choice of the cloud service provider should be made foreseeing the needs of other phases. For the two kinds of requirements – namely, user requirements and a high-level abstraction and system requirements – all relevant details have to be gathered. The requirements of the system further fall under functional, non-functional and domain-related categories. Requirements tell what the system should do and define constraints on its operation and implementation [16]. It gives a lead to choose service providers.

Selecting a suitable service provider is very much influenced by the feasibility analysis for the cloud adoption. This is a critical step as no industry standards exist as of today for choosing service providers' services. This step involves having an architectural description that gives a high-level view of the system, its structure, software elements and relationship among them [15]. Typically descriptions should cover the business domain, applications integration, technology, data and information architecture [14]. Due to lack of standards for cloud-architecture evaluation, the proposed architecture against non-functional quality attributes may not give a right evaluation result. A possible alternative is to follow Web Application Architecture Framework (WAAF) proposed by author David Lowe that categorises the architecture into Structure (what), Behaviour (how), Location (where) and Pattern (in Web applications) [17]. Apart from requirements specification document that contains precisely stated requirements, architecture description is also produced as an output.

Table 5.1 Classic life cycle model for cloud: common activities

Classic life cycle model for cloud	
Phase	Activities common to all services i.e., SaaS, PaaS and IaaS
Communication	Requirements gathering
	WHAT and not HOW of requirements
	Requirements specification
	[a]*Cloud adoption decision – taken based on risk based feasibility analysis*
	[a]*As there are few players in cloud computing arena, choose service provider in line with needs of future phases. This is critical as presently industry standards do not exist*
	Project initiation
Planning	Project schedule
	Estimation of efforts and task duration
	Tracking the activities – happens parallelly in all phases
Modelling	ANALYSIS:
	Model requirements
	Build prototype
	Evaluate alternate options
	[a]*Consider and incorporate non-functional and infrastructure requirements while modelling. Traditionally this is delayed until designing*
	DESIGN:
	Translate requirements into software construction blue print, iterate up to fine grain
	[a]*Include design goals of traditional web applications (irrespective of domain, size and complexity) for end-user interfaces*
Construction	Code and Test
	[a]*Testing to happen in a simulated or real cloud environment; hence testing to be planned accordingly*
Deployment	Deliver
	Support and maintain the deployed software

[a]Activity applied for cloud-based development

In the requirements, barring functional requirements, performance and external interface requirements, design constraints are heavily dependent on the cloud service and the respective provider for the same. This phase gives way to the next phases by a formal project initiation activity.

Planning phase [15] requires both requirements specification and architecture description as inputs for coming up with an executable plan. A plan for the processes to be followed for the entire project needs to be formulated. Based on this, the project schedule includes activities, their timelines and milestones to cross. Estimates of effort and resources can be done by taking expert opinion or through the use of models. As very little expertise exists in the industry today, and models are more suited for traditional development efforts, estimation is a challenging task. A good estimation has as its ingredients – scope of activity being estimated, work environment and usage of tools [18]. One needs to look at increasing the productivity which is an added result of environment, tools and experience. A heuristic approach along with both of the above could be a better option. Quality and configuration management

Table 5.2 Classic life cycle model: communication phase in cloud services

Phase	Services
Communication	*SaaS*
	Software is by third party provider. Important to choose appropriate service provider
	Along with domain specific standard requirements, customization as applicable are specified
	Software service may need customization as per feasibility analysis
	PaaS
	Application is to be custom built, so will be the requirements gathered
	However platform and infrastructure are by third party provider; choose appropriate provider
	Platform service to satisfy non-functional requirements as per feasibility analysis
	IaaS
	Application and platform as per customer needs, only computing environment by third party provider; customer virtually owns infrastructure
	Choose appropriate provider
	Infrastructure configuration is customized and utilization is charged accordingly
	Infrastructure service to satisfy non-functional requirements like traditionally owned infrastructure with focus on security, legal compliance and proper governance

Table 5.3 Classic life cycle model: planning phase in cloud services

Phase	Services
Planning	*SaaS*: Plan for software service customization
	PaaS: Plan for application development for the cloud platform and deployment on that platform
	IaaS: Plan for application development, deployment on specified platform and on the cloud infrastructure

plans are to be made ready. Risk management is managing of the unknown risks in the cloud development arena. To assess a project situation, use a carefully crafted monitoring plan to track activities across the development phases. This helps in comparing actual performance against the plan, and thereby ensuring the right actions at the right time to achieve the project goals. The output is a detailed plan based on these efforts and resources estimation and anticipated risks.

Modelling phase is split into analysis and design phase. Though the high-level architecture is available by now, it is of utmost importance to determine whether the suggested strategy deals with client's constraints. The obvious approach is prototyping [19]. Modular decomposition of modules is performed and prototypes constructed for chosen significant modules. Alternate options are explored, if needed using appropriate techniques to do the analysis. Consideration of non-functional requirements and infrastructure requirements during analysis is a critical step. For a

Table 5.4 Classic life cycle model: modelling phase in cloud services

Phase	Services
Modelling	ANALYSIS
	SaaS
	Based on requirements + customization specifications, identify the necessary custom interfaces for software service
	PaaS
	Based on requirements choose suitable application design architecture
	Devise deployment architecture considering the platform of the provider
	IaaS
	Based on requirements choose suitable applications design and deployment architecture
	Devise the configuration set up of the necessary infrastructure based on the offerings of the provider
	DISIGN
	SaaS: Design the identified interfaces as part of necessary customization
	PaaS and IaaS:
	Based on the architecture design interfaces that are internal as well as external to application
	Design software components as per the requirements model i.e., structured analysis model or object-oriented analysis model or both

Table 5.5 Classic life cycle model: construction phase in cloud services

Phase	Services
Construction	*SaaS*
	Code as per customization needed for the software
	Focus on regression testing of software as frills are added in the name of customization
	PaaS
	Code and Test as per design specified
	Focus on performance testing as non-functional requirements like scalability, availability etc. of web application are essential
	IaaS
	Code and Test as per design specified
	Focus on recovery testing and failover testing as recovery and failover are essential non-functional requirements. Testing becomes more significant as infrastructure is owned virtually and no physical control on them

public cloud as total infrastructure is owned by a third party, this analysis decides the success of the subsequent phases. Detailed design of the system is carved out to the level of individual methods and their interfaces for all the modules. As the application would run on distributed, heterogeneous, virtual computers on the Web, following Web engineering approach helps in successful Web-based system [20]. Web requirements like uniform look and feel, up-to-date, navigability and more have to be fulfilled within the design. For Internet-based applications, additional challenges are scalability and load balancing [20]. In an open environment like the Internet, it is not so easy to understand and predict the workload and user profiles. An unbalanced workload can become a cause for reduced system performance, reliability

Table 5.6 Classic life cycle model: deployment phase in cloud services

Phase	Services
Deployment	*SaaS*
	Deploy as per the configuration guidelines given by the provider
	Support and maintenance in line with the provider's software maintenance strategy
	PaaS
	Deploy like traditional application onto the provider's platform with configuration setting suggested by the provider
	Support and maintenance depends on the platform support by the provider
	IaaS
	Deploy like traditional application except that infrastructure is virtually owned
	Configure for cloud parameters like resource requirements, bounds for elasticity, dynamic provisioning, details for billing and metering etc.
	Support and maintenance happens as with traditional applications, depends maintenance strategy adopted by the provider for the virtual machines

and availability. A gap analysis of scalability and load balancing offerings from the provider would help in properly configuring those parameters, anything additional required must be built in-house through solutions provider.

The major concern in construction phase is vendor lock-in. Hence, the focus should be on writing interoperable, portable applications for the cloud. Applications need to be as flexible as possible and open for changes. This would in turn facilitate the maintenance phase.

Deployment phase is to deliver, deploy, support and maintain the cloud application. Stephen Schach mentions in his book [19] that maintainability should be built into the system from the beginning and not compromised any time during development. Like for any product, maintenance is like after sales service for an application; in case of cloud this is to be taken care of by all providers involved. Establishing a shared maintenance service, switching or replacing service providers are the key complex challenges faced in this phase.

Communication Phase: Apart from the common activities, choice of service provider is most important for SaaS. Unlike other digital products, plug-and-play is not the case with cloud product/software. Hence, it is also essential to specify the required customisations and describe architecture to suit the current needs with a provision to accommodate future requirements. With PaaS, it is the platform that runs on third-party-owned infrastructure that needs to be configured and customised. Application to be built by the solutions provider follows the life cycle of a typical Web application. While choosing the PaaS service providers, bear in mind the non-functional requirements. In case of IaaS, except for the infrastructure, the rest of the Web application cycle is similar to that of typical Web applications. The virtual infrastructure made available as a service is charged based on configuration and utilisation. PaaS and SaaS utilisation will be charged inclusive of the charges for the wrapped services as well. Refer to Fig. 5.1 to know what and how services are wrapped. Along with the other non-functional requirements security, legal compliance and proper governance are to be looked at without fail while choosing the service providers for all cloud services. Here, the Wrapper model can help in visualising the control that can be exercised by the customer in getting the non-functional requirements satisfied. Outer layers indicate lesser control, while inner layers can lend themselves to better control.

Planning Phase: When compared with a typical Web application that can go along with classic life cycle, the cloud services have variations as per architecture description given below. Accordingly the needed service, application or interface integration should be made part of the plan.

- SaaS – plan for the required customisation for the cloud software
- PaaS – plan for application development for cloud platform and deployment on it
- IaaS – plan for application development and deployment on specified platform and on the cloud infrastructure

Modelling Phase: After planning comes the modelling and designing of the system based on the project requirements. If prototypes are to be built, they are to be analysed and best one chosen. With SaaS, the customisation demands the necessary interfaces to be analysed and designed. In PaaS and IaaS, the application is modelled like any other web application; the deployment architecture is analysed, the internal and external interfaces are designed keeping in mind the platform and infrastructure offerings of the providers.

Construction Phase: For each service, code is written in line with the design. Focus during testing varies in services. Security testing needs to be done compulsorily. Control in SaaS needs regression testing as frills are added as part of customisation. PaaS would need performance testing on the parameters like scalability and availability, as infrastructure is virtual. In IaaS, recovery and failover have to be tested since physical resources are in the hands of third party.

Deployment Phase: SaaS deployment is based on service provider guidelines. Support and maintenance will be controlled by the provider. Depending on the support and maintenance strategy of the provider, the phase can be smooth or a roller coaster ride. In PaaS application, deployment happens on the providers' platform configured as per their guidelines. Support and maintenance is a shared responsibility between the solutions provider and the service provider. Cloud application aspect is dealt by solutions provider and that of platform is with service provider. With IaaS, the deployment activity involves the infrastructure specification in the form of configuration parameters like number of resources needed, namely, processor, operating system, storage capacity, bounds of elasticity, dynamic provisioning, monitoring and metering. Again support and maintenance is a shared responsibility, infrastructure onus is with service provider whereas platform and the application is with the solutions provider.

The complexity of any cloud project is mainly in requirements analysis and mapping those to the capabilities of the cloud environment. The emphasis is mainly on communication, planning and modelling phases of the life cycle. Compared to traditional development efforts, cloud-based development efforts and costs are lower in the construction phase. The activities listed above make it clear that cloud computing activities need tailored approach to classic life cycle model, especially for deployment and technology architecture. Lack of standards has made cloud-based developments highly platform- and vendor-specific projects. Hence, a high adaptability model is recommended for solution implementation. Other process models possible for cloud have been briefly explored in the next section.

5.2.6 Other Process Models

Process models that are suitable for cloud projects are basically iterative in nature. An incremental model can help in managing the technical risks by way of planned increments to the application. This approach is in general combined with other approaches for realising the application in quick time.

Prototyping is an iterative model wherein core requirements are realised quickly, thereby reducing the time to market. It is a mechanism to define requirements in an iterative manner till requirements are clearly understood and frozen. By itself prototyping is not a cost-effective model for large-scale complex applications. However, it is best applied in the context of other process models.

Spiral model is the best of waterfall and prototyping models. It imbibes the systematic aspect of waterfall and iterative aspect of prototyping. It is a risk-driven process model and reduces the degree of risk through iterations [21]. Though it is suitable for large-scale systems and software, it is not a convincing model for cloud projects at this stage. This is because of lack of standards and lack of expertise in the industry on cloud risks assessment.

Unified process which is driven by use-cases and centred around architecture is incremental and iterative; hence suitable for object-oriented projects. In the cloud the dynamic provision of resources and application components is inherently object oriented. This aspect of cloud can be best utilised by the model in combination with other process models [21].

As indicated earlier in the feasibility analysis section, cloud can adapt to changing business needs. One development approach that accommodates changes is the agile methodology. Some of the process models based on this methodology are Extreme Programming (XP) and SCRUM. Adaptability is the basic principle of these models. They focus on satisfying the customer's requirements as of today with a provision for long-term requirements. In this methodology, system is built over multiple releases by constantly responding and implementing requirements. It is a harmonious collaboration between customer and solutions provider teams for a sustainable application development. It includes improved communication among the working teams and thereby results in faster deployment.

5.3 Case Study

The industry service providers under the cloud platforms have many success stories. The underlying factor in most of these successes is hybrid cloud. This is considered the right choice for IT systems needing Web hosting, content delivery, e-commerce, backup and storage. NIST definition [6] of Hybrid Cloud is "the cloud infrastructure is a composite of two or more distinct cloud infrastructures (private, community or public) that remain unique entities, but are bound together by standardized or proprietary technology that enables data and application portability (e.g. cloud bursting for load balancing between clouds)". Only non-critical businesses, start-ups and one-off Web presence cases choose public cloud. The Web sites of some service providers like Amazon [22], IBM [23] and Google [24] have case studies for cloud that can be referred. A case study presented here helps understand usage of the proposed classic life cycle model.

5.3.1 Background Scenario

Back to Basics (B2B) is a not-for-profit organisation, with the stated goal of providing free education covering all age groups, through content delivered online through the Internet. The organisation has an online learning portal hosted within their country. To realise their stated goal of reaching out to all learners across the globe, they now want to re-establish themselves on the Web. The founding members of the organisation are determined to realise their stated goal and ensure the success of this online learning program. To cater to the needs of non-English-speaking countries, the organisation is planning to create video lessons in different languages and is also trying to subtitle present content videos wherever possible. As the demand for video lessons are increasing by the day, they also need to ensure portal availability 24×7 for the global audience. They also have plans to Webcast (live or recorded) important education conferences especially for university learners. All these plans call for huge infrastructure outlay.

Presently, the site offers lessons in basic science and mathematics. These are video lessons of short duration of 5–8 min. Every learning video hosted on the site goes through a process workflow. Apart from aspiring learners, there are other site users like administrator, editors, authors and reviewers.

The authors and reviewers are a large community of volunteers who contribute to the video lessons bank periodically. The site administrator oversees the need for innovations, simplicity of content and additional practice assignments. He posts artefact generation requirements to the author community after a careful scrutiny of reports. These reports are generated based on the video ratings, assessment of scores of learners and frequency of downloads of a particular artefact.

Whenever there is a post on artefact generation requirement, interested authors can nominate themselves along with a story board for the subject. This is reviewed and approved by the administrator in consultation with the editor-in-chief. Once approved, the administrator charts a schedule and updates are sent to the selected author (if there are many nominations for a particular artefact) and a corresponding reviewer is assigned. Designated authors produce the videos and upload it onto the site for review. In the first instance when the video is uploaded, both the administrator and assigned reviewer receive e-mail alerts. From now, the review activity between author and reviewer happens on the network, till final reviewer approval. The final call for any improvements or full rejection rests with the editor-in-chief, who is the designated authority to sign off the video for both the story board and hosting. As per set standards, the editor-in-chief awards credit points to both author and reviewer, based on the popularity and usefulness of the video. This ensures special recognition of the volunteers' contribution, a source of satisfaction for them.

Learners can download the video lessons of their subjects and topics of interest, practice assignments and take up assessment tests. The assessment scores are recorded for later analysis. The learners need to rate the videos on different parameters like simplicity of presentation, narrative style, topic coverage, innovative examples and sufficiency of time for a topic. Learners can also provide feedback for any improvements.

For this mammoth mission, the organisation does not want to invest on large CAPEX (capital expenditure), preferring moving to OPEX (operational expenditure) and wants to utilise the available funds more thoughtfully. So they are exploring a viable, cost-effective and scalable solution and have discussed their requirements with a solutions provider. The following section details how the solution was arrived at.

5.3.2 Classic Life Cycle Model: Application

The organisation has started the communication phase with the selected solution provider. Risk-based analysis is carried out along with other activities in this phase, and public cloud is chosen. As the project security is not critical, the whole system resides on public cloud. The solution offered is not just limited to a Web application and its associated database but comprises additional features like e-mail services, calendar service and video production workflow. The video hosting and video streaming are part of content delivery network (CDN) aimed to serve a global audience of learners. The storage needs to be scalable to meet growing future demand. The main drivers for choosing cloud for solution implementation are:

- To spend on OPEX rather than CAPEX
- Affordable and scalable storage
- Access mobility for end users
- Users resident across the globe
- Anytime availability and elasticity
- Non-critical application
- Needs collaboration

Ensuring privacy is important, as log reports, Web access reports, location, country- or continent- wise assessment reports need to be secure due to legality issues. This needs to be incorporated carefully in the contract being entered into with the service provider. It is assumed that this requirement is fully met in the contract signed between customer and service provider. The other option is to hold such critical data on premises, and opt for hybrid cloud covering the rest of the application. We proceed next to the three-step approach for feasibility analysis.

- Step 1: Assess risk involved especially with the breach of legal compliance. Study the risk profile of service provider under consideration. Get assured on the quality of their infrastructure and operations.
- Step 2: Assess own security capabilities. Opt to encrypt data that gets onto the cloud, else it may lead to legal risks. (Here it is assumed that the organisation opts for encryption and contract with service provider is entered into accordingly.)
- Step 3: Establish a governance framework to monitor the events real time, as application is targeted at a global audience. (Here it is assumed that the organisation wants to delay having a monitoring system.)

Life cycle phases follow the project initiation. Table 5.7 gives details of the phases involved. The architecture diagram along with explanation given helps understand how to choose the right cloud service as well as service provider.

In the communication phase, solutions provider selects the right service provider for the proposed high-level architecture (Fig. 5.3). As all of software, platform and infrastructure services are chosen, project schedule and plan are prepared to be run in tandem till the necessary integration points are reached. During the modelling phase, the modules and interfaces are defined; however, prototypes on integration interfaces have to be built and analysed, based on which other alternate interfaces are explored. Especially for the cloud integrator supposed to integrate SaaS, PaaS and IaaS, prototyping is required. One more prototyping needed is to understand the browser compatibility and limitations. With satisfactory prototyping, the high-level architecture is now frozen for designing.

Design phase details out the modules and interaction interfaces with other modules. This being a Web-based system, the attributes like usability, navigability, response time, interaction efficiency, localisation, mobility, accessibility, consistency and compatibility are part of the user interface design goals [25]. Since the solution provider has chosen cloud itself for the development of the system, testing happens in the public cloud environment that becomes a facilitator for this testing activity. Support and maintenance responsibility would be shared among the providers, and accomplishing this federated activity is with the solution provider. For detailed activities in each of the phases, refer to the explanations in Tables 5.2, 5.3, 5.4, 5.5 and 5.6.

Architecture: The system comprises an end-user interfacing application for accessing the video lessons, connected database for data storage, reports and exclusive video storage. Other functions like e-mail, calendar, video production workflow and content delivery network (video hosting, video streaming) are equally essential for a fully operational system. All these services have to be seamlessly integrated on the cloud. Figure 5.3 depicts a high-level architecture diagram.

Table 5.7 Classic life cycle model for case study

Back to basics – case study	
Phase	Activities carried out
Communication	Gather requirements, Specify requirements
	Choose services – email services, calendar service as SaaS video production work-flow as PaaS, Main Web Application and its database as PaaS, content delivery network as SaaS and storage as IaaS. A cloud integrator to integrate all these
	Choose the service providers – Amazon, IBM, We Video, Google Apps
	Initiate project
	Service specific activities carried out; refer Table 5.2
Planning	Schedule is ready along with estimation
	Service specific activities carried out
Modelling	ANALYSIS
	Model the requirements
	Build prototype as necessary, and evaluate alternates
	High level architecture is decided
	Service specific activities carried out; refer Table 5.4
	DISIGN
	Translate requirements to software blueprint with detailed designing
	As it is a web-based application, the design goals like usability, navigability, simplicity, consistency, compatibility etc.
	Service specific activities carried out; refer Table 5.4
Construction	Code and Test as per design
	Testing happens in real cloud environment as solution provider uses cloud for development
	Service specific activities carried out; refer Table 5.5
Deployment	Deliver i.e., deploy application live
	Support
	Service specific activities carried out; refer Table 5.6

The diagram depicts that to produce online content, the authors and reviewers community first need a collaboration medium, which also needs to be provided to the administrator and editor-in-chief. The medium is primarily for communication and planning, e-mail and calendar services. The video creation workflow needs a platform service where all stakeholders interact on work allocation, subsequent submission of the allocated work, followed by the work approval within the defined flow. Saving of the intermediate outcomes and final artefacts of video creation workflow requires for growing storage that can only be offered through infrastructure service. The videos approved are hosted on the provided storage. This huge content residing on the storage is meant for delivery via video streaming. Here a software service that offers content distribution and streaming is a must. A key need for enthusiastic learners is a Web interface that is a one-stop shop for them to access and download the video lessons, practice assignments and take up assessment tests. This Web application is built in Java and hosted on a Web server platform service. Apart from this, learners' data needs to be saved in a structured fashion for future reports generation and subsequent analysis. This calls for a relational database platform. Now with multiple services and providers in the arena, a suitable integrator

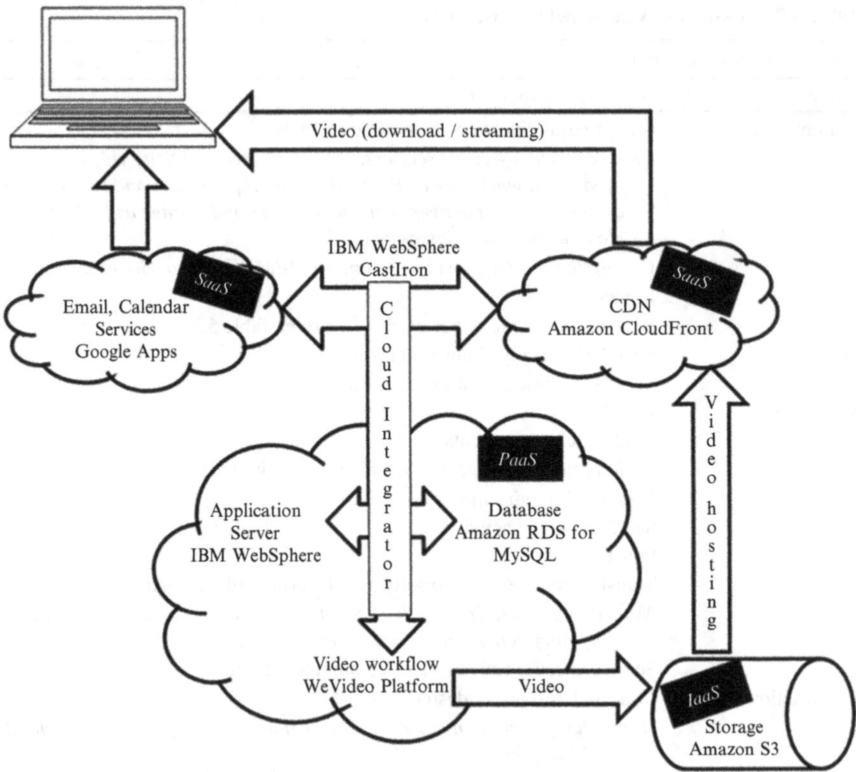

Fig. 5.3 High-level architecture diagram (Abbreviations: *Amazon S3* Amazon Simple Storage Service, *Amazon RDS* Amazon Relational Database Service, *CDN* Content Delivery Network)

that integrates them effortlessly is vital for the success of the system. The choice of providers and their services for the above functions are mentioned in the following section. The impact of the differences using life cycle model for SaaS, PaaS and IaaS is highlighted in conclusion.

- IBM WebSphere Application server [23] that is chosen for hosting the main Web application is a PaaS service. It is opted to achieve the necessary interoperability of different services. The relational database is again a PaaS service, and Amazon RDS for MySQL [22] is chosen for the same.
- The interaction among the users other than learners happens through e-mails and calendars for work scheduling. This implies need for a system that offers collaboration and mobility. Google Apps e-mail and calendar SaaS services [24] are selected for this.
- WeVideo [26], a cloud-based, collaborative video-editing platform, best fits the video creation workflow. The kinds of users, their activities and the complete workflow are catered to by this PaaS. The next functionality is to host and distribute the video content. WeVideo also has an option to export baseline videos to a hosting and distribution environment.

- Amazon CloudFront [22], a SaaS, best fits the need of content distribution network, inclusive of streaming.
- Storage for videos is achieved through IaaS, in particular storage service Amazon S3 [22].
- As there are multiple cloud players offering SaaS, PaaS and IaaS, it is crucial to have a seamless integrator that makes it a unified system. IBM WebSphere Cloud Integrator [23] is the choice here.

5.4 Conclusion

As evident from the illustrated case study, the activities of each phase are closely interconnected to the service chosen. Based on choice of services opted for during the communication phase, the span of activities for each of the functions varies in the subsequent phases. If the planning phase is not carefully thought through, the entire project may become highly risky. This means that the planning phase is extremely crucial to determine successful choice of provider, as also design and deployment on the cloud.

Any SaaS opted for mainly involves customisation that may cut down project resources and project costs in the modelling phase. However, this is not the case if PaaS and IaaS are opted for. Construction phase follows the same pattern with the exception of testing. Irrespective of the service selected, prior to final deployment on the cloud, the application is tested in a simulated environment. The extent of testing can be planned which is based on controls exercised for each service. This can be better understood with reference to the Wrapper model. The deployment with SaaS and PaaS here is as per the service providers' specifications. With IaaS, it is like traditional deployment on a virtual infrastructure. Support and maintenance for all services in deployment phase rely heavily on the cloud providers' strategy.

The development activities of the chosen cloud service follow a linear path under the classic life cycle model. If all the three services, namely, SaaS, PaaS and IaaS, are opted for, then across services within a phase, all activities happen simultaneously with varying time durations but with a lag. For instance, while SaaS is in construction phase, PaaS and IaaS could be in modelling phase.

If factors like cost, design, technology lead to a single service being chosen, IaaS leads to virtual infrastructure being used with traditional development, PaaS leads to virtual platform inclusive of infrastructure used with traditional development, while SaaS leads to using customised virtual software. The core differences among services are highlighted across activities of all the phases in the classic life cycle model.

Acknowledgements I would like to thank my colleague Mr. Krishna Prasad Srinivasa Rao for his assistance in content creation and my managers Mr. Rajagopalan P, Dr. Ramesh Babu S. and Mr. Srikantan Moorthy for their valuable guidance and support. The encouragement and support received from my husband Mr. Ravi Balasubramanyam helped me immensely in chapter presentation.

References

1. Foster, I., Zhao, Y., Raicu, I., Lu, S.: Cloud computing and grid computing 360-degree compared. Paper presented at grid computing environments workshop, Conference Publications, Austin, 12–16 November 2008
2. Dollimore, J., Kindberg, T., Coulouris, G.F.: Distributed Systems: Concepts and Design, 4th edn, pp. 206–207. Pearson Education, Harlow (2005)
3. Hurwitz, J., Bloor, R., Kaufman, M., Halper, F.: Cloud Computing for Dummies, pp. 197–208. Wiley, Hoboken (2009)
4. Velte, T., Velte, A., Elsenpeter, R.: Cloud Computing: A Practical Approach, pp. 253–258. Tata McGraw-Hill, New Delhi (2010)
5. Ramaswamy, R. (ed.): The Art and Technology of Software Engineering: A Mosaic of Models and Methods, pp. 131–139. Tata McGraw-Hill, New Delhi (2002)
6. NIST Cloud Computing Reference Architecture Version 1, March 30, 2011. http://www.nist.gov (2011)
7. Hayes, B.: Cloud computing. Commun. ACM **51**(7): 9–11. http://cacm.acm.org/ (2008)
8. Gartner Information Technology Research and Advisory Company: http://www.gartner.com
9. Mateo, L.A.: IBM IT Consulting Leader, Europe, December 13, 2011, Post named "Migration to cloud: It is all about workloads" at Thoughts on Cloud Blog sponsored by IBM. http://thoughtsoncloud.com/ (2011)
10. SETLabsBriefings, Cloud Computing, Infosys Labs Publications, vol. 7, no. 7 (2009)
11. Chakrabarti, A.: Grid Computing Security. Springer, Berlin/New York (2007)
12. Symantec, White Paper, The Secure Cloud: Best Practices for Cloud Adoption. http://www.symantec.com/
13. Pressman, R.S.: Software Engineering: A Practitioner's Approach, 7th edn. McGraw Hill, New York (2009)
14. Pradhan, A., Nanjappa, S.B., Nallasamy, S., Esakimuthu, V.: Raising Enterprise Applications: A Software Engineering Perspective, pp. 33–39. Wiley India, New Delhi (2010)
15. Jalote, P.: An Integrated Approach to Software Engineering, 3rd edn, pp. 67–211. Narosa Book Distributors, New Delhi (2008)
16. Sommerville, I.: Software Engineering, 8th edn, pp. 131–164. Pearson Education, Harlow (2009)
17. Pressman, R.S., Lowe, D.: Web Engineering: A Practitioner's Approach. Tata McGraw Hill, New Delhi, pp. 115–116, 253–258 (2011)
18. Parthasarathy, M.A.: Practical Software Estimation. Addison-Wesley, Upper Saddle River, pp. 6–22, 206–207 (2007)
19. Schach, S.R.: Software Engineering, 7th edn, pp. 332, 515–520. Tata McGraw Hill, New Delhi (2006)
20. Suh, W.: Web Engineering: Principles and Techniques. Idea Group, Hershey, pp. 1–22, 81–82 (2004)
21. Tsui, F., Karam, O.: Essentials of Software Engineering, 2nd edn. Jones & Bartlett Learning, Burlington (2010)
22. Amazon Web Services: http://aws.amazon.com/
23. IBM: http://www.ibm.com/
24. Google Cloud Platform: http://cloud.google.com/
25. Gerti, K., Siegfried, R., Brigit, P., Werner, R.: Web Engineering, pp. 219–246. Wiley, Hoboken (2010)
26. WeVideo: https://www.wevideo.com/

Chapter 6
Business Requirements Engineering for Developing Cloud Computing Services

Muthu Ramachandran

Abstract Cloud computing is an emerging paradigm that is becoming rapidly popular with business organisations. The software-as-a-service (SaaS) delivery approach is increasing in demand for yet more cloud-based services. However, this new trend needs to be more systematic with respect to software engineering (design and development) and its related processes. In this case, a valid question is: How do we change our existing user-based requirements capturing methodologies to a suitable service-based business requirements engineering? In this chapter, we present an approach to cloud requirements engineering that is based on business-oriented analysis as this is the key to a successful cloud service. This chapter explores the new requirements engineering process and relevant techniques for capturing cloud-based services. The process and techniques have been explained using a large-scale case study based on Amazon Cloud EC2.

Keywords Cloud computing • Software engineering • Requirements engineering • Cloud services • Service-oriented computing

6.1 Introduction

Cloud computing has evolved to address the availability of computing resources which can be accessed from anywhere and anytime. In particular, computing hardware and software often gets outdated, and, hence, it is wise to outsource computing resources and to manage their IT infrastructures outside of their company premises, which is more cost-effective than the case at present. Applications can be

M. Ramachandran (✉)
School of Computing and Creative Technologies, Faculty of Arts,
Environment and Technology, Leeds Metropolitan University, Leeds LS6 3QS, UK
e-mail: M.Ramachandran@leedsmet.ac.uk

Z. Mahmood and S. Saeed (eds.), *Software Engineering Frameworks for the Cloud Computing Paradigm*, Computer Communications and Networks,
DOI 10.1007/978-1-4471-5031-2_6,

leased (as pay-per-use services) rather than being purchased. Also, companies have increased their data centres due to demand (Amazon, Microsoft and IBM). Cloud computing is heavily based on 'software-as-a-service' concept and needs high-speed Web access. It provides services on demand, utilising resources more effectively within the cloud environment. The cloud architecture, its layers and its composition of components and services need to be designed for scalability, security and reconfigurability as they support services and its agreements (e.g. service-level agreements). In this scenario, the resource management of cloud computing is key to achieving potential benefits.

Cloud computing is based on Web access. Therefore, we need to design Web applications which are designed for security. Hence, it is essential to design cloud applications as Web service components based on well-proven software process, design methods and techniques such as component-based software engineering (CBSE). Wang and Laszewski [1] define cloud computing as a set of network-enabled services which provide scalable, guaranteed QoS (quality of service) and inexpensive computing platforms on demand, which are customisable (personalised), and all of which can be accessed in a simple and pervasive way. An overview of different cloud computing paradigms is presented with definitions, business models and technologies by Wang and Laszewski [1] and by many others [1–34].

Traditionally, requirements engineering is defined as a set of activities involving various stakeholders to elicit requirements for a software system. This process is further refined to provide clear classes of requirements such as functional, non-functional, governance and business. Requirements validation is another process of making sure that the requirements are clear, consistent and contextual (3Cs). Business requirements is often not clearly identified and captured as this is directly related to business level. Therefore, we can define business requirements as a process of discovering, analysing, defining and documenting the requirements that are related to enterprise-wide business objectives. This process involves identifying and capturing key business stakeholders who are mainly investors (use interviews, focus groups, ethnographic studies and current market analysis), conducting business feasibility analysis using ROI (return on investment) strategies, studying organisational objectives that should represent true value for long-term investment, analysing the impact of business change to the enterprise and forecasting profit with respect to a set time period, prioritising business requirements and producing a business requirements document to sign off.

SaaS design process involves identifying service components and artefacts that can all be mapped onto service-oriented architecture (SOA). Software components provide a good design rationale supporting various requirements of application developments, design flexibility, system composition, testability, reusability and other design characteristics. Component-based designs are customisable and interfaces can be designed supporting SLA (service-level agreement). SLAs vary between service providers which need to be customised without much effort. This can only be achieved using components which have been designed for flexible interfaces that link to a number of SLAs. Each SLA and associate business rule can be represented as a set of interfaces that can be mapped onto knowledge-based database or a data server. This also allows reuse of SLAs for any individual service providers. Some of the important characteristics of cloud computing are:

- On-demand services and pay per use
- Handling wide area multiple network addresses
- Resource grouping and management
- Efficient elasticity vs. costing
- Measurable service delivery and QoS

The first characteristic of on-demand service and pay-per-use cost efficiency model poses tremendous challenges to provide efficient support and a trustworthy cost model (provided by cloud service providers) for pay per use for every resource used by customer services automatically. Cloud computing is based on clients with high bandwidth for Internet access, and each client may have *N* number of end users or cloud application users. Therefore, it will create *N*N* multiple network addresses which need to be managed accurately as it has a strong dependency for costing users. The second characteristics of cloud computing is based on clients with high bandwidth for Internet access, and each client may have *N* number of end users or cloud application users. Therefore, it will create *N*N* multiple network addresses which need to be managed accurately as it has a strong dependency for costing users. The third characteristic on resource grouping and management has to be monitored and managed efficiently by cloud service providers both reasons of efficiency and costing. The fourth cloud characteristic on elasticity, scalability and costing poses huge challenge for cloud service providers as part of the cloud service management system. The final cloud characteristic on measurable service delivery and quality of service (QoS) has long-term implications for cloud service providers to measure and improve service quality continuously.

Our earlier work described by Ramachandran [22] on component model for Web services and service-oriented architecture (SOA), grid computing and various other systems can become an integrated aspect of any cloud computing architectures and application design. We also need to understand the basic differences amongst SOA (service-oriented architecture), grid and cloud computing. *SOA* is to offer services which are based on open standard Internet services and virtualisation technology and have been running in a different environment, *grid* offers services from multiple environments and virtualisation and *cloud* combines both. We also need to identify a specific development process for capturing requirements, design and implementation strategies, security and testing cloud applications. Cloud computing paradigm has lots to offer, but at the same time we need to consider building a secured and resilient architecture and services that are reliable and trustworthy.

This chapter has proposed a model which is based on the notion of design for scalability of the cloud architecture which is driven by business requirements. We have also identified a set of business as a service for Amazon EC2 cloud. The result shows that 20 % represents BPaaS services from business requirements.

6.2 Design for Cloud Applications

The idea of design for reuse and design for testability have emerged to address how best design can be represented in the system which reflects expected design characteristics (based on design principles) such as reusability, testability, securability (building software security in) and scalability. These are the four basic architectural characteristics that are prevalent in most systems. The main purpose of identifying them during requirements stage is to build them right from the beginning; therefore, they can exhibit themselves on-the-fly. In order to define a process model for cloud computing applications, it is useful to capture some of our thoughts on understanding the very nature of cloud characteristics and the type of services that it aims to provide. Identifying characteristics of a service-oriented system is vital for designers such that they can select, design and evaluate those characteristics that are applicable to their applications. Service-oriented computing (SoC) involves integration of several disciplines and subject areas, and, therefore, some of the characteristics will overlap. Some of the identified service components characteristics are:

- Reusable Web services and some other core services
- Enterprise integration services
- Dynamic binding and reconfigurable at runtime
- Granularity
- Publish, subscribe and discover
- Open world where components must be able to connect and plug to third-party software systems or components
- Heterogeneity supporting cross-platform applications
- Reconfigurable
- Self-composable and recoverable
- Cloud infrastructure and resources management
- Autonomic framework
- Middleware
- QoS
- Controllability
- Visibility and flexibility
- Security and privacy
- High performance and availability
- Integration and composition
- Standards

These characteristics and their underpinning design principles embody a large variety of best practices that exist widely. These best practices have evolved over the last two decades of software engineering. For example, software requirements engineering, software reuse concepts and practices have been widely adopted and are used in the industry. Therefore, the main aim of this chapter is to consider a systematic approach to capturing business requirements that can be applied to the cloud paradigm. Service design is based on the principle of loosely coupling and therefore is a good candidate for achieving service-level reuse such as business services,

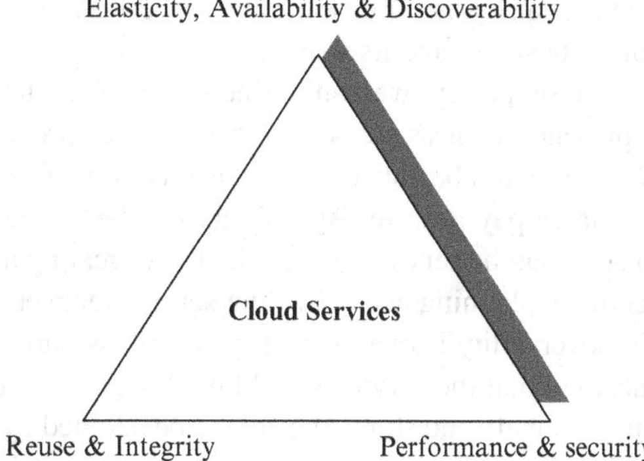

Fig. 6.1 Design for cloud applications

infrastructure services, composite services (as services are designed based on the principle autonomous), co-operation services, information services, task-oriented services, and orchestration services). Therefore, service level reuse has potential to save service development cost and cloud resource utilisation cost. The notion of design for reuse, design for test (also known as testability) and design for security exists in software engineering literatures more widely (Ramachandran [22]). Controllability, visibility and flexibility are design characteristics that can help to build and recover new services more widely. High performance, standards and availability characteristics can provide required service quality. In order to make a design for cloud applications, we need to understand various required cloud characteristics and provide a clear set of design guidelines that can be used by cloud applications engineers. Some of such guidelines are presented as:

- Make applications loosely coupled using SOA principles.
- Design for cloud will provide a value for money in the longer term.
- Use cloud and SOA design principles and characteristics as strictly as possible as discussed by Erl [10].
- Leverage three-tiered SOA architecture which will even allow you to design a database service linking to two different cloud providers.
- Make use of asynchronous messaging wherever possible as discussed by Linthicum [35].
- Avoid cloud-specific APIs wherever possible so as allowing portability across clouds.

Our work on best practice software guidelines provides a disciplined approach to service-driven software development life cycle [22]. Our previous work on this has identified guidelines on good requirements representation using use case models for identifying common requirements across a range of software product lines [22]. Reuse of service-level business requirements can yield higher-level reuse across cloud service. Making business service requirements can develop reuse across different levels in the SOA model. Therefore, Fig. 6.1 shows a model for design for reuse which focuses on elasticity, availability and discoverability, reuse and integrity and performance and security. For each business requirement, we need to conduct analysis based on main six criteria identified in this model with view to future business and its sustainability.

For simplicity, we can define some of the terms very briefly. Elasticity directly represents business focus for services which provide value proposition, and, therefore, service should be able to expand and contract resources based on demand and be able to charge pay per use. Availability can be defined with respect to business focus to ensure that the services are available by creating multiple data centres, proper disaster recovery planning and providing service recovery and failover mechanisms in place. Discoverability is one of the key criteria as part of service-oriented design principle, meaning that the service should be designed in such a way that it can be discovered automatically and should be able to be adopted by service requesters automatically or with a minimum human input. Elasticity, availability and discoverability are part of quality of service (QoS).

Service reuse can be defined as the process of linking business service together to solve an end-to-end business problem or a business process. Although this looks simple but can create reuse across cloud services with automatic discoverability and composability with strict integrity in place. Oh et al. [36] states that the reusability is a key intrinsic characteristic of cloud services and can yield a high return on investment (ROI). Services can be reused and composed to create new cloud services and applications from a set of common service directories across different cloud providers. Service integrity can be defined as the degree to which a service can be provided without excessive impairment and the degree to which it provides fair value to the business. Service reusability and integrity are part of the key criteria for measuring the quality of service (QoS).

One of the main reason for moving cloud is the cost benefit. Therefore, it is paramount for cloud providers to ensure performance is effective. There are a number of performance characteristics such as network throughput and latency. Service availability is another key factor in measuring cloud performance. This is also known as uptime. Other parameters include scalability of service applications, pay per use, load balancing, elastic load balancing, number of cloud computing created per service instance, number of cloud images created per instance, number of cloud resources created per instance and cloud profiling.

Cloud security is paramount amongst all other characteristics as cloud service is internet based. Therefore, we need to make sure that network security, denial of service attacks, software service security and other forms of security are well protected. Other aspects include cloud content management, privacy, business continuity and data recovery.

6.3 Business-Oriented Cloud Service Development Process

Identification of service requirements needs a new RE process and modelling techniques as it is highly dependent on multilevel enterprises across corporation. Identifying and knowing all requirements for all expected and even unexpected

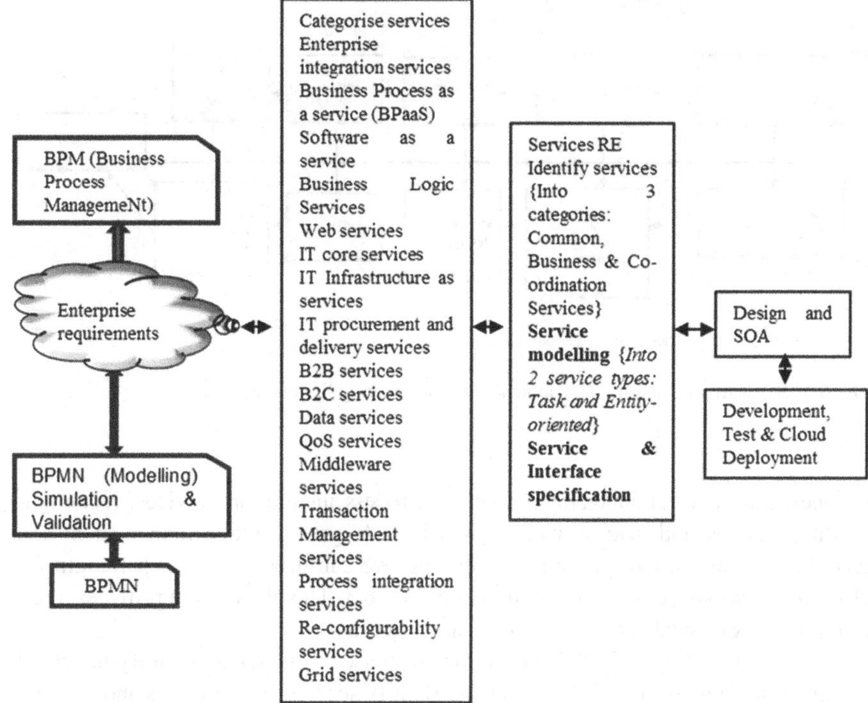

Fig. 6.2 Business-oriented cloud service development process

services is very hard. The idea in service-oriented engineering is to publish automatically new services whereby service agents can then be able request and take advantages of required services for their customers. Figure 6.2 shows a development process model for service-oriented computing where initial requirements are captured based on enterprise-wide techniques and perhaps using domain analysis which should focus on a family of products and services. The second phase (Services RE) involves identifying a set of requirements of system services. This process involves service modelling and service specification for which we can use any well-known techniques such as use case design and a template for service-level specifications.

The third phase (Categorising services) involves classifying and distinguishing services into various categories such as enterprise integration services (services across corporations, departments, other business services), BPaaS (which represents process related to businesses), software services (which represents core functionality of software systems), business logic services (which represents business rules and its constraints) and Web services (a self-contained and Web-enabled entity which provides services across businesses and customisable at runtime). IT core services include resource management, help desk systems, IT infrastructure, procurement, delivery services, B2B and B2C services, data services, QoS services, middleware

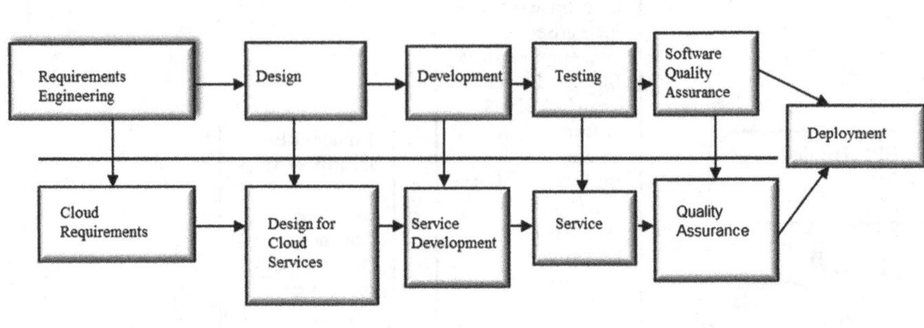

Fig. 6.3 Software engineering vs. cloud service engineering life cycle

services, transaction management services, process integration services, reconfigurability services and grid services which include grid resource management and reconfigurations. Based on the above finding, we can propose a new paradigm for cloud applications engineering as shown in Fig. 6.3. This illustration provides a relevant link to classical software engineering process.

As shown in Fig. 6.3, the requirements phase is linked to identifying cloud requirements which should, in particular, identify service requirements and relevant software security requirements so that cloud services are built with security in rather than adding security batches after release. The design phase is linked to designing services for cloud environment which are reusable. Services are designed as loosely coupled allowing high potential for reuse. The code/implementation phase is linked to service development. Likewise testing and QA are related to cloud testing strategies and quality engineering.

The key difference in cloud SE life cycle is service quality engineering/assurance (SQoS). Service quality engineering/assurance represents quality of service aspects which is different from software engineering quality. SQoS should consider parameters such as workflow management which helps to manage resources instantly, accuracy and accountability of pay-per-use, throughput, latency and service satisfactory index.

6.3.1 Business Process as a Service Paradigm

Business process as a service (BPaaS) is a top-level part of the service-level architecture (BPaaS → SaaS → PaaS → IaaS) for cloud platform. This refers to any business process such as payroll, multivendor e-commerce, advertising, printing, enterprise-wide applications and common business processes and could include contract negotiation services [37]. BPaaS services can also be designed to automate

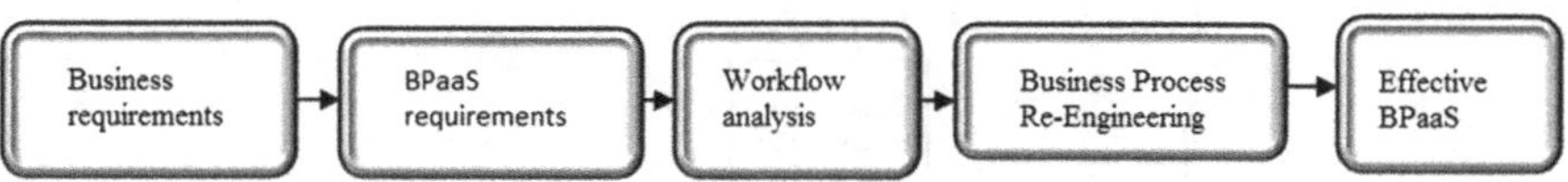

Fig. 6.4 BPaaS process scenario

certain business utility services such as billing and shipping. BPaaS can be a part of internal cloud services as well as external services from different cloud vendor types such as public, hybrid and virtual private. Gandhi [37] addresses some of the key questions that need to be addressed:

- What are the key attributes of BPaaS services to negotiate and gain new business strategies?
- How can BPaaS partnering services accelerate new businesses?
- What are the implications if we don't act now?

These are some of the key strategies and business analysis to be considered for designing BPaaS services. We should be able to use and transfer knowledge gained in business strategies and business process re-engineering and enterprise-wide applications. Figure 6.4 provides a process for capturing and designing BPaaS.

As shown in Fig. 6.4, we should be able to identify and extract business processes and business-related functions as candidate for BPaaS from business requirements capturing process. The second step is to conduct a detailed workflow and task analysis for each suitable BPaaS service. The third step is to conduct business process re-engineering (BPR) for each service which aims to identify ROI, business needs analysis, market analysis and business negotiation strategies for each task that is identified in the workflow analysis. Finally, conduct business effective analysis which interlinks internal and external cloud environment.

BPaaS's most important aspect of the service is to integrate scattered and embedded business rules together in many organisations. Often business rules are scattered and some embedded in different places within the organisations. Therefore, organisations have difficulties in dealing with constant change and evolution of new businesses. BPaaS will also act as business rule management system (BPMR).

6.4 Business Requirements Engineering Process and Framework

Businesses are striving through tough market competition to deliver value-driven products and services. The pace of business delivery has rapidly changed since well-established business practices, nature of business service with advancement and demand for technology-based business services such as e-commerce, e-government, Web services and cloud services. People are looking for value for

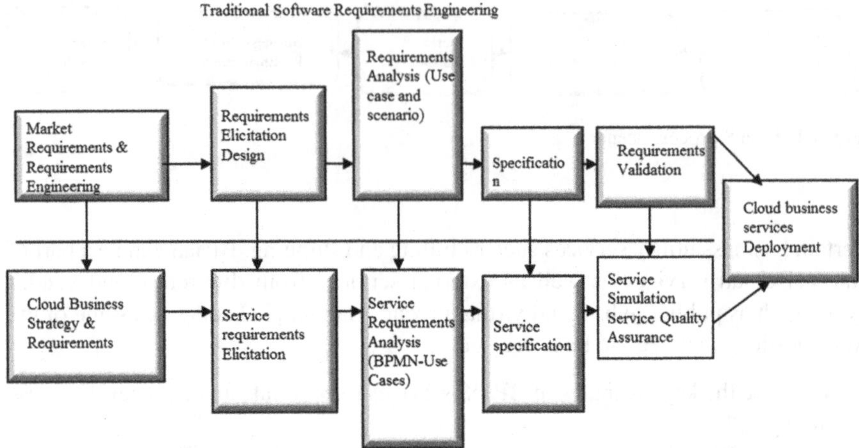

Fig. 6.5 Cloud business-oriented requirements engineering

money as well as automated results (self-driven services). Cause [38] discusses a concept known as PRAISED which is defined as follows:

- P → Productivity gains
- R → Reduced cost
- A → Avoided cost
- I → Increased revenue
- S → Service-level improvements
- E → Enhanced quality
- D → Differentiation in the marketplace

Cause [38] argues that many companies force technologies to be sold as their way of improving business value without understanding of business and market needs. Cause [38] has also proposed a feature-driven development (FDD) approach to identifying business need to drive business value as it captures required features of a business and a product. Our approach to identifying BPM using PRAISE model will enhance BPM to drive market and business values. Figure 6.5 shows cloud business-oriented requirements engineering which compares with classical requirements engineering process.

As shown in Fig. 6.5, classical market requirements process needs to be used for conducting business requirements for cloud services which will include business strategies, identifying business services requirements, market analysis and ROI. The second phase is the requirements elicitation and specification which aims to identify stakeholders and conduct requirements analysis and validation which will derive service requirements elicitation, evaluation and validation. This phase will also derive business process modelling using BPMN, and business process simulation will form the basis for service requirements validation. The final process will deliver hand-picked candidates for business services requirement.

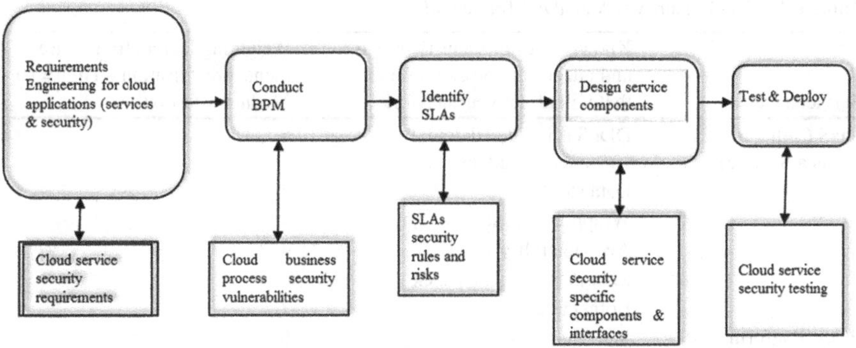

Fig. 6.6 Cloud service security development process with built-in security

Software security has emerged to build security in from requirements through to testing. Security assessment and analysis needs to be applied for each phase of the life cycle [39]. Software engineering has established techniques, methods and technology over two decades. However, due to the lack of understanding of software security vulnerabilities, we have been not successful in applying software engineering principles when developing secured software systems. Therefore, software security can't be added after a system has been built as seen in today's software applications. However, the issue here is to apply software security techniques to cloud services. Services are application system and therefore we should be able to apply those techniques to develop cloud services with built-in security.

Figure 6.6 shows a process model for the development of cloud services with built-in security. As shown in the diagram, the cloud development process model consists of a number of phases such as RE for cloud, conducting BPM modelling and specification (using BPMN 2 standard and BPEL), identifying and specifying SLAs, building software security in, designing services and testing and deploying.

As part of the cloud service requirements engineering process, we can apply software security engineering techniques all identified cloud services. This includes using security analysis tree and various other techniques specified by Ramachandran [39]. The second step is on identifying BPM (business process modelling) which should include software security analysis for each business process identified to allow us to identify potential security threats. This has been illustrated in Fig. 6.6 which starts with service requirements and business requirements (as shown in Fig. 6.5) as the input to conduct service security analysis using techniques such as Secure Quality Requirements Engineering (SQUARE) and Microsoft Secure Development Lifecycle (SDL). The outcome of this process should yield a set of cloud services security requirements with clear indication of software security issues. The second phase is to conduct business process management during this process should identify a set of business process requirements with security vulnerabilities.

The third phase is to identify service-level agreements (SLAs) which should derive a set of security specific rules. It is also a well-known best practice that eliciting and

Table 6.1 Cloud security risk analysis framework

Service layer	Known types of security threats and attacks on the cloud service that will affect your network	Weighting factors for requirements prioritisation – High = 10; Medium = 5; Low = 1
SaaS (Software as a Service)	DDoS (distributed denial of service attack)	8
	Data stealing	3
	Wrapping attack	4
	Accountability attack	4
	Man in the middle attack	6
	Botnet attack	7
PaaS (Platform as a Service)	SQL injection	6
	SSL attack	3
	Spoof attack	5
IaaS (Infrastructure as a Service)	Blackout/outage	1
	Malware injection attack	3

validating service-level requirements early can save as much as 70 % of the overall test and development costs. Typically, SLA refers to a part of service contracts defining performance attributes, message passing constraints, problem management, customer duties, warranties, disaster recovery, service termination agreements and required local and international laws etc., all of which can be embedded as part of the WSDL specifications. In the context of business-oriented requirements, we need to identify SLA with regard to B2B, B2C and business process and operational constraints. This allows services to make decision on acquiring new businesses. This can further be classified into new and existing business services, customer-driven services, market-driven services, corporate-level services and enterprise-level services. In general, we can define a good business process as

$$\text{Business Process} = \text{Business Rules} + \text{Process}$$

that results in simple processes, higher agility, trust, business integration and better risk management. This will also help business processes to define service trust which is the higher form of business quality as part of QoS performance characteristics. Building trust is the basic means of creating a branding which has been historically successful for major business across the world. Cloud security risks analysis should also be part of this process to identify risk associated with each security and business requirement. Therefore, we propose a framework for conducting security risk assessment. This is shown in Table 6.1, a risk analysis framework which can be used to systematically analyse cloud security risks. The framework provides a comprehensive structure for analysing cloud security risks. This framework consists of service layers and their type of service security attacks that are well known. For each of those security attributes, we need to assign a weighting factor from 10 to 1. The weighting factor 10 (high) has higher risks, 5 (medium) and 1 (low). At the SaaS level, the well-known security risks are DDoS, data stealing, wrapping attack, accountability attack etc.

At the PaaS level, the well-known attacks are SQL injection, SSL attack and spoof attack. At the IaaS level, the well-known attacks are blackout and malware attacks. These lists are not limited to security risks shown in our framework which are commonly known and the discovery of such security risk identification should continue to grow as we gain more user experiences. The above weighting factor for prioritising security requirements is the average of total score against its known frequency of threats, loss of business days (in terms of technical challenges associated to recover), financial loss and predictability. Ramachandran [39] discusses more detailed approaches to vulnerability analysis.

The next phase is on service design which starts with business and service requirements in order to design cloud service components, service interfaces and architecture. During this stage, we need to identify security-driven approach to design of interfaces, message descriptions and handing vulnerabilities that are identified in the previous phase. The final phase is on cloud testing and deployment. During this phase, the main aim is to identify security test strategies such as penetration testing, attack tree testing and other forms of testing. Numerous test strategies have been discussed by Ramachandran [39].

To help manage business process requirements, we have identified a generic enterprise requirements framework (ERF) as shown in Fig. 6.7. The concept of enterprise requirement is based on IT service management, business process management and software development. The main aim is to identify business goals, service concept, change management, organisational rules, enterprise economics, business analysis and software development. *Business analysis* can be defined as a set of tasks, knowledge and techniques that are required to identify business needs and to determine solution to business problems. The solutions often include system development, software development, organisational change and process improvement [40].

The ERF, as presented in Fig. 6.7, consists of three major categories:

- Customer requirements aim to identify service needs, business goals and business types. This further classified into B2B, B2C and C2C business types. Secondly, it aims to identify service requirements and, thirdly, to identify governance requirements.
- Market analysis aims to identify clear rationale for a business service and to analyse return on investment strategies. This further classified into industry strategies, opportunities, competitor analysis and business assets.
- Investment analysis aims to identify required systems, services and infrastructures. The application system refers to identifying cloud infrastructure services, content management services and service types such as SaaS, PaaS and IaaS. This further classified into identification of business application systems; *dynamic scaling* is the key basic rationale behind elasticity, the ability of a cloud to be able to add and remove capacity as and when it is required. This can also be referred as elastic scaling. Secondly, to identify infrastructure services refers to management services required to manage IaaS. Thirdly, to identify service security rationale, risk analysis, availability and resiliency is the ability to withstand security attacks and vulnerability.

The ERF framework provides a structured approach to capturing enterprise requirements. The ERF can also be used to document enterprise-wide requirements as it provides a template. This should also identify peak user performance metrics,

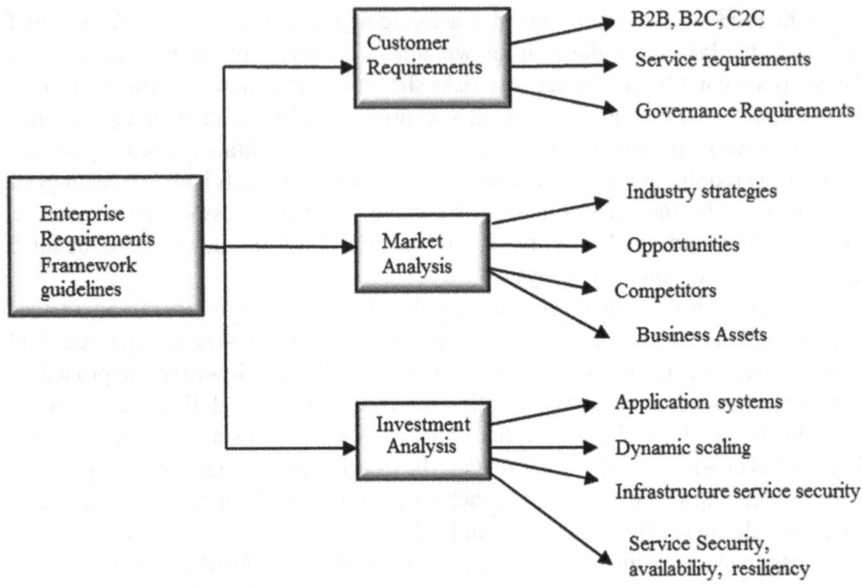

Fig. 6.7 Enterprise requirements framework

capacity planning, security and privacy, availability, response time, hours of operation, pay-per-use calculations, server load, load balancing and cloud management.

6.5 Design of Service Components

Component models and their architecture provide a framework for system composition and integration. A generic component model that is presented in this chapter provides a unique concept of two distinct set of services: *provide and requires*. Software components are the basic unit of artefact that supports service composition with the cloud computing architecture and its environment. However, each development paradigm and application demands customisable and extendable component architectures that suit the needs of their applications. Each Web service component interface is mapped onto different ports within architectural layers to request for services and offer services as and when required at runtime.

The aim is to map business requirements onto a service component that can be designed and implemented. A *service component* can be defined as the one that configures a service implementation. A service component model (UML-based service model) is shown in Fig. 6.8 which reflects service component design principle with a number of plug-in-type interfaces that allow to connect other service components, service provider type of interfaces (IServiceInterface1, 2 etc.) and IServiceContract interface which is a unique concept in our design that allows you to build and reuse business rules. The other types of interface include EntryPort, RejectedMessagePort and ExitPort. These interfaces reflect WSDL descriptions and can be automatically generated.

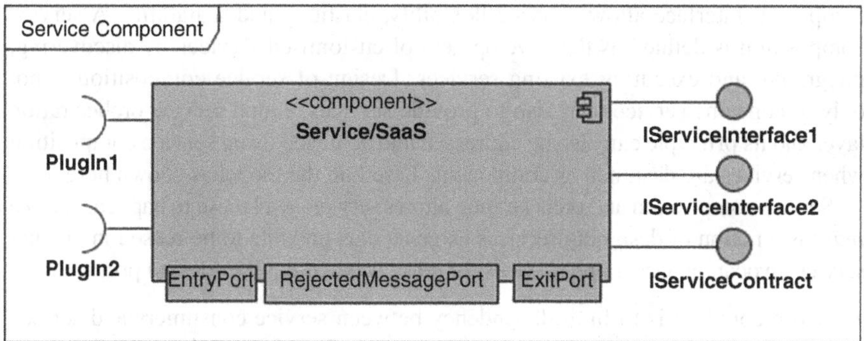

Fig. 6.8 Component model for SaaS

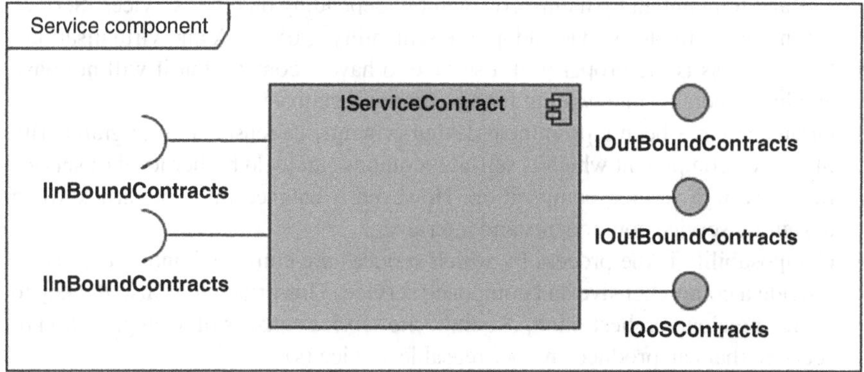

Fig. 6.9 Component model for service contract interface

The service contract interface IServiceContract is a complex class as it allows us to build component rules and be able to reuse them in another service implementation where the similar design contract applies. Due to its nature of complexity, we have designed a separate service component as shown in Fig. 6.8. The service contract component model provides plug-in interfaces such as IInBoundContracts which allows a service component to take business contracts/rules as input to the component, whereas the provider interface such as IOutBoundContracts provides business contract services to other service components. The IQoSContracts service provides services contracts on quality of service rules that are embedded within the service component implementation (Fig. 6.9).

The service component modelling and design provides a systematic approach to building cloud service components to allow on-the-fly configuration, to discover new business services and to be able to connect and disconnect service compositions. *Service composition* is one of the key principles of service design which can't be achieved without a component-based approach. The design principle of component interface allows service flexibility, elasticity and scalability. A service composition is defined as the development of customised services by discovering, integrating and executing existing services. Design of service composition is not only to consume services but also to provide services. Cloud service orchestration layer and its principle can also be addressed and achieved using service composition when services are designed as components based on the model as shown here.

Service composition and orchestration allows service-level reuse to happen. *Service reuse* is a notion of designing services as generic as possible to be reused in another service invocation. Designing services for reuse is based on SOA design principles:

- Loose coupling is to limit dependency between service consumers and service providers. This can be achieved by service interface design which has been part of a service component model as discussed.
- Autonomy is the key principle that enables service reuse. This can be achieved by designing services that can manage their own resources as database and legacies and to maintain by themselves without depending on other services. Service autonomy facilitates service adoption, scalability, QoS, SLA and virtualisation.
- Statelessness is the property of a service to have a context, but it will not have any intermediary state waiting for an event or a callback.
- Granularity has been a prominent design principle of reuse. A large granularity of service component which is self-autonomous can yield higher level of service reuse through service composition. However, a balance must be struck when designing service components and interfaces.
- Composability is the process by which services are combined and integrated to provide a comprehensive and composite service. This principle is also the key to achieving cloud orchestration. A composite service consists of an aggregation of services that can produce another reusable service (s).
- Discoverability is an important means of mandating service time (design time reuse and runtime discoverability) notion when designing service components so that component can be called on when required. Service component interface concept allows components to be discovered and connected.

Designing reusable services can save cost as it is a well-known benefit of reuse. Cost reduction is one of the key aspects of cloud computing which aim to reduce cost for consumers by allowing pay-per-use cost model. The design rationale and service component model discussed in this section will help to improve cloud service reuse experiences.

6.6 Case Study: Amazon EC2

Amazon has three main businesses that are consumer business, seller business and IT infrastructure business. Firstly, let's look at initial business requirements set out by Amazon to create a new cloud as a new business venture. It is aimed to build a

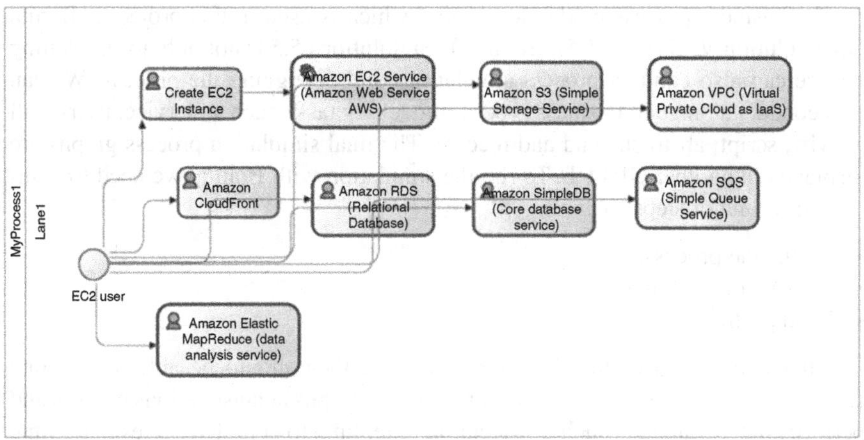

Fig. 6.10 Amazon Web services (business process modelling)

powerful cloud with features supporting scalability, failure resilient and enterprise applications including (EC2 2012 [41]):

- Elastic and scalable means users can increase or decrease computational power and other resources within minutes and are charged per use.
- Flexible means users have the choice to choose type of OS, platforms, multiple instances and applications packages.
- Designed for use with other Amazon Web services such as Amazon S3 (a simple storage service), RDS (relational DB services), SimpleDB and Amazon SQS (simple queue service).

These are the examples of non-functional requirements. There are more than 100 business processes, also known as functional requirements, identified from this study which are of typical nature such as account creation, pay-per-service metre, resource management and usage, billing and payment, data storage and maintenance and security and privacy related. Some of the currently offered Amazon Web services are, as part of the AWS, shown in Fig. 6.10 and explained as follows:

- Higher level business processes for Amazon EC2 which consists of composite business services such as RDS, MapReduce, S3, SimpleDB, VPC and SQS.
- Each of these business services can be decomposed into a number categories of business services such task-oriented, infrastructure-oriented, and business service-oriented.

We have developed a number of business services using Bonita software for business process modelling using BPMN notation.

The business process model design tool which is used in this project is Bonita OpenSolution-v5.5 (BOS 5.5). Bonita Open Solutions 5.5 is not only for modelling but we can also conduct process simulations and debugging the process. We can also conduct a range of business process modelling tasks such as service, users, call activity, script, abstract, send and receive. The final simulation process graphs are displayed in another GUI tab. To run the simulation with Bonita, we need to complete three major steps such as:

- Define the process.
- Manage the resources.
- Load profiles.

After completion of the three processes, we then should be able to generate reports of the designed process. We can generate graphs against various process and performance parameters such as execution time, time to completion, response time and raise alarm to study any intrusion during a specific time period.

Amazon S3 (Simple Storage Service) provides a simple Web services interface that can be used to store and retrieve any amount of data, at any time, from anywhere on the Web. It provides a discoverable WSDL document describing service operations that can be implemented using RESTful HTML as well as SOAP RPC interfaces. In this experiment, we have attempted to describe its basic functionality using a subset of the available services. Basic executable SOA business models were created based on assumptions made from information provided by online Amazon AWS documents. The Amazon S3 Web Service is just one piece of entire Amazon AWS SOA structure. Other than discoverability, none of the SOA Design concepts can really be applied to the Amazon S3 service on its own. Some of the AWS business services are identified as follows (EC2 2012 [41–42]):

- Amazon S3 (Simple Storage Service) provides a simple Web services interface that can be used to store and retrieve any amount of data, at any time, from anywhere on the Web.
- Amazon EC2 (Elastic Compute Cloud) is a Web service that provides resizable compute capacity in the cloud.
- Amazon CloudFront is a Web service for content delivery. It integrates with other Amazon Web Services to give developers and businesses an easy way to distribute content to end users with low latency, high data transfer speeds and no commitments.
- Amazon Route 53 is a highly available and scalable DNS service designed to give developers and businesses an extremely reliable and cost-effective way to route end users to Internet applications.
- Amazon RDS (Relational Database Service) is a Web service that makes it easy to set up, operate and scale a relational database in the cloud.
- Amazon SimpleDB (Simple Database Service) is a Web service providing the core database functions of data indexing and querying in the cloud.

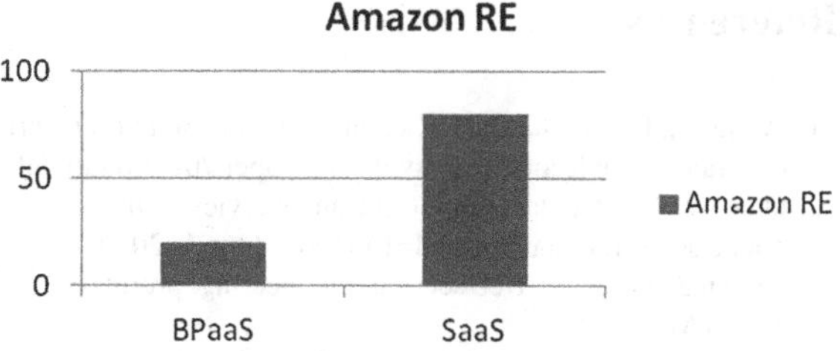

Fig. 6.11 Amazon BPaaS requirements

- Amazon SQS (Simple Queue Service) is a reliable, highly scalable, hosted queue for storing messages as they travel between computers.
- Amazon SNS (Simple Notification Service) is a Web service that makes it easy to set up, operate and send notifications from the cloud.
- Amazon Elastic MapReduce is a Web service that enables businesses, researchers, data analysts and developers to easily and cost-effectively process vast amounts of data.

These services have been considered as a whole to meet the multiple SOA Design criteria by being business-driven, enterprise-centric, loosely coupled, discoverable, stateless and flexibly contractable, and they promote vendor neutrality. The services are provided by Amazon but they can be accessed by any language running on virtually any platform. They are highly scalable and the pricing structure is set up on a cost-per-use basis. Services can be scaled almost instantly when needed and reduced just as fast providing the best of both worlds for businesses, on-demand access without the associated overhead and the delay that would otherwise be required for local on-site implementation. Figure 6.11 shows a bar chart of 100 business processes, out of which we have discovered about 20 BPaaS processes, which is about 20 %.

This is an interesting outcome for our research, in particular, how many BPaaS requirements that can be extracted to evaluate business process service exclusively. BPaaS has a growing strength in making cloud a success with respect to business as a service.

6.7 Conclusion

Cloud computing is emerging rapidly with increasing demand for service-oriented computing and associated technologies. This is the right time to explore what works better and what doesn't work for cloud environment. Therefore, the proposed model helps to understand how it should be developed to avoid classical issues related to software development projects. We believe the proposed model will help us to develop cloud applications systematically. This project has explored some of the process described using Amazon EC2 case study, and we have discovered that there are 20 % of the service requirements that belong to BPaaS as it is a growing business entity for cloud services.

References

1. Wang, L., Laszewski, V.G.: Scientific cloud computing: early definition and experience. http://cyberaide.googlecode.com/svn/trunk/papers/08-cloud/vonLaszewski-08-cloud.pdf (2008)
2. Creeger, M.: Cloud computing: an overview. Distributed computing. ACM Queue. http://queue.acm.org/detail.cfm?id=1554608, June 1, 2009
3. Aoyama, M., et al.: Web services engineering: promises and challenges. In: ICSE'02, Orlando, 19–25 May 2002
4. Bertolino, A., et al.: Audition of web services for testing conformance to open specified protocols. In: Stafford, J., et al. (eds.) Architecting Systems with Trustworthy Components. Springer, Berlin/New York (2006)
5. Bias, R., Cloud Expo Article, Cloud Computing: Understanding infrastructure as a service. Cloud Comput. J. http://cloudcomputing.sys-con.com/node/807481. January 2009
6. Chesbrough, H., Spohrer, J.: A research manifesto for services science, Special issue on services science. CACM **49**(7), 30–87 (2006)
7. Cobweb: http://www.cobweb.com/ (2009)
8. Curbera, F.: Component contracts in service-oriented architectures, Special issue on service-oriented computing. IEEE Comput. **40**(11), 74–80 (2007)
9. Clarke, R.: User requirements for cloud computing architecture. In: 10th IEEE/ACM International Conference on Cluster, Cloud and Grid Computing, Melbourne, 17–20 May 2010
10. Erl, T.: Service-Oriented Architecture: Concepts, Technology, and Design. Prentice Hall, Upper Saddle River (2005)
11. Farrell, J., Ferris, C.: What are web services? (Special issue). CACM **46**(6), 31 (2003)
12. Khaled, L.: Deriving architectural design through business goals. Int. J. Comput. Sci. Inf. Secur. (IJCSIS) **7**(3), 20–26 (2010)
13. Helbig, J.: Creating business value through flexible IT architecture, Special Issue on service-oriented computing. IEEE Comput. **40**(11), 80–89 (2007)
14. IaaS, Cloud computing world forum. http://www.cloudwf.com/iaas.html (2010)
15. IThound Video Whitepaper. http://images.vnunet.com/video_WP/V4.htm (2010). Accessed Feb 2010
16. Lakshminarayanan, S.: Interoperable security service standards for web services, IT pro. IEEE CS Press USA (2010)
17. Nano, O., Zisman, A.: Realizing service-centric software systems, Special issue on SoC. IEEE Softw. **24**(6), 28–30 (2007)
18. Naone, E.: Computer in the cloud, technology review. http://www.technologyreview.com/Infotech/19397/?a=f (2007)
19. NIST: http://csrc.nist.gov/groups/SNS/cloud-computing/index.html (2009)
20. PaaS. Types of PaaS solutions http://www.salesforce.com/uk/paas/paas-solutions/ (2010)
21. Papazoglou, P.M., et al.: Service-oriented computing: State of the art and research challenges, Special issue on service-oriented computing. IEEE Comput. **40**(11), 38–45 (2007)
22. Ramachandran, M.: Software Components: Guidelines and Applications. Nova, New York (2008)
23. SaaS: SaaS http://www.saas.co.uk/ (2009)
24. Science Group, 2020 Science Group: Toward 2020 science, tech. report, Microsoft. http://research.microsoft.com/towards2020science/downloads/T2020S_Report.pdf (2006)
25. Serugendo, G., et al. (eds): Self-organisation: paradigms and applications. In: Engineering Self-Organising Systems: Nature-Inspired Approaches to Software Engineering. Springer, Berlin/New York (2004)
26. Taiyuan, S.: A flexible business process customization framework for SaaS. In: WASE International Conference on Information Engineering, Taiyuan, 10–11 July 2009
27. Tyagi, S.: RESTful web services. http://www.oracle.com/technetwork/articles/javase/index-137171.html (2006)

28. Venkataraman, T., et al.: A model of cloud based application environment. Int. J. Comput. Sci. Inf. Secur. (IJCSIS) **7**(3) (2010)
29. Verizon: http://www.zdnet.co.uk/news/cloud/2010/10/08/the-cloud-lessons-from-history-40090471/. October 2010
30. Vouk, M.A.: Cloud computing – issues, research and implementations. J. Comput. Info. Technol. (CIT) 16, 40–45 (2008)
31. Wilson, C., Josephson, A.: Microsoft office as a platform for software + services. Archit. J. (13). www.architecturejournal.net. 98–102 (2007)
32. Weiss, A.: Computing in the clouds. http://di.ufpe.br/~redis/intranet/bibliography/middleware/weiss-computing08.pdf, December 2007
33. Yang, J.: Web service componentisation. Commun. ACM **46**(10), 35–40 (2003)
34. Zhang, L-J., Zhou, Q.: CCOA: Cloud Computing Open Architecture. In: IEEE International Conference on Web Services, Bangalore, 21–25 September 2009
35. Linthicum, D.: Application design guidelines for cloud computing. InfoWorld. http://www.infoworld.com/d/cloud-computing/application-design-guidelines-cloud-computing-784?page=0,0. November (2009)
36. Oh, S.H., et al.: A reusability evaluation suite for cloud services. In: Eighth IEEE International Conference on e-Business Engineering. IEEE CS Press USA (2011)
37. Gandhi, B.: Business Process as a Service (BPaaS) delivered from the cloud. http://thoughtsoncloud.com/index.php/2011/12/business-process-as-a-service-bpaas-delivered-from-the-cloud/. December (2011)
38. Cause, G.: Delivering real business value using FDD. http://www.methodsandtools.com/archive/archive.php?id=19. Accessed April 2012
39. Ramachandran, M.: Software Security Engineering: Design and Applications. Nova Science, New York, ISBN: 978-1-61470-128-6. https://www.novapublishers.com/catalog/product_info.php?products_id=26331 (2012)
40. Longo, T., Hass, K., Cannon, D.: ITIL, business analysis and the enterprise requirements hierarchy. http://h10076.www1.hp.com/education/ITIL_BusAnalysis_Enterprise_Req_Hierarchy.pdf (2012)
41. EC2: http://aws.amazon.com/ec2/ (2012). Accessed April 2012
42. What is Cloud Computing – A complete engineering of design and implementation of cloud computing. http://www.keendirect.com/blog/cloudcomputing/. Accessed April 2012

Chapter 7
Testing Perspectives for Cloud-Based Applications

Inderveer Chana and Priyanka Chawla

Abstract Cloud computing is often used to describe a model for ubiquitous, convenient, and on-demand network access to shared pool of configurable computing resources that can be rapidly provisioned and released with minimal management effort or service provider interaction. Cloud computing heralds the trend of service provider companies in comparison to traditional software licensing era. As the Cloud-based services are increasing and businesses catered through software services require reassurances, so there is a need to test those services and applications before offering them to the customers. Cloud-based testing offers reduction in the unit cost of computing with test effectiveness, on-demand flexibility, freedom from holding assets, enhanced collaboration, greater levels of efficiency, and, most significantly, reduced time-to-market for key business applications. This chapter largely quantifies on testing related to Cloud computing, elaborates fundamentals of testing and differentiates between traditional software testing techniques and software testing in Cloud environment. It also emphasizes on analysis of the existing Cloud-based testing models and their limitations and Cloud-based application frameworks. The chapter concludes with the discussion on need of automated test case generation techniques, potential research directions, and technologies for testing approaches in Cloud environments.

Keywords Cloud-based applications • Testing in the Cloud • Cloud applications framework

---

I. Chana (✉) • P. Chawla
Computer Science and Engineering Department, Thapar University, Patiala, India
e-mail: inderveer@thapar.edu; priyankamatrix@gmail.com

Z. Mahmood and S. Saeed (eds.), *Software Engineering Frameworks for the Cloud Computing Paradigm*, Computer Communications and Networks,
DOI 10.1007/978-1-4471-5031-2_7,

7.1 Introduction

Software testing ensures correctness, robustness, reliability, and quality in software and is thus fundamental to software development. Testers often execute software under a stipulated environment as well as out of bounds with the intent of finding errors in it [1]. According to IEEE, software testing is the process of analyzing a software item to detect differences between existing and required conditions and to evaluate the features of the software item [2]. Software testing is considered to be a critical element of software quality assurance due to the following reasons [3]:

- To test a developed system for its performance, reliability, and quality
- To ensure long-lasting working of the software without failures
- To detect the bugs and deviations from specifications before delivering it to the customer

Software testing comprises verification and validation tasks. Verification is the process of evaluating a system or component to determine whether the products of a given development phase satisfy the conditions imposed on that phase. Validation is the process of evaluating a system or component during or at the end of development process to determine whether it satisfies specified requirements [IEEE/ANSI]. Hence, software testing is not limited to executing software to find defects only but also to test documents and other non-executable forms of a software product and does often become bottleneck in software development.

7.1.1 Software Testing in the Cloud

Testing is a challenging activity for many software engineering projects, especially for large-scale systems. The amount of test cases can range from a few hundred to several thousands, requiring significant computing resources and lengthy execution times. Cloud computing offers resources like virtualized hardware, effectively unlimited storage, and software services that can aid in reducing this execution time of large test suites in a cost-effective manner. Many organizations like SOASTA, Microsoft, Rackspace, Sogeti, IBM, CloudTesting, Wipro, and HP provide Cloud-based testing services such as performance testing, load testing, and Web-based application testing. Following factors account for the migration of testing to the Cloud [4]:

(a) Testing is a periodic activity and requires new environments to be set up for each project. Test labs in companies typically sit idle for longer periods, consuming capital, power, and space.
(b) Testing is considered an important but non-business-critical activity. Moving testing to the Cloud is seen as a safe bet because it doesn't include sensitive corporate data and has minimal impact on the organization's business-as-usual activities.

(c) Applications are increasingly becoming dynamic, complex, distributed, and component based, creating a multiplicity of new challenges for testing teams. For instance, mobile and Web applications must be tested for multiple operating systems and updates, multiple browser platforms and versions, different types of hardware and a large number of concurrent users to understand their performance in real time. The conventional approach of manually creating in-house testing environments that fully mirror these complexities and multiplicities consume huge capital and resources.

According to the Software Testing in the Cloud (STITC) [5], a special interest group, there are three categories of Cloud testing as enumerated below:

(a) Testing in the Cloud: Leveraging the resources provided by a Cloud computing infrastructure to facilitate the concurrent execution of test cases in a virtualized environment. Testing in the Cloud is about utilizing the Cloud for testing, such as for configuration testing and load testing.
(b) Testing of the Cloud: Testing applications that are hosted and deployed in a Cloud environment.
(c) Migrating testing to the Cloud: Moving the testing process, test assets, and test infrastructure from their current state to facilitate either testing in the Cloud or testing of the Cloud.

However, migrating testing to Cloud does not come without cost, nor is it necessarily the best solution for all testing problems. The two perspectives that have to be considered before migration of software testing to the Cloud are the characteristics of an application under test and the types of testing performed on the application [6].

7.1.2 Benefits and Challenges of Cloud-Based Testing

The benefits of Cloud-based testing can be enumerated as mentioned below [7–10]:

(a) Testing in the Cloud leverages the Cloud computing infrastructure reducing the unit cost of computing, while increasing testing effectiveness.
(b) Cloud-based testing service providers offer a standardized infrastructure and pre-configured software images that are capable of reducing errors considerably.
(c) The non-cost factors include utility like on-demand flexibility, freedom from holding assets, enhanced collaboration, greater levels of efficiency, and, most important, reduced time-to-market for key business applications.

On-demand Cloud provisioning addresses the issues of software testing with one click. Moreover, the effort and resources saved in the development and testing area can be utilized for core business needs. Recent research from Fujitsu [11] (as shown in Fig. 7.1) suggests that testing and application development rank second (57 %) as the most likely workload to be put into the Cloud after Web sites (61 %). Although,

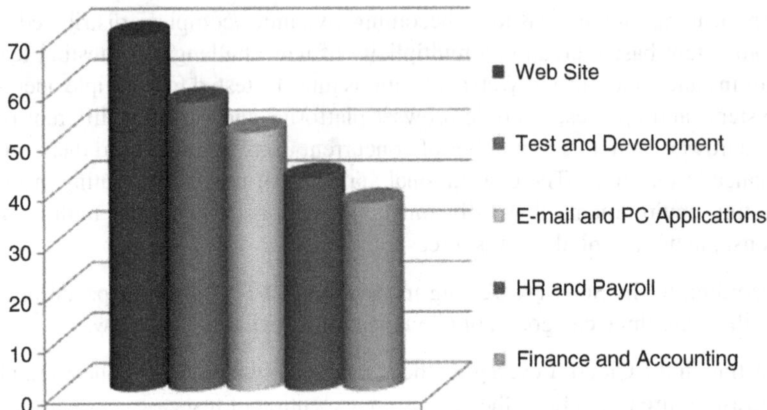

Fig. 7.1 Top application of Cloud [11]

numerous benefits can be accounted for Cloud-based testing, following challenges [6, 12–14] also need to be addressed to fully exploit the benefits:

(a) Lack of standards: There is no universal/standard solution to integrate public Cloud resources with user companies' classic data center. Cloud providers have their own architecture, operating models, and pricing mechanisms and offer limited interoperability.
(b) Security in the public Cloud: Security is currently addressed through encryption techniques, which is not sufficient.
(c) Service Level Agreements (SLAs): There is no standard procedure to define terms and conditions of Cloud service providers. Existing procedures are generally not precise, misleading and biased toward the providers.
(d) Infrastructure: Limited types of configurations, technology, servers and storage, networking, and bandwidth are provided by some providers, which make it difficult to create real-time test environments.
(e) Usage: Usage is directly dependent on the estimations made by the users. Any error in the estimates can lead to extra costs.
(f) Planning: Planning is very crucial for the testing teams before migrating testing in a Cloud as it will consume additional CPU and memory. Testing teams should be aware of all the expenses like cost of encrypting data.
(g) Performance: Service provider may suddenly announce disruption of service due to a maintenance window or network outage, which can cause long waiting time for the service users.

7.2 Cloud Applications Frameworks

Computing paradigms have evolved from dummy terminals/mainframes to PCs, network computing, to Grid and Cloud computing [15]. Cloud computing helps to build a model for on-demand network access to a shared pool of computing resources

Table 7.1 Traditional apps vs. Cloud-based applications

Parameters	Traditional applications	Cloud-based applications
User base	Known at design time	May not be known and could be dynamic
Multi-tenancy	Not required	Assumed
Security	Enforced by application architecture	Service contracts like WS-Security, SAML provided by Cloud providers
Deployment	Only traditional tools	Requires knowledge and utilization of vendor specific Cloud API and tools
Downtime	Upgrades and enhancements are associated with downtime	No downtime
Infrastructure	Structured and controlled	Unstructured and is managed by Cloud fabric
Components	Components co-located in same environment	Components are mostly scattered around one or many Clouds
Testing	In controlled environment	Application (integration) is tested on the Cloud to ensure seamless orchestration between services on one or many Clouds
User base	Known at design time	May not be known and could be dynamic

that requires minimal management effort or service provider interaction [16]. The Cloud model as defined by NIST promotes availability and is composed of five essential characteristics, namely, on-demand self-service, broad network access, resource pooling, rapid elasticity, and measured service [17]. The building blocks of Cloud computing are essential characteristics, service delivery models, deployment models [17], and enabling technologies [18, 19]. For Cloud applications, the enabling technologies are the set of technological advances that made the appearance of Cloud computing possible. The service delivery model identifies the services that are delivered on each implementation, while the deployment models identify how those services are deployed. Essential characteristics and enabling technologies are common to every Cloud service implementation, while the delivery and deployment models differentiate each one of the implementations.

7.2.1 Traditional Applications vs. Cloud-Based Applications

Cloud computing environment is unlike a traditional environment in terms of applications deployment, configuration, execution, and management. Traditional applications and Cloud-based applications differ considerably and have been compared on the basis of type of users, multi-tenancy, security, etc., in Table 7.1.

Cloud applications can also be categorized on the basis of the degree of multi-tenancy required for an application; multi-tenancy is enabled by the concept of virtualization, which supports sharing of compute, storage, and network resources among multiple clients. In a Cloud, a client (tenant) could be a user, a user group, or an organization/company.

Cloud-Hosted Applications: Cloud-hosted applications are the one that can be executed on the Cloud. In Cloud-hosted applications, multi-tenancy is at the infrastructure layer, that is, only infrastructure would be shared by providers to support multiple client applications, for example, Amazon EC2 and Rackspace.

Cloud-Optimized Applications: Cloud-optimized applications are the one that can leverage the Cloud to its fullest potential. These applications meet the stringent requirements and deliver the maximum return on the Cloud investment. In Cloud-optimized application multi-tenancy is supported at the different layers like infrastructure, application, and database by leveraging a PaaS platform, for example, Salesforce.com's Force.com.

7.2.2 Traditional Software Testing vs. Cloud Testing

Traditional software testing cannot be applied to test applications in a Cloud environment as traditional software testing is designed for on-premise single-tenant applications and cannot support multi-tenant applications. Traditional software testing does not support new business requirements and risks that come with Cloud environment. Test engineers that are trained to perform traditional software testing need special training to perform testing in Cloud.

New business needs and associated challenges should be properly understood before migrating to Cloud environment in order to meet Cloud testing requirements. Organizations need to be equipped with additional infrastructure such as different testing skills required by test engineers to perform the job of testing in a Cloud [20, 21].

To identify the type of testing to be performed, an understanding of Cloud characteristics and the risks/challenges involved is required. Right testing strategy should be selected by addressing the following challenges:

- Quality risks of Cloud computing such as reliability, flexibility, multi-tenancy, self-healing, pricing band on SLA's and location independence.
- Inherited risks associated with Cloud computing like data governance, data security, virtualization security, reliability, monitoring, and manageability.
- Applicable Cloud models to be tested like Software-as-a-Service (SaaS), Platform-as-a-Service (PaaS), and Infrastructure-as-a-Service (IaaS).

Cloud testing exemplifies testing on demand and is perceived as future of testing services. The following testing types are performed in general for Cloud testing:

- System Integration Testing/User Acceptance Testing: The Cloud platform must be integrated with all platforms and infrastructure services so that a user can build up his data online.
- Interoperability Testing: Interoperability refers to moving Cloud applications from one infrastructure to another Cloud infrastructure. Any application on Cloud must have the ability to be operated on multiple platforms and environments. It should be able to get executed across any Cloud platform.
- Performance Testing/Load Testing: Elasticity refers to using minimum resources and producing maximum usage for end users. The performance of Cloud should remain intact even if there are increasing inflows of requests.

- Stress Testing/Recovery testing: In case a failure occurs, disaster recovery time should be as less as possible. Services must be retrieved online with minimum adverse effects on client's business.
- Security Testing: Unauthorized access to data must be strictly prohibited. Shared data integrity and security must be maintained all times as client trusts the Cloud platform for securing his information.

The infrastructure requirement for test environment is another important consideration for Cloud testing. The two possible options for choosing the right test environment are:

- Simulating in-house Cloud test environment
- Choosing the right Cloud service provider

Apart from identifying applicable testing types, testing team must also focus on the specific requirements of the application to be tested because of being in a Cloud environment (as enumerated below):

- Supporting multiple browsers
- User session management related issues
- Test against security vulnerabilities
- In a multi-tenant environment, restricting users to access their data only
- Test engineer's skill

7.2.3 Applications Suitable for Cloud

Classes of applications that can be benefited with Cloud computing and contribute further to its momentum are:

(a) Mobile interactive applications: These applications reside on the mobile device, which connects all organizations to all types of consumers and employees. They are highly available and generally rely on large data sets that are most conveniently hosted in large data centers. Such applications respond to information provided either by their users or by nonhuman sensors in real time [22].

(b) Parallel batch processing: Batch processing is execution of programs in some specified sequence on a computer without manual intervention. Parallel processing is use of more than one CPU or processor core to execute a program at the same time. Parallel batch processing is the execution of programs using more than one CPU or processor core to make the execution faster. Cloud computing is very useful for batch processing and analytics jobs that analyze terabytes of data and can take hours to finish. By making application that is equipped with enough data parallelism one can take care of using hundreds of computers for short time costs. For example, Peter Harkins, a Senior Engineer at The Washington Post, used 200 EC2 instances (1,407 server hours) to convert 17,481 pages of Hillary Clinton's travel documents into a form more friendly to use on the WWW within 9 h after they were released [23]. Programming abstractions such as Google's MapReduce [24] and its open-source counterpart Hadoop [25] allow programmers to express such tasks while hiding the operational complexity of choreographing parallel execution across hundreds of Cloud computing servers.

(c) Business analytics: It is a special case of compute-intensive batch processing which is expending large share of computing resources to understand customers, supply chains, buying habits, ranking, and so on. Hence, while online transaction volumes will continue to grow slowly, decision support is growing rapidly, shifting the resource balance in database processing from transactions to business analytics.

(d) Extension of compute-intensive desktop applications: Cloud computing is being used to extend the basic versions of the mathematics software packages MATLAB and Mathematica to perform expensive evaluations. For example, symbolic mathematics involves large amount of computing per unit of data. An interesting alternative model might be to keep the data in the Cloud and rely on having sufficient bandwidth to enable suitable visualization and a responsive GUI back to the human user.

(e) Web Applications: Web applications are the applications that can be accessed from anywhere via the Web browser. Web application development through Cloud computing provides cost-effective solution to provide specialized services to customers without having to build, maintain, or host the applications. Businesses can depend on Cloud service providers to collect, maintain, and store their data. For example, multitiered Web applications like RUBiS [26] and Media Wiki [27] can also be ported to Cloud platform [28].

(f) Scientific Workflow Applications: Scientific workflow applications can be executed efficiently over utility computing platforms such as Amazon Elastic Compute Cloud, Google App Engine and academic Cloud like Nimbus Science. A few examples of scientific workflow applications are now listed below:

- In astronomy, scientists are using workflows to generate science-grade mosaics of the sky [29], to examine the structure of galaxies to understand the structure of the universe [30].
- In bioinformatics, workflows are used to understand the underpinnings of complex diseases [31, 32].
- In earthquake science, workflows are used to predict the magnitude of earthquakes within a geographic area over a period of time [33].
- In physics, workflows are used to try to measure gravitational waves [34] and model the structure of atoms [35].

7.2.4 Cloud Application Architecture and Process Models

Cloud application development is different from traditional application development, as for the development of Cloud-based applications, architectural, and operational considerations should be taken into account [36].

Software application architecture involves the process of defining a structured solution that meets all of the technical and operational requirements. It concerns with a series of decisions based on a wide range of factors, and each of these decisions can have considerable impact on the quality, performance, maintainability, and overall success of the application. Application architecture seeks to build a bridge between business requirements and technical requirements by understanding use cases and then finding ways to implement those use cases in the software.

A good design is sufficiently flexible to be able to handle the natural drift that will occur over time in hardware and software technology, as well as in user scenarios and requirements. To fully attain architectural goals, structure of the system can be fully exposed, hiding the implementation details, and thus should be able to realize all user cases and scenarios. Architecture of Cloud-based application must possess the following attributes:

(a) Support for service-based model: Once an application is deployed, it needs to be maintained. In the past this meant using servers that could be repaired without or with minimal downtime. Today it means that an application's underlying infrastructure components can be updated or even replaced without disrupting its characteristics including availability and security.
(b) Incorporating elasticity to dynamically scale and support large number of users: Applications designed for Cloud computing need to scale with workload demands so that performance and compliance with service levels remain on target. In order to achieve this, applications and their data must be loosely coupled to maximize scalability. The term elastic often applies to scaling Cloud applications because they must be ready to not only scale up but also scale down as workloads diminish in order to not run up the cost of deploying in the Cloud.
(c) Supporting parallel processing: Reliability, in today's arena, means that applications do not fail and most importantly they do not lose data. The way that architecture addresses this characteristic today is to design applications so that they continue to operate and their data remains intact despite the failure of one or more of the servers or virtual machines onto which they are decomposed.
(d) Support for multi-tenancy: The single-tenant model has a separate, logical instance of the application for each customer, while the multi-tenant model has a single logical instance of the application shared by many customers. It's important to note that the multi-tenant model still offers separate views of the application's data to its users.
(e) Security of data: Applications need to provide access only to authorized, authenticated users, and those users should be able to trust that their data is secure. Security in today's environments is established using strong authentication, authorization, and accounting procedures, establishing security of data at rest and in transit, locking down networks, and hardening operating systems, middleware, and application software.
(f) Cloud orchestration: Cloud orchestration involves interconnecting processes running across heterogeneous systems in multiple locations. Its main purpose is to automate the configuration, coordination and management of software and

software interactions. Tasks involved include managing server runtimes, directing the flow of processes among applications and dealing with exceptions to typical workflows. Vendors of Cloud orchestration products include Eucalyptus, Flexiant, IBM, Microsoft, VMware, and V3 Systems.

(g) Persistent software licensing issues: The different types of license models are pay-as-you-go, subscription-based licenses, licenses based on number of users, and Bring Your Own Software and License (BYOSL). For example, Amazon's software license models in the Cloud are often pay-as-you-go and/or subscription-based licenses. Salesforce.com charges according to the number of users on a subscription basis. Microsoft has created dedicated software license models for Cloud service providers based on Processor License (PL) or Subscriber Access License (SAL), which is based on the number of end users connected. Both of these are licensed on a monthly basis to service providers.

Process model used for developing Cloud-based application should be chosen appropriately so as to enhance the benefits of Cloud computing like flexibility, availability, and adaptability and assisting the testing of Cloud apps. Let us have a look on the most popular process models adopted by the software development companies and find out which process models support the above discussed features and requirements of Cloud-based application development.

Agile Methodology: In an agile paradigm, every phase of development – requirements, design, etc. – is continually revisited throughout the life cycle. It gives more importance to customers, collaborations over contracts, and working software over documentation and responds to changes at any time during the development. The results of this approach lead to reduction in both development costs and time-to-market. Team's work cycle is limited to 2 weeks; customer involvement is given the highest priority at each phase, which results in the development of right product as per the requirements of the customers. Widely used agile processes in Cloud application development are Scrum and Extreme Programming (XP).

Waterfall Model: In this model, development of software occurs just like a waterfall from one phase to other in a downward fashion. Various phases of the software development like requirements and analysis and design become sequential phases. Each and every phase is highly dependent on the document exchange between the phases. This process model is good for repetitive work, but not for Cloud-based application development because of the risks associated that increase with time.

Iterative Model: In an iterative process, various phases of software development like requirements and analysis and design are distributed within iterations, which occur in a sequential manner and are often combined into phases. This process model is good for exploratory work and risk associated is less. Widely used iterative process models are IBM's Rational Unified Process (RUP) and Eclipse's Open Unified Process (OpenUP).

Out of these three models, agile methodology is the most preferred process model for Cloud-based application development as it can facilitate quick discovery and assembly of resources and services available within the Cloud in order to build a software application and thus help in easy development and testing of software applications.

7.2.5 *Cloud Application Development and Testing Platforms*

A Platform is very important element for application development and deployment, which includes hardware architecture, and a software framework that facilitates developers to build, deploy, and manage custom applications. This feature applies to the traditionally licensed platforms and platforms that are provided as a service. Earlier vendors like IBM, Microsoft, and Oracle provided platform products through a traditional on-premise licensing model, but nowadays they are moving toward delivery of Platforms as a Service (PaaS). Vendors like Google and Salesforce.com provide computing resources as services.

Cloud-based application development and testing platforms provide highly reliable, scalable, and low-cost infrastructure platform by which users can build, deploy, test, and manage applications with great ease. Applications can be built using any language; tool or framework and public Cloud applications can be integrated with existing IT environment. There is also no need to maintain servers.

Cloud computing platforms not only provide its users with various innovative technologies but also offer lucrative businesses to its investors. Today, these platforms have successfully been able to build up, customize, and deploy applications befitting user's requirements exactly.

Cloud-based application testing platforms mainly facilitate unit testing and load/performance testing. During software development process, unit testing allows testing of small and reusable modules of code. Unit testing framework works as a test runner, runs user's test binary, track progress via a progress bar, and displays a list of test failures [Google Test].

Load testing is the process of putting demand on a system or device and measuring its response. It is performed to determine a system's functional behavior and performance under both normal and anticipated peak load conditions. Load testing frameworks build tests by simulating large number of virtual visitors, each with their own unique user name/login and task.

Currently there are many Cloud-based application development and testing platforms such as Google, Microsoft, Amazon, Rackspace, Right Scale, EngineYard Cloud, Terremark Worldwide, Enki, and XCalibre Flexi Scale [37–45].

In the next section, we discuss the current academic research in the area of Cloud-based testing and various testing techniques focused by the researchers.

7.3 Cloud-Based Testing Models: State of the Art

Cloud-based testing can be divided into seven categories based upon the type of research models [17]. Following testing techniques are currently being used for testing in Cloud environment. A comparative analysis of these techniques is presented in Table 7.2.

Virtualization-Aware Automated Testing Service (VATS): VATS is a framework that facilitates automated performance testing and configuration of services in Cloud

Table 7.2 Comparison chart of Cloud-based testing models

Techniques/parameters	SUT	Virtualization technology	Benefits
VATS	SAP/R3 System	Xen	Improved service performance
D-Cloud	Distributed/parallel	QEMU; Eucalyptus	Cost and time
Yeti	Java.lang,iText	Hadoop; Amazon EC2	Test execution speedup
AST	Communication Virtual Machine (CVM)	Microsoft Windows Server 2008; R2 operating system	Fault detection from the interaction between services
PreFail	HDFS	Cassandra; Zookeeper	Reduced testing time
NMS	Simulation of large-scale networks	Amazon EC2	Less expensive and more scalable implementation
FATE and DESTINI	HDFS	–	Build robust, recoverable systems
LSTS	Symbian S60	–	Easy to deploy; tester's task minimized
TSaaS	–	–	Elastic resource infrastructure; provides various kind of testing services to users
Bare-Bone	–	–	Conduct analysis on Cloud composition and detection of anomalies
Cloud9	UNIX utilities	Eucalyptus; Amazon EC2	On-demand software testing service; speedup

computing environments. It executes tests, manipulates virtualized infrastructure, and collects performance information. VATS complements a Service Lifecycle Management system named SLiM. SLiM is a model-driven service for managing the configuration, deployment, and runtime management of services operating in Clouds. VATS works with SLiM and supports the testing of other services that are compatible with SLiM. VATS uses HP LoadRunner as a load generator and provides the foundation for an automatic performance evaluator for Cloud environments.

York Extensible Testing Infrastructure (*YETI*): The York Extensible Testing Infrastructure (YETI) is Cloud enabled automated random testing tool with the ability to test programs written in different programming languages [8]. While YETI is one of the fastest random testing tools with over a million method calls per minute on fast code, testing large programs or slow code – such as libraries using intensively the memory – might benefit from parallel executions of testing sessions. It relies on the Hadoop package, and it does map/reduce implementation to distribute tasks over potentially many computers. Cloud version of YETI can be distributed over Amazon's Elastic Compute Cloud (EC2).

Model-Based Testing Using Symbolic Execution: Symbolic execution [46] is a fully automatic technique for generating test case to achieve high testing coverage. It is performed by executing programs with symbolic, rather than concrete inputs. The paths followed during symbolic execution form a symbolic execution tree, representing all the possible executions through the program. However, exploring all the possible program executions is generally infeasible, thus restricting the application of symbolic execution in practice. Scalability of symbolic execution can be addressed through parallelization as done in Cloud9 [14, 47, 48]. Cloud9, an automated testing platform that employs parallelization to scale symbolic execution by harnessing the resources of commodity clusters. Cloud9 helps cope with path explosion. It can automatically test real systems. Doing so without Cloud9 is hard, because single computers with enough CPU and memory to symbolically execute large systems either do not exist today or are prohibitively expensive. Besides single-threaded single node systems, Cloud9 also handles multi-threaded and distributed software, and it provides an easy-to-use API for writing "symbolic tests." Developers can specify concisely families of inputs and environment behaviors for which to test the target software, without having to understand how symbolic execution works.

D-Cloud: It is a software testing environment for dependable, parallel, and distributed systems using the Cloud computing technology, namely, D-Cloud. D-Cloud includes Eucalyptus as the Cloud management software and FaultVM based on QEMU as the virtualization software and D-Cloud front end for interpreting test scenario. D-Cloud enables not only to automate the system configuration and the test procedure but also to perform a number of test cases simultaneously and to emulate hardware faults flexibly.

Autonomic Self-Testing (AST): It is based on the concepts of autonomic computing to software testing of adaptive systems which is called as autonomic self-testing (AST). It deploys test managers throughout the software to validate dynamic adaptations and updates. AST is designed with flexible strategies for incorporating the approach into systems with different performance and availability requirements. It supports replication with validation strategy that can provide a highly transparent runtime testing process in distributed environments. AST is supplemented with TSaaS that allows testing to cross administrative boundaries in the Cloud [48].

Cloud-Based Performance Testing of Network Management Systems: It is a method for NMS performance testing, which is based on off-the-shelf "Infrastructure-as-a-Service" Cloud computing service. The method involves preparing and storing images of managed elements on the Cloud which can be run later in large numbers using the Cloud computing service in order to simulate large-scale networks for NMS testing purposes. It is used to test distributed system that consists of thousands of VoIP private branch exchange (PBX) networked through SIP. Emulation agents have been used instead of recorded HTTP(S) traffic, which have many advantages like writing application level test cases instead of low-level scripts, emulation of element-specific business logic, and flexibility in the communication protocols [49].

Model-Based Testing Using Bare-Bone Cloud: Bare-Bone Cloud is a directed graph of providers and consumers in which computing resource such as services or intellectual property access rights acts as an attribute of a graph node, and the use of a resource as a predicate on an edge of the graph. Author has proposed algorithms to compose Cloud computations and a family of model-based testing criteria to support the testing of Cloud applications [50].

Test-Support as a Service (*TSaaS*): TSaaS is a new model to provide testing capabilities to end users. Scheduling and dispatching algorithms are developed to improve the utilization of computing resources. Authors evaluate the scalability of the platform by increasing the test task load, analyze the distribution of computing time on test task scheduling and test task processing over the Cloud, and examine the performance of proposed algorithms [50].

Model-Based Testing Service Using Labeled State Transition Systems (*LSTSs*): It is a model-based GUI testing service for Symbian S60. The server encapsulates the domain-specific test models and the associated test generation heuristics. The testers, or test execution specialists, order tests from the server, and the test adapter clients connect to the phone targets under test. It is easy to deploy in industrial environments; in practice, the tasks of the tester are minimized to specifying the coverage requirement [51].

PreFail: It is a programmable failure injection tool that supports failure abstractions and executions profiles that helps testers to write policies to prune down large spaces of multiple-failure combinations. It facilitates the automatic sorting of failed experiments depending upon the bugs that caused them and parallelization of test workflow for further speedup. PreFail has been integrated to three Cloud software systems like HDFS, Cassandra, and Zookeeper [52].

FATE and DESTINI: It is testing framework which has been integrated to several Cloud systems like HDFS, for Cloud recovery which consists of different modules: Failure Testing Service and DESTINI (Declarative Testing Specifications). FATE facilitates systematic multiple-failure testing of recovery, whereas DESTINI specifies the way to recover from failures [18].

7.3.1 Limitations of the Existing Models

Various Cloud testing techniques have been proposed that mainly focus on automatic test case generation [8–10, 14, 47, 48, 53], runtime virtualization [8, 14, 48, 51, 53], checking interoperability of multiple application level services [48], etc., but still there is a need to increase the overall testability of Cloud applications and provision of metrics related to test set size and breakdown, item pass/fail results, and code coverage which may act as a measure of confidence in the hosted service.

Potential providers of Cloud have so far been focused on flexibility; cost-effectiveness [12]; easy obtain ability, on-demand access [12, 13, 54–57]; dynamicity, scalability, security [36]; and provision of testing service across multiple browsers in the Cloud [58]. However, quality checks for applications that have been tested on the Internet have not been addressed yet.

Pricing models and service description for online software testing services need to be well elaborated so that customers are well informed and able to estimate costs. In order to achieve transparent pricing models, different factors and metrics should be considered while calculating the value of a Cloud-based testing service. Therefore, transparent pricing models based on appropriate metrics and different factors should be designed [6, 10, 14, 48, 53].

Testing vendors and customers interested in testing in the Cloud would want to be aware of the characteristics of an application like test case dependency and the operating environment under test and the types of testing that can be performed on the application [6].

The transformation of Capital Expenditure Model (Cap-Ex) to Operating Expenditure Model (Op-Ex) has not been yet fully achieved. Therefore, there is a need to shift to a flexible Op-Ex to avail the benefits of Cloud computing like cost reduction, on-demand flexibility, freedom from holding assets, enhanced collaboration, greater levels of efficiency, and reduced time-to-market for key business applications [4, 11].

As we have observed that various researchers have worked on automation Cloud-based testing, so we will discuss the need and importance of automatic test case generation and various existing automated testing frameworks in the next section.

7.4 Automatic Test Case Generation

Software testing can be roughly divided into automated and manual testing. Automated software testing implies automation of software testing activities and tasks [59]. Increased automation of the testing process supports a more continuous approach to software quality. These activities include the development and execution of test scripts, the verification of testing requirements, and the use of automated test tools. Testing a software product forms a considerable expense, but so do the costs caused by faults in the software product. By automating at least some of test process phases and directing available resources toward additional testing can result in gains [60]. Most of the test cases in one project are executed at least five times, and one-fourth over 20 times [61]. For example, smoke tests, component tests, and integration tests are repeated constantly, so there is a dire need for automation development.

Test automation is a significant area of interest in current testing research, with the aim to improve the degree of automation, either by developing advanced techniques for generating test inputs or by finding support procedures to automate the testing process itself [62]. The main benefits of test automation are quality improvement, the possibility to execute more tests in less time and fluent reuse of testware. The major disadvantages are the costs associated with developing test automation especially in dynamic customized environments. Optimal case for automated software testing would be a standardized product with a stable, consistent platform and cases that yield unambiguous results which can be verified with minimal human intervention [59].

Nowadays, complexity of applications further increases due to adoption of technologies like Cloud or Big Data, which results in insufficient test coverage by the existing traditional automation strategies. Hence, there is a need to define an effective Test Automation strategy that focuses on maintenance of test scripts and the learning curve associated with it along with improved test coverage.

Following are some of most popular existing automation frameworks used in distributed environment:

JAT: It is a test automation framework for Multi-Agent Systems based upon aspect-oriented techniques and is implemented using the agent platform JADE. It has very high fault detection effectiveness [63].

HadoopUnit: It is distributed execution framework which is built upon Hadoop for JUnit test cases for creation and execution of JUnit test cases. It is very useful for data-intensive application testing and has shown reduction in the test execution time when tested experimentally [64].

STAF (*Software Testing Automation Framework*): It is multi-platform, multi-language approach based on the concept of reusable services that can be used to automate major activities in the testing process [65].

Test Automation in Agile Projects: It is an established fact that automated testing facilitates change and delivers working software in agile. Practices such as Test-Driven Design or Test-Driven Development as well as Continuous Integration are all complemented by the automated tests. Impetus believes that the need for automation is reflected in the agile principles. Organizations must incorporate the following key attributes into their automation strategy [66]:

- Testing across multiple levels to ensure optimum test coverage and save time and costs.
- Regular updating of storyboards to include acceptance tests before automation.
- Knowledge of appropriate automation tools to match up with changing requirements, which changes with time.
- Making of system in iterations, which helps customers, has more control over the system and measurement of automation scripts.
- Exchange of ideas, plans, or problems through sprint planning by the whole team to facilitate required automation at all the levels.
- Continuous Integration to ensure code links and compiles correctly.

7.5 Future Research Directions

Organizations use testing in the Cloud to overcome their limitations of testing infrastructure. They are then able to test traditional/on-premise resident applications over the Clouds. There is no distinct or ideal approach for Cloud testing. This is primarily due to the fact that when an organization uses Cloud testing, various factors like the Cloud architecture design, and non-functional and compliance requirements need to be taken into account to ensure successful and complete testing. Cloud infrastructure for setting up test environment can be very useful in the scenario where there is requirement of distributed servers and distributed load generators. Setting up actual test infrastructure in different geographic locations can be very difficult, time-consuming, and expensive, but in case of Cloud this would be very quick and less expensive. Also, number of load generators required for testing can be easily increased and decreased in case of Cloud, which otherwise becomes difficult in case of in-house test environment.

Cloud computing can provide online access to testing infrastructure with quality attributes like availability, reliability, security, performance, scalability, and elasticity. There is a need to migrate software testing to Cloud owing to reasons like paradigm shift in the provision and use of computing services, reduction in cost of software development, shorter development cycles, flexibility, on-demand basis, and access to global markets for both providers and customers. Furthermore, online software testing is required to support agile development methods by providing continuous testing services. Largely the companies are providing performance testing, functional testing, and unit testing as Cloud test services but, very few companies are providing security testing, recovery testing, and fault-tolerance testing. There has not been much progress by the academia also in the Cloud-based testing techniques especially in security testing, fault-tolerance, and recovery testing. There is also lack of standards in test tools and their connectivity and interoperability to support Test-Support as a Service (TSaaS).

Furthermore, pricing models and service description for online software testing services need to be well elaborated so that customers are well informed and able to estimate costs. Transparent pricing models based on appropriate metrics and different factors need to be designed. In future it can be concluded that though initial steps have been taken, but much more effort needs to be accomplished in order to facilitate Cloud-based software Test-Support as a Service.

References

1. Harrold, M.J.: Testing: a roadmap. In: Proceedings of the Conference on the Future of Software Engineering, ICSE'00, pp. 61–72. ACM, New York (2000)
2. IEEE Computer Society: IEEE Standard Glossary of Software Engineering Terminology. Technical Report. IEEE, New York (1990)
3. Ahamad, S.: Studying the feasibility and importance of software testing: an analysis. ETRI J. **1**(3), 119–128 (2009)
4. Cognizant: Taking Testing to the Cloud. Cognizant Whitepaper. http://www.cognizant.com/InsightsWhitepapers/Taking-Testing-to-the-Cloud.pdf (2012). Accessed May 2012
5. Software Testing in the Cloud (STITC). http://www.stitc.org/
6. Parveen, T., Tilley, S.: When to migrate software testing to the Cloud? In: Proceedings of the 2010 Third International Conference on Software Testing, Verification, and Validation Workshops, ICSTW'10, pp. 424–427. IEEE Computer Society, Washington, DC (2010)

7. Gaisbauer, S., Kirschnick, J., Edwards, N., Rolia, J.: VATS: Virtualized-Aware Automated Test Service. In: Quantitative Evaluation of Systems, 2008. QEST'08. Fifth International Conference,] pp. 93–102, IEEE St Malo, France, September 2008
8. Oriol, M., Ullah, F.: Yeti on the Cloud. In: 2010 Third International Conference on Software Testing, Verification, and Validation Workshops (ICSTW), pp. 434–437, IEEE Paris, France, April 2010
9. Candea, G., Bucur, S., Zamfir, C.: Automated software testing as a service. In: Proceedings of the 1st ACM Symposium on Cloud Computing, SoCC'10, pp. 155–160. ACM, New York (2010)
10. Ciortea, L., Zamfir, C., Bucur, S., Chipounov, V., Candea, G.: Cloud9: A software testing service. SIGOPS Oper. Syst. Rev. **43**, 5–10 (2010)
11. Fujitsu: Confidence in Cloud Grows, Paving Way for New Levels of Business Efficiency. Fujitsu Press Release, November 2010. http://www.fujitsu.com/uk/news/ (2010). Accessed May 2012
12. Sogeti: STaaS – Software Testing as a Service. Sogeti Cloud Testing Tool, September 2011 http://www.sogeti.com/looking-for-solutions/Services/Software-Control-Testing/STaaS-/ (2011). Accessed May 2012
13. IBM: CloudBurst: Cloud Testing Tool. http://www-304.ibm.com/. Accessed May 2012
14. Banzai, T., Koizumi, H., Kanbayashi, R., Imada, T., Hanawa, T., Sato, M.: D-Cloud: design of a software testing environment for reliable distributed systems using Cloud computing technology. In: Proceedings of the 2010 10th IEEE/ACM International Conference on Cluster, Cloud and Grid Computing, CCGRID'10, pp. 631–636. IEEE Computer Society, Washington, DC (2010)
15. Voas, J., Zhang, J.: Cloud computing: new wine or just a new bottle? IT Prof. **11**(2), 15–17 (2009)
16. Mell, P., Grance, T.: NIST Definition of Cloud Computing. National Institute of Standards and Technology, 7 October 2009. www.nist.gov/itl/cloud/upload/cloud-def-v15.pdf (2009)
17. Priyanka, C.I., Rana, A.: Empirical evaluation of cloud-based testing techniques: a systematic review. SIGSOFT Softw. Eng. Notes **37**(3), 1–9 (2012). doi:10.1145/180921.2180938 http://doi.acm.org/10.1145/180921.2180938
18. Gunawi, H.S., Do, T., Joshi, P., Alvaro, P., Yun, J., Hellerstein, J.M., Arpaci-Dusseau, A.C., Arpaci-Dusseau, R.H., Sen, K., Borthakur, D.: FATE and DESTINI: a framework for Cloud recovery testing. EECS Department, University of California, Berkeley, Tech. Rep. UCB/EECS-2010-127, Sept 2010. http://www.eecs.berkeley.edu/Pubs/TechRpts/2010/EECS-2010-127.html (2010)
19. Jin, H., Ibrahim, S., Qi, L., Cao, H., Wu, S., Shi, X.: Tools and technologies for building Clouds. In: Antonopoulos, N., Gillam, L. (eds.) Cloud Computing: Principles, Systems and Applications, pp. 3–20. Springer, London (2010)
20. AppLabs: Approach to Cloud Testing. Applabs Whitepaper. http://www.applabs.com/html/. Accessed May 2012
21. Ghag, S.: Software Validations of Application Deployed on Windows Azure. Infosys Whitepaper. www.infosys.com/cloud/. Accessed May 2012
22. Siegele, L.: Let it rise: a special report on corporate IT. The Economist. www.economist.com/node/12411882 (2008)
23. Washington Post Case Study: Amazon Web Services. http://aws.amazon.com/solutions/case-studies/washington-post/
24. Dean, J., Ghemawat, S.: Map reduce: Simplified data processing on large clusters. In: OSDI'04: Proceedings of the 6th Conference on Symposium on Operating Systems Design & Implementation, pp. 10–10. USENIX, Berkeley (2004)
25. Bialecki, A., Cafarella, M., Cutting, D., O'Malley, O.: Hadoop: a framework for running applications on large clusters built of commodity hardware. http://lucene.apache.org/hadoop (2005)
26. RUBiS: Rice University Bidding System. http://rubis.ow2.org/index.html. Accessed May 2012
27. MediaWiki: http://www.mediawiki.org. Accessed May 2012
28. Li, A., Zong, X., Zhang, M., Kandula, S., Yang, X.: CloudProphet: towards application performance prediction in Cloud. ACM SIGCOMM Comput. Commun. Rev. SIGCOMM '11 **41**(4), 426–427 (2011)

29. Montage: http://montage.ipac.caltech.edu
30. Taylor, I., Deelman, E., Gannon, D., Shields, M. (eds.): Workflows in e-Science. Springer, London (2006)
31. Stevens, R.D., Robinson, A.J., Goble, C.A.: MyGrid: personalised bioinformatics on the information grid. In: Bioinformatics (11th International Conference on Intelligent Systems for Molecular Biology) **19**, i302–i304 (2003)
32. Oinn, T., Li, P., Kell, D.B., Goble, C., Goderis, A., Greenwood, M., Hull, D., Stevens, R., Turi, D., Zhao, J.: Taverna MyGrid: aligning a workflow system with the life sciences community. In: Taylor, I., Deelman, E., Gannon, D., Shields, M. (eds.) Workflows in e-Science. Springer, New York (2006)
33. Deelman, E., Callaghan, S., Field, E., Francoeur, H., Graves, R., Gupta, N., Gupta, V., Jordan, T.H., Kesselman, C., Maechling, P., Mehringer, J., Mehta, G., Okaya, D., Vahi, K., Zhao, L.: Managing large-scale workflow execution from resource provisioning to provenance tracking: the CyberShake example. In: E-SCIENCE '06: Proceedings of the 2nd IEEE International Conference on e-Science and Grid Computing, p. 14, IEEE Washington, DC (2006)
34. Brown, D.A., Brady, P.R., Dietz, A., Cao, J., Johnson, B.A., McNabb, J.: A case study on the use of workflow technologies for scientific analysis: gravitational wave data analysis. In: Taylor, I., Deelman, E., Gannon, D., Shields, M. (eds.) Workflows for e-Science. Springer, New York (2006)
35. Piccoli, L.: Lattice QCD workflows: a case study. In SWBES08: Challenging Issues in Workflow Applications, Indianapolis, IN (2008)
36. Sun Microsystems: Introduction to Cloud Computing Architecture. Sun Microsystems Whitepaper. eresearch.wiki.otago.ac.nz/images/7/75/Cloudcomputing.pdf. Accessed May 2012.
37. Google AppEngine. http://developers.google.com/AppEngine. Accessed May 2012
38. Amazon Web Services: aws.amazon.com/. Accessed May 2012
39. Microsoft Azure: www.windowsazure.com. Accessed May 2012
40. Enki: http://www.enki.co/. Accessed May 2012
41. XCalibre FlexiScale: www.flexiscale.com. Accessed May 2012
42. RackSpace: www.rackspace.com. Accessed May 2012
43. RightScale: www.rightscale.com/. Accessed May 2012
44. Terremark Worldwide: www.terremark.com. Accessed May 2012
45. Engine Yard Cloud: www.engineyard.com. Accessed May 2012
46. King, J.C.: Symbolic execution and program testing. ACM Commun. **19**, 385–394 (1976)
47. Bucur, S., Ureche, V., Zamfir, C., Candea, G.: Parallel symbolic execution for automated real-world software testing. In: Proceedings of the Sixth Conference on Computer systems, EuroSys'11, pp. 183–198. ACM, New York (2011)
48. King, T.M., Ganti, A.S.: Migrating autonomic self-testing to the Cloud. In: Proceedings of the 2010 Third International Conference on Software Testing, Verification, and Validation Workshops, ICSTW'10, pp. 438–443. IEEE Computer Society, Washington, DC (2010)
49. Ganon, Z., Zilbershtein, I.E.: Cloud-based performance testing of network management systems. In: Computer Aided Modeling and Design of Communication Links and Networks, 2009. CAMAD'09, IEEE 14th International Workshop, pp. 1–6. IEEE Germany (2009)
50. Yu, L., Tsai, W., Chen, X., Liu, L., Zhao, Y., Tang, L., Zhao, W.: Testing as a service over Cloud. In: 2010 Fifth IEEE International Symposium on Service Oriented System Engineering, pp. 181–188. IEEE Nanjing, China (2010)
51. Jaaskelainen, A., Katara, M., Kervinen, A., Heiskanen, H., Maunumaa, M., Tuula, P.: Model-based testing service on the web. In: Suzuki, K., Higashino, T., Ulrich, A., Hasegawa, T. (eds.) Testing of Software and Communicating Systems. Lecture Notes in Computer Science. Springer, Berlin/Heidelberg (2008)
52. Joshi, P., Gunawi, H.S., Sen, K.: PreFail: a programmable tool for multiple-failure injection. In: Proceedings of the 2011 ACM International Conference on Object Oriented Programming Systems Languages and Applications, pp. 171–188. ACM Portland (2011)

53. Das, D., Vaidya, K.: Taking Testing to the Cloud. CSC Whitepaper. http://assets1.csc.com/lef/downloads/CSC_Papers_2011_Agile_Process_Framework.pdf. Accessed May 2012
54. Zephyr: Zephyr Cloud Testing Tool, September 2011. http://Zephyr.com/ (2011). Accessed May 2012
55. Skytap: SkyTap Cloud Testing Tool. http://skytap.com/. Accessed May 2012
56. uTest: uTest Cloud Testing Tool. http://utest.com/. Accessed May 2012
57. VMLogix: VMLogix Lab Manager Cloud Testing Tool. http://vmlogix.com/. Accessed May 2012
58. SauceLabs: On Demand Cloud Testing tool. http://saucelabs.com/. Accessed May 2012
59. Taipale, O., Kasurinen, J., Karhu, K., Smolander, K.: Trade-off between automated and manual software testing. Int. J. Syst. Assur. Eng. Manag. **2**(2), 1–12 (2011)
60. Ramler, R., Wolfmaier, K.: Economic perspectives in test automation: balancing automated and manual testing with opportunity cost. In: Proceedings of the 2006 International Workshop on Automation of Software Test, AST'06, pp. 85–91. ACM, New York (2006)
61. Berner, S., Weber, R., Keller, R.K.: Observations and lessons learned from automated testing. In: Proceedings of the 27th International Conference on Software Engineering, ICSE'05, pp. 571–579. ACM St. Louis, MO, USA (2005)
62. Bertolino, A.: Software testing research: achievements, challenges, dreams. In: 2007 Future of Software Engineering, FOSE'07, pp. 85–103. IEEE Computer Society, Washington, DC (2007)
63. Coelho, R., Cirilo, E., Kulesza, U., Von Staa, A., Rashid, A.: JAT: a test automation framework for multi-agent systems. In: 2007 I.E. International Conference on Software Maintenance, vol. 34, pp. 425–434 (2007)
64. Parveen, T., Tilley, S., Daley, N., Morales, P.: Towards a distributed execution framework for JUnit test cases. Software Maintenance, 2009. ICSM 2009. IEEE International Conference, pp. 425, 428, 20–26 September 2009
65. Rankin, C.: The software testing automation framework. IBM Syst. J. **41**(1), 126–139 (2002)
66. Impetus: Using Test Automation to Address Agile Testing Challenges, Impetus Whitepaper. www.impetus.com/Home/Downloads. Accessed May 2012

Chapter 8
Testing in the Cloud: Strategies, Risks and Benefits

Olumide Akerele, Muthu Ramachandran, and Mark Dixon

Abstract Testing in the cloud, commonly referred to as cloud testing, has revolutionised the approach adopted in traditional software testing. In the literal terms, it refers to testing Web applications in the "cloud" – leveraging a service provider's ready-made testing resources. The customer boycotts the hassle and expense of procurement, setup and maintenance of test environment setup on premise. Previously, accustomed solely with non-functional testing such as performance and load testing, recent advancements have made it possible to write test scripts and modify and automate test suites – all in the cloud environment. This chapter provides an in-depth overview of contemporary cloud testing, the types and its best practices. The benefits and risks are fully discussed with recommended methods to abate these risks. A methodological approach to govern an organisation migrating to cloud testing is also presented. A unique model, which shows the complex and dynamic interrelationship among active factors and their effect on the major project success factors in a cloud testing environment, is designed and presented. These project success factors include productivity, quality and cost. This model will help management to make strategic decisions on the adoption of cloud testing and the impact of their policy adoption on the productivity, quality and cost of software development projects.

Keywords Cloud computing • Cloud testing • Testing-as-a-Service • Agile software development

O. Akerele (✉) • M. Ramachandran • M. Dixon
School of Computing and Creative Technologies, Faculty of Arts, Environment and Technology, Leeds Metropolitan University, Headingley Campus, Caedmon Hall, LS6 3QS Leeds, UK
e-mail: o.akerele@leedsmet.ac.uk; m.ramachandran@leedsmet.ac.uk; M.Dixon@leedsmet.ac.uk

Z. Mahmood and S. Saeed (eds.), *Software Engineering Frameworks for the Cloud Computing Paradigm*, Computer Communications and Networks,
DOI 10.1007/978-1-4471-5031-2_8,

8.1 Introduction

Cloud computing has been a coveted buzzword in the computing industry and has been trending since the year 2005. Cloud computing is the technology behind the provision of software applications, data storage, computation and data access by service providers to their customers (businesses or individuals) – leveraging the Internet as the deployment medium [1] making the traditional infrastructure acquisitions necessary for on-premise computing operations unwarranted. The cloud service provider is typically located remotely, and the customer is charged proportionally to the amount of service or infrastructure usage.

Software development has been suggested to be improved by the introduction of cloud computing [2]. Apparently, every individual development phase and activity in the software projects can now be executed in the cloud; this includes coding, testing, deployment and maintenance of software projects. An area of viable potential research is the impact of the evolved synergy achieved from the adoption of cloud testing on a software development process methodology, particularly agile-based processes such as the Test-Driven Development (TDD).

Testing in the cloud, mostly referred to as cloud testing in this chapter, is the practice of carrying out the "testing" phase of the software development process in the cloud, hence preventing the need for the vast capital expenditure on acquiring infrastructure, licences and setup on customer site. The most popular applicability of cloud testing has been in carrying out performance and load testing where there is the vital need to generate multi-user traffic from various locations – which would ideally need numerous high-configuration servers for the traffic simulation. For example, a project needing to carry out load testing by hitting the test server with 30,000 users simultaneously will require a sizeable amount of infrastructure – with direct implicit soaring costs of test environment setup.

The ease and agility of the testing environment setup, reduced cost and maximum efficiency of the leveraged testing environment in cloud testing makes it an alluring option for both big- and small-sized software development teams. This chapter provides an overview of cloud testing and its various modes of deployment – with special emphasis on cloud testing in the context of non-functional Web applications testing in the cloud. Section 8.2 presents an overview of cloud testing, classes of cloud testing and the benefits, risks and a proposed best practice model for testing software applications in the cloud. Section 8.3 discusses the various ways in which cloud testing boosts the "agility" of a software development team. Section 8.4 describes a unique cloud testing causal loop model which summarises the activities, benefits and risks of adopting cloud testing.

In this chapter, the terms "software development organisation", "customer", "user" and "development team" are all used interchangeably. They all apply to the purchaser and adopter of the cloud testing service. Likewise, the terms "service provider" and "cloud vendor" are used in the same context, and both refer to the provider of the cloud test platform and services. In most parts of this chapter, cloud testing infers to performance, stress and load tests carried out in the cloud. However, it is implicitly specified at instances when it is used in the context of performing functional tests in the cloud.

8.2 Cloud Testing

Cloud testing is the carrying out of traditional testing practices using test resources situated in the cloud – made possible by the technology of virtualisation. This encompasses carrying out tests on both enterprise and Web applications in the cloud environment. Cloud testing can be classified under the three modes of cloud computing depending on the test activity requirements.

8.2.1 Types of Cloud Testing

Broadly, cloud computing is categorised under Infrastructure-as-a-Service (IaaS), Platform-as-a-Service (PaaS) and Software-as-a-Service (SaaS) [2]. The author has further classified cloud testing under these three categories of cloud computing as Cloud Testing Infrastructure-as-a-Service (CTIaaS), Cloud Testing Platform-as-a-Service (CTPaaS) and Cloud Testing Software-as-a-Service (CTSaaS). Figure 8.1 shows the types of cloud testing which are proposed and examples of the service providers and are defined and described as follows:

8.2.1.1 Cloud Testing Infrastructure-as-a-Service (CTIaaS)

This category provides organisations secured access to storage, hardware, networking components (including load balancers) and servers over the Internet for testing and development purposes. The infrastructure is the property of the service provider and is usually housed, run and maintained by the same. Customers pay for the amount of infrastructure needed for testing purposes, and this is maintained solely for the customer use by the service provider. All major testing activities are done on the customer site. Organisations have a high level of control over their instances and this category is deemed the most secured albeit it is the most capital intensive. The ease and low cost of racking up and tearing down the server makes it a very attractive option for organisations who are concerned about their data security. Customers are priced on a pay-as-you-go basis with the prices varying linearly with the number of "instances" of the server (Windows or Unix) and the software environment

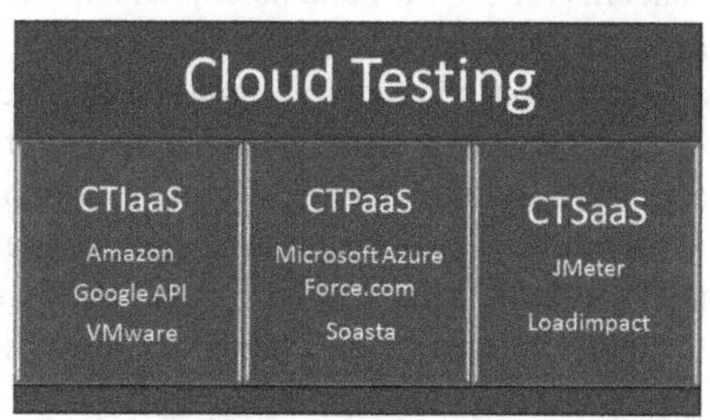

Fig. 8.1 Classifications of cloud testing

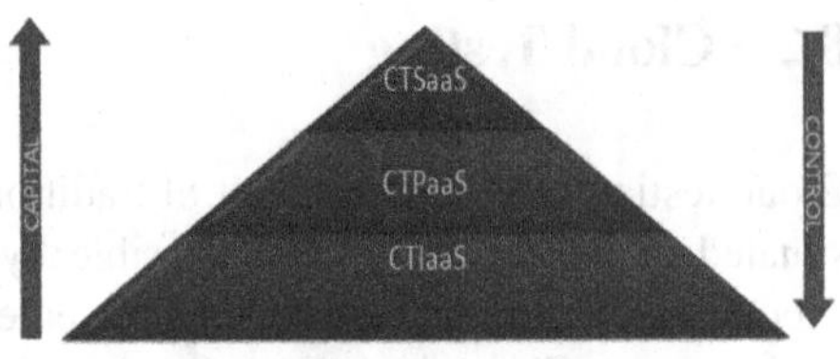

Fig. 8.2 Cloud testing stack

installed on them. The network traffic on the server as well as the volume of the data hosted on the server also influences the pricing. Typical examples of such service providers are VMware and Amazon. Figure 8.2 presents an overview of the three major modes of deploying cloud testing and their relative cost and control proportional relationships. The figure indicates CTIaaS is the most flexible category which provides organisations full control of their resources while CTSaaS is the least capital intensive as organisations do not require infrastructure or resource of their own for testing purposes.

8.2.1.2 Cloud Testing Platform-as-a-Service (CTPaaS)

CTPaaS provides a platform to development teams for functional testing purposes. This enables development teams leverage Cloud Integrated Development Environments (IDEs) with inbuilt unit frameworks to perform various functional tests and edit test scripts for test automation. CTPaaS vendors provide a subtle platform for operational facilities ranging from application development, testing and deployment environment. In other words, CTPaaS could be regarded as a platform for cloud-computing system development.

CTPaaS obliterates the need for the substantial capital that would otherwise be needed to set up a testing/development environment by helping to deliver the specific platform configurations through the Web browser interface. Hence, without any hardware or software investment, the platform of the service provider can be fully leveraged for software testing purpose. For instance, if development and testing requirements of a new application are Asp.net and SQL server database, an organisation would ideally need the following: VS.Net developer's licence, SQL server licences and deployment on a production server. The cost implication and configuration time of setup can all be done away with now! Also eliminated are the concerns for the staff and personnel expertise necessary to acquire and maintain the necessary infrastructure. CTPaaS enables users to select the testing requirement configurations via the Web browser interface presented by the service provider.

In some cases, such tests have to be written in the service provider's Domain-Specific Language (DSL). A typical example of this platform is the force.com with its proprietary programming language Apex Code. The major disadvantage of this is "Vendor Lock-In" [3] – which is literally the power the service provider possesses to lock customers into the service provision due to the customer's high cost of

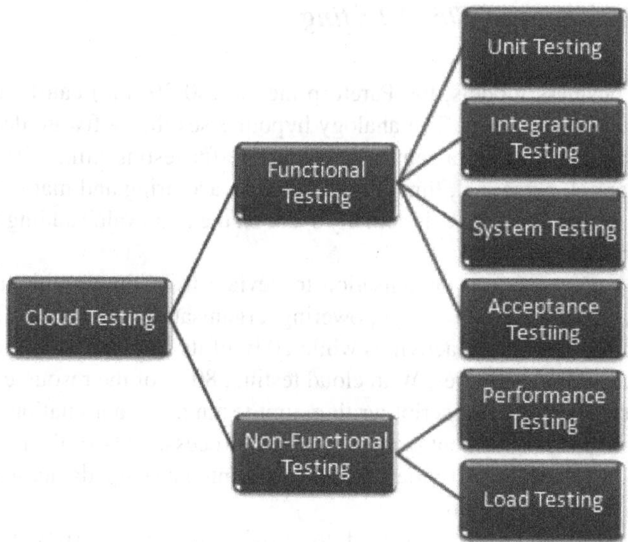

Fig. 8.3 Types of testing in the cloud

migrating to another provider or platform. The high costs of rewriting all the tests scripts in another programming language and the cost of training new personnel on a new platform make it an expensive option for customers to source other service providers.

8.2.1.3 Cloud Testing Software-as-a-Service (CTSaaS)

This is the most popular and adopted category of cloud testing and often illusively understood as the only application of cloud testing [4, 5]. Non-functional tests, particularly load and performance tests, are run on browsers offered by the service providers. Users enjoy the privilege of choosing the operating systems, browser types and versions, number of simultaneous Web traffic users as well as the various geographical locations of the mimicked generated traffic. This category allows Web application testing in the cloud by running the tests using real-life generated data traffic as input. The generated traffic is applied over the same communication channels as a Web browser, i.e. HTTP and HTTPS over ports 80 and 443, respectively. Examples of such platform are Loadimpact and JMeter. Figure 8.3 below broadly categorises the types of testing that are done in the cloud into functional and non-functional tests.

Cloud testing is used to apply solely to load and performance tests; recent advancements have seen it applied in numerous forms for functional testing such as unit tests, integration tests, system tests and user acceptance tests.

8.2.2 Economics of Cloud Testing

As in other business models, the Pareto principle (80-20 rule) can be effectively applied to software projects. The analogy hypothesises that software development teams running their own data centre infrastructure for testing utilise 80 % of their resources (capital, personnel, time, floor space) on acquiring and maintaining their own infrastructure, while 20 % is actually spent on the main value adding test activities of the project.

Cloud testing enables an organisation to deviate from this traditional "80-20" ratio described to a "20-80" – empowering organisations to swap 80 % of its resources on the actual core activities while 20 % of its resources are now spent on the non-value adding activities. With cloud testing, 80 % of the resources are spent on crucial activities like test script writing, unit testing, test automation and developing continuous improvement strategies for test process; 20 % of the resources are spent on less value adding activities like test environment setup, database configurations and browser installations.

Cloud testing has been suggested to provide up to 50–70 % testing cost savings – when appropriately adopted and integrated into software development organisations [4]. A significant amount of savings is made on infrastructure, licence purchase, storage mediums, multiple operating systems and experienced QA team. This also includes savings in labour for designing as well as building hardware and software platforms.

Fixed costs from the high investment on servers, network equipment and licence purchases are converted to variable costs as customers are charged on a "pay-as-you-go" basis. The evolved variable cost varies proportionally to the amount of the service provider's leveraged resource usage by the customer. Flat monthly/yearly fees charged to customers by service providers are no more the case, and customers hence do not pay for underutilised resources.

The reduction or eradication of the total cost of ownership is the most obvious attraction to cloud testing. The capital intensity of acquiring the infrastructure and platform for testing is avoided – making software development a more hospitable industry for start-ups and SMEs. The unused capital can then be diverted to fund more value adding and prioritised needs.

8.2.3 Benefits of Cloud Testing

The advantages of cloud testing to software development organisations and teams are systematically divided in three sections. The financial benefits to the organisation were discussed in Sect. 8.2.2. The third section is discussed later in this chapter in Sect. 8.3. The general impact of cloud testing is now discussed.

8.2.3.1 Improved Quality

Cloud testing reduces defects in web applications as compared to traditional on-premise testing [6]. There are two main factors responsible for this: the closeness of the simulation environment to the actual production environment making it easy to capture any bugs that will be encountered in real case scenario. Secondly, being the cloud vendor's area of expertise and core activity, they are more aware of the recent challenges faced, particularly security-wise, and are therefore able to put these into consideration during development and maintenance of their platforms.

8.2.3.2 Improved Accuracy

The cloud testing platform explored provides an environment with little or no variation from the actual production environment. Consequently, there is notable improvement in the predictability and accuracy of testing. There is also a higher degree of accuracy in the test. This makes the software quality more controllable, and this is a huge step for companies trying to adopt Six Sigma and achieve CMM levels 4 and 5 accreditation [3].

8.2.3.3 Waste Reduction

Another valuable benefit of cloud testing is that the organisation is charged on a pay-as-you-go basis by the cloud vendor. The scalability of the "rented" platform makes it possible for the organisation's price to vary linearly with the amount and time of cloud platform usage. This helps to reduce waste that occurs when infrastructure is redundant and helps the organisation to go "lean". This invention reduces the much valued time and effort spent by QA in creating the appropriate development and testing environment, hence greatly improving the Time-to-Market (TTM) of the developed software.

8.2.3.4 Improved Return-on-Investment (ROI)

Return-on-Investment will take a considerable leap when cloud testing is adopted appropriately. On-site QA team can now focus on improving quality and testing features instead of spending time acquiring, setting up and configuring infrastructure. They can now devote their time on process improvement activities. There is immense improvement in reliability of the tested application. The defect density and maintenance cost of the software would also subside consequently – improving the reliability of the software system. Substantial savings are made on maintenance costs on finding and fixing bugs on released software. The risk of losing customers and competitive advantage due to complaints and damaged reputation is also reduced. Improvement in product quality improves customer satisfaction, retention and advocacy. Non-conformance cost is also reduced due to reduced resource to deal with customer complaints. As reported by a leading bank in 2009, their software projects adopted cloud testing and made overwhelming cost savings with a predicted ROI of 474 % over the following 3 years [7].

8.2.3.5 Green Testing

There is the ever-increasing need for industries to be environmentally responsible by going "green" and the IT industry is no exception. Cloud testing organisations enhance green testing. By sharing test resources in the cloud, businesses use IT resources solely on demand and this eliminate wastes by eradicating infrastructure idleness. In addition, organisations using cloud data centres can minimise energy use and deliver environmental savings in CO_2 by up to 80 % [8].

8.2.3.6 Easy Barrier to Exit

In the event the software development organisation decides to stop operation due to financial or strategic reasons, it is easier for the organisation to opt out as there is not much resources "locked-in", if at all any. This is unlike the difficulty to exit operations faced by an organisation that has made a lot on investment in acquiring these infrastructures, storage and operating systems to carry out its testing activities on site.

8.2.4 Best Practices for Migrating to Cloud Testing

Migrating to cloud testing has to be a systematic process otherwise it could turn out to be a fiasco. A shrewd and meticulous approach has to be adopted to avoid failure and reap the maximum benefits of cloud testing. The recommended sequential activities during the migration process are represented in Fig. 8.4.

Figure 8.4 depicts the diagrammatic flow of the best practices before migrating to cloud testing. They are explained below.

8.2.4.1 Cost-Benefit Analysis

This is the most crucial and fundamental process in the roadway to leveraging cloud test platform. It involves the preliminary feasibility study and an in-depth breakdown of the benefits and the cost associated with its adoption in the organisation. This is usually handled by a cloud broker who will be conducting full auditing of

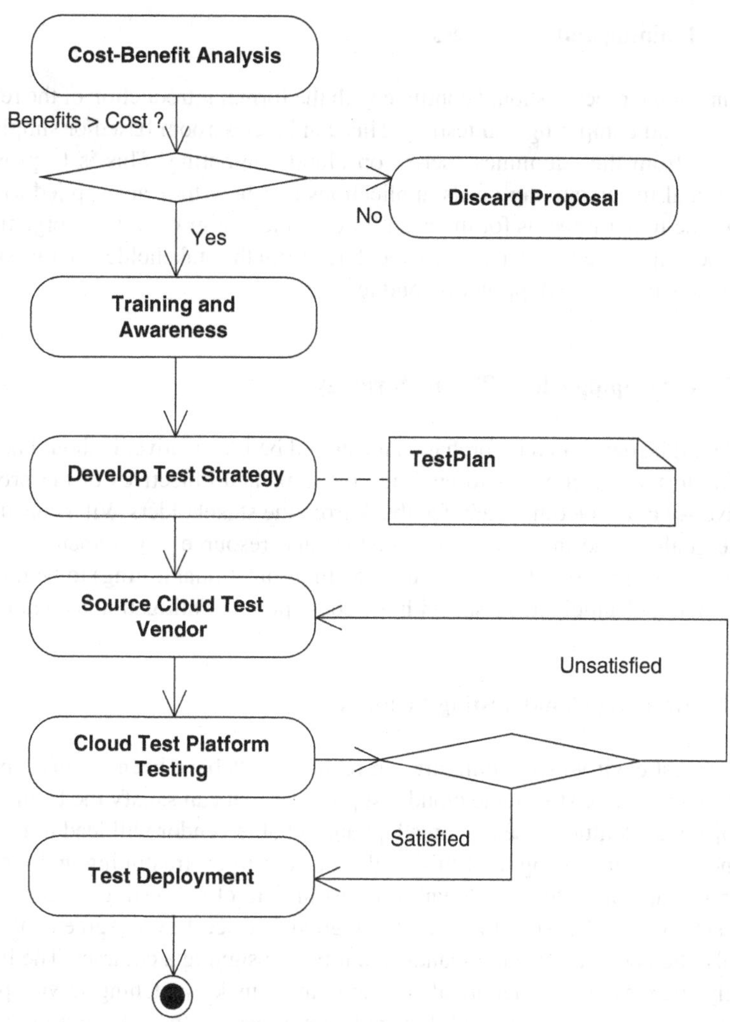

Fig. 8.4 Cloud testing migration model

the entire testing infrastructure requirements of the organisation. Ideally, a 2-year ROI analysis should be enough to give an insight into its viability. Some organisations however require a minimum of 5-year ROI projection. It is a common illusion that cloud-computing testing is generally cheaper. Ongoing intrinsic costs associated with cloud testing include the cost to support privacy regulation policy, cost to build auditing processes in the system and recovery service cost [8]. Before such conclusion could be reached, all the related cost associated should be considered holistically. It is easy for organisations to fall for "Management-by-Magazine" approach particularly with new computing innovations and cloud testing is one of them.

8.2.4.2 Training and Awareness

The transitional process should continue with the formal introduction of the relevant teams to cloud computing and testing. This can be classroom based or simply provide texts from the "dummies" series on cloud computing. This is to provide a foundational understanding on its applications and how they are applied to cloud testing. The major impetus for the need for cloud test migration in the organisation should be emphasised, and necessary feedback from the stakeholders at this stage is vital to the successful adoption of cloud testing.

8.2.4.3 Developing Cloud Testing Strategy

This should be developed beforehand and should be informative. It should be made available to the stakeholders to envisage the aims and objectives of the proposed initiative – while welcoming any feedback from the stakeholders. Vital constituents include goals of the initiative, infrastructure and resource requirements, types of tests (load testing, stress testing, security testing, functional testing) to be migrated to the cloud and anticipated risks with the corresponding mitigation techniques.

8.2.4.4 Sourcing Cloud Testing Vendors

After the test environment configuration requirements have been elicited, the next step is to find the most suitable cloud test provider that can satisfy the team's goals and objectives. Failure to secure an adept and reliable vendor will lead to inconsistent and erroneous testing, and this could turn out to be frustrating and regretful. The "ramp-up" and "tearing down" time to initiate cloud testing should also be considered when choosing the vendor. A good Service Level Agreement (SLA) must also be negotiated by the management before signing a contract. The barriers to easily change the provider are also paramount to make switching service providers easy and must be considered. Figure 8.5 summarises the selection process for the right cloud test vendor.

8.2.4.5 Cloud Test Platform Testing

Equally important is the testing of the cloud test environment to ensure the cloud vendor can perform to meet with the development team's goals. Adequate testing also helps to alleviate possible risks that may occur during testing. Vigorous testing performed should be aimed at determining the cloud environment's level of security, scalability, reliability and performance. These tests should be fully run before an agreement is signed with the cloud provider and before executing any tests. Other aims of testing the platform should focus on data governance, manageability, availability, latency, connectivity, regulatory compliance, uptime and privacy. There are

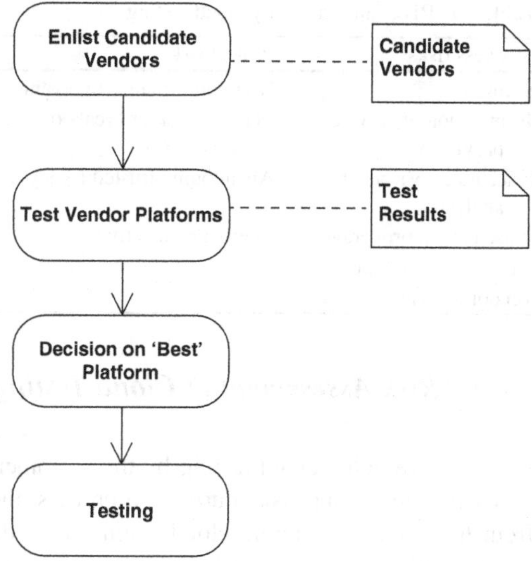

Fig. 8.5 Platform sourcing process

third-party tools such as Cloudstone and Cloud Harmony that can be utilised in testing the performance of the cloud test environment.

8.2.4.6 Test Execution

It is imperative that the test environment is configured correctly before test execution. Thirty percent of all defects are reported to be caused by wrong test environment configurations [5]. Following the success of the previous steps, test activities can now be securely carried out on the vendor's platform. A good practice is to start the initiation process with the more experienced testers who can quickly grasp the dissimilarities between cloud testing and the traditional on-premise testing – and use this to mentor the less experienced ones on the best practices in the new environment.

Following the successful migration of the testing activities to the cloud, activity monitoring, analysis and reporting must be continuously ensured. The performance of cloud testing must be evaluated constantly by the development organisation – particularly during real-time simulations. Productivity of cloud testing might be lower initially considering the learning process of getting used to the new test environment but will improve significantly with time if this approach is followed diligently. A major factor is the learning curve of the testers in learning the DSL of the service provider's platform (if any). Metrics such as defect density, test coverage and the likes should also be closely monitored – while being alert at any eyebrow-raising variability in the system performance. The SLA should be closely monitored to ensure the vendor is keeping to their part of the agreement. It is a good practice to hold regular meetings with the cloud test vendor to highlight any areas of concerns, risks or issues that might arise during the course.

Table 8.1 Risks introduced by cloud testing

Business risks	Project risks
Security	Non-conformance to organisational policy, strategy and methodology
Termination of service provision	Vendor's server breakdown/availability
Inaccurate cost-benefit analysis	Abandoning trusted legacy testing resources
Biased cloud brokerage	Internet connectivity
Industrial espionage	
Vendor lock-in	

8.2.5 Risk Assessment in Cloud Testing

Risks in leveraging cloud testing by the customer are bidirectional: while the customer transfers some risks during the process, they are also prone to certain risks from the vendor. Adopting cloud testing must therefore be meticulously planned with proactive measures to reduce the occurrence of the highlighted uncertainties [9].

For the purpose of clarity, these risks are classified into business risks and project risks. Business risks in this context are those that have a direct impact on the profitability and reputation of the organisation, while the project risks have a direct impact on the success of the software engineering project. Table 8.1 outlines the risks the customer is prone to when adopting cloud testing:

The risk items tabulated above are further explained in the following section.

8.2.5.1 Non-conformance to Organisational Policy, Strategy and Methodology

The testing processes of the service provider might not be following the principles governing the customer's organisation. Service providers usually have separate regulations governing their operations and infrastructure management. This might be difficult to verify even when specified in the SLA due to the limitation of the customer's involvement in cloud vendor's activities. This is unlike the on-premise sites where there is a governance system to ensure compliance. This can be mitigated by emphasising on compliance on the contract agreement and strictly outlining the organisations' specific policies.

8.2.5.2 Security

The major disgruntlement and concern in cloud testing revolves around security – especially when the user's sensitive data will be stored in the production environment sat in the cloud. The utilisation of a second party's platform creates an atmosphere for paranoia because organisations usually cede control of the platform and data to the vendor. This is exacerbated when part of the cloud services is federated to a third party by the cloud vendor. A couple of infamous let-downs by cloud vendors that epitomise the above security concerns are:

- Amazon's "glitch" in April 2011 which was responsible for numerous Web sites' malfunction.
- Sony of Japan revealed that about 100 million of PlayStation customer accounts had been hacked.

This risk is abated by adoption of security testing tools and vigorous hacking techniques. A disaster recovery test also helps to have an insight into the reliability and dependability of the testing service provider. These tests should be ongoing and should also precede the test execution process as discussed earlier.

8.2.5.3 Industrial Espionage

This is also a major concern particularly when the testing activities are completely outsourced to a cloud test service provider. The cloud vendor's personnel could be easily "tapped" for information about the development organisation's product and be offered a reward for such unscrupulous act. For example, the cloud vendor's staff could trade in significant features of a product yet to be released to the rival organisations. The rival company could then strategically match or even better the feature and incorporate this into their similar product. This puts the development organisation in severe risk of losing their competitive advantage in such scenario. To reduce this risk, consequences of information divulgence must be reasonably severe, explicitly communicated and stated in a non-disclosure agreement offered to cloud vendor personnel.

8.2.5.4 Termination of Service Provision

In the event the service provider terminates service provision due to financial or strategic reasons, the user could potentially be in trouble if adequate provision and flexibility for adopting a "plan B" is not in place. Strategic decisions could be due to merger and diversification or simply the company's decision to concentrate on more profitable business activities. Service providers reserve the arbitrary right to terminate customer's account without notice due to policy violations; this however happens in exceptional cases. This risk can be reduced by checking the vendor's history to ensure it has been sustainable and fairly successful in operations for a reasonable length of time – to give some assurance on its reliability in the industry. Also, the signed contract should indicate a fair notice period for termination of contract by either party.

8.2.5.5 Inaccurate Cost-Benefit Analysis

Risk of unanticipated soar in operation cost associated with cloud testing is also a possibility when the cost-benefit analysis is not done correctly with all latent costs unravelled. This could make the decision of adopting cloud testing a regrettable one should the costs outweigh the benefits on the long run. These costs should include, if applicable, cost of writing or modifying the entire test cases should the cloud test platform require applications tested in its own discrete language. The opportunity cost of such activities should also be considered. The analysis and comprehensive cost projection should be cross-checked by a second cloud expert – who could be an insider so as to reduce cost.

8.2.5.6 Biased Cloud Brokerage

Cloud brokers act as intermediaries between cloud vendors and individuals or businesses purchasing there service. They help the potential users to understand their needs and source the possible best cloud service providers in return for an agreed premium. This involves the end-to-end audit of the entire incumbent testing process of the customer and the network infrastructure and usually putting up the cost-benefit analysis as well as the expected ROI necessary to make the business case for cloud testing. This consultancy service is usually costly but it is a vital process and must be done regardless if it is done in-house or outsourced. The challenge is actually in getting an unbiased broker because most cloud brokers usually have some sort of affiliation with specific cloud vendors and they are rewarded for their referrals. Hence, there is the tendency for brokers to always recommend adopting cloud testing as the best solution to customers even when that is not the case. Also, cloud brokers advocate the "best" cloud vendors to their customers, and these vendors are usually the ones they have affiliation with, not necessarily the best service providers to meet the customer's needs. Getting acceptable references from the broker's customers is a way of reducing this risk. Also, ensuring that the final decision of the choice of the vendor is in the user's hands helps to reduce getting "sold" to a cloud vendor.

8.2.5.7 Abandoning Trusted Legacy Testing Resources

Discarding the old testing infrastructure and resources poses a huge risk to an untested technology in an organisation. Though the on-premise testing requirements are quite expensive to maintain, replacing them with untested technology could be disruptive, more expensive and potentially risky. Retraining of staff on the new cloud vendor's system and also learning the service provider's DSL (if any) take a lot of time, and an initial reduced productivity should be expected. This risk can be controlled by avoiding the big bang approach to cloud test migration. Selecting a vendor that utilises the user's familiar application language is also very important and helpful.

8.2.5.8 Vendor Lock-In

Many cloud platform vendors, like force.com using Apex Code [10], offer services on their platform in their Domain-Specific Language (DSL) – making it difficult to move applications to another CTPaaS. Due to the high switching costs (time, effort and other resources as well as cost already spent on personnel learning the proprietary language) in migrating to a new platform, customers are tied down to the vendor. This gives the vendor the power to increase the subscription rates at any time, and this would have an adverse effect on the ROI. Google, another example of vendor that provides app engine CTPaaS in its proprietary language, recently announced a shocking increase of 100 % in their pricing which caused an intense backlash from users. The best way of eliminating this risk is avoiding lock-ins by all means. Choosing programming languages that are easier and faster to modify can also reduce the impact of this risk.

8.2.5.9 Cloud Vendor's Server Breakdown

The breakdown of the testing platform server entirely paralyses the testing activities of the customer. This affects not only the testing activities but all other activities dependent on the testing phase. Hence, the server needs to be up and running as well as being available at all times to prevent this period of no activity. Running availability tests before choosing the vendor can help reduce this risk.

8.2.5.10 Internet Connectivity

The success of the testing activity is fully reliant on the provision of fast, reliable, dependable and robust Internet connection. Necessary network infrastructure to provide this is a prerequisite to venturing into cloud testing with a service provider. This is because should the Internet connection fail, testing activities cannot be run on the vendor's platform and this could result in substantial loss as there will not be connection to the host server.

8.3 Impact of Cloud Testing on Software Development Agility

Agile software development values quick feedback to customers, collocation and easy collaboration between team members and customers. This reduces idleness by capitalising on the "just-in-time" approach of the development activities and flexibility to user requirements at any stage in the development process. Cloud testing ticks the fore-mentioned features to enhance the "agility" of a software development process and is therefore considered a good match – particularly to distributed agile teams. The relative impact of cloud testing on agile development projects is detailed below:

8.3.1 Reduced Time-to-Market (TTM)

Feedback is vital in agile processes. Cloud testing significantly reduces the test cycle times of software projects and consequently the deployment cycle. Cloud testing not only has a major impact on the TTM, it also improves the flexibility of the system to accommodate changes and requirement creep [5]. The type of agile methodology adopted also has an impact on the impact of cloud testing on the deployment cycle. For example, when TDD is adopted, concise and just enough code needed to design and test a function is written. With this, even more time is saved in coding and testing by avoiding extraneous coding and this will positively impact the TTM for the software.

8.3.2 Support for Geographically Dispersed Teams

Cloud testing eradicates the problem of proximity in dispersed development teams. It bridges the geographical distance between global teams – enabling easy interchange and handover of feature development among teams as if they were collocated. Teams can now collaborate globally with a self-defined user interface. The omnipresent accessibility of the cloud test platform via a common URL makes it possible for distributed teams to perform testing without geographical barriers and makes handing over easier.

8.3.3 Visibility and Accessibility

Teams can now collaborate in real time; this overcomes the problem of delay in hours or even a day in sending and receiving data between offshore and onshore colleagues. Every testing activity can be revealed and made visible in real time and accessed from anywhere via a custom URL for the organisation.

8.3.4 Support for Automated Testing

There is an increasing demand for automation in software development due to its significant time savings on the development cycle [5]. Automation is now being applied in development, testing and even software deployment. Cloud testing fully supports agility in testing by creating a welcoming platform for writing and importing automated scripts for functional testing. Cloud test platforms usually have plug-ins that allow the recording of the test activities to be analysed after test completion. Valuable time can now be spent investigating new possible bugs instead of exhausting time on running repeated tests manually. Cloud testing also provides an environment to concurrently run tests with different configurations on the same machine. This produces financial savings due to customers being charged on time consumed for testing.

8.3.5 *Requirement Volatility Support*

Cloud testing encourages frequent changes to requirements as it provides testing accessibility anywhere and testing the modified system is made possible anywhere. The effect (estimated finish date) of the frequent changes in the requirements and requirement creep is offset by the reduced test cycle achieved by cloud testing. Also, the scalability of the system makes it possible to test each iteration feature as each iteration feature might require the ramping up and scaling down of the system requirements.

8.3.6 *Bug Reproduction*

Another vital importance of cloud testing is the quick ability to reproduce bugs for further analysis. This has been a major issue in traditional testing. There is a constant need to regenerate bugs that were detected in an environment for further investigation. During simulation, snapshots at the point of software failure could be taken to show the entire configurations when bugs are found – enabling testers to quickly revert to the configuration needed to reproduce the bugs and they can start debugging in no time.

8.3.7 *Support for Test-Driven Development*

Cloud testing creates synergy by being fully supportive of agile development techniques such as the TDD. Automatic unit tests are written to fail, pass and refactor – all in the cloud. This yields great time savings and fosters quick customer feedback while guaranteeing improvement in software quality.

8.3.8 *Parallel Testing*

Agility is improved by allowing tests to be run in various scenarios concurrently without having to test consecutively on the same physical machines. It also facilitates testing various components simultaneously. This increases throughput and coverage while reducing test cost. It enables the tester to create different configurations such as the operating system database and storage to meet the actual production environment specification.

8.4 Cloud Testing Model

The cloud testing model described in this section diagrammatically summarises the entire cloud testing system – giving an instant high-level view of the processes, advantages, risks and consequences of actions within a cloud testing environment. All the components within the cloud test platform are modelled as interrelated factors in feedback loops. This model succinctly describes the variables, influencing factors and the dynamic influence of cloud testing activities in a software organisation. It shows the interrelationships and continuous nature of the actions performed in cloud testing and the resulting positive and negative impacts in the cycle.

The model provides a high-level general overview of cloud testing to management for decision-making purposes regarding adoption of cloud testing in the software organisation. The model can be used to trace the root causes of irregularities as well as improvements achieved when leveraging cloud testing platform. It provides an instant insight into the risks the potential users become susceptible to when testing applications in the cloud and also presents the opportunities. A significant portion of this model can also be applied to cloud computing in general. The positive and negative polarities indicate constructive and degenerative impact on the variables respectively. A number of assumptions have been made in constructing this causality model:

- Testing is fully automated.
- All other activities before development and after testing are performed on premise.
- Iteration-based development approach is adopted.
- The cloud vendor uses a DSL.

This dynamic model is presented in Fig. 8.6. The positive and negative polarities in the designed model indicate constructive and degenerative impacts on the directional variables respectively.

For brevity, a brief explanation of the major variables in this causal model diagram is explained below. The factors referenced in the model are italicised.

8.4.1 Productivity

The *Corporate IT Governance* in an organisation should encourage the provision of up-to-date training on cloud testing, thus improving the *organisation cloud awareness*. This earns the *stakeholder support* as well as better *understanding cloud*

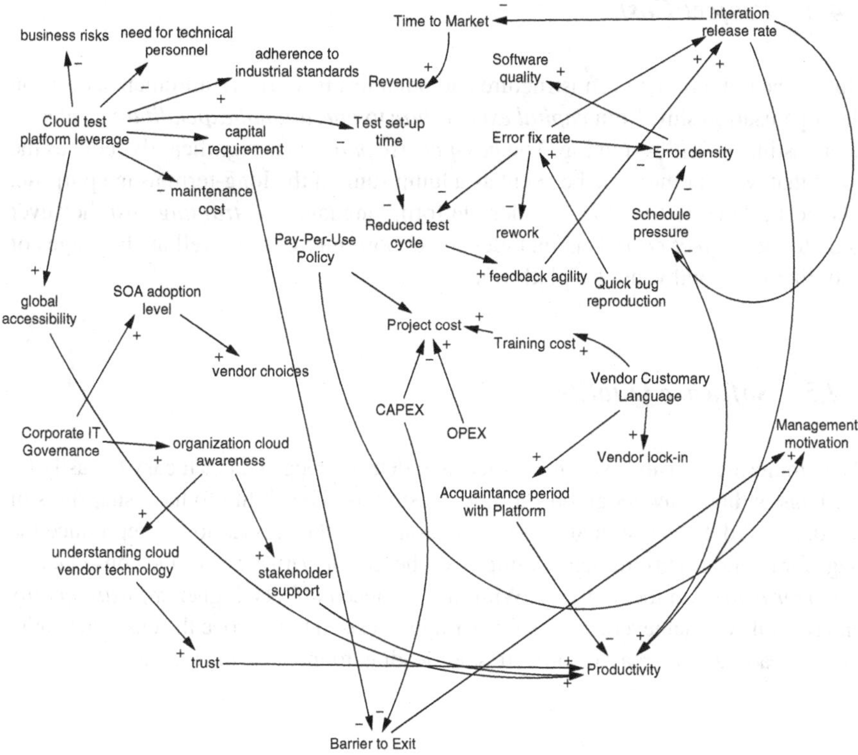

Fig. 8.6 The cloud testing model in software development

vendor technology for its potential adoption. *Stakeholder support* greatly favours *productivity* due to the motivation given by the stakeholders. *Trust* is built in the software development organisation when the cloud vendor technology is fully understood and supported which is extremely vital to maximise productivity in software testing.

The *global accessibility* of the cloud test platform also helps to keep the work going at anytime from anywhere to boost *productivity*. The short test cycles enhance agility and make the entire development cycle reduced, and teams can meet their deadlines better while attaining better productivity. This reduces the schedule pressure and undue tension in teams hence improving productivity.

The only degenerative factor into this variable is *Acquaintance Period of New Platform*. This is the time it takes to get used to the new interface as well as the *vendor customary language* (*DSL*) of the cloud test provider. The time spent to learn the customary language reduces the time that could actually be spent performing testing, hence reducing team productivity.

8.4.2 Project Cost

Due to the reduction on infrastructure and other test resource requirements, costs on the organisation shift from *capital expenditure* to *operational expenditure* needed to keep testing activities running. The *pay-per-use policy* also significantly reduces the costs that would otherwise be spent as a lump sum on the long-term usage purpose. The cost related to the cloud vendor platform language, i.e. *training cost*, however adds to the *project cost*. This includes the opportunity cost as well as the wages of adopting the cloud vendor's platform.

8.4.3 Software Quality

The omnipresent visibility of the project and detected bugs makes it easy to easily fix the bugs without any geographical time constraints. The ability to have snapshots of the detected defects also makes it easy to configure the application to reproduce the bugs for fixation. This immensely improves the *rate of error fixation* and consequently the *error density* in the software. With these reduced effects, higher *software quality* and reliability is achieved. This is further hypothesised to improve the customer satisfaction leading to increased software sales leading to increase in revenue.

8.5 Conclusion

Cloud testing is relatively new in the industry but gradually growing popularity particularly in the application of performance and load testing. In a number of ways, cloud testing enhances the "agility" of the testing process in terms of the reduced development cycle, improved quality and faster ROI. Cloud testing, when integrated well into software projects, accounts for vast savings due to the avoidance of total cost of ownership (TCO) and also helps to reduce TTM. This invention is however not a silver bullet and has a tangible number of risks, particularly security-wise, when companies have to put vital information in the cloud to create a production environment for testing.

There are steps that need to be ensued to determine its profitability, relevance and alignment with an organisation's goals. A unique model has been presented in this chapter which includes all the variables in a cloud test environment – including the risk factors, benefits and causal effects of decisions taken in an organisation adopting cloud testing. Cloud testing is steadily making its mark and software teams are now realising the benefits of testing their software applications in the cloud. Based on the present trend of the pervasiveness of cloud testing, it is expected that cloud testing will have a monumental indelible impact on software testing and development over the next few years.

References

1. Barry, C.: 70+ ways to reduce costs, increase productivity and improve customer service. http://www.fcbco.com/Portals/163466/docs/FCBCO-Cost-Reduction (2008). Accessed 4 May 2012
2. Bykov, S., Geller, A., Kliot, G., Larus, J.R., Pandya, R., Thelin, J.: Orleans: cloud computing for everyone. In: Proceedings of the 2nd ACM Symposium on Cloud Computing, SOCC'11, pp. 16:1–16:14. ACM, New York (2011)
3. Salkever, A.: 5 ways to protect against vendor lock-in in the cloud. http://gigaom.com/2011/09/24/5-ways-to-protect-against-vendor-lock-in-in-the- cloud/ (2011). Accessed 23 Feb 2012
4. Linthicum, D.S.: Cloud Computing and SOA Convergence in Your Enterprise. Addison-Wesley Professional, New York (2009)
5. Jun, W., Meng, F.: Software testing based on cloud computing. In: 2011 International Conference on Internet Computing Information Services (ICICIS), pp. 176–178. IEEE, Los Alamitos (2011)
6. Weidong, F., Yong, X.: Cloud testing: the next generation test technology. In: 10th International Conference on Electronic Measurement Instruments (ICEMI), pp. 291–295. IEEE, Piscataway (2011)
7. David, J.S., Schuff, D., St Louis, R.: Managing your total IT cost of ownership. Commun. ACM **45**(1), 101–106 (2002)
8. Ebbers, M.: Cloud Computing: Save Time, Money and Resources with a Private Test. IBM Redbooks. Raleigh, North Carolina, USA (2009)
9. Kantarcioglu, M., Bensoussan, A., Hoe, S.: Impact of security risks on cloud computing adoption. In: 49th Annual Allerton Conference on Communication, Control, and Computing (Allerton), pp. 670–674. IEEE, Piscataway (2011)
10. Mountjoy, J.: An introduction to Force.com Apex Code. http://wiki.developerforce.com/page/An_Introduction_to_Apex_Code_Test_Methods (2012). Accessed 2 Mar 2012

Part III
Software Design Strategies for Cloud Adoption

Chapter 9
Feature-Driven Design of SaaS Architectures

Bedir Tekinerdogan and Karahan Öztürk

Abstract An important service delivery category of cloud computing is the Software-as-a-Service (SaaS) domain in which software applications are made available through the cloud environment. In general, when describing SaaS, no specific application architecture is prescribed but rather the general components and structure is defined. However, it appears that SaaS architectures vary widely according to the application category and the number of tenants. To define a proper SaaS architecture, it is important to have both a proper understanding of the domain and the architecture design. In this chapter, we provide a domain-driven design approach for designing SaaS architectures. We provide a family feature model of the SaaS domain that models both the common and variant parts of SaaS architectures. For deriving the application architecture based on selected features from the family feature model, we also provide a systematic approach and the corresponding tool support. Our approach and the framework tool aim to support the SaaS architect in generating a proper SaaS architecture.

Keywords Software-as-a-Service • SaaS • Feature modeling • Reference architecture • Application architecture • Design decisions • Tool support

9.1 Introduction

Different from traditional enterprise applications that rely on the infrastructure and services provided and controlled within an enterprise, cloud computing is based on services that are hosted by providers over the Internet. Hereby, services are fully

B. Tekinerdogan (✉)
Department of Computer Engineering, Bilkent University,
Ankara 06800, Turkey
e-mail: bedir@cs.bilkent.edu.tr

K. Öztürk
British Sky Broadcasting, London, UK

Z. Mahmood and S. Saeed (eds.), *Software Engineering Frameworks for the Cloud Computing Paradigm*, Computer Communications and Networks,
DOI 10.1007/978-1-4471-5031-2_9, © Springer-Verlag London 2013

managed by the provider, whereas consumers can acquire the required amount of services on demand, use applications without installation, and access their personal files through any computer with Internet access. Recently, a growing interest in cloud computing can be observed, thanks to the significant developments in virtualization and distributed computing, as well as improved access to high-speed Internet and the need for economical optimization of resources.

The services that are hosted by cloud computing approach can be broadly divided into three categories: Infrastructure-as-a-Service (IaaS), Platform-as-a-Service (PaaS), and Software-as-a-Service (SaaS). Research on cloud computing has focused on different issues. Obviously, an appropriate cloud computing architecture design will play a fundamental role in supporting the cloud computing goals. In the literature, the basic components required for cloud computing and its conceptual reference architecture are given. However, designing a cloud architecture is not a trivial task and involves many different design decisions. For a given reference architecture, one may derive various different application design alternatives , and each design alternatives, may meet different functional and nonfunctional requirements. It is important to know the feasible architecture design so that a viable realization can be selected.

To enhance the understanding of cloud computing applications and support the architect in designing cloud computing architectures, we propose defining a feature-driven design approach for deriving the cloud computing architecture. Since the domain of cloud computing is quite broad, we focus on the domain of SaaS architectures. Feature modeling is an approach in the domain analysis process whereby the common and variant properties of a domain or product are elicited and modeled. In addition, the feature model identifies the constraints on the legal combinations of features, and, as such, a feature model defines the feasible models in the domain. To design a SaaS application architecture, we first propose the feature model for SaaS domain that includes the common and variant features. The feature model has been derived after an extensive literature study to SaaS architectures. Together with the feature model of SaaS, we define a reference architecture for SaaS applications that represents the common components and their interactions with various cloud computing platforms. Using the reference architecture, we propose an approach for (1) modeling the design space of SaaS architectures (2) and guiding the selection of these design alternatives based on the particular requirements. We explain the derivation of the architecture using the developed toolset.

The remainder of the chapter is organized as follows. In Sect. 9.2, we describe the notion of domain analysis and feature modeling. In Sect. 9.3, we present the reference architecture for SaaS based on the literature. Based on the reference architecture, in Sect. 9.4, we present the feature model for SaaS that defines the common and variant features. In Sect. 9.5, we present the tool support for deriving and generating SaaS application architecture based on the feature model and the reference architecture. In Sect. 9.6, we present the related work. Sect. 9.7 concludes the chapter.

9.2 Feature Modeling

Domain analysis can be defined as the process of identifying, capturing, and organizing domain knowledge about the problem domain with the purpose of making it reusable when creating new systems [1–4]. The UML glossary provides the following definition of the term domain: *Domain* is an area of knowledge or activity characterized by a set of concepts and terminology understood by practitioners in that area.

A survey of domain analysis methods shows that these methods include the similar kind of activities. Domain analysis is an important activity in software architecture design methods [5]. Figure 9.1 represents the common structure of domain analysis methods as it has been derived from survey studies on domain analysis methods [1, 3, 6].

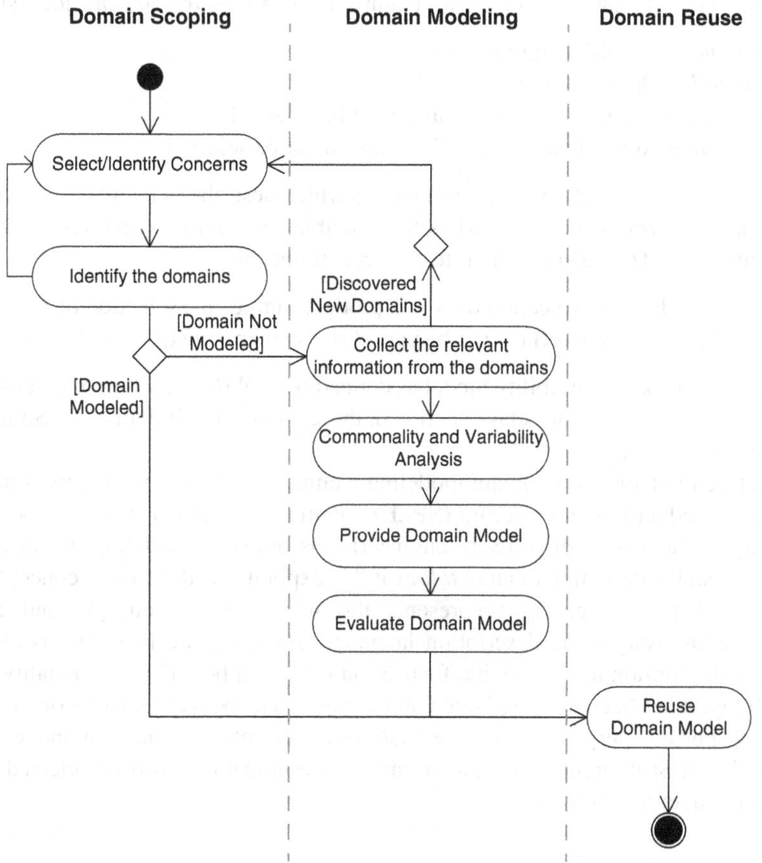

Fig. 9.1 Common structure of domain analysis methods

Conventional domain analysis methods consist generally of the activities known as *domain scoping* and *domain modeling*. *Domain scoping* identifies the domains of interest, the stakeholders, and their goals and defines the scope of the domain. *Domain modeling* is the activity for representing the domain, or the *domain model*. The domain model can be represented in different forms such as object-oriented language, algebraic specifications, rules, and conceptual models. Typically, a domain model is formed through a commonality and variability analysis to concepts in the domain. A *domain model* is used as a basis for engineering components intended for use in multiple applications within the domain.

One of the popular approaches for domain modeling is *feature modeling*. A feature is a system property that is relevant to some stakeholder and is used to capture commonalities or discriminate between. A *feature model* is a model that defines features and their dependencies. Feature models are usually represented in feature diagram (or tables). A *feature diagram* is a tree with the root representing a concept (e.g., a software system), and its descendent nodes are features. Relationships between a parent feature and its child features (or sub-features) are categorized as:

- *Mandatory* – Child feature is required.
- *Optional* – Child feature is optional.
- Or – At least one of the sub-features must be selected.
- *Alternative* (xor) – One of the sub-features must be selected.

A *feature configuration* is a set of features which describes a member of an SPL. A *feature constraint* further restricts the possible selections of features to define configurations. The most common feature constraints are:

- A requires B – The selection of A in a product implies the selection of B.
- A excludes B – A and B cannot be part of the same product.

Besides the basic variability model as defined by FODA [3], different extensions have been proposed. A nice classification of these approaches is defined by Sinnema and Deelstra [7, 8].

Feature modeling is a domain modeling technique, which is widely used in the software product line engineering (SPLE) community. Another domain modeling technique that is used in software engineering is ontology modeling [9]. A commonly accepted definition of an *ontology* is "an explicit specification of conceptualization" [10]. An ontology represents the semantics of concepts and their relationships using some description language. Basic feature modeling is also a concept description technique that focuses on modeling both the commonality and variability. It has been indicated that feature models can be seen as views on ontologies [9]. For our purposes, since we wish to model both the common and variant properties of SaaS architectures, adopting feature modeling has been selected as a feasible modeling approach.

9.3 Reference Architecture for Cloud Computing

Based on the literature we have studied [11–14], the reference architecture for SaaS is given in Fig. 9.2. Besides the theoretical papers, we have also looked at documentation of reference architectures as defined by SaaS vendors such as Intel [14], Sun [15], and Oracle [16].

In principle, SaaS has a multi-tier architecture with multiple thin clients. In Fig. 9.2 the multiplicity of the client nodes is shown through the asterisk symbol (*). In SaaS systems the thin clients rent and access the software functionality from providers on the Internet. As such the cloud client includes only one layer, User Layer, which usually includes a web browser and/or the functionality to access the web services of the providers. This includes data integration and presentation. The SaaS providers usually include the following layers: Distribution Layer, Presentation Layer, Business Service Layer, Application Service Layer, Data Access Layer, Data Storage Layer, and Supporting Service Layer.

Distribution Layer defines the functionality for load balancing and routing. *Presentation Layer* represents the formatted data to the users and adapts the user interactions. The *Application and Business Service Layer* represents services such as identity management, application integration services, and communication

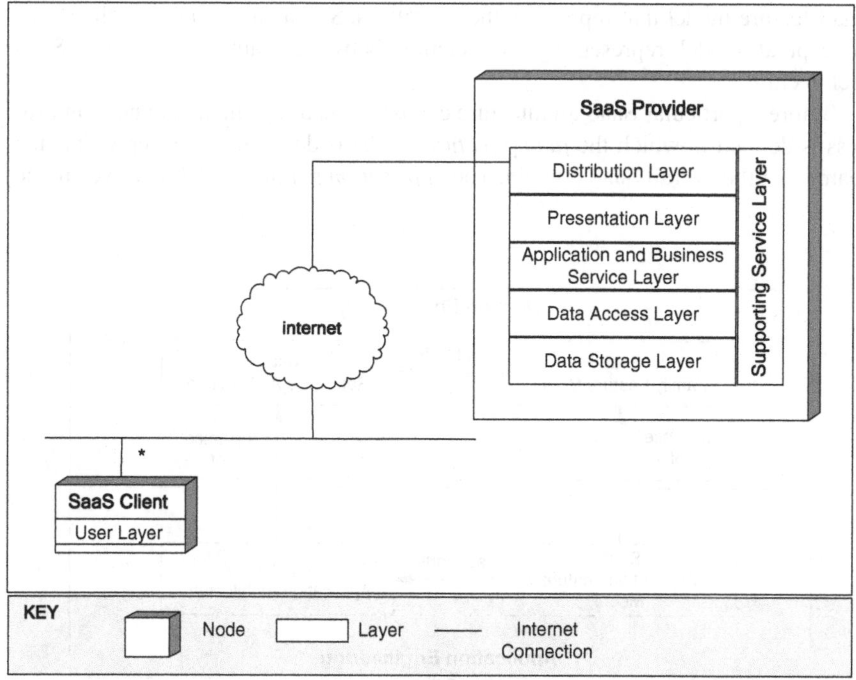

Fig. 9.2 SaaS reference architecture

services. *Data Access Layer* represents the functionality for accessing the database through a database management system. *Data Storage Layer* includes the databases. Finally, the *Supporting Service Layer* includes functionality that supports the horizontal layers and may include functionality such as monitoring, billing, additional security services, and fault management. Each of these layers can be further decomposed into sub-layers.

Although Fig. 9.2 describes the common layers for SaaS reference architecture, it deliberately does not commit on specific *application architecture*. For example, the number of clients, the allocation of the layers to different nodes, and the allocation of the data storage to nodes are not defined in the reference architecture. Yet, while designing SaaS for a particular context, we need to commit on several issues and make explicit design decisions that define the application architecture. Naturally, every application context has its own requirements, and likewise these requirements will shape the SaaS application architecture in different ways. That is, based on the SaaS reference architecture, we might derive multiple application architectures.

9.4 Feature Model of SaaS

To support the architect in designing an appropriate SaaS application architecture, a proper understanding of the SaaS domain is necessary. In this section we define the SaaS feature model that represents the overall SaaS domain. Figure 9.3 shows the conceptual model representing the relation between feature model and SaaS architecture.

Before a particular SaaS architecture can be defined, a domain engineering process is defined in which the *family feature model* is defined, which represents the features of the overall SaaS domain. The *application feature model* is derived in the

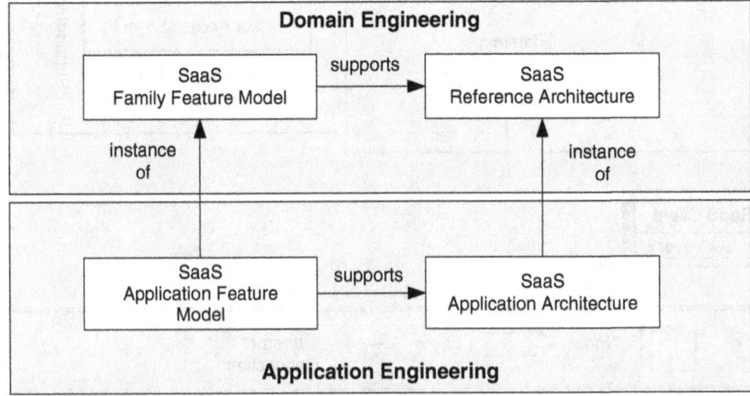

Fig. 9.3 Conceptual model representing relation between feature model and SaaS architecture

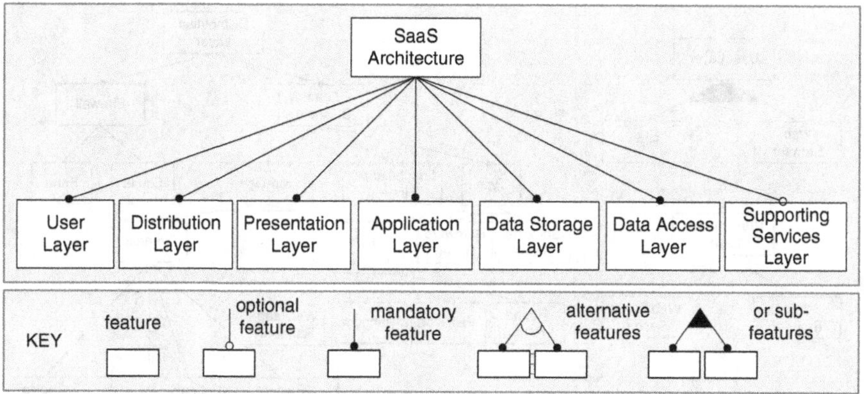

Fig. 9.4 Top-level family feature model for SaaS

application engineering process and represents the features for a particular SaaS project from the family feature model. The features in the feature model typically refer to the architectural elements in the SaaS architecture. As discussed in the previous section, we also distinguish between *SaaS reference architecture* and *SaaS application architecture*. For designing the SaaS application architecture, first the required features need to be selected from the family feature model resulting in the application feature model. The application feature model will be used to support the design of the SaaS application architecture. In the following sections, we elaborate on the family feature model.

9.4.1 Top-Level Feature Model

The top-level feature diagram of SaaS that we have derived is shown in Fig. 9.4. The key part represents the different types of features including *optional*, *mandatory*, *alternative*, and *or features* [17]. Note that the features in Fig. 9.4 denote the layers in the SaaS reference architecture as defined in Fig. 9.2. All the layers except the Support Layer have been denoted as mandatory features. The Support Layer is defined as optional since it might not always be provided in all SaaS applications. Each of these layers (features) can be further decomposed into sub-layers. The feature diagram for each of the layer is shown in Fig. 9.5. We explain each layer in the following subsections.

9.4.1.1 User Layer

User Layer is the layer that renders the output to the end user and interacts with the user to gather input. In principle, the User Layer might include a *web browser* or

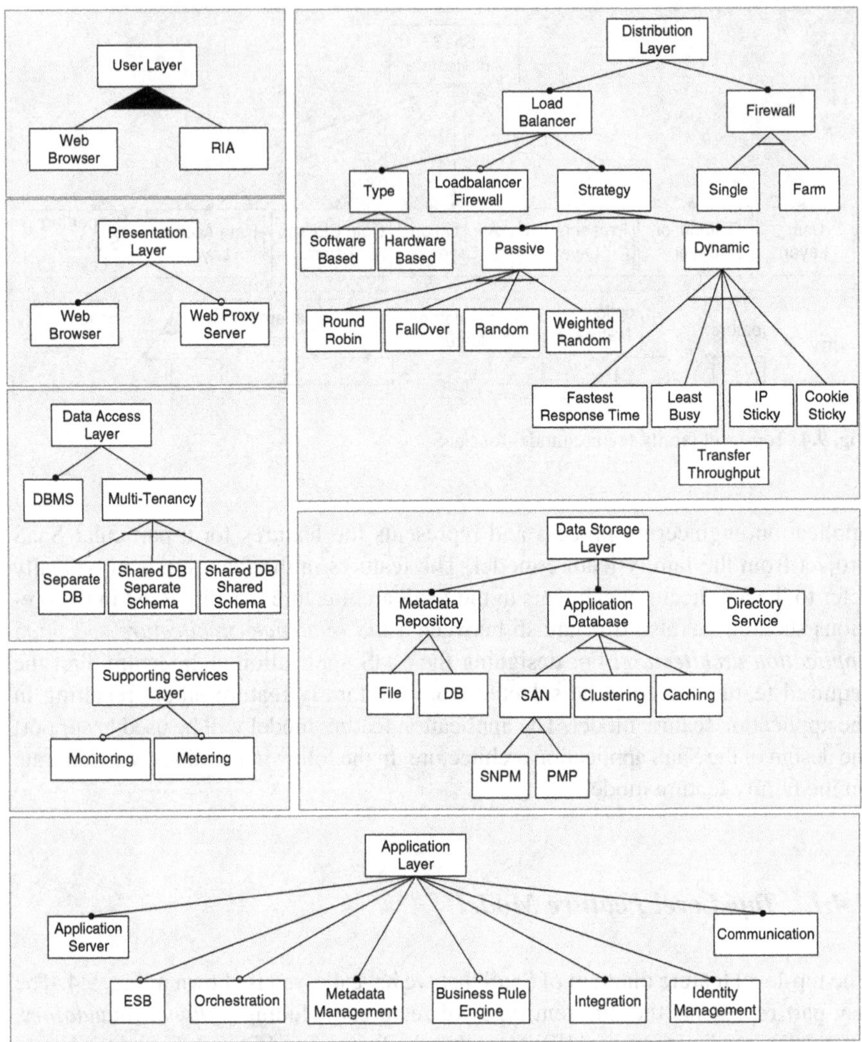

Fig. 9.5 Feature diagram for layers

Rich Internet Application (RIA) or both of these (or features). RIA is especially used on mobile platforms.

9.4.1.2 Distribution Layer

This layer is the intermediate layer between the Internet and the SaaS application. The main concerns of the layer are scalability, availability, and security. The mandatory features of this layer are load balancers and firewalls [18].

A firewall inspects the traffic and allows/denies packets. In addition to this, firewalls provide more features like intrusion detecting, virtual private network (VPN), and even virus checking. The Distribution Layer can have a single firewall or a firewall farm. A firewall farm is a group of connected firewalls that can control and balance the network traffic.

Load balancers divide the amount of workload across two or more computers to optimize resource utilization and increase response time. Load balancers are also capable of detecting the failure of servers and firewalls and repartitioning the traffic. Load balancers have the mandatory features of *Type* and *Strategy* and an optional feature *Load Balancer.Firewall.* There are two types of load balancers, *hardware based* and *software based.* Load-balancing strategies decide how to distribute requests to target devices. *Passive* load-balancing strategies use already defined strategies regardless of the run time conditions of the environment. Some of the most used passive strategies are *Round-Robin, Failover, Random,* and *Weighted Random. Dynamic* load-balancing strategies are aware of information of the targets and likewise route the requests based on traffic patterns. Some of the most used passive strategies are *Fastest Response Time, Least Busy, Transfer Throughput, IP Sticky*, and *Cookie Sticky.*

The optional *Load Balancer.Firewall* can be used as firewall by providing both packet filtering and stateful inspection. Using load balancer as a firewall can be an effective solution for security according to network traffic and cost requirements. This feature excludes the *Distribution Layer.Firewall* feature.

9.4.1.3 Presentation Layer

The Presentation Layer consists of components that serve to present data to the end user. This layer provides processes that adapt the display and interaction for the client access. It communicates with application layer and is used to present data to the user.

The Presentation Layer feature includes two sub-features, the mandatory *web server* and optional *web proxy server* features. A web server handles HTTP requests from clients. The response to this request is usually an HTML page over HTTP. Web servers deal with static content and delegate the dynamic content requests to other applications or redirect the requests. *Web proxy server* can be used to increase the performance of the web servers and Presentation Layer, caching web contents and reducing load is performed by web proxy servers. Web proxy servers can also be used for reformatting the presentation for special purposes as well as for mobile platforms.

9.4.1.4 Application Layer

The Application Layer is the core layer of the SaaS architecture including the sub-features business logic and main functionalities, Identity Management, Orchestration, Service Management, Metadata Management, Communication, and Integration.

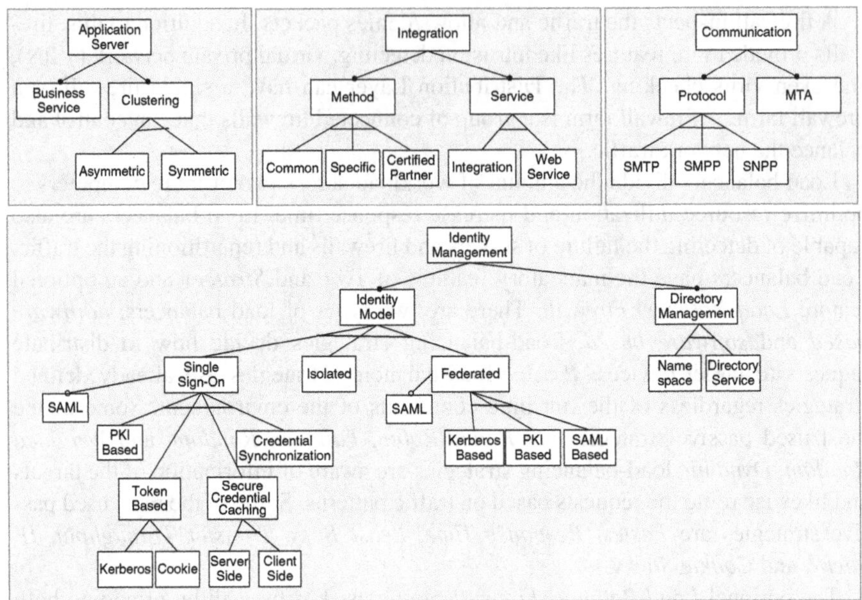

Fig. 9.6 Sub-feature diagrams for application layer

Especially in the enterprise area, SaaS platforms are usually built on SOA technologies and web services. *Application Server*, *Integration*, *Metadata Management*, *Identity Management*, and *Communication* are mandatory features for the application layer. In case of using SOA, some other features – *ESB*, *Orchestration*, and *Business Rules Engine* – are used in this layer. The sub-feature diagrams of the features of the Application Layer are shown in Fig. 9.6. In the following subsections, we describe these features in more detail.

9.4.1.5 Application Server

An Application Server is a server program that handles all application operations between users and an organization's back end business applications or databases. The Application Server's mission is to take care of the business logic in a multi-tier architecture. The business logic includes usually the functions that the software performs on the data. Application Servers are assigned for specific tasks, defined by business needs. Its basic job is to retrieve, handle, process, and present data to the user interface and process any input data whether queries or updates, including any validation and verification and security checks that need to be performed.

SaaS applications have to have continuous uptime. Users around the world can access the application anytime. Application failure means customer and monetary loss. The application should be prevented from single point of failure. In addition to availability issues, there are performance and scalability capabilities to overcome for SaaS applications. Integrating a number of computers to provide a unified virtual resource can solve these problems. This technique is called server clustering. There are two techniques for server clustering: *asymmetric* and *symmetric*. In asymmetric clustering, a standby server exists to take control in case another server fails. In symmetric clusters, every server in the cluster does the actual job. The first technique provides more available and fault-tolerant system but the latter is more cost-effective.

9.4.1.6 ESB

When we discuss SaaS applications and service-oriented architecture, the requirement is providing an infrastructure for services to communicate, interact, and transform messages. Enterprise Service Bus (ESB) is a platform for integrating services and provides enterprise messaging system. Using an ESB system does not mean implementing a service-oriented architecture, but they are highly related and ESB facilitates SOA.

9.4.1.7 Orchestration

Orchestration is a critical mission in SOA environment. A lot of tasks should be organized to perform a process. Orchestration provides the management, coordination, and arrangement of the services. BPEL is, for example, an Orchestration language that defines business processes. Some simple tasks may be performed by ESB but more complex business processes could be defined by BPEL. To interpret and execute BPEL, a BPEL engine is needed.

9.4.1.8 Metadata Management

SaaS has a single instance, multi-tenant architecture. Sharing the same instance to many customers brings the problem of customization. In SaaS architecture, customization is done using metadata. Metadata is not only about customization (e.g., UI preferences), it is also intended to provide configuration of business logic to meet customers need. Updating, storing, and fetching metadata is handled through metadata services [30]. This feature requires *Metadata Repository* feature.

9.4.1.9 Business Rules Engine

As mentioned before, SaaS applications can be customized and configured by metadata. Workflow may differ for each customer. Business Rules Engine is responsible of metadata execution. It consists of its own rule language, loads the rules, and then performs the operations.

9.4.1.10 Integration

In the context of SaaS, all the control, upgrade, and maintenance of user applications and data are handled by SaaS providers. An important challenge in SaaS is the data integration. SaaS applications usually need to use client data which resides at the client's node. On the other hand, each client may use more than one SaaS application or on-premise application using the same data. The data may be shared among several applications and each application may use different part of it or in different formats. Manipulating the data will usually have an impact on the other applications. Data accuracy and consistency should be provided among those applications. Re-entering or duplicating the data for any application is not a feasible manner to provide data.

There are three different approaches for providing consistent data integration including *common integration*, *specific integration*, and *certified partner integration*. In the common integration approach, services are provided for all clients. This feature requires *Integration.Services.Web Services* feature. In the specific integration, services are customized for each customer. This feature requires *Integration.Services.Integration Services* feature. Finally, in the *Certified Partner* approach the SaaS vendor delegates the integration to another vendor which is a specialist for SaaS integration. The SaaS vendor still needs to provide web services, but it leaves the control to other entities and focuses itself on the application. This feature also requires *Integration.Services.Web Services* feature.

The Integration feature describes either *Integration Service* or *Web Service*: In *Integration Service* approach, the SaaS vendor provides custom integration services for customers. Although this is the easiest way for customers, it is hard to manage adding integration service for different needs for vendors, and increasing number of customers causes scalability problems. In the *Web Service* approach, the SaaS vendor provides a standard approach for customers as web services. The customers themselves take responsibility for SaaS integration. Compared to the Integration Service approach, customers have to do much more and need extensive experience. On the other hand, this is a more scalable solution for vendors.

9.4.1.11 Identity Management

Identity Management deals with identifying individuals in a system and controlling access to the resources in the system by placing restrictions on the established identities of the individuals [32]. The *Directory Management* is responsible for managing the identities. Identify Management includes two mandatory features *Identity Model* and *Directory Management*. Identity Model can be *Single Sign-On*, *Isolated*, or *Federated*. *Isolated Identity Management*: The most common and simplest Identity Management model is the isolated one. Hereby, each service provider associates an identity for each customer. Despite its simplicity, this model is less manageable in case of the growth of number of users who should remember their log-in and passwords to their accounts for each service. Single Sign-On is a centralized

Identity Management model, which allows users to access different systems using a single user ID and password.

Single Sign-On Identity Management model [19] can be *PKI-Based, SAML-Based, Token-Based, Credential Synchronization,* or Secure *Credential Caching.* SAML stands for Security Assertion Markup Language and defines the XML-based security standard to enable portable identities and the assertion of these identities. The *Token-Based* approach can be either based on *Kerberos* or *Cookie.* The *Secure Credential Caching* can be on the *Server Side* or *Client Side.*

The *Federated Identity Model* is very close to Single Sign-On but defined Identity Management across different organizations [11]. There are three most used approaches, *Kerberos-based Federation, PKI-based Federation,* or *SAML-based Federation. Directory Management* feature includes two mandatory features, *Namespace* and *Directory Service. Namespace* maps the names of network resources to their corresponding network addresses. *Directory Service* represents the provided services for storing, organizing, and providing access to the information in a directory (e.g., *LDAP).*

9.4.1.12 Communication

SaaS vendor needs to provide a communication infrastructure both for inbound and outbound communication. Notification, acknowledging customers, sending feedbacks, and demanding approvals are useful for satisfying users. The most common approach for communication is e-mailing. To transfer mails between computers, a *Mail Transfer Agent* (*MTA*) can be used which requires *Simple Mail Transfer Protocol* (*SMTP*). Besides mailing, other protocols such as *Short Message Peer-to-Peer Protocol (SMPP)* and *Simple Network Paging Protocol* (*SNPP*) can be used.

9.4.1.13 Data Access Layer

This layer provides the database management system (DBMS) consisting of software which manages data (database manager or database engine), structured artifact (database), and metadata (schema, tables, constraints, etc.). One of the important, if not the most important, SaaS feature is multi-tenancy [20, 21]. Multi-tenancy is a design concept where a single instance of software is served to multiple consumers (tenants). This approach is cost saving, scalable, and easy to administrate, because the vendor has to handle, update or upgrade, and run only single instance. Multi-tenancy is not only about data; this design can be applied in all layers, but the most important part of the multi-tenancy is multi-tenant data architecture. Based on the latter, different kinds of multi-tenancy can be identified. Multi-tenancy with *Separate Databases* means that each tenant has its own data set which is logically isolated from other tenants. The simplest way to data isolation is storing tenant data in separate database servers. This approach is best for scalability, high performance, and security but requires high cost for maintenance and availability. In the *Shared Database, Separate Schemas* approach, a single database server is used for all tenants. This approach is more cost-effective but the main disadvantage is restore is difficult to achieve. Finally, the *Shared Database, Shared Schema* approach involves using one database and one schema for each tenants' data. The tables have additional columns, tenant identifier column, to distinguish the tenants. This approach has the lowest hardware and backup costs.

9.4.1.14 Data Storage Layer

The Data Storage Layer includes the feature for metadata storage, Application Database, and Directory Service. Metadata files can be stored either in a database or in a file-based repository. Application Database includes the sub-features of Storage Area Network (*SAN*), *Clustering*, and *Caching* [20]. SAN is a dedicated storage network that is used to make storage devices accessible to servers so that the devices appear as locally attached to the operating system. SAN is based on fiber channel and moves the data between heterogeneous servers.

Clustering is interconnecting a group of computers to work together acting like a single database to create a fault-tolerant, high-performance, scalable solution that is a low-cost alternative to high-end servers. By caching, disk access and computation are reduced while the response time is decreased.

Directory Service stores data in a directory to let the Directory Service look up for Identity Management. This data is read more often than it is written and can be redundant if it helps performance. Directory schemas are defined as object classes, attributes, name bindings, and namespaces.

9.4.1.15 Supporting Services Layer

Supporting Services Layer is a crosscutting layer that provides services for all layers. As known, SaaS applications have quality attributes such as scalability, performance, availability, and security. To keep the applications running efficiently and healthy, the SaaS system needs to have monitoring system to measure metrics. The monitoring infrastructure can detect failures, bottlenecks, and threats and alert the administrators or trigger automatic operations. Furthermore, SaaS systems may be built on service-oriented architecture and may need metering process for service level agreements and billing. Example metrics are CPU usage, CPU load, network traffic, memory usage, disk usage, attack rate, number of failures, and mean time to respond.

9.5 Tool Support and Example

Although, the steps of the process in the previous section can be performed manually, we have developed a set of tools to assist the SaaS application design process. Figure 9.8 depicts the data flow and order of the steps including the tools. In the following subsections, we explain the tool support activities together with a running example.

```
User Layer
------------------
User.Client
User.Certified Partner

Distribution Layer
------------------
Distribution Layer.Firewall
Load Balancer.Technique.Direct Routing
Load Balancer.Type.Hardware Based
Load Balancer.Pairing

Application and Business Service Layer
------------------
Application Layer.Enterprise Service Bus
Application Layer.Orchestration
Identity Management.LDAP
Identity Management.Single Sign On
Single Sign On.Kerberos
Single Sign On.SAML
Communication Server.Protocol.SMTP
Communication Server.Reporting
Application Server.Clustering
Integration.Common Integration
Integration.Web Service

Data Access Layer
------------------
Data Access.Cache Server
Data Access.Multitenacy.Shared

Data Storage Layer
------------------
Data Storage.Storage Area Network
```

Fig. 9.7 Example feature model derived from family feature model

9.5.1 Feature Modeling

An important part of the process consists of feature modeling. We have used the tool XFeature (developed at ETH-Zürich) [33] to define both the SaaS reference feature model and to derive the application feature model. In Fig. 9.8, the family feature modeling is defined as step 1, while the application feature modeling is defined in step 4.

Using XFeature, it is possible to edit and extend the feature diagram. XFeature has a graphical editor and represents the hierarchical structure visually. The resulted family feature model is stored in XML files. The family feature model is stored in the file SaaS-FM.xfm; the application feature model is stored in Application-FM. xfm. XFeature allows defining constraint through the features. In case of deriving an application feature model from the family feature model, the tool checks these constraints and warns the user if there is any inconsistency. So, XFeature guarantees that the application feature model is valid and consistent.

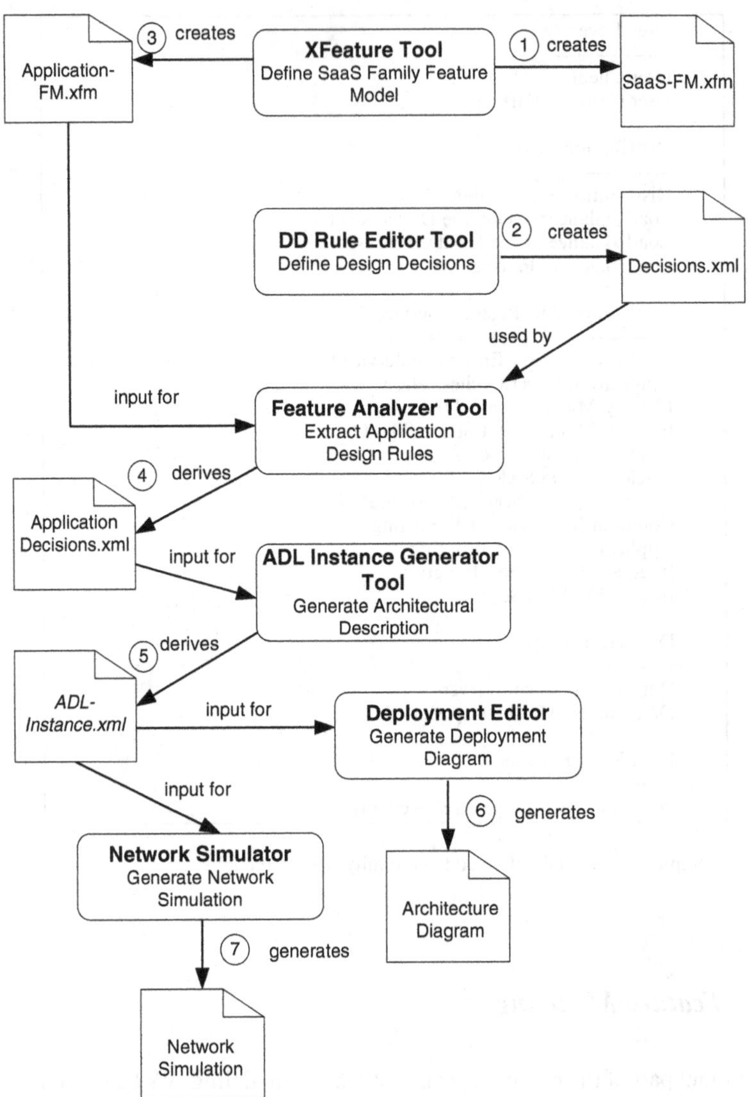

Fig. 9.8 Tool support data flow

In Fig. 9.7, we illustrate the feature modeling example with selected features based on the family feature model.

Note that in Fig. 9.7 there are no variant features; the features for the specific business requirements have determined the selected features. As an example, we can observe that for the Distribution Layer the features Firewall, Direct Routing, Hardware Based, and Paring have been selected.

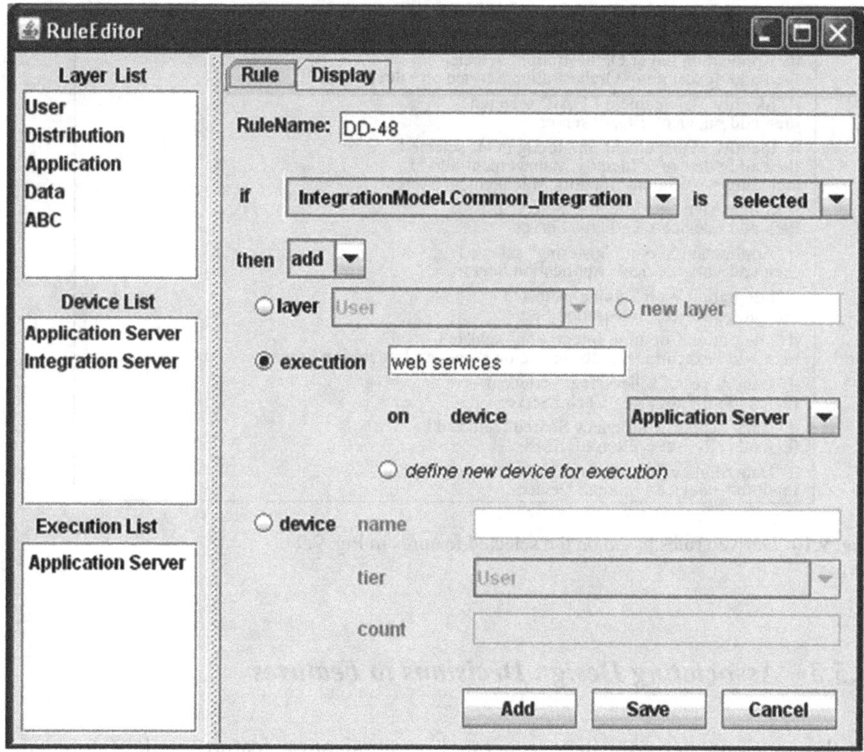

Fig. 9.9 Design decision rule editor

9.5.2 Design Rule Modeling

To represent design rules we have developed a tool called Design Rule Editor which is shown in Fig. 9.9. The tool supports the earlier defined Design Rule Definition Language, and we can use it to specify the design rules for the features in the family feature model.

Design Rule Editor uses the SaaS Family Feature Model file (SaaS-FM.xfm) created in the previous step. All features from the feature model are listed, and the user selects one of the features and defines the rule about that feature.

As an example, in Fig. 9.9, we show the definition of the rule "if Integration Model.Common_Integration is selected then add execution 'Web Service' on device Integration Server." In this case, the designer aims to provide web services for data integration to its clients instead of implementing customer-specific integration services, and the rule dictates that there should be a piece of software as web services on the specified device. In the Display tab of the tool, the human-readable form of the rule is showed and the user can add note or a description of the rule. With this rule editor we have specified all the reference rules based on the family feature model which is stored in the file Decisions.xml as shown in Fig. 9.8.

```
if "Application Layer.Enterprise Service Bus" selected
then add <device> ESB including <execution> ESB Services
if "Application Layer.Orchestration" selected
then add <execution> Orchestration Service on <device> ESB
if "Identity Management.LDAP" selected
then add <device> LDAP server
if "Identity Management.Single Sign On" selected
then add <device> "Identity Management Server"
including <execution> Identity Management System
if "Single Sign On.Kerberos" selected
then add <device> Kerberos Server
if "Application Server.Clustering" selected
then add <n> <device> Application Server
if "Integration.Web Service" selected
then add <device> Integration Server
if "Integration.Common Integration" selected
then add <execution> Web service on <device> Integration Server
if "Data Access.Cache Server" selected
then add <n> <device> Cache Server
if "Data Access.Multitenacy.Shared" selected
then add <1> <execution> DBMS
if "Data Storage.Storage Area Network" selected
then <n> <device> Storage Device
```

Fig. 9.10 Derived rules based on the selected features in Fig. 9.9

9.5.3 Associating Design Decisions to Features

In the previous steps we have generated an application feature model (stored in Application-FM.xfm) and we have defined the design decision rules (stored in Decisions.xml). In this step we use the Feature Analyzer Tool to determine which design rules will be used for the features of the application feature model. The Feature Analyzer Tool first reads the selected features from the Application-FM.xfm file. Then it checks the condition parts of the design decision rules to determine whether there are matching rules. After the tool scans all the design rules, it brings only the matching ones.

For the example application feature model in Fig. 9.9, the design rules have been derived by checking the reference design rules and matching it with the selected features. We show, as an example, the set of the derived rules for the Application and Business Layer and the Data Access and Storage Layer features, as shown in Fig. 9.10. After correlation of the design rules and features, the next step is creating an instance of the family, which is called the application model.

9.5.4 Generation of the Application Architecture

In this study, we aimed to provide guidance for reasoning about alternative SaaS architectures. So far, we were able to define an application model from the family, and we need to represent the corresponding architecture of the application model.

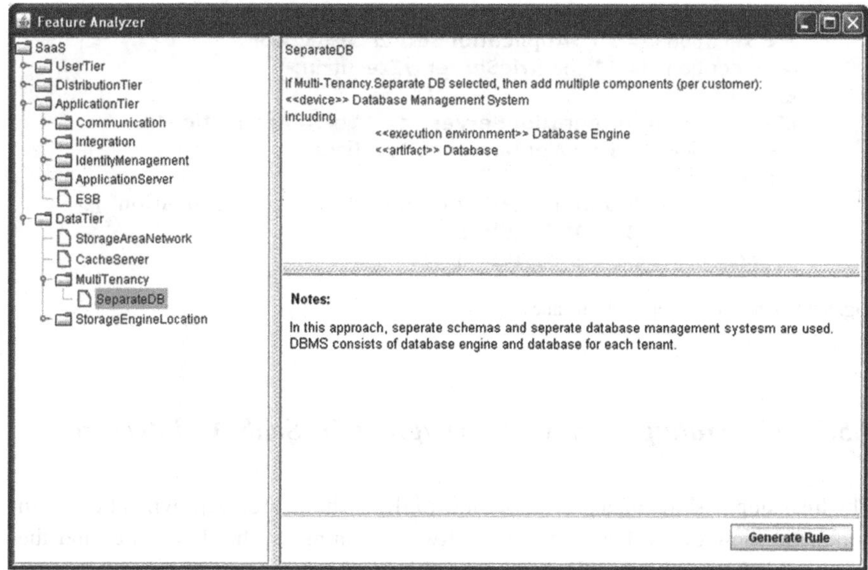

Fig. 9.11 Feature analyzer tool

The design decision rules, we mentioned before, are useful for exposing the architecture. Since application model derives from the family model, it also inherits the existing attributes. Within the application model features, there are references to design rules as attributes. Here, we introduce another tool, Feature Analyzer, which takes as input both the application model file (Application-FM.xfm) and design decision rules file (Decisions.xml). The tool automatically extracts the attributes of the features, finds references to design rules, and links it to those rules. As a result, all features of the application model are represented graphically as a treelike hierarchical structure and the corresponding design decision rules are displayed.

As shown in Fig. 9.11, on the left side of the panel, the features are displayed for a specific alternative application model. In the case of selecting a feature, the corresponding design rule is displayed at the right side. Remember that Design Rule Editor allows adding notes for the features and the notes are also displayed on the panel.

The next step is transforming these design rules to an architecture specification. For this, we have developed a simple architecture description language (ADL) [22]. This language has only basic types for describing the architecture: device, execution, and connection. The ADL instance is used internally, that is to say, the user does not write a description manually. We have developed another tool, Architecture Generator, which takes application-specific design rules and converts them to architectural description in XML format. A part of the architectural description is shown in Fig. 9.12 which is generated by the Architecture Generator Tool.

```
- <Device name="AppServer" id="0" tier="Application">
    <Execution id="10">ApplicationServer</Execution>
    <Execution id="11">MetricServer</Execution>
  </Device>
- <Device name="IntegrationServer" id="1" tier="Application">
    <Execution id="12">WebServer</Execution>
  </Device>
  <Device name="CommunicationServer" id="2" tier="Application" />
  <Connection srcID="0" destID="1" />
  <Connection srcID="2" destID="0" />
```


Fig. 9.12 An example of ADL instance

9.5.5 Generating Deployment Diagram for SaaS Architecture

The final step is showing a graphical view of the architecture. Deployment diagram is a static view of the hardware, the software running on that hardware, and the relationship between them. We have chosen the deployment view of the architecture to display, because deployment diagram is also very useful for system engineering. It can be used for analyzing quality attributes such as scalability, performance, maintainability, and portability [23]. We have developed an Eclipse plug-in [24], an editor, which is capable of both drawing deployment diagram automatically from ADL instance and enabling user for editing the generated diagram.

Similar to Protégé [8], which is a free, open source ontology editor, Eclipse is a framework for which various other projects can develop plug-ins. Protégé provides tool support for ontology modeling but feature modeling and the mapping to architecture design is missing.

We used Model-Driven Architecture (MDA) and Eclipse Graphical Modeling Framework (GMF) [25] for developing a deployment diagram editor. MDA provides high-level abstraction and platform-independent modeling approach and uses a Domain-Specific Language. GMF helps to define domain models and represent them graphically based on MDA.

In our ADL, we have basic elements to define architecture. To develop the deployment diagram, we also need Domain-Specific Language (DSL) elements that correspond to the ADL elements. Thus, device, execution, and connector model and meta-model files are defined in GMF. By using the model and meta-model files, GMF generates the tool code.

The graphical editor generates the deployment diagram automatically from the architectural description which is generated in the previous step. First, the editor parses the ADL instance components and then determines the layout of the components and arranges the position of the components.

After the deployment diagram is generated automatically, the user can modify the diagram arbitrary. Figure 9.13 illustrates the visual representation of the architecture by the deployment diagram editor for the example application feature model of Fig. 9.9 and the derived application design rules of Fig. 9.10.

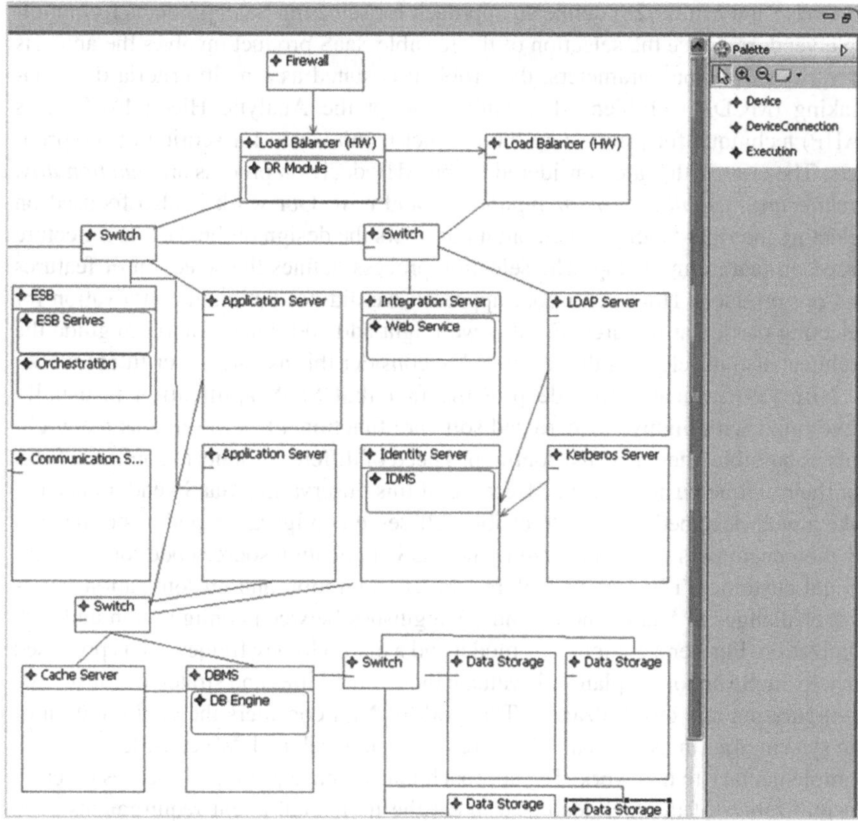

Fig. 9.13 Deployment diagram editor

9.6 Related Works

Despite its relatively young history, different surveys have already been provided in the literature on cloud computing and many chapters have been published on SaaS. An example survey chapter is provided by Goyal and Dadizadeh [26]. However, to the best of our knowledge, no systematic domain analysis approach has been carried out to derive a feature model for SaaS.

La and Kim [27] propose a systematic process for developing SaaS systems highlighting the importance of reuse. The authors first define the criteria for designing the process model and then provide the meta-model and commonality and variability model. The metamodel defines the key elements of SaaS. The variability model is primarily represented as a table. The work focuses more on the general approach. The metamodel could be complementary to the reference architecture in this chapter and as presented by SaaS providers. Although the goal seems similar, our approach appears to be more specific and targeting the definition of a proper modeling of the domain using feature modeling.

Godse and Mulik [28] define an approach for selecting SaaS products from multiple vendors. Since the selection of the feasible SaaS product involves the analysis of various decision parameters, the problem is stated as a multi-criteria decision-making (MCDM) problem. The authors adopt the Analytic Hierarchy Process (AHP) technique for prioritizing the product features and for scoring of the products. The criteria that are considered in the AHP decision process are *functionality*, *architecture*, *usability*, *vendor reputation*, and *cost*. Our work is also focused on selecting the right SaaS product, but it considers the design of the SaaS architecture based on feature modeling. The selection process defines the selection of features and not products. However, in our approach we did not outline the motivation for selecting particular features. For this we might add additional criteria to guide the architect also in selecting the features. We consider this as part of our future work.

Nitu [29] indicates that despite the fact that SaaS application is usually developed with highly standardized software functionalities to serve as many clients as possible, there is still a continuous need of different clients to configure SaaS for their unique business needs. Because of this observation, SaaS vendors need to take a well-designed strategy to enable self-serve configuration and customization by their customers without changing the SaaS application source code for any individual customer. The author explores the configuration and customization issues and challenges to SaaS vendors and distinguishes between configuration and customization. Further a competency model and a methodology framework is proposed to help SaaS vendors to plan and evaluate their capabilities and strategies for service configuration and customization. The work of Nitu considers the configuration of the system after the system architecture has been developed. We consider our work complementary to this work. The approach that we have presented focuses on early customization of the architecture to meet the individual client requirements. The approach as presented by Nitu could be used in collaboration with our approach, that is, by first customizing the architecture based on the potential clients and then providing configurability and customization support for the very unique business needs.

9.7 Conclusion

Different research topics have been addressed in the literature concerning cloud computing in general and SaaS in particular. In general, the design of the SaaS architecture from a reference architecture however seems to have not been directly addressed. In this chapter we have provided a domain-driven design approach to model both the SaaS domain and to support the SaaS architect in deriving an application architecture. The mechanism for distinguishing the modeling between family modeling and application modeling appeared to be very useful. In the family modeling part, we actually applied a domain engineering process and defined the reference architecture, the family feature model, and the reference design rules. The reference architecture actually defines the space of application architectures.

The family feature model defines the possible features for SaaS applications, and it appeared that we can relate these to specific architectural decisions. Based on the derived architectural decisions, we could derive the specific application architecture. The approach has been supported by a set of tools to support the selection of the feature model and the automatic generation of the application architecture.

Hereby, the application features, the derived design rules, and the eventual application architecture are linked to each other, and as such the design decisions and the requirements feature selection for the application architecture can be easily traced. By defining multiple application architectures based on different application feature models, we can even compare multiple alternatives and based on this select the most feasible alternative. We can derive several important lessons from this study. First of all, feature modeling appeared to be very useful to make explicit the common and variant concerns of SaaS. This is not only important for novice designers but also for experienced architects who wish to derive an application architecture. In addition, the corresponding tool support appeared to be necessary to cope with the complexity of the domain and the generation process. In our future work, we will focus on multiple architecture views [31], enhance the tool further, and apply the tool in a real industrial context.

References

1. Aksit, M., Tekinerdogan, B., Marcelloni, F., Bergmans, L.: Deriving object-oriented frameworks from domain knowledge. In: Fayad, M., Schmidt, D., Johnson, R. (eds.) Building Application Frameworks: Object-Oriented Foundations of Framework Design, pp. 169–198. Wiley, New York (1999)
2. Arrango, G.: Domain analysis methods. In: Schäfer, W., Prieto-Díaz, R., Matsumoto, M. (eds.) Software Reusability, pp. 17–49. Ellis Horwood, New York (1994)
3. Kang, K., Cohen, S., Hess, J., Nowak, W., Peterson, A.: Feature-Oriented Domain Analysis (FODA) feasibility study. Technical Report, CMU/SEI-90-TR-21. Software Engineering Institute, Carnegie Mellon University, Pittsburgh, PA, November 1990
4. Tekinerdogan, B., Aksit, M.: Synthesis based software architecture design. In: Aksit, M. (ed.) Software Architectures and Component Technology: The State of the Art in Research and Practice, pp. 143–173. Kluwer Academic, Boston (2001)
5. Tekinerdogan, B., Aksit, M.: Classifying and evaluating architecture design methods. In: Aksit, M. (ed.) Software Architectures and Component Technology: The State of the Art in Research and Practice, pp. 3–27. Kluwer Academic, Boston (2001)
6. Czarnecki, C., Eisenecker, U.: Generative Programming: Methods, Tools, and Applications. Addison-Wesley, Boston (2000)
7. Sinnema, M., Deelstra, S.: Classifying variability modeling techniques. Inf. Softw. Technol. **49**(7), 717–739 (2007)
8. Protégé: Official web site. http://protege.stanford.edu/. Accessed 2012
9. Czarnecki, K., Kim, C.H.P., Kalleberg, K.: Feature models are views on ontologies. In: Proceedings of the 10th International on Software Product Line Conference, 2006. pp. 41–51. IEEE Computer Society (2006)
10. Gruber, T.R.: Towards principles for the design of ontologies used for knowledge sharing. Technical Report KSL93-04. Stanford University, Stanford, August 1993
11. Chong, F., Carraro, G.: Architecture Strategies for Catching the Long Tail. Microsoft, MSDN Architecture Center (2006)

12. Wikipedia: Cloud computing. http://en.wikipedia.org/wiki/Cloud_computing
13. Laplante, P.A., Zhang, J., Voas, J.: What's in a name – distinguishing between SaaS and SOA. IT Prof. **10**(3), 46–50 (2008)
14. Spence, C., Devoys, J., Chahal, S.: Architecting software as a service for the enterprise. IT@ Intel White Chapter url: http://www.intel.com/content/dam/doc/white-paper/cloud-computing-intel-it-architecting-software-as-a-service-paper.pdf (2009)
15. Sun Cloud Computing Primer: http://www.scribd.com/doc/54858960/Cloud-Computing-Primer. Accessed 2011
16. Joshi, S.: Architecture for SaaS Applications – Using the Oracle SaaS Platform. Oracle White Chapter. http://www.oracle.com/us/technologies/saas/ (2009)
17. Lee, K., Chul Kang, K., Lee, J.: Concepts and guidelines of feature modeling for product line software engineering. In: Proceedings of the 7th International Conference on Software Reuse: Methods, Techniques, and Tools, pp. 62–77, 15–19. Springer, April 2002
18. Kopparapu, C.: Load Balancing Servers, Firewalls, and Caches. Wiley, New York (2002)
19. de Clercq, J.: Single sign-on architectures. In: Proceedings of the International Conference on Infrastructure Security, pp. 40–58, 1–3. Springer, October 2002
20. Chong, F., Carraro, G.: Building Distributed Applications: Multi-Tenant Data Architecture. MSDN Architecture Center. Microsoft Developer Network (MSDN), http://msdn.microsoft.com/en-us/library/aa479086.aspx (2006)
21. Kwok, T., Nguyen, T., Lam, L.: A software as a service with multi-tenancy support for an electronic contract management application. In: Proceedings of the 2008 IEEE International Conference on Services Computing – Vol. 2 (SCC '08), vol. 2, pp. 179–186. IEEE Computer Society, Washington, DC (2008)
22. Medvidovic, N., Taylor, R.N.: A classification and comparison framework for software architecture description languages. IEEE Trans. Softw. Eng. **26**(1), 70–93 (2000)
23. Balsamo, S., Di Marco, A., Inverardi, P., Simeoni, M.: Model-based performance prediction in software development: a survey. IEEE Trans. Softw. Eng. **30**(5), 295–310 (2004)
24. Eclipse official web site. http://www.eclipse.org. Accessed 2012
25. Eclipse: Modeling Framework web site. http://www.eclipse.org/gmf/. Accessed 2012
26. Goyal, A., Dadizadeh, S.: A survey on Cloud computing. Technical Report. University of British Columbia, Vancouver (2009)
27. La, H.J., Kim, S.D.: A systematic process for developing high quality SaaS Cloud services. In: Proceedings of the 1st International Conference on Cloud Computing. Springer LNCS, vol. 5931/2009, pp. 278–289. Springer, Berlin/Heidelberg (2009)
28. Godse, M., Mulik, S.: An approach for Selecting Software-as-a-Service (SaaS) product. In: IEEE CLOUD, pp. 155–158 (2009)
29. Nitu: Configurability in SaaS (software as a service) applications. In: Proceedings of the 2nd India Software Engineering Conference (ISEC '09), pp. 19–26. ACM, New York (2009)
30. Brandt, S.A., Miller, E.L., Long, D.D.E, LanXue: Efficient metadata management in large distributed storage systems. In: Mass Storage Systems and Technologies, 2003. (MSST 2003). Proceedings. 20th IEEE/11th NASA Goddard Conference on, vol., no., pp. 290, 298, 7–10 (2003)
31. Clements, P., Bachmann, F., Bass, L., Garlan, D., Ivers, J., Little, R., Merson, P., Nord, R., Stafford, J.: Documenting Software Architectures: Views and Beyond, 2nd edn. Addison-Wesley, Boston (2010)
32. FIDIS: Structured Overview on Prototypes and Concepts of Identity Management Systems. Future of Identity in the Information Society (No. 507512)
33. XFeature: Official web site. http://www.pnp-software.com/XFeature. Accessed 2012

Chapter 10
Impact of Cloud Adoption on Agile Software Development

Sowmya Karunakaran

Abstract Cloud computing provides a wide range of core infrastructure services such as compute and storage, along with building blocks which can be consumed from both on-premise environments and the Internet to develop cloud-based applications. It offers Platform as a Service capability which allows applications to be built, hosted and run from within managed data centres using programmable APIs or interoperable services exposed by the platform. The objective of this chapter is to study the effects of cloud adoption on software development projects that use agile methodologies. Agile methodologies involve iterative and incremental approaches to software development. The ubiquitous nature of cloud computing makes it an enabler of agile software development. This chapter highlights various aspects of cloud provision that can catalyse agile software development. The chapter provides directions for agile teams that are keen on exploiting the potential of cloud to alleviate the challenges currently faced by them. A case study of an agile development team which adopted cloud is discussed to articulate the real-time benefits and challenges in adopting the cloud environment.

Keywords Cloud computing • Agile software development • Distributed development • Collaboration • Software testing

10.1 Introduction

Agile is a software development methodology that dramatically reduces the lead time for development. Features and capabilities demanded by software product owners and end users of the software are made available to them almost as rapidly as they

---

S. Karunakaran (✉)
Department of Management Studies, Indian Institute of Technology (IIT), Madras, India
e-mail: sowmya.karu@gmail.com

Z. Mahmood and S. Saeed (eds.), *Software Engineering Frameworks for the Cloud Computing Paradigm*, Computer Communications and Networks,
DOI 10.1007/978-1-4471-5031-2_10, © Springer-Verlag London 2013

need them. Agile teams achieve this by breaking down the prioritised requirements backlog, commonly referred to as the product backlog, into smaller chunks achievable in 2–4 weeks' time frame. The software development team then focuses on each chunk individually. As each chunk is designed, coded and tested, it forms an *iteration*. Each iteration entails release of potentially shippable software that can be made available to end users immediately. The software development team moves on to the subsequent iteration. At every point during development, product owners, developers, testers, analysts, architects and users collaborate. A relationship that is built on trust and transparency prevails between the software development team and the users/product owners. Above all, no useless functionality is built.

Agile and cloud computing can be considered complementary concepts. According to Computer Sciences Corporation (CSC) Cloud Usage Index survey, 21 % of the respondents quote agility as the driver for cloud adoption [1]. One of the key benefits of agile development methodologies is faster time to market. Similarly, the cloud can catalyse the development process. This implies that new features and capabilities can now be made available to users instantly, as soon as the software development team has implemented them. There is no necessity for detailed, lengthy deployment procedures, patches and multiple installations. Integration issues are handled, change management is addressed and overall risks are minimised. Users can use the new features and updates seamlessly.

The following sections of this chapter provide insights into how cloud positively impacts agile software development. Collaboration is critical for success of any agile project. The first section deals with collaboration and how cloud enables collaboration among agile teams that are geographically dispersed. The impact of cloud on various steps involved in a typical software project like setting up infrastructure, development, testing, deployment and project management is discussed in subsequent sections from the context of agile. The later sections focus on cost and time implications of cloud on agile teams and the potential challenges in implementing cloud for agile projects. A case study of an agile team that adopted cloud is discussed to understand the real-time benefits and issues. The last section provides a summary of various tools that support agile software development in the cloud.

10.2 Agile, Cloud and Collaboration

Agile development involves bringing stakeholders from across the entire life cycle together—from business analysts to developers to QA managers to IT operations personnel—more frequently and collaboratively than ever before. Agile requires high-velocity feedback from these stakeholders throughout the process, which the cloud enables with ease.

Geographical distance affects the ability of teams to collaborate [2]. Moreover, it has been found that as the distance between two working locations increases, communication and collaboration decline [3]. Also, physical distance removes the opportunity for face-to-face communication.

Practitioners and researchers in information technology are of the opinion that cloud is important not just for the technologists but also for businesses as it provides

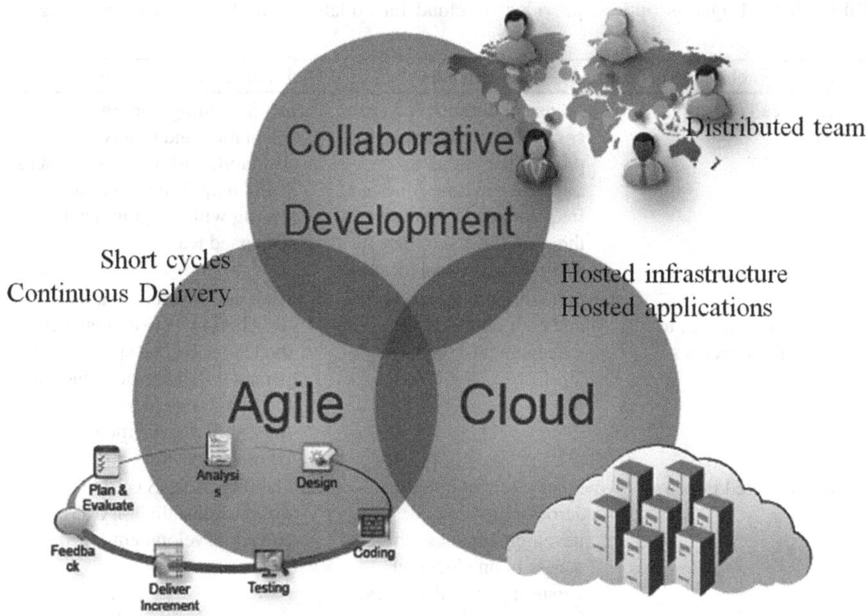

Fig. 10.1 Agile, cloud and collaboration

an opportunity for improving and accelerating collaboration. Collaboration within teams and across stakeholders including the business is particularly relevant for successful adoption of agile practices (see Fig. 10.1).

Project management and project collaboration tools have been one of the earliest tools to be available as Software as a Service (SaaS) within the domains of cloud computing. This can be attributed to the pervasive nature of the Internet which has enabled subscription-based IT. The Internet offered IT services as utility at much lower prices. However, the biggest advantage that SaaS in the cloud offers is that it takes care of owning most of the hardware and the software resources required.

As the project progresses, agile teams can expand or contract in size within and across multiple geographical locations. This calls for quick scalability in terms of collaboration and project management software. With SaaS-based project management and collaboration, scalability becomes easier with a few clicks of a button, without heavy investments in software and hardware. The transition is smoother because of the subscription-based collaborative IT services.

Table 10.1 summarises the collaboration challenges faced by agile teams and mitigation options provided by cloud adoption [16].

Cloud collaboration has been rapidly evolving. In the past, cloud collaboration tools have been primitive with basic and limited features. Recent solutions have a document-centric approach to collaboration. Even more sophisticated tools allow users to "tag" specific areas of a document for comments which are delivered real time to those viewing the document. In some tools, the collaboration software can be integrated into other tools like Microsoft Office, SharePoint and Adobe Photoshop. Using a single software tool to suit all the collaboration needs of an

Table 10.1 Mitigation options provided by cloud for collaboration challenges faced by agile teams

Collaboration challenges	Impact on agile team	Facilitating by using cloud
Geographically distributed team	The physical distance can cause communication gaps and project delays due to difference in time zones and frequent handoffs (during the start and end of day at every geographical location)	Dynamic binding, runtime adaptation and timely availability of required services could help deal with issues arising with geographically dispersed teams
Lack of trust/ understanding due to cultural differences	Unequal distribution of work and poor skill set management	Services could maintain a fair distribution of work between the teams. Only a specific person will be responsible for the task assigned to him or her; thus, skill management would be easier too
Logistics-related issues	Unequal levels of quality across software development sites, direct access in one location versus a poor VPN access in other location	Availability of SaaS could diminish installation overheads at each development location
Time-based issues	Ineffective project management, lack of visibility into project progress, difficulty in project configuration management	The cloud service models imply that the data resides on a centralised location where inventory of services is maintained. Services maintain a registry where all of them are stored. This attribute could be used to store and retrieve configurations

agile team could be a good option rather than having to liaise with multiple different tools and techniques.

SaaS-based models have features that enhance collaboration and project management. They include:

- Managing multiple projects
  - Dashboard
  - Ticket management
  - Access controls for each project
- Online document management
  - History/version control
  - Backup
- Time tracking of the team
  - Task-level tracking

- Ensuring proper allocation of resources
- Generating reports
  - Predefined templates
  - Custom templates

The ubiquity of cloud computing services is another key advantage for distributed teams. In a hot site, the provider typically gives only a few sites needing dedicated network connectivity; however, in a cloud-enabled hot site, the provider can offer access to multiple sites effortlessly across the Internet [4]. This benefit can also make flexible workspace arrangements possible. Team members can work from an alternate work location. They could access the resources on the cloud via a web browser and thereby eliminate the need to have the required connectivity setup at the alternate work location [5].

Aligning with the agile manifesto, agile project management encourages involvement of software development teams in iterative and collaborative requirements gathering process. This process is embraced by utilising hosted collaboration tools, particularly in case of a distributed team. For example, let us examine a cloud-based collaboration tool: BootstrapToday (see Fig. 10.2). The features include file sharing, file organising, walls for companywide announcements and sharing ideas, project wiki to create and manage project knowledge base for each project, email integration, notifications and activity streams.

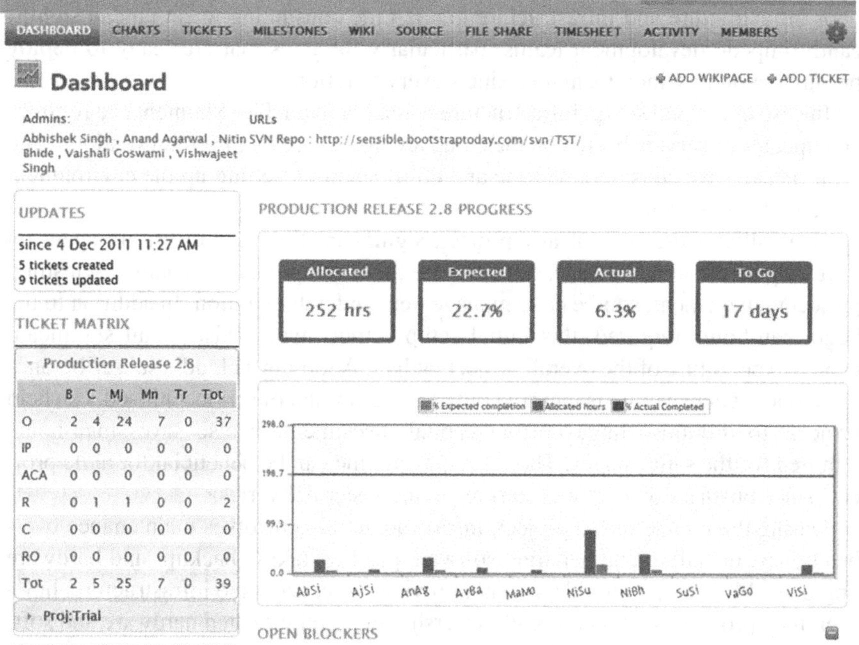

Fig. 10.2 Screenshot of the tool BootstrapToday (digitizor.com)

Agile manifesto also emphasises face-to-face collaboration. In a distributed team, the only way to make this happen on a daily basis is to make use of videoconferencing (VC). Few distributed agile teams have started leveraging videoconferencing to improve their collaboration. However, they would have gone through many hiccups to procure, set up and use VC systems. In most cases, it is a shared asset and teams may not be able to get access to VC on demand. Traditional VC systems also require upfront capital investment in equipment, particularly if the system is expected to scale. In addition to this constraint, VC units are also required at each user location. A dedicated, secure network with a huge bandwidth is required to have good-quality calls. This has made many small- to medium-sized businesses to postpone their investments in VC. There have been instances where teams have abandoned VC usage due to frequent glitches. A cloud-based VC service eliminates costs involved in possessing the technology required for VC sessions and can aid in setting up and managing calls. In addition, it can provide the much needed reliability. Certain providers also offer transcoding services which make the usage agnostic of the videoconferencing protocol being used and improve the interoperability.

10.3 Setting Up Infrastructure

Agile methods require infrastructure to be in place before development starts since poor infrastructure and infrastructure that is time consuming to set up can significantly impede development teams, particularly the ones that are ready to deploy production quality incremental products every iteration.

In case of a cloud setup, infrastructure is readily available. Maintenance routines and updates of servers hosted on the cloud are taken care by the cloud vendor. Agile projects can save considerable time and effort spent on setting up the environment through this mechanism.

Generally, at the start of any project, significant time and effort are spent on acquiring hardware and licences of software for development environments, testing, project management, source code management and collaboration. In addition to the huge man-hours required, this initial setup activity would also entail significant capital expenditure of the overall project budget. Adopting a cloud's subscribe-and-use model, where capital is incurred only for the amount of service utilised, can help projects to minimise huge upfront capital investment. It also saves man-hours required for the setup stages. These savings in time can be beneficial for agile projects since business owners will start receiving faster deliveries.

During the course of the project, infrastructure also involves maintenance overheads, say, installing and handling software patches, taking backups and hardware upgrades. Most cloud providers do not provide direct access to infrastructure; however, they provide permissions and ownership of a prefabricated hardware and software infrastructure. This provides the much needed consistency for an agile team to deploy and run an application directly without incurring maintenance overheads.

The top most level of configuration option available in cloud is infrastructure. Most cloud service providers offer many infrastructural services including message queues, static content hosting, virtual machine hosting, streaming video hosting, storage and load balancing.

10.4 Distributed Development

In a global software development team, a team member from across the geographically distributed agile team should be able to perform typical software development activities like coding, testing, deployment and release to production without any difficulties during their respective working hours (in their time zones). However, distributed software development approaches have several concerns like cultural differences, collaboration and communication mechanisms, which can destabilise the overall development success if not handled efficiently [6]. Distributed work items appear to take about two and a half times as long to complete as compared to similar items in a colocated work environment [7]. Cloud enables centralised hosting of tools for agile project management, continuous integration, test dashboard, testing environment and all other software and hardware instances needed for a typical development team. Because of these features, software development teams would be comfortable developing their software using cloud-based development platforms that allow their teams to collaborate and manage various project artefacts like product backlogs and user stories, burn-down charts, task lists, bug information, documentation and release notes irrespective of where they are located.

The Platform as a Service representation can provide a development platform with set of services to assist application development and hosting on the cloud. It does not require any kind of software downloads and installations [8] and, because of its characteristics, has the capacity to support geographically distributed teams.

Software development teams can benefit by rapidly provisioning SCM repositories in the cloud in minutes with secure, 99.9 % or better uptime SLAs [9]. In addition to being available at all times, development platforms on cloud can also scale on demand from a workgroup to the entire enterprise providing services across several sites and projects.

10.4.1 Setting Up Environments

Services in the cloud support establishment of different virtual environments. The most common use of the cloud includes the setting up of an environment consisting of several virtual servers. These virtual servers can then be used for development and testing. Certain types of cloud services are also beginning to support modern, multitier application architectures. When the development in a virtual cloud environment is completed, the images of virtual servers can be moved to the production environment. The production environment can also be set up in the cloud; in this case, only the images have to be moved to another virtual environment marked for production [10].

10.4.2 Continuous Integration

In addition to development, agile teams will want to exploit virtualisation to provision for build images in the cloud, automate SCM-to-build links and provide frequent feedback to stakeholders on the health of code from their continuous integration servers.

Continuous integration (which involves frequent integration of new code/changes into the code repository) was first proposed as part of extreme programming. Continuous integration is one of the difficult tasks that can be implemented on the cloud. This is obvious due to the fact that constant building and testing place enormous demands on hardware. However, many widely used continuous integration tools are now cloud ready. For example, Hudson (Jenkins), one of the popular continuous integration tools, has options for configuration which can be used to effectively manage dynamic demands by spinning slaves up and down on demand. As a result, setting up Hudson in the cloud might be more efficient to meet impulsive demands instead of running a huge swarm of servers.

The cloud enhancement on Hudson enables it to work with cloud services and virtualisation technologies so that development teams can improve resource utilisation, reduce maintenance overhead and handle spiky system loads. Hudson cannot only start as many nodes as needed but also turn them off when they are unnecessary [11]. By means of programmable APIs, Hudson can also talk to Amazon's EC2 (see Fig. 10.3). Hudson's EC2 plug-in runs on top of a Java client library, Typica, for a variety of Amazon Web Services. Typica takes care of automatically provisioning slaves on EC2 on demand and also shutting down unused instances.

10.4.3 Software Testing

Testing is another key activity in any software project. In case of a project that uses agile, testing is not carried out as a separate phase in the project life cycle. Testing is predominantly impulsive in nature. Developers and testers will continually want resources for multiplatform testing, unit and functional testing and in parallel execute effective load testing. Hence, testing is another key activity that can greatly benefit from cloud migration, as they tend to use the cloud assets in spikes and have fluctuating demands over a period.

Even if cloud is not used for the production infrastructure, it can still be an exceptionally useful tool for accelerated software delivery process. Figure 10.4 shows a sample setup for acceptance testing in the cloud. Cloud makes it simpler to

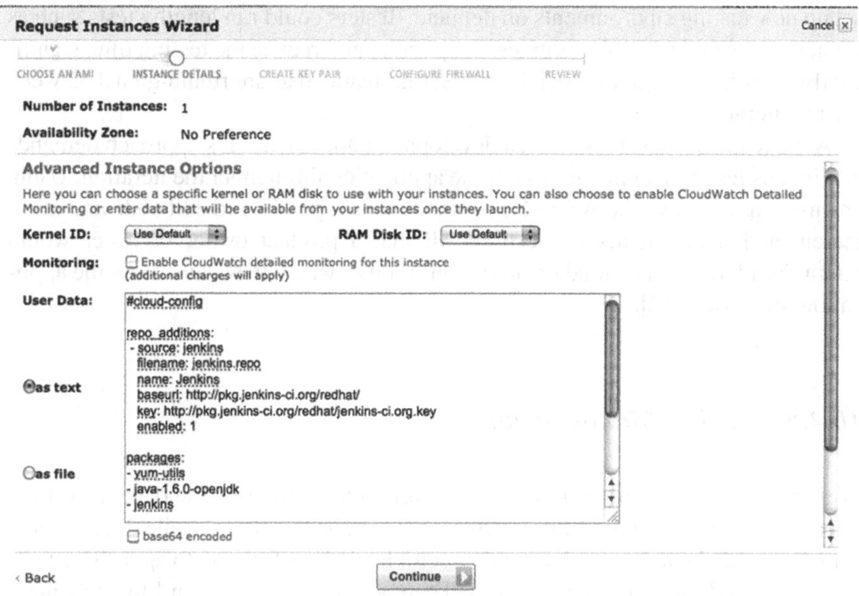

Fig. 10.3 Amazon EC2 create instance—Jenkins GUI

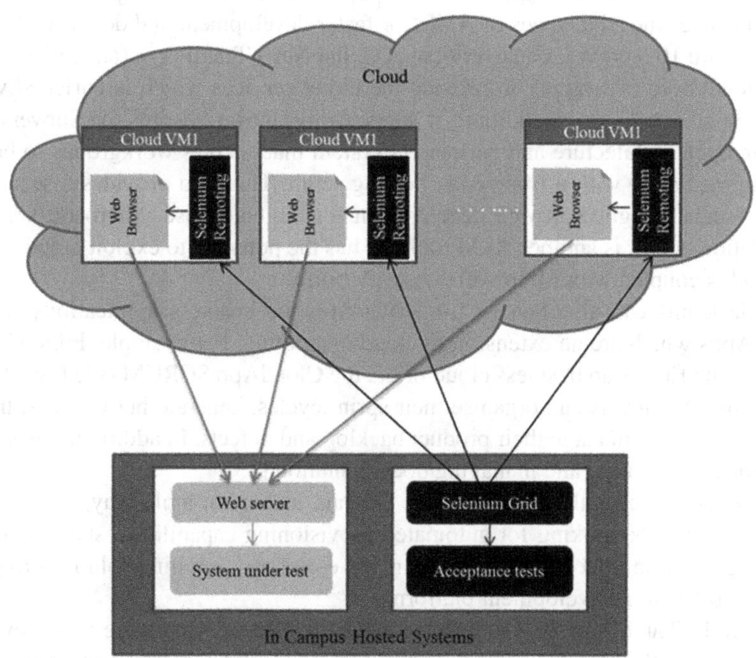

Fig. 10.4 A sample setup for acceptance testing using cloud

set up new testing environments on demand. Testers could run lengthy tests such as capacity tests and multiplatform tests in parallel and reduce the testing time significantly. This is important especially for Scrum teams that are running on 1–2 week sprints (iterations).

Agile teams follow a test-driven development approach. This approach demands continuous testing and integration of the application throughout the iteration. Using an environment, say, like Azure for testing makes it possible to edit code and make incremental deployments for testing. All that a product owner or tester would require is a URL of the cloud environment through which they can access the application for testing [12].

10.4.4 Project Management

Project management in cloud can allow agile teams to create and manage their releases, sprints, backlogs, burn-down charts, etc., on the cloud. Agile development is maturing, and many organisations are completely transforming to agile. This calls for enterprise-level management tools. There are many application life cycle management (ALM) tools in the market which provide this capability. These tools provide an end-to-end solution for all the needs of enterprise-wide agile adoption.

For example, CollabNet's ScrumWorks Pro provides flexible, hosted cloud environment, which is well integrated with popular source code and deployment tools. This enhances the advantages of Agile for faster development and delivery of software. Figure 10.5 provides an overview of CollabNet's TeamForge (an Agile ALM) and CloudForge (a wrapper to provide the cloud services which is enriched with major cloud vendors). In addition, it supports instant-on hosting for Subversion, with an open architecture and partner ecosystem that enables workgroups to bootstrap immediately with a basic code hosting setup. This also provides a seamless path to scalable agile software development for the enterprise. Microsoft's Team Foundation Server is another ALM tool that has the potential to exploit cloud offerings and is coupled with Microsoft Azure platform.

Agile teams can also benefit from custom-made business applications called CloudApps which are an extension to cloud computing. For example, Folio Cloud which is the European business cloud offers the CloudApp SCRUM (see Fig. 10.6). Using this app, teams can organise their sprint cycles, generate burn downs, track their velocity and manage their product backlog and defects. In addition, it has features for collaboration and managing documentation [13].

To quickly access these services on demand and in an agile way, application developers will be looking for automated provisioning capabilities, such as "one-click" application selection, provisioning and e-commerce billing solutions as part of their application development platforms.

Figure 10.7 and Table 10.2 summarise the above discussions. Figure 10.7 provides suggestions on the type of activities to move to cloud, and Table 10.2 provides a list of considerations to make before migrating to cloud.

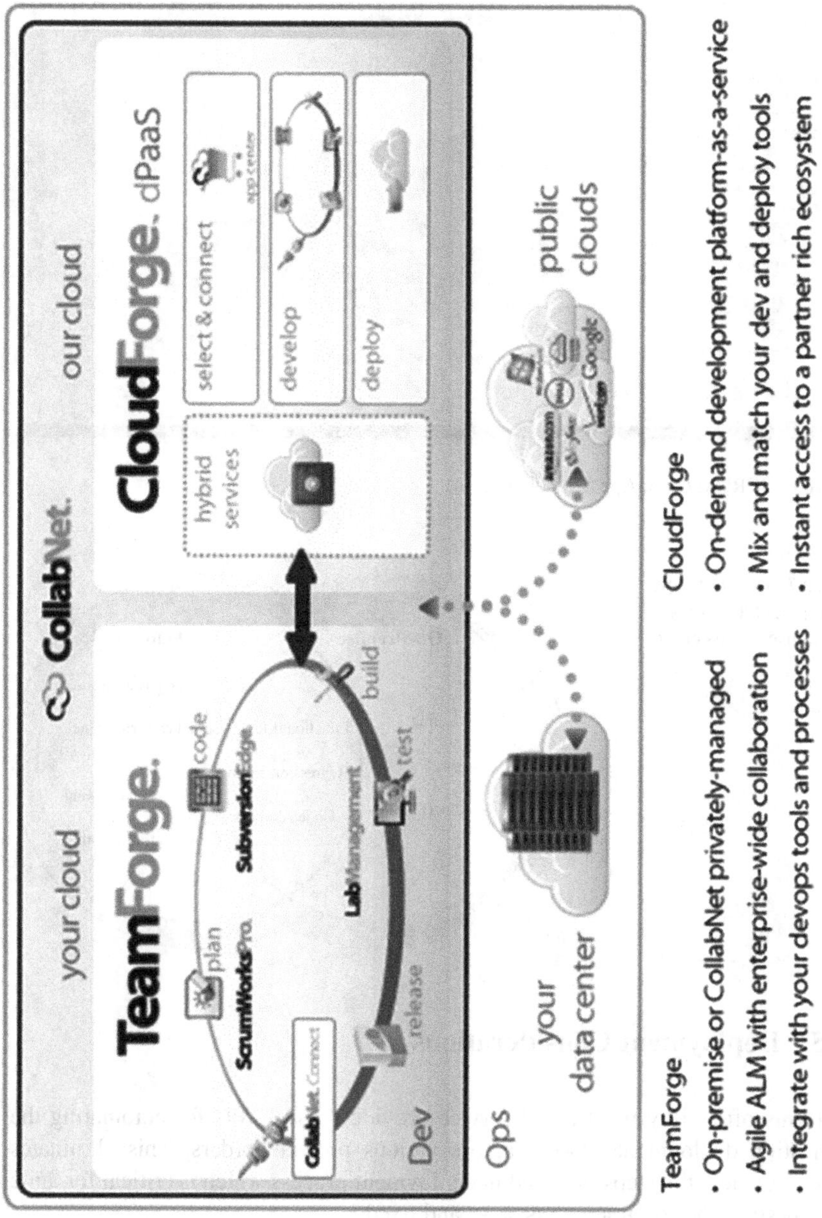

Fig. 10.5 CollabNet cloud platform—TeamForge and CloudForge [14]

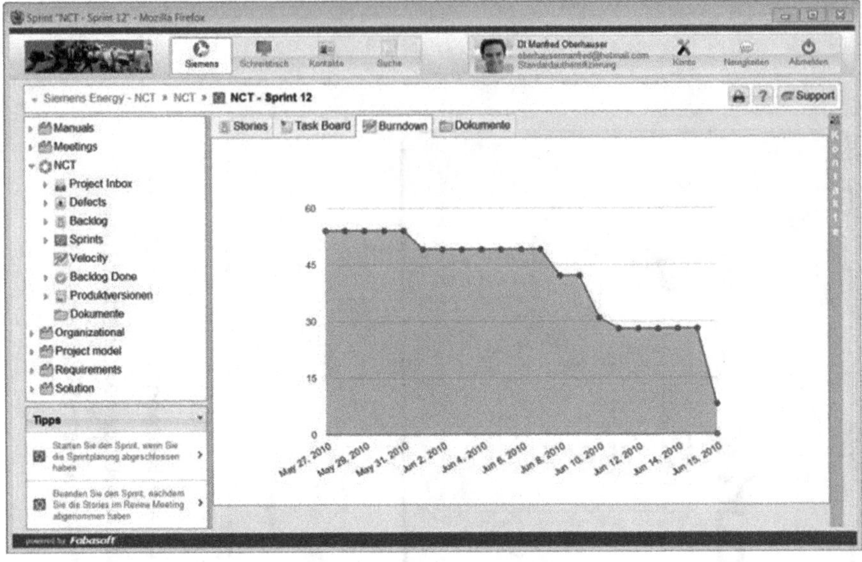

Fig. 10.6 SCRUM CloudApp (foliocloud.com)

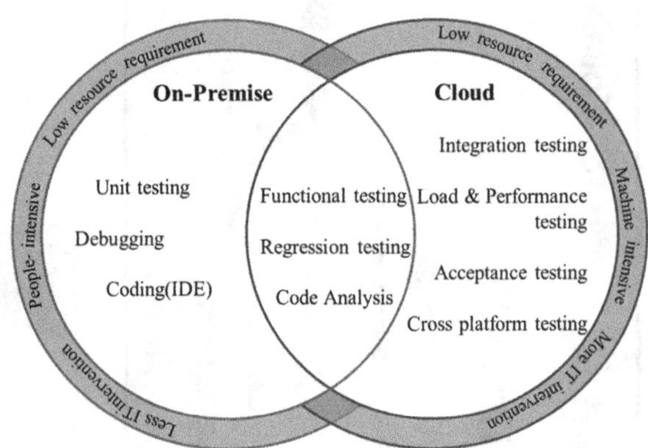

Fig. 10.7 Key software development activities—on-premise versus cloud

10.5 Deployment Considerations

Platforms offered by most cloud service providers have APIs for automating the application deployment process across various project borders. This eliminates some of the lengthy steps involved in deployment process which is critical for agile projects since the sprint length is short and fixed.

The capability that is most sought after in recent times on cloud-based development platform is the ability to support production deployment. Agile teams need to set up environments quickly, automate deployment into the live environment, schedule their jobs between private and public clouds and execute on flexible cloud platforms.

Table 10.2 Considerations for application assessment parameters

Characteristics	Parameters
Application type	Business applications
	Consumer applications
	Enterprise applications
Build type	COTS
	Custom
Functional	Domain
	Criticality
	Location
	Customer facing
Data	Data privacy
	Data volume
Non-functional characteristics	Availability
	Latency
	Security
	Scalability
Elastic requirements	Network
	Compute
	Storage

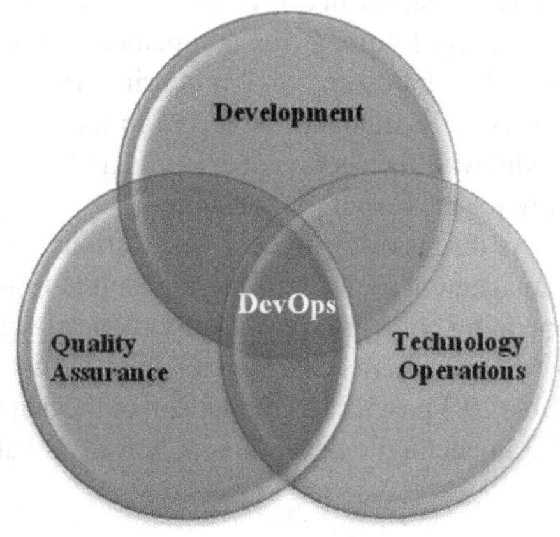

Fig. 10.8 DevOps as the intersection of development, technology operations and quality assurance

There will be a growing need for cloud analytics and management capabilities that provide visibility to development organisations as well as ability to quickly address changes typically triggered by trouble tickets and new software releases and to address the challenges of releasing new services and applications into production.

Agile software development has been in the industry for more than a decade, and agile development in the cloud is becoming a norm. Iterative and incremental development is now being applied for deployment too and popularly being known as DevOps. This is an agile operations concept that uses agile techniques to link up departments—Development (Dev) and Operations (Ops)—together, which traditionally operated in silos. Figure 10.8 summarises the DevOps concept.

The foundation of DevOps is established on the premise that all aspects of technology infrastructure can be managed through code. This may not be entirely possible without cloud. Repeatability is crucial for the success of DevOps. Once a setup is made available on the cloud, every task on that setup becomes repeatable. For example, starting a server becomes a repeatable testable process [15]. Scalability is another aspect of DevOps in the cloud, as it dramatically improves the server to admin ratio. Setting up a server is usually maintained as a set of lengthy procedures that are poorly documented and often demand manual intervention. However, with DevOps cloud combo, these steps are written down as a piece of software. This improves speed of setting up a server and at the same time reduces the need for manual intervention and thereby consequent errors. DevOps in the cloud also enables self-restoration; i.e. failures can be automatically detected, and backup systems can be brought to forefront seamlessly.

10.6 Cost and Time Implications of Agile in the Cloud

Pressures faced by businesses are increasing day by day; this in turn puts tremendous pressure on software development projects both in terms of time and cost. We have discussed earlier in this chapter that adopting cloud helps distribute the costs over a period into future, as the companies do not have to incur huge initial costs for provisioning hardware and procuring the software. The subscribe-and-use model allows for instantaneous access to the necessary resources, and the pay-as-you-go model with the service provider is a utility-based pricing scheme that allows to pay only for the resources consumed.

As discussed in the various sections throughout this chapter, collaboration and management tools in the cloud result in lesser economic investment. Overheads and operating costs are significantly reduced without compromise on instant availability of service which helps businesses to realise faster and higher return on investments. Table 10.3 provides a comparison of the nature of costs incurred due to various factors that impact agile development before and after cloud adoption.

10.6.1 The Case of Start-Ups and SMEs

Agile project management in the cloud can benefit small- and medium-sized enterprises (SMEs) and start-ups which are typically cash starved. The key enabling benefits are:

- Almost zero software installations and hardware setups
- Reduced time to market
- Access to extendable team of providers, partners and employees
- Avoid maintenance of server racks (needs skilled manpower and space)
- Offer flexible work from home options to their team members
- Save on overheads further by reducing the usage of the office space

Table 10.3 Nature of costs before and after cloud adoption

Factors impacting agile development	Traditional costs	Nature of costs with cloud adoption
Admin and maintenance people for handling in house infrastructure	High	Negligible, since most infrastructures are moved to cloud and managed by the cloud provider
Development effort	High	Low, SaaS-based licences used for various development software like IDEs, management and collaboration software
On-demand team ramp up/ramp down	High	Low, elasticity is one of the biggest advantages of cloud; payment is only for the services utilised
Demo	Moderate	Low, setting up demo environments can be done on a virtualised instance
Deployment	High	Low
Creating and managing test environments	High	Low
Creating and managing production environments	High	Low
Prototyping and continuous feedback	High	Low, risk associated with failure of prototypes would be minimal as compared to on-premise deployment wherein considerable investments have to be made on setting up the infrastructure and making the prototypes accessible

10.7 Challenges Using Cloud for Agile Software Development

The various benefits that cloud can offer to embrace agile software development were discussed in the previous sections. However, teams need to understand the challenges in adopting cloud. The challenges need to be weighed against the potential benefits before migrating to cloud. This section discusses the various challenges that need to be considered.

A system may be implemented with a wide range of services and applications. For example, static content could be on Google App Engine, and the streaming content could be on AWS. To make these possible, applications need to be specifically designed to work in such heterogeneous environments.

Each cloud vendor offers a different set of services. Choosing the right vendor is crucial since there is significant lock-in once a vendor has been chosen. Unlike other traditional development methodologies like waterfall, agile teams will not be able to re-evaluate a vendor and change the cloud provider during the course of the iterations. This can prove to be costly in terms of time. Outages could be another challenge. Although this is true even for self-owned data centres, the team has very little control and knowledge in the event of an outage in this case.

Compliance could be another constraint when using cloud computing. However, regulations and compliance bodies do not completely hinder the use of cloud computing. The implications for cloud computing while complying with the regulations should be understood. It is possible to reconcile through both careful planning and risk management. For example, in order to remain HIPAA compliant, one of the projects encrypted its data so that it can be hosted on a cloud platform.

As far as security and performance are considered, service levels are particularly important when the entire or most parts of the infrastructure are outsourced to a cloud provider.

At this moment, there is no common standard used by utility computing services. Depending on the type of product and application being built, the economic aspects need to be worked out. The costs and savings of moving to cloud versus owning the infrastructure need to be carefully weighed.

There are different cloud-based tools that allow us to work together, but these tools may need a tool of their own to work together better. It is a fact that teams struggle to manage the multiple communication streams they are connected to. For example, 300 mg is a tool that pulls all the business information from various cloud services together in one place; Hojoki lets all of a customer's CloudApps work as one.

10.8 Case Study of an Agile Project That Adopted Cloud

This case study is about a software solution to a telecom service provider (TSP). TSP had solutions and products which could be offered by the parent business or any of its partners. The solutions and products were offered across diverse geographical locations, and the partners offering the solutions were scattered across the world. The key issues and the core requirements of the project are listed below:

- Each of the partners wanted a portal from which the solutions and products could be offered.
- Existing customers of the partner wanted a mechanism to manage their products.
- Develop the ability to set up new partner portals in minimum time duration taking into account the customisation needs of the new partner.
- Provide integration with interfaces for ease of management and provisioning of products and solution packages.

These problem areas were impacting the business already. As more partners were being added across the geographies, partner portals needed to be designed and deployed. Infrastructure costs and development efforts were beginning to increase. The effort required in order to come up with a single partner portal was around 12 person months on an average. This directly correlated to an increased turnaround time before a partner could start offering the products and solutions.

These challenges would be true in any business which offers products and solution packages through a network of partners based in different locations. In addition to the above challenges, the development team was distributed and spread across the USA, India and China. Collaboration was difficult to achieve, and lack of sufficient collaboration could lead to integration problems and delay the project significantly.

The solution approach which was proposed to cater to the problem areas mentioned above involved:

- Development of a portal framework which could address the customisation needs of the partner and support an XML template-based GUI customisation and has the ability to integrate with the exposed product and solution interfaces.
- The portal framework would be hosted on a cloud platform like Amazon EC2 or Microsoft Azure.

The high-level architecture diagram for the solution is given in Fig. 10.9. The solution provided key administrator roles—super admin, partner admin and customer admin. The super admin could create instances of the portal for the different partners. The entire portal framework was hosted inside a cloud environment.

Hosting the portal inside a cloud platform provided the following benefits:

- Better scalability—scaling of the portal instance depending on the load of incoming traffic on the partner portal instance.
- Complete control of instances—instance management is provided through a single interface.
- Elastic load balancing—automatically distributes incoming application traffic across multiple instances. It enables greater fault tolerance.
- Multitenancy—the cloud platform provided inbuilt multitenancy, thus providing partner instances.
- The framework had support for XML-based template customisation and also provided localisation support.
- Reduction in infrastructure cost—leveraging a cloud platform resulted in drastic infrastructure cost reduction (close to 25 %).
- Reusable and customisable framework.
- Efficient load balancing and instance management.

In addition, the project management tool, source code repositories and continuous integration servers were maintained on the cloud. The team also practised test-driven development (TDD). Cloud enabled TDD by making it possible to edit code and make incremental deployments for testing. Table 10.4 lists the benefits that the team got through continuous integration and TDD. The teams across the geographies collaborated on a daily basis via a cloud-enabled videoconferencing system (see Fig. 10.10). Frequent demos and reviews were set up throughout the iteration. Adoption of cloud made it possible to set up in progress working software for demo purposes within short setup times.

10.9 Tools for Agile Software Development in the Cloud

Throughout this chapter, different activities and tools were discussed. Table 10.5 provides a snapshot of various tools and the activities they support along with few examples. Some of the tools in this space in the industry as well as the ones listed in

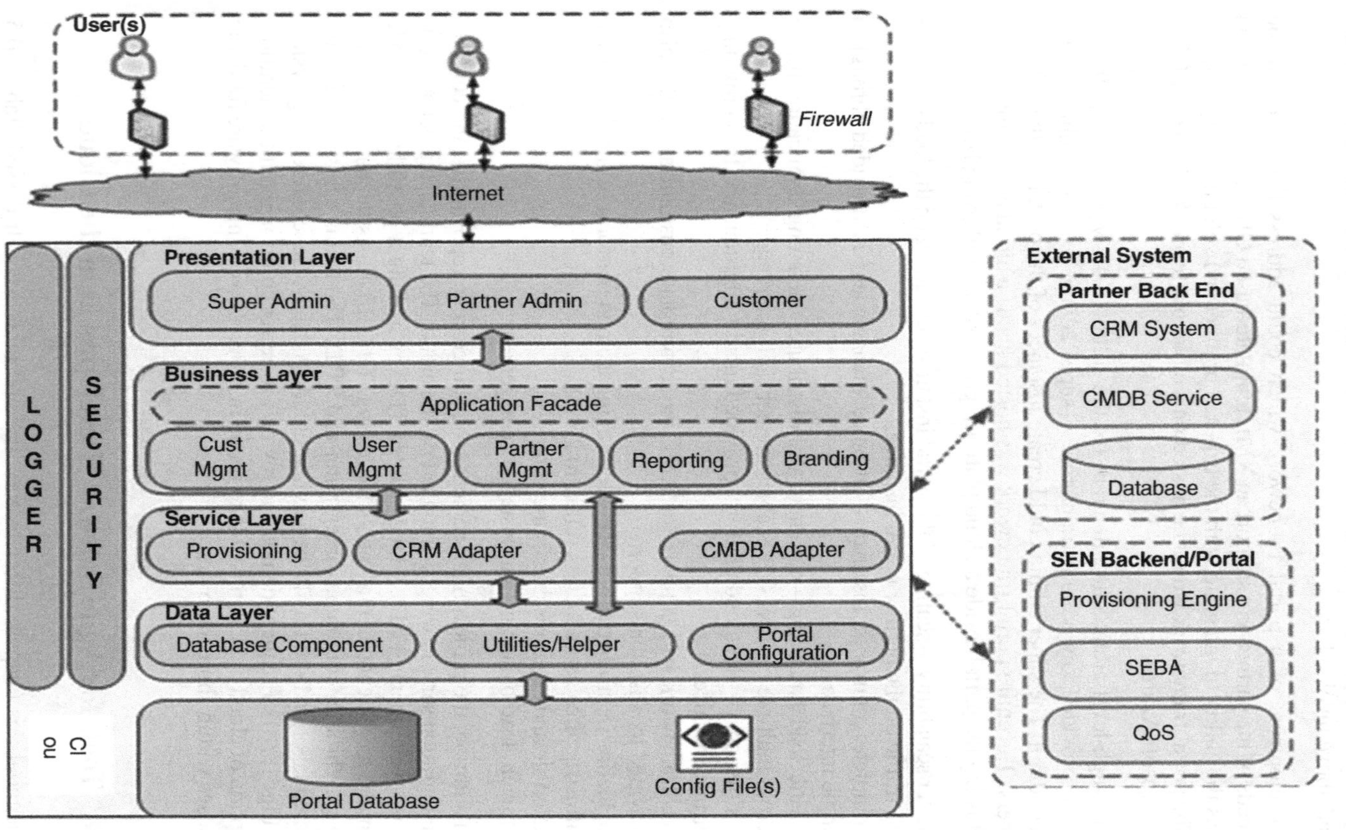

Fig. 10.9 High-level architecture diagram

Table 10.4 Effects of continuous integration and test-driven development before and after cloud adoption

Continuous integration	
Before	*After*
A dedicated build engineer takes care of the build	The entire process is automated by means of continuous integration tool
In addition to the actual build time, the build engineer is involved in cleaning up previous builds, restoring last known good build in case of failures, debugging and deploying builds	Productivity improvement: 7 h/day
Build time: approx. 2 h 40 min	Build time: 30 min
Build frequency: once per day	Build frequency: 4 times per day
Test-driven development	
Before	*After*
Manual unit tests were written and maintained on a spreadsheet	Test cases were written using an xUnit framework
Code coverage ratio: <0.20	Code coverage ratio: 0.84
(Could not be measured precisely; the number was derived based on input from the team)	(This metric was calculated precisely using the code coverage tool Cobertura)
No. of unit test cases: 176	No. of unit test cases: 3,552
No. of defects: 13 (in user acceptance testing), 4 (postproduction)	No. of defects: 4 (in user acceptance testing), 0 (postproduction)

Fig. 10.10 Collaboration through videoconferencing setup hosted on cloud

Table 10.5 List of tools for agile development in the cloud

Tool categories	Purpose	Example
Project management	An integrated suite for web-based project management—sprint planning, generating reports, tracking estimates and task breakdowns	Atlassian-GreenHopper, CollabNet-TeamForge
Collaboration	Collaboration through wikis, online discussion forums, instant chat and document management	Basecamp, Microsoft SharePoint
Continuous integration	Automated continuous builds through continuous integration	Jenkins, TeamCity
Test automation	Automated regression, performance and load tests	Selenium Grid, HP LoadRunner
Defect management	Tracking and managing defect category, status, description, steps to reproduce, etc.	Bugzilla, Atlassian-JIRA
Requirements management	Managing product backlog—epics and user stories	Microsoft Team Foundation Server, Pivotal Tracker
Source code management	Committing coding, version control, branching, change management	Subversion, Git
Integrated development environment (IDE)	Writing code, debugging and unit testing	Eclipse, Visual Studio
Videoconferencing	Face-to-face discussion among geographically distributed members	IVCi, Nefsis
DevOps	IT operations management for continuous delivery	Puppet, Chef
Virtual Private Cloud Management	Physical and virtual machines that can be adaptably used by project teams	enStratus, CUBiT

the example column in Table 10.4 also have ALM capabilities. For businesses that practise enterprise-scale agile, using an ALM tool may be a good option as the integration issues are almost invisible.

10.10 Conclusion

Combining agile development together with the capabilities of cloud computing dramatically accelerates the pace of business development. Agile methods emphasise on involving the end users in the software development process. Each requirement is built exactly the way the user wants it. As development progresses, the project moves in an incremental manner with a strong feedback loop that reprioritises the work based on the real-time business needs. Agile software development powered by cloud gives superior control over the process, helps realise faster ROI, strengthens the firm's competitive edge and above all enables preservation of agility as defined by the agile manifesto.

Agile methods are continuously evolving; agile teams have broken the barriers to communication and have taken agile development from small pockets to global software development. The number and size of distributed teams that collaborate and embrace agile across time zones and geographies are increasing. These teams have begun exploiting the capabilities of cloud computing. Due to the advent of cloud, agile practices which were applied to development and testing are now being applied for IT operations.

A software development team that is planning to adopt cloud can identify different types and spheres of issues faced by the team in case of global software development and investigate the potential of the cloud to address those issues. Evaluation of service model is crucial to determining the service providers. The integration requirements with current on-premise systems need to be considered. Classification of the applications based on security and confidentiality could be a useful step before migration. Frequent and preferably automated review of service-level agreements and performance requirements is important to ensure there is no degradation in service. Teams should also be aware of the additional collaboration and coordination efforts requirement with the cloud service provider. In addition, project managers need to understand the contractual implications that have been established with the cloud vendors.

Cloud can simplify software development as a product as well as a process. The process could have implications for the software development business model in which service providers are organisations and services are parts of a global software development process.

In summary, agile and cloud together make a valuable combination as it can aid software teams to produce useful functionality that can be taken to the customers instantaneously, collate feedback and make quick changes based on that feedback. Software development teams will need to make use of the potential that agile and cloud together offer and provide better software products.

References

1. Ahead in the cloud: CSC Cloud Usage Index Report, BusinessWire (2011)
2. Herbsleb, J.D.: Global software engineering: the future of socio technical coordination. In: Proceedings of the Future of Software Engineering (FOSE'07), pp. 188–198. IEEE, Washington, DC (2007)
3. Allen, T.J.: Managing the Flow of Technology. MIT Press, Cambridge, MA (1977)
4. Linthicum, D.: Leveraging cloud computing for business continuity. Disaster Recovery J. **23**(3), 28–30 (2010)
5. Halpert, B.: Auditing Cloud Computing – A Security and Privacy Guide. Wiley, Hoboken (2011)
6. Herbsleb, J.D., Mockus, A.: An empirical study of speed and communication in globally distributed software development. IEEE Trans. Softw. Eng. **29**(6), 481–494 (2003)

7. Ciccozzi, F., Crnković, I.: Performing a project in a distributed software development course: lessons learned. In: Proceedings of the 5th IEEE International Conference on Global Software Engineering (ICGSE), pp. 187–191, 23–26 Aug 2010. IEEE, Princeton (2010)
8. Grinter, R.E., Herbsleb, J.D., Perry, D.E.: The geography of coordination: dealing with distance in R&D work. In: Proceedings of the International ACM SIGGROUP Conference on Supporting Group Work (GROUP '99), pp. 306–315. ACM Press, New York (1999)
9. Ensell, J.: Agile development in the cloud. Agile J. http://www.agilejournal.com/articles/columns/column-articles/6018-agile-development-in-the-cloud (2011). Last Accessed May 2012
10. Zrnec, A.: Software engineering in the cloud for reducing the application time-to-market. Elektroteh. Vestn. Electrotechnical Society of Slovenia, Ljubljana, Slovenia **78**(3), 123–127 (2011)
11. Kawaguchi, K.: Continuous integration in the cloud with Hudson (TS-5301). In: Proceedings of the JavaOne Conference (2009).
12. Dumbre, A., Ghag, S.S., Senthil, S.P.: Practising Agile Software Development on the Windows Azure platform, Infosys Whitepaper (2011)
13. Folio Cloud: www.foliocloud.com (2012). Last Accessed May 2012
14. Collabnet TeamForge: www.collab.net (2012). Last Accessed May 2012
15. Reese, G.: DevOps in the cloud explained. http://devops.com (2011). Last Accessed May 2012
16. Hashmi, S.I., Clerc, V., Razavian, M., Manteli, C., Tamburri, D.A., Lago, P., Nitto, E.D., Richardson, I.: Using the cloud to facilitate global software development challenges. In: Proceedings of the Global Software Engineering Workshop 2011 (ICGSEW). IEEE, Helsinki, Finland (2011)

Chapter 11
Technical Strategies and Architectural Patterns for Migrating Legacy Systems to the Cloud

Sidharth Subhash Ghag and Rahul Bandopadhyaya

Abstract With the advent of Internet, information has crossed the realms of books and gone digital, requiring data to be easily accessible and delivered anywhere speedily. There are myriads of formats in which data is currently available, such as videos, images, documents and Web pages. Accordingly, handling datasets in various formats has made the task of designing scalable and reliable application really challenging. Building the applications of tomorrow would need architects and developers to construct applications that can meet the needs that would demand handling high volumes of data and deliver substantial throughput. In today's enterprises, there are legacy applications which may have been developed several years or even decades ago. At the time, the business may have been in its infancy, and so applications may have been designed to satisfactorily handle workloads prevalent in those times with some average growth factors built in. However, owing to the new emerging trends in the technology space, such as mobile and big data, the workloads at which businesses operate today have grown manifold. Also, the monolithic legacy systems serving those workloads have failed to keep pace, often struggling to deliver the SLAs (Service-Level Agreement). Although cloud is not a panacea for all kind of new demands, we believe that with some appropriate architectural restructuring, existing applications may go a long way in serving the demands of new growing businesses. Applications redesigned on the lines of parallel computing patterns such as master/worker or MapReduce and implemented on cloud platforms can be leveraged to add new life or re-energise legacy applications that can scale much better. In this chapter, we discuss an approach to transform legacy applications, designed to handle high-volume requests, by using re-engineering techniques and modern design patterns so as to effectively realise the benefits of cloud environment.

S.S. Ghag (✉)
Infosys Labs, Infosys Limited, Pune, India
e-mail: sidharth_ghag@infosys.com

R. Bandopadhyaya
Infosys Labs, Infosys Limited, Bangalore, India
e-mail: rahul_bandopadhyaya@infosys.com

Z. Mahmood and S. Saeed (eds.), *Software Engineering Frameworks for the Cloud Computing Paradigm*, Computer Communications and Networks,
DOI 10.1007/978-1-4471-5031-2_11,

Keywords Application migration • Distributed application • Parallel processing • SOA • Cloud engineering • Windows azure • Azure • Model-driven architecture

11.1 Introduction

Service-oriented architecture (SOA) is a key architectural concept in the field of service computing. SOA design principles are used as guidance to develop service-oriented applications [1]. A *service* forms the basic construct of SOA which enables rapid creation, ease of publication and seamless assimilation for developing distributed applications across a heterogeneous system environment. The World Wide Web Consortium (W3C) defines SOA as "*A set of components which can be invoked, and whose interface descriptions can be published and discovered*" [2]. As per a Microsoft article, SOA can be simply defined as "*A loosely-coupled architecture designed to meet the business needs of the organization*" [3]. In short, SOA aids to deliver agility. Globally, enterprise IT is adapting to SOA in order to bring in efficiencies and responsiveness within the internal as well external processes and systems. Agile IT systems help businesses tackle and exploit change by delivering faster, better and cheaper services.

For enterprises to truly benefit from SOA, best-in-class SOA practices have to be established. Service-oriented principle applied to service design improves service reusability and infuses desirable characters such as agility, interoperability and flexibility [4]. However, applying service-oriented principles come with their own set of design challenges [5]; e.g.:

- Existing SOA frameworks do not guide developers towards proper application of these principles and thus cannot help in establishing best practices in service-oriented design.
- SOA principles are violated by binding services tightly to specific technologies and middleware, which lock systems into the specific product.

The application being discussed in this chapter, "service modelling workbench", has been developed to effectively address the challenges highlighted.

In the rest of the chapter, we begin by providing a background and discuss the AS-IS architecture along with challenges faced by the application to meet the growing demands of SOA in Sects. 11.2 and 11.3. Then, in Sect. 11.4, we discuss the overall technical adoption strategy, identify a suitable design pattern and propose a cloud-driven future-state solution architecture with a detailed view into the different components developed to address the challenges highlighted. Further, in Sect. 11.5, we identify the Windows Azure cloud service components which have been utilised to develop the target application. Section 11.6 lists the benefits gained from this new proposed cloud-based architecture. We also share best practices which have been compiled from our learnings and experiences in this process in Sect. 11.7. A brief summary is provided in Sect. 11.8.

11.2 Background

"Service modelling workbench" is a service modelling tool which provides its users (architects, analysts and developers) a design environment to model and build service-oriented applications in a *standards-oriented* approach. The tool is used to enhance service engineering life cycle by providing best practices and guidances around service design and development practices. It presents a workbench environment to design, develop and deploy services on the lines of SOA. Using this application, a user is able to model service-oriented definitions and implementations without having to touch a single line of source code. This is possible as the application, based on predefined templates and configurations specified by the user, automates the low-level code generation of the entire architecture stack of a typical service-oriented application as depicted in Fig. 11.1.

The process of realising the services is driven by the design specifications defined in the model and is implemented using a template-based code generation process. This approach requires a lot of code churning to generate low-level code from the high-level models. Based on the complexity of the business functionality and as demands of service orientation begin to grow in enterprises, so did the need to process high volume of requests. The services modelled could range anywhere from one to thousands of services, and, hence, it was required for the application as well as the infrastructure to scale and handle the load variations in a consistent and time-bound manner. In some of our deployments, when demands to process requests began to increase rapidly, we observed that the application took 3–4 h to generate around 300–400 services. Also, the processing time would rise linearly as the number of services expanded. This high processing time and the inability of the application to scale were unacceptable. The scalability of the application was limited due the monolithic nature of the existing architecture and also the infrastructure it ran on. More details on the state of the earlier architecture and its challenges are explained in the next section (Fig. 11.2).

11.3 AS-IS Architecture

The traditional architecture of the legacy service modelling application consisted of a monolithic stand-alone desktop client running within a single app domain [6]. This design constrains the application to execute in one single process with limited ability to scale. Similar patterns have been significantly observed with legacy applications in several enterprises which have evolved in the context of their businesses. As the business continued to grow, so would have the workloads on such applications outgrown the planned expectations.

The different steps involved and their order of execution which constitute the process of service modelling and subsequent code generation are depicted in Fig. 11.3 and explained below:

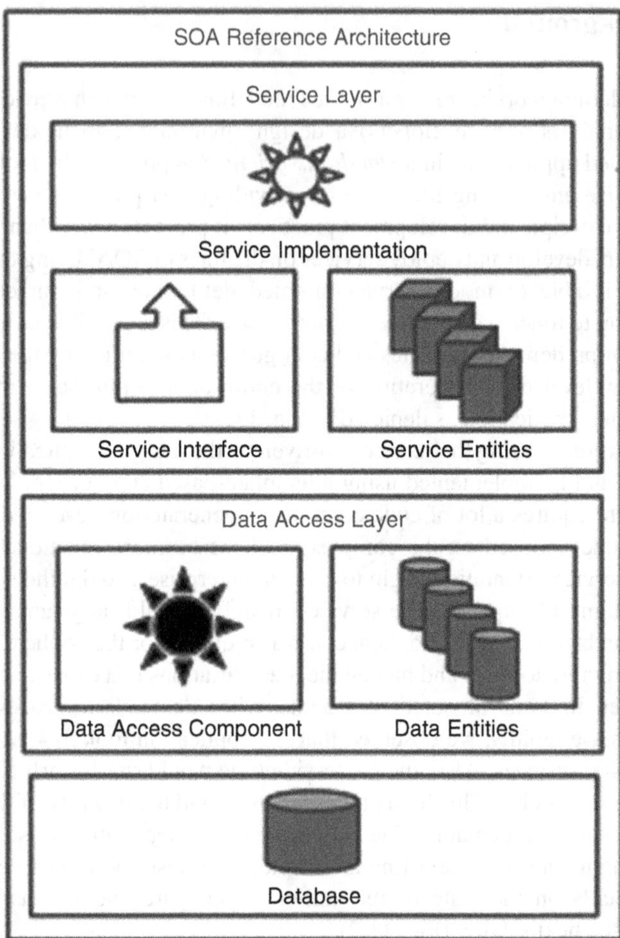

Fig. 11.1 SOA reference architecture

- *User interactions* – service modelling workbench:
  1. Using the application workbench, the analyst or architect designs the service model providing information such as the data contracts/information models, service contracts, service binding, policies, the target back-end database type and optional information regarding the final hosting environment such as Windows Azure™ and on-premise.
  2. Once the model is finalised, the model is persisted for future reference, and, subsequently, the code generation process is initiated.
- *Process* – code generation process:
  1. Based on the service model, data contracts and service contracts are generated by using code template files stored in the template store.

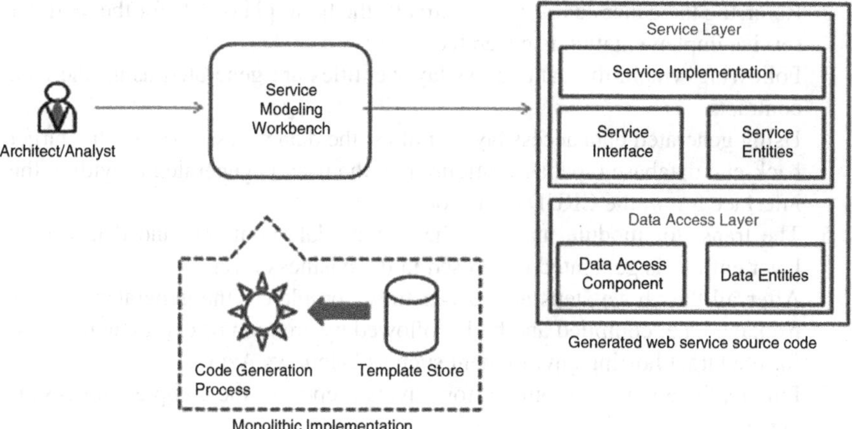

Fig. 11.2 Application overview

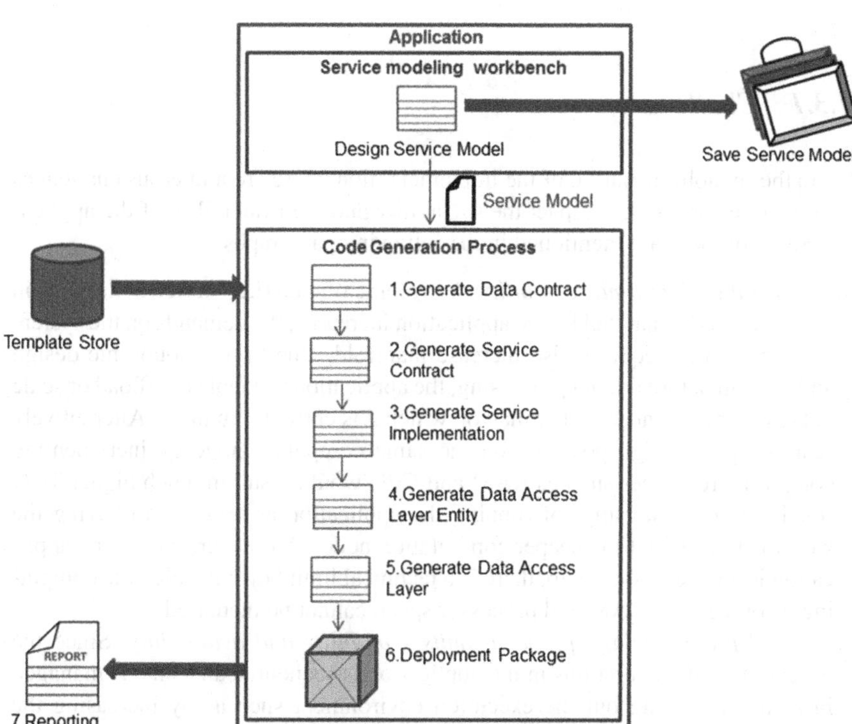

Fig. 11.3 Tasks and interdependencies in the legacy application

2. Referring the generated service contracts, the boilerplate code for the modular service implementation is generated.
3. Following which, the data access layer entities are generated using the data contracts.
4. Using generated data access layer entities, the data access layer for the target back-end database type, as configured by the user, is generated providing the interface for all the CRUD operations.
5. The translator module mapping the service data contracts and data access layer entities is generated to be used in the business layer.
6. After all the above steps are successfully completed, the generated code is packaged, i.e. compiled and built, followed by creation of deployment file(s) for the target hosting environment such as Windows Azure.
7. Finally, the quality and other effort savings report of the complete process is generated.

Though the code generation process has clear separation and abstraction, there is close dependency among the above operations, i.e. dependency on the state or output of the previous operation. Due to this and in its monolithic implementation approach, if any operation crashes for any reason, the entire application is brought down. That is, there is less opportunity for the application to quickly heal itself for attending to subsequent requests.

11.3.1 Challenges

Due to the monolithic nature of the implementation, there are numerous challenges in the architecture which impact the scalability and the availability of the application. Some of these are mentioned in the following paragraphs.

Architectural choices limit scalability: As volume of data (i.e. service definitions in the model) to be handled by the application increases, the demands on the system to process such requests also increase manifold. Due to the monolithic design and stateful nature of data processing, the application is unable to offload or scale out to computing nodes other than on which it is currently running. Alternatively scaling up, although possible, on the same computing node by incrementing computing resources such as RAM and CPU would result in much higher TCO (total cost of ownership) of running the application as opposed to having the workloads scale out to cheaper computation nodes. Moreover, even if the application is allowed to scale up, there is a technical limit beyond which the computing resources like RAM and processor speed cannot be increased.

Traditional programming approach limits scalability and availability: Since the execution of the operations in the application is sequential and state is managed in memory, scaling out the execution environment such as by increasing the number of processor or machine count may also not help the application to scale to handle high volumes. The sequential nature of the code execution also forces the system to be rendered unavailable to process additional requests for the entire duration of the code generation cycle.

Lack of isolation boundaries impacts software reliability: The different operations are executed in a single application domain; any faulty operation affects the entire application execution. The moment any operation crashes for any reason, the application aborts all the subsequent operations and simultaneously also flushes out the state of all the operations which may have successfully completed prior to the exception. The application is left in a faulty state, and it is highly unlikely that it will quickly heal itself unless the entire process is restarted afresh.

Consumption of system level resources in an uncontrolled manner results in system conflicts: Since the code generation process requires high-compute resources, its execution may affect the normal execution of other applications/services in the same machine.

11.4 Technical Adoption Strategy

Now that we understand the issues with the legacy application, let us discuss on the approach adopted to re-engineer the application for achieving the desired benefits of scalability, reliability and availability. We now discuss in detail the strategies adopted to migrate a monolithic stand-alone desktop application to a distributed cloud-hosted application.

11.4.1 Application Re-engineering

With the new application design, re-engineering was done only for part of the application where major performance bottlenecks had been observed, which being the code generation process, while the client interface was mainly left untouched. In the application re-engineering process, basic operations (as described in the Sect. 11.3) were re-factored to be stateless by design, i.e. not to rely on information about operations being stored between interactions, so that, given a task, it can be executed independently in a different processor or machine as may be the case to enable scale-up or scale-out conditions. Here are the steps followed to re-factor the application:

11.4.1.1 Draw Flowcharts

In case the program is not properly documented, a first step in the migration process is to draw out the flow of your program using flowcharts. Flowcharts are a very useful tool to help understand complex or intertwined code flows. A flowchart helps to identify code inefficiencies or code smells [7] such as duplicate code, long methods and variable interdependencies. Using the flowchart, a visual representation of the different steps traversed by the program to complete a certain operation is presented to the analyst. This provides the analyst opportunities to "*extract methods*", as is discussed in the next step.

11.4.1.2 Breakout Granular Operations

This is usually the first step in *re-factoring* [7]: decomposition of monolithic implementation of the application into granular and independent operations which are modular. An appropriate granular definition of an operation can be arrived by first drawing out the use case of the overall process as a series of activities required to be done to achieve the end state. Each activity can be considered as potential operation candidate. If there is scope for further refinement of any particular activity, sublevel use cases can be further created at the activity level and aid in the process of refining the operations definition. In our case, the key operations identified were data contract generation, service implementation generation, data access layer entity generation, data access layer generation and package deployment. This was derived based on the use case as depicted in Fig. 11.3. The approach we discuss here is considering a top-level view of the application to extract granular operations. Other low-level code re-factoring strategies can also be adopted to extract modules from monolithic software code [8].

11.4.1.3 Define Input/Output Operation Parameters

Each operation should have its input or output parameters defined explicitly. Private variable references, if used, in the legacy code to run across multiple pieces of code statements should be extracted and be explicitly included as a part of the operations parameter. This will enable the operation to be executed in an independent manner. *Data Transfer Object* (*DTO*) *pattern* is best suited to realise operations which can meet this requirement. A DTO pattern is simply a container for carrying aggregated data that needs to be transferred across process or network boundaries. It should not contain any business logic [9, 10]. The DTO pattern helps provide abstraction from object or function internals, thereby increasing potential for reuse.

11.4.1.4 Define and Coordinate Interactions Asynchronously

Interactions between the operations have to be achieved asynchronously. Since there would be dependencies between operations in the application (i.e. not all the operations can be run simultaneously), such operations can be made to communicate or share information/data using asynchronous mechanisms such as queues. When the prerequisite information/data which may be the output of some other

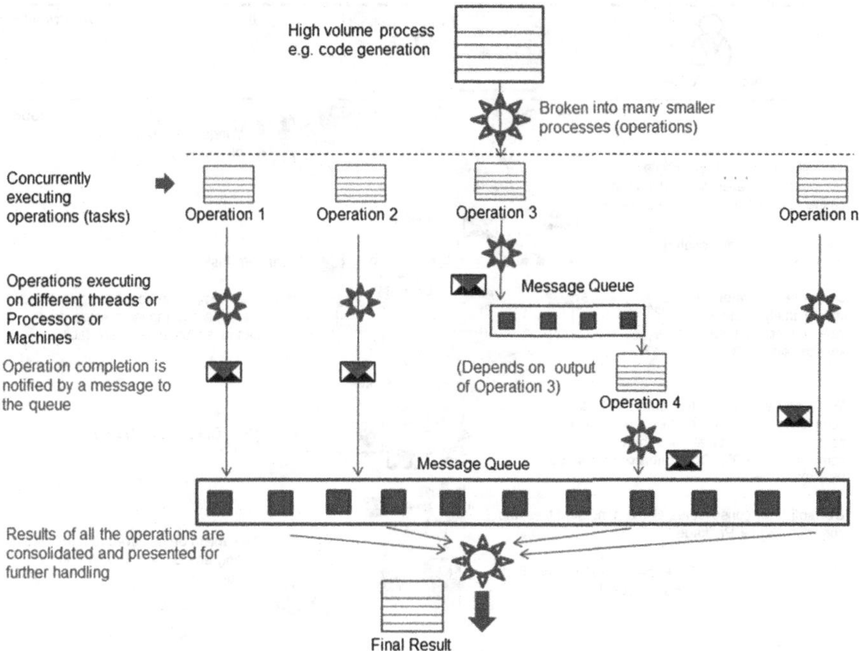

Fig. 11.4 Parallel processing design pattern

operation is available, the following operation in the process is communicated asynchronously using an event notification message. This approach helps in scaling the overall implementation both in a scale-up as well as scale-out manner.

11.4.2 Identification of Design Patterns

The code generation process is re-engineered on the lines of the parallel processing design pattern. Parallel processing design pattern is a well-known implementation approach to scale an application so as to handle high volume of requests. Parallel processing is the execution of one or more task(s), usually in parallel and independently, with the objective to achieve a common goal by a group of executing entities (machines, processors) engaged to do the parts of a high-volume process. This is applied in the cases where it is possible to break a large process into group of tasks/operations, and each task can be executed independently without having any dependency on the other task(s) during the course of its execution. Some popularly known examples of implementation of the parallel processing design patterns are master/worker and MapReduce (Fig. 11.4).

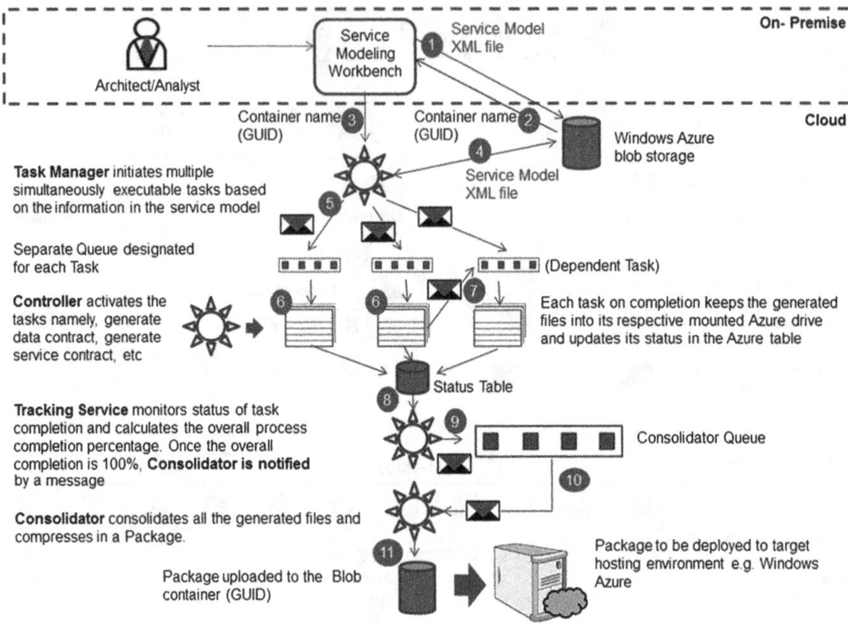

Fig. 11.5 Cloud-enabled application architecture

11.4.3 Future-State Solution Architecture

As the legacy code is re-factored, we are in a good position to implement the parallel processing design pattern in the application. In our case, we realised the future-state solution architecture by leveraging cloud computing building blocks and infrastructure offered by Windows Azure [11]. Here we provide detail of the same. We have tried to keep our explanation in context of design patterns so that techniques discussed here may be applied equally well on other cloud computing platforms having similar set of services.

The future-state solution was implemented as depicted in Fig. 11.5.

The key components of the architecture include the following.

11.4.3.1 Service Modelling Workbench

A service model is prepared in the service designer using the client workbench. The task manager Web service is invoked by the client to initiate the code generation. A pointer to the model is passed as one of the input parameters to the service request. Following are the steps which describe the process of forwarding the service model to the task manager (also refer to Fig. 11.5):

- The service model is persisted as an XML file by the service modelling workbench.
- The workbench generates a Globally Unique Identifier (GUID) for every new request raised. A Windows Azure blob storage container uniquely identified by the GUID name is created. The XML file is then uploaded to this container. This GUID depicting the container name is then sent to the task manager using the Web service interface.
- The task manager using the GUID accesses the blob storage and downloads the service model XML file which is contained in the Azure blob storage container created in step 2 (Fig. 11.5).

Based on the service designed by the user in the client workbench, the service model file can range to a few hundreds of megabytes in size. The pattern discussed above provides a more efficient and reliable approach to processing large volume datasets. Without having the initiating Web service to handle large datasets, we free up the task manager services from accepting additional requests received from other users and in turn improve the throughput of the application. Also, in case a failure occurs while uploading the service model to the blob storage, say if the storage services are unavailable or it goes down during the upload process, the user is immediately prompted of the inability to process the request at the time. This happens without having to initiate the code generation process request with the task manager, freeing it from having to worry about failures of other services not really within its direct control.

11.4.3.2 Task

A task is a basic unit of work scheduled by the task manager. As discussed in the application re-engineering section, each granular operation extracted from the legacy code after being identified as being an autonomous part of the code generation process is defined as a separate task, namely,

- Generate data contract.
- Generate service contract.
- Generate service implementation.
- Generate data access layer entity.
- Generate data access layer.
- Create and deploy the deployment package.

These granular operations defined as tasks are considered to be modular functions which can operate independently without relying on external resources such as shared variables or shared database to complete its assigned task. This design philosophy of building modular functions is one of the key principles of SOA which aid to maximise reuse. These tasks are the concurrently executable operations activated by the controller.

11.4.3.3 Task Manager

The next component in the architecture is the task manager. A task manager is responsible for the following:

- Receiving and validating the request from the client with the metadata used to process the request
- Creating a new entry in the service model processing database indicating the service request received from the user
- Based on the service model specification, creating separate entries of all the files which are to be generated by the respective tasks
- Preparing the task message for the respective task in the code generation process
- Distributing the messages using queue to different tasks configured in the controller

The task manager initiates task by posting job initiation messages to the respective task queues. The message contains information regarding the job to be executed by the task. In our solution, the task manager is implemented as a WCF (Windows Communication Foundation) Web service configured as a Windows Azure Web role. This task manager Web service exposes a service end point to receive the information regarding the service model code generation request from the client.

11.4.3.4 Controller

A controller will centrally manage and activate all the required tasks to successfully execute the code generation process. The controller is implemented as a Windows Azure worker role component, which is primarily used to handle batch or offline operations on Windows Azure, and the information regarding the tasks to be activated is configured through the worker role configuration settings. A controller configuration setting contains the following information:

- Task module path: A pointer to the module (say a dynamic link library, .dll) which exposes the entry point for activating the task.
- Task queue: A queue name to raise event triggers for task defined in the module path to initiate its job. The task would be listening for specific events on this queue for any message. The message would contain information required by the task to process its job. Essentially through this message, the task is given a job to execute.
  - Queues help in achieving loose coupling between the task manager, explained later, and the tasks.
  - Queues also enable loosely coupled interactions between dependent tasks. In case of dependent tasks where it is needed to maintain the order of execution, once one task is completed, it drops a message with required information in the queue of the subsequent task to be executed.

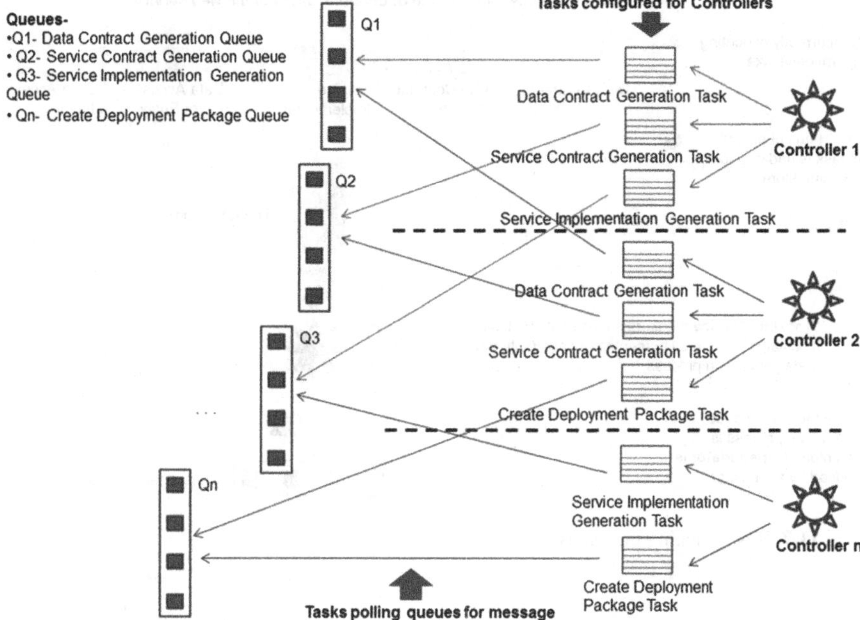

Fig. 11.6 Scaling out of controller to increase application throughput

- Task storage drive: A Windows Azure drive letter, where the files generated by the respective tasks are persisted. A Windows Azure drive is automatically mounted by the controller for the respective tasks, during the activation process based on the storage drive letter configured here.

Configuring tasks in the controller helps in spawning tasks across more than one controller. On Windows Azure, this is seamlessly achieved by configuring a separate worker role, which instantaneously provisions VMIs (Virtual Machine Images) while hosting the app on Windows Azure. This configuration provides flexibility to scale out the controller both at design time as well as runtime (Fig. 11.6).

With this approach of scaling out the controller, we are fundamentally able to scale out the task handler and hence able to achieve high throughput.

11.4.3.5 Tracking Service

On completion of respective code generation tasks, each task updates its status of execution to a centralised status table. This tracking service tracks the task status and calculates the overall code generation process completion percentage. On overall completion of all tasks, it notifies the consolidator (Figs. 11.5 and 11.7) by posting a message in the designated queue.

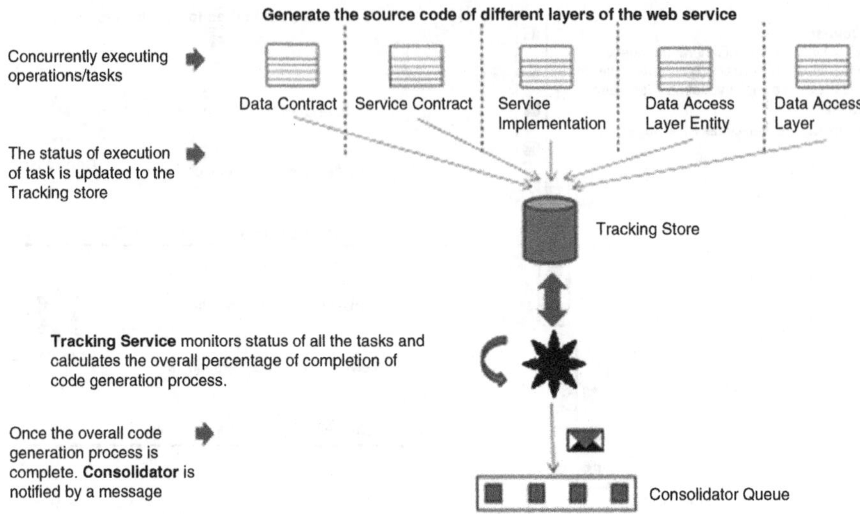

Fig. 11.7 Task-tracking mechanism

The tracking service maintains a log which it continuously updates with the current processing percentage completed and also the current status of overall code generation. The service model workbench using this log provides the details on the dashboard to monitor the overall completion percentage and the status of the code generation process. Accordingly in case of any anomaly, corrective steps may be initiated.

Once all the tasks are completed, which will be identified by the tracking service, the tracking service notifies the same to the consolidator by posting a message in the designated queue for further consolidation of all the generated different code files.

11.4.3.6 Consolidator

On being notified by the tracking service, the consolidator process consolidates the generated source code files from all the task-specific Azure drives into a well-structured .net solution and subsequently packaging these into a single compressed file. The compressed file is then uploaded to the same container in the blob storage where the service model had been uploaded earlier during the initiation process by the client, i.e. the service modelling workbench. The consolidator component is implemented as a Windows Azure worker role.

The status of the entire process is monitored from the service modelling workbench. Once all the tasks are completed and the compressed file is uploaded by the consolidator, the file is available for download from the workbench client.

The resultant heterogeneous system is highly scalable, available and reliable capable of handling high-volume request and provides high throughput.

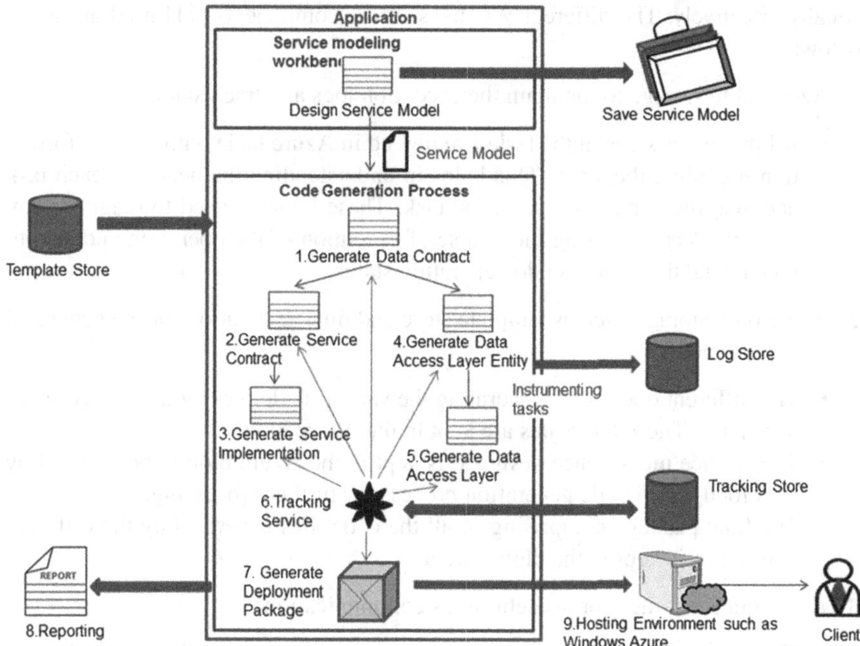

Fig. 11.8 Tasks and interdependencies in the re-engineered application

A brief summary of what has been discussed so far is depicted in Fig. 11.8. A reference of the designed service model is passed to the code generation process. The code generation process on the basis of the model received activates the tasks, namely, generate data contract, generate service contract, generate service implementation, generate data access layer entity and generate data access layer. All these tasks update their execution status in a tracking store which is monitored by the tracking service to trigger the completion of the code generation process. Once the code generation is completed, all the generated files are consolidated and compressed in a package for download or deployment to a hosting environment like Windows Azure. In this pattern, all the driving services like task manager, controller and consolidator and also the different tasks are designed so that they may be elastic as the workload demands and dynamically scale to handle varying workloads.

11.5 Windows Azure Cloud Components to Implement the Proposed Architecture

The cloud-based architecture explained above leverages the building blocks provided by Windows Azure. But as discussed earlier, similar building blocks from other cloud computing infrastructure like Amazon and Google can also be leveraged equally effectively. The different Windows Azure components [11] used are given below:

1. Azure table storage to maintain the execution logs and track status
   - All the major steps in the tasks are logged in Azure table with some information regarding the steps. This helps in understanding the health of each task and also the current status of the task. These logs are used to diagnose any issue if it occurs during the course of execution of the operation and also to understand the overall code generation status.
2. Azure blob storage used as template store and final destination for the generated code package
   - The different operations generating the various code files by using text-based templates. These templates are kept in the Azure blob.
   - The service model once designed is kept in the Azure blob to be referred by the cloud-based code generation process for further processing.
   - The final package comprising of all the code files generated by the different operations is kept in the blob storage.
3. Azure queue storage for asynchronous communication
   - The communications between the task manager and the different tasks and also between the dependent tasks are achieved by dropping messages into the respective Azure queues.
4. Azure drive as intermediate store for generated code files
   - Each task has their dedicated Azure drive mounted to be used to temporarily store the files generated. The consolidator then consolidates all the files from all the drives in a proper .net solution format and packages in a single compressed file.
5. Azure Web and worker roles for implementing the task handlers
   - Web role is used to build the task manager which is used to handle task distribution responsibilities.
   - Worker role is used to build the controller which activates all the tasks.
   - Worker role is used to build the tracking service to monitor the execution of all the tasks assembled by the controller.
   - Worker role is also used to build the consolidator which is responsible to create the final deployment package.

11.6 Benefits Realised

Apart from leveraging the benefits of cloud infrastructure such as elastic scalability, better reliability and higher availability, the following additional benefits are also achieved:

Improved process isolation: Since the operations are distributed across separate VM nodes and seconded by the fact that all the communications between different components are asynchronous, any faulty operation does not affect the entire operation. The moment a task is aborted for any reason, only that particular task needs to be restarted without affecting the rest of the process.

Improved application throughput: Unlike in the earlier procedural-driven processing approach, new requests could not be processed by the system unless the entire process had been completed, which limited the throughput of the application. With the new design, the moment any task is completed, it is already available to serve the next request in the queue. Hence, overall processing time required to serve the request is shortened which enhances the overall throughput of the system.

Better workload management: Since in this approach, the activation of different tasks is driven by a configuration of the controller, the task distribution can be achieved even across controllers for better load handling.

- Separate worker roles may be started with different set of tasks configured. In case a task demands more resources, it can be moved to a separate worker role where few or no other tasks have been configured by the controller. This helps in an efficient utilisation of the computing resources on the cloud and effective optimisation of operating costs.
- Some tasks can be repeated across more than one controller so that if a particular task in a controller crashes for any reason, there will be other instances of the same operation active to support the new request. Higher availability and fault tolerance are thus achieved.

SaaS-ification of traditional desktop applications: Separating the desktop-based, process-intensive, service engineering code generation operation to the cloud offers the ability of offering the application as a multi-tenant "SaaS" (Software as a Service)-enabled application. In our case, service engineering capabilities are now available as scalable on-demand service to the end consumer.

11.7 Best Practices

Here we share some of the best practices learnt during the course of our experience in moving an on-premise monolithic application to a modern cloud-based application architecture.

Loose coupling: Make the application/service components loosely coupled. Loose coupling could be best achieved using messaging technologies such as queues. This improves the scalability and hence the overall performance of the system in concern.

Design to handle idempotency: If a queue is used for asynchronous communication, avoid the messages to be processed more than once by multiple worker processes.

If the same message reappears in the queue for any reason after it has been successfully processed, there must be a mechanism to understand that the message has been already processed and accordingly either delete or ignore it.

Design for failure: Developing applications targeted for public cloud is about "designing for failure". In the traditional approach of deploying an application in the data centre, applications are designed and developed by relying on the underlying infrastructure such as reliable memory and high-speed reliable networks to meet their SLAs primarily because they rarely tend to fail. However, moving to a public cloud infrastructure would require some unlearning and understanding of the cloud environments. On the cloud, applications would need to be designed and developed under the assumptions that cloud infrastructures would tend to fail more often than not. Hence, each subsystem of your application would need to be designed and developed with this basic premise in mind.

Handle poison messages: For any reason if the message read from a queue is not processed properly and the processing application fails/aborts, then the message is returned back to the queue (probably after some timeout duration). If there is any issue with the information in the message, then this message has to be removed; otherwise, any other instance of the processing application will again try to process it and will eventually fail.

Think asynchronous: Move from a synchronous online processing to an asynchronous offline processing. This approach would help to free up client resources and push the heavy processing computation tasks to a more scalable platform like cloud.

Adopt parallel processing pattern: One of the best practices to build high-performance application is to avoid long-running resource-exhaustive task; instead, if possible, break it into small tasks and run these tasks simultaneously, e.g. in different threads and processors.

Short-running transactions: Keep duration of tasks short. Tasks needing a lot of time block the resources, resulting in messages being piled up in the queue. Short-running tasks can release resources quickly and help optimise the utilisation of the resources in a uniform and efficient manner. If the tasks are running long or you find messages being piled up in the queues, then there could be a possible opportunity to re-factor the code into a separate operation. Another way of running transactions for shorter duration could be to look at the intensity of the transaction being processed. For example, if a task is processing ten files, you may want to reduce the file size to a smaller chunk so as to shorten the queue lengths.

Use cloud resources cautiously: The usage of cloud infrastructure provides scalability, availability, etc., but suboptimal use of the same may lead to high cost of execution. So when there is less demand, relinquish the unused resources. For example, to handle the increase in the load, the instance count of a Windows Azure role can be increased, but as soon as the load decreases, decrease the instance count accordingly.

Avoid chatty communication: Avoid this between components especially when using cloud resources like Windows Azure table. The cost for using such resources also depends on the number of transactions done on such resources. If possible, try to implement transaction in batches during a single call.

Configure proximity deployments: While leveraging Windows Azure, make use of affinity groups. Resources within the same affinity group are kept as close as possible in the data centre, and this reduces the communication time between the different cloud resources.

Use local compute storage facility: While using Windows Azure roles, leverage local storage for temporary data, i.e. data which need not to be persisted and needed only for short duration. This can help minimise transactions to the storage service and hence transactions cost to the storage service.

Instrument your code: Moving from a stand-alone to a distributed environment such as the cloud, manageability of the application can be highly impacted. As observed with the target architecture discussed in this chapter, with an increase in the heterogeneous nature of the design, the overall complexity of the system would tend to also increase. Further with the code generation process being deployed in a public cloud, administrators would tend to lose the flexibility of managing and control the target environment. This can lead to a lot of unknowns. It thus becomes imperative to instrument application code which provides regular runtime updates on the services executing the process. This will help developers as well as administrators to take corrective measures as and when an incident occurs. For instance, when there is sudden surge in the workload, the instrumentation code can help the administrator take evasive action and scale out the executing task nodes. Another instance could be for developers to investigate issues in code, say to investigate on a particular task/process which ends abruptly.

11.8 Summary

In this chapter, we have discussed in detail the process of *re-engineering* a monolithic stand-alone application to a distributed cloud application so as to be able to seamlessly scale and handle rapid growth in workload by leveraging cloud infrastructure and services.

We have discussed the traditional architecture of a typical legacy application and some of the key challenges faced to support scalability. Subsequently, we covered the technical adoption strategy to migrate the application to a distributed cloud model by leveraging the *parallel processing pattern*. A detailed future-state architecture was proposed on the lines of the parallel processing pattern utilising the cloud infrastructure and services offered by Windows Azure. Some of the important benefits realised such as elastic scalability, SaaS-ification and process isolation were highlighted as a result of the re-hauling of the application. We finally concluded by briefly listing down some of the best practices from the lessons learnt during the implementation of this project.

References

1. Artus, D.J.N.: SOA realization: service design principles. Retrieved from http://www.ibm.com/developerworks/webservices/library/ws-soa-design/ (2006). Accessed on 15 July 2012
2. Haas, H., Brown A. (eds.): "Web services glossary" W3C Working Group Note (2004). Accessed on 15 July 2012
3. MSDN: Service Oriented Architecture (SOA), Microsoft MSDN Library. Retrieved from http://msdn.microsoft.com/en-us/library/bb833022.aspx (2010). Accessed on 15 July 2012
4. MSDN: Design considerations for S+S and cloud computing, Microsoft MSDN library. Retrieved from http://msdn.microsoft.com/en-us/architecture/aa699439 (2009). Accessed on 15 July 2012
5. Burton: A guidance framework for applying SOA design principles. Retrieved from http://www.gartner.com/id=1405628 (2009). Accessed on 15 July 2012
6. MSDN: Application domains. Retrieved from http://msdn.microsoft.com/en-us/library/2bh4z9hs(v=vs.100).aspx (2012). Accessed on 19 July 2012
7. Fowler, M., Beck, K., Brant, J., Opdyke, W., Roberts, D.: Refactoring: Improving the Design of Existing Code. Addison-Wesley, Reading. http://www.pearsoned.co.uk/Bookshop/detail.asp?item=166518 (1999)
8. Terra, R., Valente, M.T., Bigonha, R.: An approach for extracting modules from monolithic software architectures. In: IX Workshop de Manutenção de Software Moderna (WMSWM), pp. 1–8. http://www.ricardoterra.com.br/publications/2012_wmswm.pdf (2012).
9. Fowler, M.: Patterns of Enterprise Application Architecture. Addison-Wesley, Boston. http://www.pearsoned.co.uk/Bookshop/detail.asp?item=312697 (2003)
10. MSDN: Data Transfer Object, Microsoft MSDN library. Retrieved from http://msdn.microsoft.com/en-us/library/ff649585.aspx (2010). Accessed on 15 May 2012
11. Ghag, S.: Primer – Windows Azure. Retrieved from http://www.infosys.com/cloud/resource-center/Documents/primer-windows-azure.pdf (2010). Accessed on 16 July 2012

Chapter 12
Cloud-Aided Software Engineering: Evolving Viable Software Systems Through a Web of Views

Colin Atkinson and Dirk Draheim

Abstract Cloud computing is currently generating tremendous excitement in the IT industry. However, most cloud initiatives to date have focused on the delivery of computing services to end users, rather than on improving the engineering and governance of software systems. The cloud has the potential to revolutionize the way software is developed and governed and to consign much of the artificial complexity involved in software engineering today to history. It not only holds the key to reducing the tensions between agile and "heavyweight" methods of developing software, it also addresses the problem of software license management and piracy – software in the cloud cannot be copied! The cloud also promises to unlock the potential of large, heterogeneous distributed development teams by supporting social interaction, group dynamics, and key project management principles in software engineering. In this chapter, we outline the motivation for a cloud-driven approach to software engineering which we refer to as Cloud-Aided Software Engineering (CASE 2.0) and introduce some key innovations needed to turn it into reality. We also identify some of the main challenges that still need to be addressed and some of the most promising strategies for overcoming them.

Keywords Cloud computing • Enterprise computing • Distributed software engineering • CASE

C. Atkinson
Software Engineering Group, University of Mannheim,
Mannheim, Germany
e-mail: atkinson@informatik.uni-mannheim.de

D. Draheim (✉)
IT Service Management Division, University of Innsbruck,
Innsbruck, Austria
e-mail: draheim@acm.org

Z. Mahmood and S. Saeed (eds.), *Software Engineering Frameworks for the Cloud Computing Paradigm*, Computer Communications and Networks,
DOI 10.1007/978-1-4471-5031-2_12,

12.1 Introduction

Cloud computing is currently generating tremendous excitement in the IT industry, and hardly a day goes by without the announcement of a major cloud initiative by one of the big IT companies. However, most initiatives to date have focused on leveraging the cloud for supporting the delivery of computing services to end users, rather than on the advantages that can be gained by using the cloud to improve the engineering and governance of software systems. We believe the cloud has the potential to revolutionize the way software is developed and governed and to consign much of the artificial complexity involved in software engineering today to history.

Many strands of Internet-based, distributed computing are converging around the notion of "the cloud" [1]. These range from the Internet-based provision of virtual platforms (platform-as-a-service) and utility-level services (infrastructure-as-a-service) to fully fledged, customized software applications (software-as-a-service) [2]. This accelerating convergence is having a dramatic impact on the whole IT industry and has energized all big IT companies to leverage the cloud in their product portfolios. However, the cloud revolution has so far focused almost exclusively on the "use" and "packaging" of software rather on its development and engineering. Although software engineering is arguably one of the most critical strategic competences of businesses and society today, applying the benefits of the cloud to software engineering has received relatively little attention.

The impact of cloud-based software engineering is driven by two main forces:

- Empowerment of large, heterogeneous, distributed software engineering teams
- Ability to better control of software usage and distribution and thus avoid copyright infringement and misuse of software

However, this potential must be unlocked. "Cloudifying" existing tool suites and using them with traditional working practices will not take off. The key enablers for successful cloud-based software engineering are:

- Strict integration of all aspects of software development and run-time maintenance through genuinely view-based software visualization metaphors
- Strict awareness and systematic treatment of group dynamics in software engineering projects

In many ways, the landscape of challenges and opportunities resembles that which preceded the first revolution in software engineering infrastructures that took place in the 1980s under the banner of Computer-Aided Software Engineering (CASE). However, we believe the impending revolution will be more far reaching and has a much deeper impact than the first – we think it will radically change the way software engineers think, work, and interact. To highlight the contrast with the first revolution, we suggest the banner Cloud-Aided Software Engineering (CASE 2.0) for the impending changes in the way software is engineered.

The 1990s saw a major trend toward off-shoring projects [3]. Overall, off-shoring did not take off because distributed teams were not properly supported – both with respect to artifact organization and work organization. Superficially, the main problem faced in off-shoring projects is the extra effort needed to coordinate distributed, heterogeneous teams. In fact, however, the main problem is the hidden passive resistance of many project participants to the consequences of off-shoring. Since off-shoring initiatives are effectively sourcing initiatives, they have the potential to provoke power shifts in enterprises and this can easily provoke resistance. Major tool vendors who are turning their tool suites into cloud-based services are currently failing to take this fact into account. To overcome this problem, underlying software description views need to be supported by sophisticated navigation and process enactment approaches that are aware of group dynamics and team management principles.

Another fundamental problem is copyright infringement which places an enormous burden on both software vendors and software customers. The former have enormous auditing challenges, while the latter have complex software license management challenges. Ensuring authorized use of software is therefore becoming and increasing obstacle to the development of vibrant software markets with robust investment into new products. Since the cloud-based delivery of software eliminates the copyright infringement problem, it will have a major impact on the economics of software markets and encourage a new wave of investment in new software products.

The organization of this chapter is as follows. In the next section, we set the stage by describing the current state of the art in software engineering (SE) in general and with respect to the emerging challenges of globalization, highly distributed teams, and software asset management. We also discuss the past and future economics of the software industry including a discussion of off-shoring and outsourcing initiatives. Section 12.3 characterizes today's concept-tool gap (i.e., the challenge presented by the complexity of today's software engineering tool landscapes) and reviews the current cloud-based utilization of software engineering tools. Section 12.4 is devoted to our vision of tool-related key enablers of tomorrow's cloud-based software engineering, that is, the orthographic software modeling approach with its single underlying model and on-demand view generation. Section 12.5 is devoted to the process-related key enablers. Important topics that are addressed by this section are group dynamics and team management principles, the viable software engineering life cycle, the viable software product, artifact and project management integration, and, last but not least, the necessary focus shift toward management. We discuss related work throughout the chapter. The chapter concludes with Sect. 12.6.

12.2 Challenges in Today's Software Engineering Projects

The opportunity to leverage cloud computing in software engineering (SE) could not have come at a better time. In recent years, software engineering researchers, methodologists, and tool vendors have come up with several powerful new "paradigms" for engineering software systems that individually offer significant benefits over first-generation development methods. However, these methods are largely incompatible with one another and are difficult if not impossible to use together. On the one side, we have the "heavyweight" methods which add extra concepts and artifacts to the traditional ingredients of software engineering in order to optimize the way in which certain core concerns are addressed such as model-driven development (abstraction), component-based development (composition), and product-line engineering (variation). On the other side, there are the agile methods, which discourage the use of any software description artifacts other than "code" and shun any activities that do not directly lead to the production of "software." The core issue is the very notion of what software is (traditional code or more sophisticated, higher-order constructs) and how it is described (via traditional programming languages or higher-level "models").

When applied in an appropriate way, the cloud offers radical solutions to these problems and has the potential to revolutionize the way in which software is engineered and managed. In fact, engineering and management could become just one of the many concerns associated with cloud-hosted software applications, alongside the concerns of other stakeholders including owners and end users. The key insight needed to unlock the potential of the cloud for software engineering is to adopt a genuinely view-based metaphor supported by a sophisticated navigation paradigm and process enactment mechanisms aware of group dynamics and team management principles.

12.2.1 Complexity in Today's Software Engineering Projects

Forty years after the NATO conferences [4], we still encounter massive time and cost overruns in today's software engineering projects. We are convinced that what we eventually need in software engineering is a focus shift onto the full spectrum of management issues that eventually takes into account the whole management body of knowledge [5]. There are two basic challenges: the first is to deal with problems of group dynamics in the customer-encompassing project team and the second is to deal with the problems of cultural change management at the customer's enterprise.

The social context in which software is engineered is complex. Large organizations can rarely arrange for their software to be developed by small, ring-fenced teams with few external interaction points. Today, the components of large software systems are brought together from many places, including formally outsourced subprojects and informally reused open source software, and the number of communication paths of the individuals involved has exploded through collaboration tools (e.g., wikis), social media [6], and professional networking Web sites such as LinkedIn. All these trends raise the importance of optimally leveraging and managing the group dynamics involved in the engineering of software.

Figure 12.1 shows a typical software development scenario. Large projects can consist of numerous teams distributed between a main contractor, several

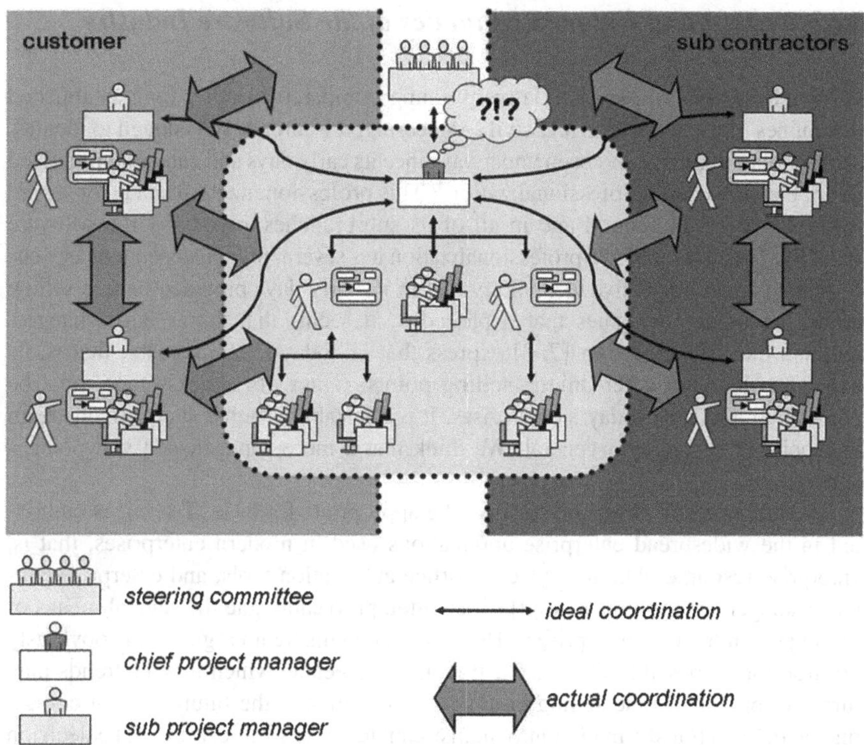

Fig. 12.1 Seasoned view of large software development projects

sub-contractors, and customers. A steering committee is often needed to track the project activities and costs from a governance perspective. A key role is played by the chief project manager who should ideally be the central hub for coordination, communication, and control in order to streamline all the activities in the project. However, in practice, project managers are usually overwhelmed by the informal coordination needs of project teams leading to constant crisis fighting or even chaos. The ideal communication pattern is visualized by the thin arrows in Fig. 12.1.

In the chief project manager's organization, which is considered the project host, this ideal communication pattern is a kind of hierarchical information flow. The role of the chief project manager and his office is to orchestrate the employees, customers, and sub-contractors. Of course, in large projects, it would not be possible for a project manager to serve as a kind of facade to the organization without becoming a bottleneck. All stakeholders must clearly be allowed to communicate directly with one another. However, what we tried to visualize by the thick arrows in Fig. 12.1 is a scenario in which the pair-wise communication between individual stakeholders starts to overwhelm coordination through the chief project manager. This is a severe risk for project success.

12.2.2 Past and Future Economics of the Software Industry

Although the IT industry is relatively young compared to other long-established disciplines like construction and civil engineering, it is already old enough to identify an important trend that has been underway since its early days and can be summarized under the buzzword "professionalization." This professionalization can be observed in the IT sector in general and in all of its sub-branches, especially the software industry. The observable IT professionalization has several mutual dependent aspects. IT started as an innovative technology that in its early days provided unique selling points for those companies that exploited it. It seems that things have changed. Authors like Nicholas Carr [7, 8] express that IT today is mainstream; that is, its existence does not offer unique selling points, rather, its nonexistence must be considered a risk for today's enterprises. It is debatable whether such a mainstream viewpoint is adequate in general. We think that a more sophisticated viewpoint is appropriate.

The mainstream viewpoint seems to be appropriate for base IT services embodied in the widespread enterprise applications used in modern enterprises, that is, enterprise resource planning systems, office automation tools, and enterprise content management systems (see [9] for an attempt to catalogue the several means of IT support in today's enterprises). However, the mainstream argument is obviously not true for all possible IT support. It is not foreseeable which new IT trends may turn into proven unique selling points for companies in the future and, of course, may undergo a transformation into mainstream technology afterward. Take decision support systems as an example. Decision support system initiatives – from data mart and data warehouse [10] approaches to high-end active data warehouse [11] approaches – have not taken off in many companies that tried them. Also, the production sector [12] still shows the potential to create unique selling points by the strategic exploitation of information technology (see [13] for a discussion).

Nevertheless, it is fair to say that the mainstream argument is appropriate for basic IT support. In parallel to IT technology becoming a commodity, IT support has become more and more professional over the years. IT support started in enterprises with relatively small, agile expert teams. Even in otherwise very strictly organized organization, the IT support teams often formed work cultures similar to those described as expert organizations by Henry Mintzberg [14]. Against this background, it is possible to understand why the transformation to an improved and adequate business alignment of IT support groups has been and still is often accompanied by tensions and often must be subject to substantial change management efforts.

12.2.3 Cloud as an Aid Against Copyright Infringement

The software industry is challenged by copyright infringements. A key ingredient of cloud computing is the fact that software in the cloud is not copyable. This sounds very trivial but actually is highly profound and important. Note that it is a center pillar of the free software philosophy [15] that *software is copyable*. However, in the cloud, software is *not* copyable. The free software community [15] is a sub-culture [16] that massively overlaps the hacker's community [17], the younger Internet networking communities [18], and the digital piracy movement [19] and shares with these groups certain ethics and visions concerning society and economics. The free software community, built around enthusiastic programmers, is currently gaining impetus from the rapidly growing Internet community movement. The basic philosophy of the free software community is that since software products are totally different from other products because they are immaterial and copyable, software should not be possessed by anybody. The free software community builds software based on this alternative approach with a strong motivation to demonstrate what is possible without profit motivation. In fact, hard-core advocates of open source software are in favor of changes to copyright law, so that ultimately the arbitrary copying and exchanging of software would be legal. More moderate strands of opinion also exist, which regard copying of somebody else's software as a minor transgression. However, until software producers are forced to give away their code (i.e., executable code or source code) which is not realistically foreseeable, the cloud is the only effective way of tackling copyright infringement. At the same time, we do not believe that the existence of the cloud threatens proven open source business models [20] and therefore do not think that it will rule out these business models.

Since the access to software in the cloud is account based, it offers perfect, 100 %-safe copy protection. Of course, customers can pass around their account data, and it is questionable whether any cloud license model should forbid that. However, the cloud provider can technically detect if an account is used simultaneously by more than the entitled person. It might be technically possible to circumvent the software provider's security with respect to this and actually have some access for more than the entitled person; however, such misuse of the account would be risky and even more important would not scale at all so it would not be cost effective. Even if parts of the cloud-based software product rely on mobile code (e.g., the client interface description and active client interface code), crucial parts of the cloud-based software (e.g., the business logic) will never become visible as code to the customer.

Of course, all this is only true for those software products that are *cloudifiable* (i.e., amenable to migration to the cloud). It is not true, for example, for embedded code or mobile code. It is also not true for code that is distributed as part of an open source business model [20]. It is also not true for hardware-related code. Even if hardware itself is subject to *cloudification* by virtualization, because more and more server hardware vanishes from private data centers and appears more and more in the on-demand data centers of the cloud, it is not true for hardware-related code in general. Ubiquitous computing [21] is based on the vision of more and more processor-based devices around us in everyday life, and with current mobile devices and computers, the first wave of ubiquitous computing is becoming a reality. However, a large class of software products is cloudifiable and encompasses crucial parts of the software supporting today's enterprises: ERP (enterprise resource planning systems), office automation tools, ECM (enterprise content management systems), many instances of established CSCW (computer-supported collaborative working) and emerging social software [22], decision support, BI (business intelligence), workflow technology [23] and BPM suites (business process management) [13], PPS (product planning systems), even MES (manufacturing execution systems), B2C portals (business-to-customer), and B2B (business-to-business).

The possibility of copyright infringement is not only a burden for the software vendor but also for the customer. It is the customer's duty to comply with copyright laws and also to prevent copyright infringements by its employees. A copyright infringement is not necessarily the result of software piracy, that is, the deliberate bootlegging of a software product. It can happen as the result of lack of awareness or slackness. Paradoxically enough, it is often the software producers themselves that foster this slackness at the customer's side by the presales and sales teams that often suggest that slight copyright infringements are acceptable in pricing processes and license negotiations.

It is the software customer's duty to appropriately inform and instruct its employees about copyright issues. In order to be on the safe side, a professional software asset management system [24] must be established in the customer's enterprise. The objectives of software asset management are systematic alignment of the software strategy with business goals and the professional procurement of software. However, once enterprises get beyond a certain size, they struggle simply to get the copyright problem under control. The larger and more heterogeneous a company, the greater the challenge it faces to keep track of its software installations. In strictly administered organization, that is, machine organizations [14] like banks or insurance companies, it might be easy to keep track of the installed software regardless of how large a company is. However, in organization with individually and distributed administered workplaces, software management can easily become a nightmare. Software producers often contract auditors with copyright surveillance, creating extra workload for the customer in terms of regular audits.

With an effective copy protection mechanism, investments into, and exploitation of, software products become substantially more calculable and much easier to handle, with consequent long-term decreases of software. Therefore, we are convinced that this copy-protecting aspect of the cloud will further boost investments into software development and will result in a more vibrant, competitive software market.

12.3 Accidental Complexity in SE Tools and Environments

Federick Brooks introduced the terms essential complexity and accidental complexity in the 1970s to distinguish between the complexity that is inherent in the underlying problem and the complexity that results from the suboptimal nature of the tools (including conceptual tools) used to build IT solutions [25]. Still today, software engineering can be characterized as a constant battle with accidental complexity, at all levels, phases, and concerns of a project. The problems with accidental

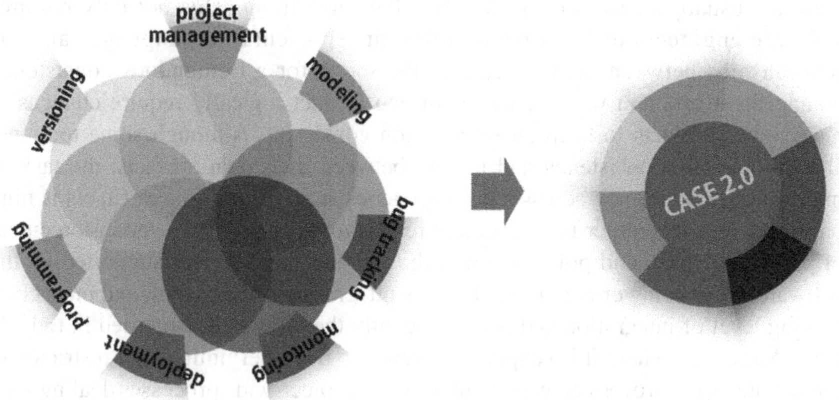

Fig. 12.2 Normalization and alignment of CASE tool services

complexity become immediately apparent when setting up the infrastructure for a modern software engineering project. In addition to a core set of programming tools, a modern integrated development environment usually includes a vast array of additional tools dealing with all kinds of concerns ranging from requirement elicitation and system modeling to bug tracking, deployment, and software transportation. In fact, it is generally accepted that a typical software engineering environment today should include tools to support:

- Artifact production
- Artifact management
- Artifact change management
- Product deployment and transportation management
- Artifact quality management
- Project management
- System monitoring

Using tools providing such a wide range of facilities would not be a problem if their facilities were orthogonal and consistent. However, this is rarely if ever the case. The tools populating a modern software development environment are invariably purchased from a variety of different vendors, and each usually has its own proprietary representation format and artifact navigation approach. Moreover, they invariably overlap in the functionality they provide, as illustrated on the left-hand side of Fig. 12.2, so that there are usually many solutions for the same task. In contrast, as illustrated by the right-hand side of Fig. 12.2, the services offered by a software engineering infrastructure should ideally be complete, consistent, and redundancy-free.

Further artificial complexity becomes apparent as soon as software engineering artifacts are developed using such heterogeneous environments. In particular, there is usually a large overlap in the information captured by artifacts, which means there are usually many ways to describe the same thing. This not only requires software engineers to learn many different representation languages and the relationships between them, it creates the scene for a tremendous consistency management problem where changes in one artifact logically require changes to many other artifacts to keep all information consistent. Although some tools are able to maintain consistency and tracing between their own artifacts, the task of maintaining consistency across a heterogeneous suite of tools and artifacts is nigh on impossible. The other main problem relates to the support for and enforcement of processes, rules, and policies across the artifacts and services supported by the software engineering environment. Process integration is the highest and most challenging level of integration and is consequently the least well supported in today's tools. Moreover, where it is supported, it tends to be rather limited and restricted to immediate usage process management. Deeper, project-wide processes dealing with fundamental project and people management issues are rarely if ever supported. Not only do they transcend individual tools, they deal with the interaction within and between teams. The lack of such support therefore becomes particularly problematic in larger projects, where the need to support teamwork and manage group dynamics is particularly acute.

An ideal, mature software development environment is a tool suite that possesses certain characteristics – namely, completeness, consistence, and process awareness. Completeness and consistency means that all the needs for tool support should be satisfied, and all developers should use the same feature to support the same issue. Process awareness means that the software project should be governed by a mature software development process. The tool suite should support this process, that is, the relationship of the tool suite and the software process should be well understood. We coin the term normalized software development environment for such an ideal tool suite. The tool suite should offer not only support for the complexity of the artifacts but also support for the complexity of the teamwork, that is, team coordination, team control, and team knowledge management [6, 9].

The tool integrator's contribution to project success is crucial and immensely challenging. In concrete projects, the plethora of tools can become a maintenance nightmare. To overcome this problem, a strictly view-based approach to software development is needed. Each tool materializes a view onto the artifacts, activities, and problems in the projects. A future-generalized software engineering platform must realize these views but must overcome technical and conceptual redundancies and inconsistencies.

12.4 View-Driven Software Engineering

The first key step needed to fully leverage the cloud for software engineering is to move to a paradigm in which "everything is a view." This tenet has to be applied universally and rigorously, so that all engineers, indeed all stakeholders, can only access or visualize information about the system via a view. Moreover, the views

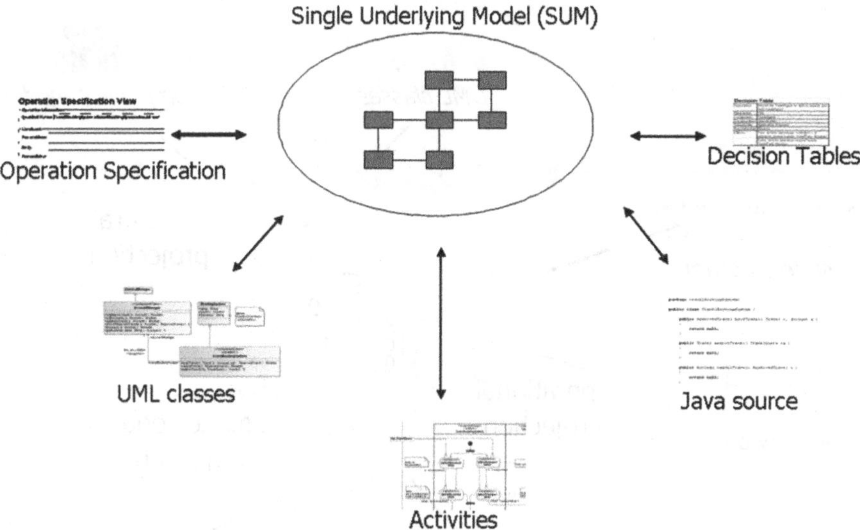

Fig. 12.3 On-demand view generation

must be genuine in the sense that they are windows onto, or derived from, a single underlying source of information. They must not be parts of a lattice of information sources in which each represents a small piece of the overall puzzle. On the contrary, as illustrated in Fig. 12.3, each view must be generated on demand from the single underlying information source, or single underlying model (SUM), and all updates performed via views must be synchronized with the SUM in the style of a configuration management system such as SVN or CVS. Obviously, the idea is that the SUM would be hosted on the cloud, while the views are generated on demand for visualization via clients.

Notice that traditional high-level source code such as Java no longer plays a special role in such a vision of view-based software development projects. If an engineer wishes to work with a code view of (part of) the system under development, this is simply created as "just another view." Tracing and round trip engineering are therefore automatically taken care of as a side effect of the view-generation and SUM-update transformations rather than a multitude of pair-wise correspondence rules between individual views.

A move toward a strictly view-based software engineering environment of this kind would have major benefit for developers. First and foremost, it would free them from any artificial complexity related to the integration of heterogeneous representation formats and overlapping diagram types because views could easily be optimized for individual stakeholders. Second, as long as the format of the SUM (i.e., the SUM metamodel) is an open standard, software engineers can relatively easily add their own customized views by writing the appropriate transformations to and from the SUM and, if necessary, extending the SUM with new model elements.

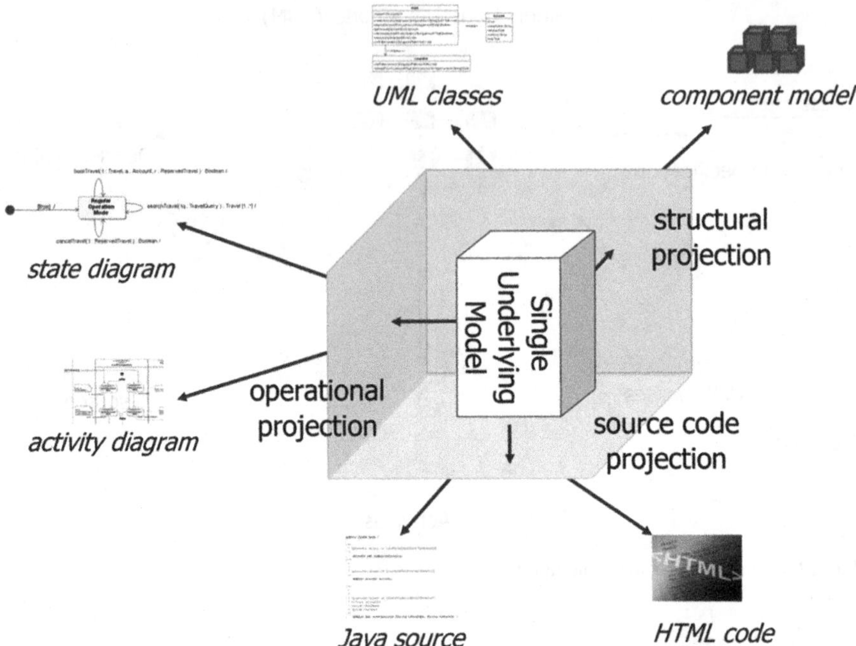

Fig. 12.4 Distinct OSM views

In fact, over time what we call "tool vendors" today will become "view vendors" who sell sophisticated off-the-shelf views for visualizing and/or editing the information in the SUM in new ways.

Finally, if a single transcending navigation metaphor could be found which allows all defined views to be accessed in a clean, simple, and coherent way, software engineers would be freed from the artificial complexity of having to learn and work with the idiosyncratic navigation approaches of the many tools in large industrial suite. They could, instead, create and work with views as if they were working with a single, unified, super-integrated software engineering environment.

Based on our project experiences with multidimensional modeling in the KobrA method as described in [26], we have elaborated a strictly view-driven software engineering tool at the University of Mannheim in which view navigation is inspired by the orthographic projection metaphor that underpins CAD tools [27]. We therefore refer to the approach as orthographic software modeling (OSM). Figure 12.4 shows three distinct views of a software system being projected along three dimensions, to highlight the analogy with the CAD of physical artifacts. However, in the software space, there is no restriction on the number of dimensions that can be defined and the number of choices that can be made in each dimension. Of course, time represents a very important dimension which captures the development history and versioning evolution of systems. The pervasive reuse of software assets has been studied by SOA governance in the past [28, 29] and underpins the need for a systematic treatment of software versioning beyond the frontiers of a single silo project.

The dimensions organize the views onto the SUM. The SUM is the core, the dimensions form the inner shell, and the views form the outer shell. In a transitional stage of the technology, we eventually envision OSM as an ideal metaphor that tool integrating platforms should approximate as closely as possible. As first approximations, implementations can be based on a protocol-based integration of existing tools as long as the realization strictly targets the maintenance of model consistency; however, the ultimate implementation is a unifying model database, actually a model data warehouse, and this is also the realization approach of our prototypical implementation. In the full vision, the defined dimensions rule all the views. Today's programming languages crosscut the dimension we naturally find in today's software modeling bases so that today's source code, as a legacy problem, impedes the pure realization of OSM. We foresee the advent of new programming languages that are systematically governed by a separation of concerns along the aforementioned naturally existing dimensions. Until then we can pragmatically realize a substantial step forward by integrating source code projections into our tool and modeling approach as is shown in Fig. 12.4.

12.4.1 Models at Run-Time

The OSM approach was designed primarily with software development in mind, with the result that the views and dimensions it supports are primarily focused on development time concerns. This is also the focus of most tools populating typical software engineering environments today. However, if we assume that the cloud will increasingly be used to execute and host software systems, as well as develop them, it makes sense to simplify the transition from development to run-time. In fact, ideally, it makes sense to remove the distinction between development and run-time altogether and simply view the cloud as the host for all parts of a software system's life cycle, from birth to cradle.

Although it sounds simple, this idea has profound consequence if carried through to its full extent. First, it means that the software engineering views and concerns become just one among many other sets of views and concerns, related to other stakeholders such as the owner, administrator, and end user. All these stakeholders would be supported through the same infrastructure driven by the same underlying information source. Moreover, the different interfaces used by other stakeholders, such as end users, would also be considered as different kinds of views. In terms of SUM-based software engineering, the SUM would become the life cycle spanning information source for all information related to the system, including its run-time execution state and real-time attribute values. This would in turn mean that behavioral aspects of the system, including information about all running process instances, would also need to be stored in the SUM. In a very real sense, therefore, the SUM represents the code as well as the trace of the ongoing run-time execution of the system as it evolves.

Moreover, the provision of information about the run-time status of the system, such as that provided by process monitors and debuggers, would essentially correspond to the demand of new types of views, albeit at run-time.

With the systematic integration of run-time models into a unified framework, we would truly arrive at cloud-empowered software engineering life cycle management. The software engineering life cycle is more than software development in that it also encompasses software operation. Much more is said about this in Sect. 12.5 on life cycle and stakeholder awareness, where we broaden the discussion even beyond technological issues in the direction of social issues. Software operation has always been the poor cousin of software engineering approaches and research although the tight dependency of software development and operation was already clear at NATO conferences [4] which regarded operation as an integral part of the software life cycle. Nevertheless, important aspects of software operation like availability management and capacity management have been regarded as part of IT service management as represented by the ITIL (IT Infrastructure Library) [30] and ISO20000 [31] community. Now is the time to systematically integrate operations as a subject of investigation into software engineering.

12.4.2 On the Realization of the SUM

The notion of the SUM expresses our two main convictions on future software engineering tools, that is, a focus shift onto abstract syntax of artifact descriptions and the conceptualizing power of a hub-and-spoke architecture for artifact descriptions. Particularly, the latter might raise questions on how and whether the SUM can be actually realized and implemented. In fact, the notion of the SUM has existed for some time in proven but proprietary technology stacks, albeit in an implicit form. We characterize a SUM as a systematically extensible, conceptual deep standardization of a domain. For instructive purposes, we distinguish between two facets of the SUM, that is, the so-called normalizing SUM on the one hand and streamlining SUM on the other. The normalizing facet of the SUM addresses the aspects of conceptualization, domain specificness, and deep standardization, whereas the streamlining SUM addresses systematic extensibility.

12.4.2.1 The Normalizing SUM

The normalizing SUM aims at capturing, at a particular point in time, the body of knowledge in a domain of application development. It then realizes this body of knowledge as a database against which tools operate as views. We emphasize the domain specificness in order to make clear that not each domain of application development is amenable to be supported by a SUM. However, for the time being, we are only interested in the domain of enterprise application development and sub-domains of it, for example, the domain of workflow-intensive information systems.

12.4.2.2 Deep Standardization

The SUM captures the state of the art of the domain of application development. The SUM can be considered the outcome of a standardization process. We coin the term deep standardization for such an effort to distinguish it from the rather shallow standards that usually emerge in the area of software development. A shallow standardization addresses the artifact of one tier or one component in the many possible multi-tier complex application architectures of today's software applications, for example, HTML5, CSS3, Java, and XML. A deep standardization might fix a whole standard architecture for a domain or might even fix the artifacts for all the tiers and components of such a standard architecture. An even deeper standardization might also fix the development processes and development tools for the indicated domain.

The fact that the typical standards in the software engineering world represent rather shallow standardization efforts by no means means that we have not seen mature and working standardization efforts in this field. Deep standardization examples do exist, but they are usually proprietary and are rarely referred to as standardization efforts. A good example, which is very close to our current CASE tool discussion, is the former SAP platform. From the beginning, the SAP platform defined an environment for the development, distribution, and operation of ERP (enterprise resource planning) applications. The SAP platform defined an integrated development environment with ABAP-4 encompassing a domain-specific 4GL programming language but much more. It also defined system architectures consisting of dedicated development, testing, and operating systems and provided the necessary deployment mechanisms (i.e., the so-called transport system) to orchestrate the code. Furthermore, it provided a worldwide application monitoring and customer feedback system. As this example shows, it is possible to integrate all necessary ingredients for successful application development in one domain at one point in time into a single platform. Of course, from time to time it becomes necessary to review whether such a platform still offers support for the necessary features, because the environment is always evolving. For example, the SAP platform needed total refactoring when the Internet boomed and brought in new requirements driven by the B2C hype.

Another example of deep standardization in the field of ERP system development, but with other emphases, is the AS400 midrange computer technology stack [32]. This provides a solid platform for the development and operation of ERP systems based on a well-integrated architecture encompassing the fully integrated operating and database system OS400/DB2, a virtual machine tier TIMI (technology-independent machine interface), and the 4GL programming language RPG (Report Generator). All the rapid development technologies, ranging from the database-related RAD (rapid development) tools of the 1980s through object-oriented, visual integrated development environments to today's elaborate Web application frameworks and tool sets, show that the concept of deep standardization and the realization of such deep standardizations is a working concept. The same is true for the early transaction monitors and workflow management systems as well as today's business process management suites.

We believe that the software engineering field needs to show more systematic efforts in deep standardization in the future. In other engineering fields, there are many mature deep standardization examples. For example, in the field of hardware manufacturing, numerous working standards span several tiers of abstraction (e.g., VHDL at the register-transfer level and SPICE at the gate level) in such a way that they can be supported by powerful development and simulation tools as well as production processes. In the field of construction works, the so-called Eurocodes [33] provide a full range of working standards for the structural design of different kinds of structures.

We believe that the SUM concept is very promising for the field of enterprise applications. This belief is reinforced by the existence of a huge body of knowledge for this domain in the form of workflow-intensive information systems [34–36].

12.4.2.3 Orientation Toward Abstract Syntax

An instance of the SUM embodies a deep standardization of a domain. It does so by implementing the domain knowledge as a database that realizes the abstract syntax of all the artifacts needed to describe applications in the application domain. All the artifacts that describe the various aspects of an application together form one composite artifact in our paradigm. We associate artifacts with system description and system descriptions with models. In orthographic modeling, each description of an aspect of a system is considered a model, including source code, which is nothing but a description of system behavior with a completely defined operational semantics. The various models that together describe an application form a composite model, and the several aspects they model form the dimension of the SUM. A software developer gains access to the information via appropriate tools which can be regarded as editable views.

The purpose of these updatable views is to establish the concrete syntax for the various dimensions of the SUM. It is possible to have different views realizing different concrete syntaxes for the same dimension. For example, one could have a visual class diagram view that presents the class structure of the application in the form of a typical UML class diagram and a view that presents the class structure textually, for example, as stubs in partial Java pseudo. The updatable views shield the SUM from issues related to the concrete syntaxes involved. The human-computer interaction of a view can be designed in such a way that it gives the user the impression of being tightly connected to the SUM, or it could be designed in more conventional way so that a concrete compilation step is executed on the command of the user. The first option resembles a strictly syntax-directed client that allows the user to construct only syntactically correct models. Editors for such views resemble syntax-directed programming language editors. It is also possible to realize a generic, unified, syntax-directed browser and editor for all possible dimensions of the SUM. An example of such a unified, integrated source code model [46], called AP1, has been developed at the University of Auckland [37].

12.4.2.4 The Streamlining SUM

An obvious counterargument against the notion of a SUM is that "one size does not fit all." It is based on the practice in today's projects that developers want to select the best tool for each representational artifact and assemble a heterogeneous tool suite from third-party products. However, first, we believe that the SUM vision is realistic given the many existing examples of deep standardizing technologies and, second, that the advantages of the SUM (i.e., redundancy freeness and normalization) more than compensate for these potential disadvantages. Artifact versioning is a very instructive example of this principle. It is common in today's projects to have an inbuilt versioning feature in each of the tools within a tool suite. When this is the case, it is necessary to develop guidelines for how to use these features to trace version across the different tools. In practice, today's tools offer auxiliary interfaces to the standard versioning systems. In our approach, versioning would only be addressed in one place as a dimension of the application domain's SUM.

The "one size does not fit all" argument is partially valid, but more in the form of the "no one can foresee everything" argument. The normalizing SUM captures the notion of deep standardization. We call a SUM that is not extensible a strictly normalizing SUM. If we add a view to a strictly normalizing SUM, this view only provides a new concrete syntax for a dimension of the SUM. However, we do not forbid the extension of a SUM, because we want to stay flexible with respect to the unforeseeable new requirements. Therefore, we want to consider the normalizing SUM as the outcome of an initial standardization that forms the starting point for an ongoing standardization process that we call the streamlining SUM. The streamlining SUM evolves through the continuous addition of new views. However, these new views should be added in a systematic and disciplined way. As in the process of building the normalizing SUM, avoidance of redundancy must be the most important guideline in this process.

In the streamlining SUM approach, a new view not only adds new concrete syntax to the domain but also new information to the SUM. We believe that there is the need for extra mechanisms to streamline the extension of the SUM by new views such as the maintenance of meta-information and a moderation process. The meta-information should describe the purpose of each information snippet in the SUM and its relation to the existing information in the SUM so that it is possible to understand whether a feature that a tool vendor wants to introduce is really new and needed. It is the purpose of the moderation process to reject views that would introduce redundant or otherwise useless features. The design of the meta-information and the moderation process is beyond the scope of this chapter.

12.5 Life Cycle and Stakeholder Awareness

The concentration and integration of all software, system state, project state, and user information into a single SUM hosted on the cloud provides a unique opportunity to significantly improve software projects performed by large, heterogeneous, distributed teams. However, enhanced support for software projects must be coupled with improved management techniques in order for this to be successful. Initiatives in cloud-based software engineering will not take off unless they systematically address management issues. The challenge is twofold – it is not only necessary to address the problems of group dynamics in the customer-encompassing project team but also cultural change management within the customer's enterprise. We believe that this needs to be addressed by adherence to two fundamental principles:

- Artifact and project management integration. The IT support for process issues needs to be unified with IT support for artifact creation and management.
- Focus shift toward management. Management issues need to be brought to the fore by explicitly integrating a project design stage into the software engineering life cycle.

12.5.1 The Viable Software Engineering Life Cycle

So far, we have discussed the artifact-related aspects of cloud-aided software engineering, but it is also important to address the process and management-related aspects as well. These cannot be defined merely in terms of the interplay of activities – management issues have to be treated as first-class citizens so that they can be supported explicitly and in a flexible manner. This is particularly important for large projects which have a significant impact on the business process landscape of enterprises [13]. Large projects therefore need to be subject to IT strategy and business alignment and, in extreme cases, need to be treated as part of corporate reengineering. In short, large projects need organization [38].

Since software development has been considered in a systematic way, there has always been a focus on the process nature of the software engineering life cycle. But it is not enough to approach the software development challenge merely in terms of a defined interplay of activities. This is because successful software development is about management. As always with management, the management of software development involves planning, organization, coordination, and control of people. In traditional software processes, there are many different, ad hoc strategies for addressing management issues. For example, the surgeon team approach [25] by Frederick Brooks discusses an organizational pattern, while the best practices agile programming [39] embodies important human relationship-oriented management principles such as pair programming, 40 h/week, and "customer on the team." As another example, the Rational Unified Process [40] embodies organizational

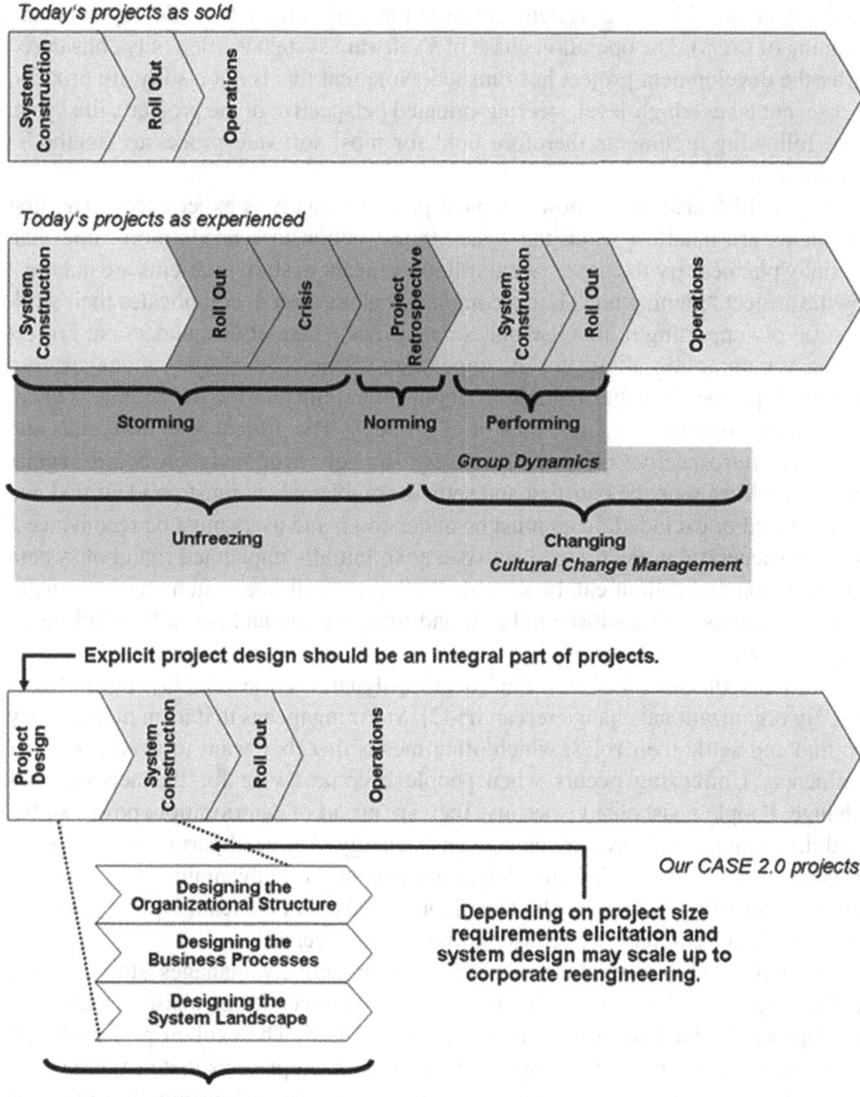

Fig. 12.5 The software engineering life cycle reconsidered

knowledge in the definition of roles. The problem with existing software processes is that management issues are not first-class citizens. They are approached implicitly and therefore in a non-flexible manner, that is, each process provides ad hoc solutions to an arbitrary combination of management problems.

Figure 12.5 reconsiders the software engineering life cycle in the context of a typical concrete project. Large projects are often regarded as consisting of two major phases addressing system construction and rollout (i.e., deployment and training of users). The operation phase of a software system is often only considered after the development project has finished. Note that this is not a software process, per se, but takes a high-level, steering-oriented perspective of the project's life cycle. The following arguments therefore hold for most software processes (methods) used today.

Figure 12.5 also shows how a typical project actually is experienced. The first problems are manifest when the system construction task needs more time than initially planned. By the time system rollout is meant to start, problems are manifest by the project "running hot." Users complain that the system complicates their work instead of supporting it, that it violates data privacy regulations, and so on; project managers complain about the incompetence of the chief project manager; and the chief project manager complains about inflexibility in the development team, resistance from the users, and lack of IT strategy. The project runs into crisis and a project retrospective becomes necessary. To get "everybody on board" again, responsibilities must be clarified and settled, troublemakers must be identified and remotivated or excluded, fears must be understood, and users must be reconvinced. After a successful project retrospective, a next, initially unplanned round of system construction and rollout can be started. If all goes well, the system can eventually start operations with a substantial cost and time overrun and partially fulfill initial expectations.

Formally, this is called "storming" in group dynamics research [41] and "unfreezing" in organizational change research [42]. Storming means that team members try to find and settle their roles, which often means that they want to maximize their influence. Unfreezing occurs when people become aware for the necessity for change. People resist change because they are afraid of deterioration, power shifts, and disorientation. Therefore, change costs energy. A crucial part of this energy is needed for unfreezing. Unfortunately, problems in group dynamics and in cultural change mutually reinforce each other. Troublemakers in the team typically encourage troublemakers in the target user group and vice versa.

A viable software engineering life cycle proactively manages storming and unfreezing. Therefore, it explicitly incorporates a project design phase as a first step as depicted by the last project life cycle in Fig. 12.5. The explicit project design phase replaces the project retrospective experienced in projects that run into crisis. The extra efforts put into project design minimize risks and eventually save costs and time. The purpose of project design is to identify and address potential resistance in the team and the enterprise as early as possible. The concrete task of the project design phase is to achieve full commitment of the stakeholders in the project, in particular, of the project managers, and to organize sufficient and appropriate resources for the chief project manager. For example, a team of appropriate experts, a kind of clearing house, could help the chief project manager deal with group dynamics and cultural change.

The essence of the viable software engineering life cycle is also evident in the types and forms of requirement elicitation efforts needed. In small projects, requirement elicitation aims at grasping and understanding the future system features at the level of work-organization and human-computer interaction. However, in the early stages of the project, highly complex and creative problems must be resolved. It is fair to say that high-end engineering tasks must be fulfilled. Note that Hammer and Champy [43] use the word corporate engineering for restructuring an organization. Of all the activities that might be still viewed as requirement elicitation from the perspective of a software engineering project, the design of a system landscape is one of the most trivial (refer to Fig. 12.5).

12.5.2 Viable Software Life Cycle Instruments

Today's software processes address management of large teams with respect to division of labor. The fields that are addressed are the classical fields of management and project management, that is, organization of the team, coordination of the work forces, and control of the outcome. Important phenomena of really large software introductions are often not considered in today's projects, and these are the problems of true leadership as opposed to mere management, that is, problems of group dynamics and cultural change management.

A viable software life cycle is aware of group dynamics in the development team and the cultural change that is catalyzed by the introduction of the new application. Where the awareness of group dynamics and cultural change is a step forward, it does not yet answer how to actually address the discussed problems. Here are a few instruments that can help to enable a viable software life cycle:

- Explicit project design
- Meta project handbook
  - Project type identification
  - Troublemaker identification
  - Diligent project organization
- Systematic stakeholder incorporation
  - Steering committee
  - Employees' committee
  - Project clearing house
  - Builders' hut
- Cultural change management
- Anticipation of software operations

The explicit project design phase that we have motivated in Sect. 12.5.1 is a direct consequence of the demand for dealing explicitly with group dynamics and cultural change. First, it is important to identify the type of project in terms of these challenges. For this purpose, question like the following should be posed: Is the project a strategic project that has the target to change crucial parts of the business processes or the organizational structure, that is, is it a part of or does it drive business reengineering efforts [43]? Is the project an even more strategic project that has the target to change the organizational culture? Is the project perceivld as such a strategic project, even if it has not been explicitly stated that it is? Will the project impact the way people work so substantially that systematic training efforts are needed?

It is also important to proactively identify possible sources of troubles, in particular, in the involved development teams. Based on these questions, the project's organizational structure should be designed with diligence. The correct persons should be assigned to correct tasks. Possible problems should be addressed from the outset, and systematically, appropriate funds and people should be made available to address them.

Diligence in project organization also requires software operation to be anticipated. An important issue is to proactively bridge the gap between different software development processes established in the various heterogeneous teams involved. If a company is under time pressure, it usually cannot normalize the processes and development approaches of all teams in every project since the processes involved may range from ad hoc through agile to heavyweight. The least that can be done is to make all project guidelines from all the teams available to all project leaders to motivate them to invest some time in understanding each other's working practices. Another basic step is to create common language in the form of a meta-glossary for the most important issues in the company.

Similarly, if one cannot steer the working processes in the distributed teams, it is at least necessary to strictly define the interfaces of the teams and the interplay between the teams by a meta-project handbook.

12.5.3 Viable Software Products

A viable software product is a software product that embodies cultural change. If a system is developed for an enterprise, it evolves. Some changes become necessary, because the functionality of the system does not fulfill the requirement specification. Other changes become necessary, because the users want to have some minor dialogues to be improved. But there are also those changes that crucially extend the functionality of the system or embody major changes of existing functionality. Each major release in an enterprise represents a maturity level with respect to the supported business processes.

We believe that large software products should also support several releases, each representing a maturity level (refer to Fig. 12.6). Introducing a full-fledged product that contains the features that evolved in the product over all the years of its product life cycle might be too heavyweight, simply too feature rich and sophisticated, to be introduced at once in an enterprise. The cultural change caused by the introduction of a large software product should be handled in a step-by-step way and should be realized using a predefined software version road map.

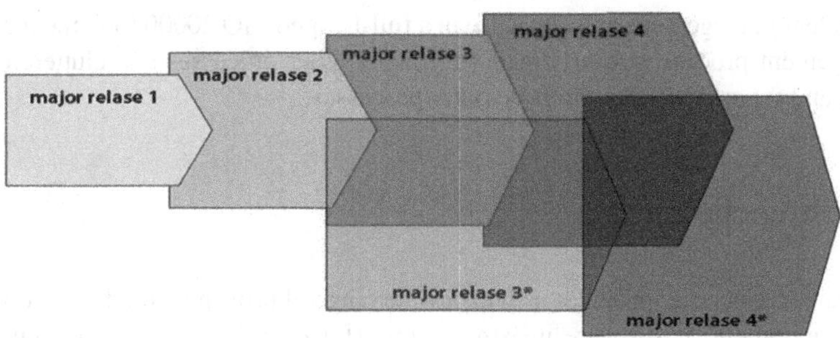

Fig. 12.6 A viable software product

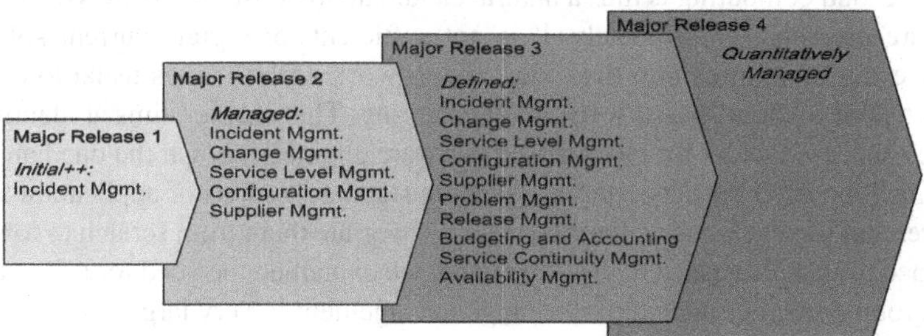

Fig. 12.7 A viable IT service management ERP system

A viable software product can be regarded as a systematically evolving software product. The notion of viable software product perfectly fits to and can be unified with the notion of software product-line engineering [26], which is depicted by the lower branch in Fig. 12.6.

A viable software product is designed to drive organizational change. Take an integrated IT service management software platform [9] as an example. It is known that the processes of IT service management, that is, such as documented by, for example, ISO20000 and ITIL, should be introduced one after the other. Usually, you start with the formalization of incident management, and then you continue with the formalization of problem management before you proceed with other processes from service delivery management, service control, and so on. Figure 12.7 proposes several stages in the IT service management of a viable software product. The several major releases are based on the maturity levels of the CMMI (Capability Maturity Model Integrated) [44] and are specified as sets of ISO 20000 processes. For example, a first version of an IT service management should only provide a targeted support for incident management. The point is that support for incident management can be tailored and simplified if there is no context of surrounding features for other processes. This means that it is simply not appropriate to use a tool with full support for ISO 20000 (i.e., across all of its processes) for the purpose of incident management only, because in a full-fledged ISO 20000 tool, the incident management process is intertwined with many other processes and cluttered with forms and reports concerning those other processes.

12.6 Conclusion

Software engineering provides us with a wide range of proven methods and tools for the development of software in large teams. However, in software projects with heterogeneous, distributed teams, we are still challenged with time and cost overruns or even failure. From a technological viewpoint (i.e., considered as an approach to combine latest network and virtualization technologies), cloud computing is here to stay. Cloud computing is thus a natural candidate to boost tomorrow's distributed software projects. Unfortunately, it is not sufficient to migrate current software engineering tool suites into the cloud and to work with them as usual to exploit the potential of cloud-based software engineering. This chapter aims at identifying the key success factors for cloud-based software engineering. On the one hand, we explained the need for deep, domain-specific standardizations of application architectures and life cycles as well as the need to integrate them from scratch to robustly designed tool landscapes. On the other hand, we explained the need for a focus shift onto group dynamics and cultural change management in very large software engineering projects and, simultaneously, the integration of appropriate project management tools into the respective tool landscape. We have discussed the following key observations and concepts:

- *Software in the cloud cannot be copied*! We have explained how this will deeply impact and boost the software industry.
- The *single underlying sum* (SUM) as the essence of next-generation integrated development environments.
- *Deep standardization* as the normalizing aspect of the SUM.
- The *streamlining SUM* as the aspect of systematic extension of the SUM, realized by, for example, maintenance of meta-information and a defined moderation process.
- *Orthographic software modeling* as an enabler for next-generation cloud-aided software engineering.
- *CASE 2.0 – Cloud-Aided Software Engineering* as the integration of next-generation view-based technologies and a focus shift toward management best practices.
- The *viable software engineering* life cycle that closes the gap between project management, organizational change management, and corporate governance.
- The *viable software product* as a product that embodies and drives organizational change.

In the 1980s, Computer-Aided Software Engineering (CASE) drove a major revolution in the way software systems were developed and maintained. We have made the case for how Cloud-Aided Software Engineering (CASE 2.0) promises to spawn a new revolution that will extend these benefits to the full software life cycle and encompass all concerns related to the engineering and running of viable software systems. The "2.0" emphasizes the fact that this will include group dynamics and advanced management concerns involving all stakeholders (from owners and end users to developers, managers, and administrators) not just the traditional development and maintenance concerns of software engineers and project managers. We have explained how the key to unlocking the power of the cloud for software engineering is to adopt a strict, fully-fledged view-based approach to visualization and have presented some innovative strategies for supporting views in a cloud-based environment.

In the future, low-level technology issues related to hardware platforms and software infrastructures will become less important for Software-as-a-Service stakeholders, as more of the responsibility for providing a reliable and robust Platform-as-a-Service is assumed by cloud providers. Moreover, the integration of new functionality into such platforms will be more generalized and standardized than it is today and will become more data oriented than message oriented. Software engineering environments will also merge with enterprise architecture environments [45] which provide related information about all aspects of how software applications are integrated into, and aligned with, an enterprise IT landscape. By consolidating all artifacts and concerns related to a software application, across its full life cycle, the cloud makes every work package, historical version, product-line version, and deployment instance, etc., dynamically visualizable on demand. In other words, all stakeholders will experience a software application through a web of real-time views.

References

1. Buyya, R., Yeo, C.S., Venugopal, S., Borberg, J., Brandic, I.: Cloud computing and emerging IT platforms: vision, hype, and reality for delivering computing as the 5th utility. Future Gener. Comput. Syst. **25**, 599–616 (2009)
2. Mell, P., Grance, T.: The NIST Definition of Cloud Computing, version 15. National Institute of Standards and Technology, Information Technology Laboratory (2009)
3. Stiglitz, E.: The Roaring Nineties: A New History of the World's Most Prosperous Decade. W.W. Norton, New York (2003)
4. Naur, P., Randell, B. (eds.): Software Engineering ~ Report on a Conference Sponsored by the NATO Science Committee, Garmisch, October 1968. NATO Science Committee, January 1969
5. Project Management Institute: PMBOK Guide – A Guide to the Project Management Body of Knowledge, 4th edn. Project Management Institute, Newtown Square (2008)
6. Drakos, N.: Magic Quadrant for Team Collaboration and Social Software. Gartner RAS Core Research Note G00151493. Gartner, October 2007
7. Carr, N.G.: IT doesn't matter. Harv. Bus. Rev. **81**(5), 5–12 (2003)
8. Carr, N.: The Big Switch – Rewiring the World, from Edison to Google. W.W. Norton & Company, New York (2008)

9. Draheim, D.: Smart business process management. In: Fischer L. (ed.) 2011 BPM and Workflow Handbook, Digital Edition. Future Strategies, Workflow Management Coalition, February 2012
10. Westerman, P.: Data Warehousing – Using the Wal-Mart Model. Morgan Kaufmann Publishers, San Francisco (2001)
11. Hahn, B., Ballinger, C.: Tpump in Continuous Environment – Assembling the Teradata Active Data Warehouse Series. Active Data Warehouse Center of Expertise, April 2001
12. Browne, J., Harhen, J., Shivnan, J.: Production Management Systems. Addison-Wesley, Boston (1996)
13. Draheim, D.: Business Process Technology – A Unified View on Business Processes, Workflows and Enterprise Applications. Springer, Berlin (2010)
14. Mintzberg, H.: Mintzberg on Management – Inside Our Strange World of Organizations. The Free Press, New York (1989)
15. Stallman, R.M.: Free Software, Free Society. Free Software Foundation, Boston (2010)
16. Gelder, K.: Subcultures: Cultural Histories and Social Practice. Routledge, New York (2007)
17. Levy, S.: Hackers: Heroes of the Computer Revolution. Penguin, New York (1984)
18. Castells, M.: The Internet Galaxy: Reflections on the Internet, Business, and Society. Oxford University Press, Oxford (2001)
19. Strangelove, M.: The Empire of Mind: Digital Piracy and the Anti-Capitalist Movement. University of Toronto Press, Toronto (2005)
20. Raymond, E.S.: The Cathedral and the Bazar. O'Reilly & Associates, Sebastopol (1999)
21. Weiser, M.: The computer for the 21st century. Sci. Am. **265**(3), 66–75 (1991)
22. Drakos, N., Mann, J., Rozwell, C.: Magic Quadrant for Social Software in the Workplace. Gartner RAS Core Research Note G00207256. Gartner, October 2010
23. Hollingworth, D.: The Workflow Reference Model. Technical Report TC00-1003, Workflow Management Coalition, Lighthouse Point, FL, USA (1995)
24. International Organization for Standardization: International Standard ISO/IEC 19770–1:2006. Information Technology – Software Asset Management – Part 1. ISO (2006)
25. Brooks, F.P.: The Mythical Man-Month – Essays on Software Engineering. Addison-Wesley, Reading (1975)
26. Atkinson, C.: Component-Based Product Line Engineering with UML. Addison-Wesley, New York (2002)
27. Atkinson, C., Stoll, D., Tunjic, C.: Orthographic service modeling. In: Second International Workshop on Models and Model-driven Methods for Service Engineering, pp. 67–70. IEEE Computer Society (2011)
28. Holley, K., Palistrant, J., Graham, S.: Effective SOA Governance. IBM White Paper, IBM Corporation, March 2006
29. Draheim, D.: The service-oriented metaphor deciphered. In: Lee I., Park J.C., Song I. (eds.) Journal of Computing Science and Engineering, vol. 4, no. 4. KIISE, December 2010
30. Cartlidge, A., Lillycrop, M. (eds.): An Introductory Overview of ITIL V3. ISBN 0-9551245-8-1. The IT Service Management Forum (2007)
31. International Organization for Standardization: International Standard ISO/IEC 20000–1:2005(E). Information Technology – Service Management – Part 1: Specification. ISO (2005)
32. Soltis, F.: Fortress Rochester. The Inside Story of the IBM I series. 29th Street Press, July 2001
33. European Committee for Standardisation: Eurocode – Basis of Structural Design, EN 1990:2002 E, CEN, November 2001
34. Dadam, P., Reichert, M., Rinderle-Ma, S., Lanz, A., Pryss, R., Predeschly, M., Kolb, J., Ly, L.T., Jurisch, M., Kreher, U., Göser, K.: From ADEPT to AristaFlow BPM Suite: a research vision has become reality. In: Business Process Management Workshops 2009, Lecture Notes in Business, Informatics, pp. 529–531. Springer (2009)
35. Dadam, P., Reichert, M.: The ADEPT project: A decade of research and development for robust and flexible process support. Comput. Sci. Res. Dev. **23**(2), 81–97, Springer (2009)

36. Dumas, M., van der Aalst, W.M.P., ter Hofstede, A.H.M.: Process-Aware Information Systems – Bridging People and Software Through Process Technology. Wiley, New York (2005)
37. Lutteroth, C.: AP1 – A platform for model-based software engineering. Ph.D. thesis, University of Auckland (2008)
38. Gillette, W.: Managing megaprojects: A focused approach. In: Software, vol. 13, no. 4. IEEE (1996)
39. Beck, K.: Extreme Programming Explained ~ Embrace Change. Addison-Wesley, Reading (2000)
40. Kruchten, P.: The Rational Unified Process. Addison-Wesley, Reading (1999)
41. Lewin, K.: Resolving Social Conflicts: Selected Papers on Group Dynamics. Harper & Row, New York (1948)
42. Schein, E.H.: Organizational Culture and Leadership. Wiley, San Francisco (2004)
43. Hammer, M., Champy, J.: Reengineering the Corporation: A Manifesto for Business Revolution. HarperCollins Publishers, New York (1993)
44. CMMI Product Team: CMMI for Development, version 1.3. Technical Report CMU/SEI-2010-TR-033. Carnegie-Mellon-University, Software Engineering Institute, November 2010
45. Lankhorst, M.: Enterprise Architecture at Work. Springer, Berlin/Heidelberg (2009)
46. Draheim, D., Weber, G.: Form-Oriented Analysis – A New Methodology to Model Form-Based Applications. Springer, Berlin (2005)

Chapter 13
Development of Cloud Applications in Hybrid Clouds with Support for Multi-scheduling

Lucio Agostinho Rocha

Abstract Development of cloud applications must consider many aspects inherent in the distributed nature of clouds, mainly those related to elasticity, high access level to computational resources, multi-tenant behavior, transparency, pay-per-use model, and resource scalability. In addition, portability is a key feature that must be present in any development framework to allow extensions and simplify resource sharing by standardized interfaces. Open source approaches can be used, but the model must be composed of independent parts to optimize the availability of active components in the infrastructure. Hybrid cloud models are interesting because widely acceptable solutions can be developed without "reinventing the wheel." Private clouds are more suitable for keeping restricted data or supporting services of small enterprises or institutions. However, their infrastructure must offer alternatives to provide services outside their own domain. In this context, a private cloud can use frameworks of public clouds and aggregate services to support the development of new applications. This generally occurs in PaaS models, where the platform offers pre-configured tools to interact with services of other domains. Security issues must also be considered at all stages of development, as most of the communication takes place among services located in different domains, linked by Internet connections. Solutions such as OpenID guarantee that public cloud services are used for the purpose of authentication, but additional security features in the source domain must be assured. In this chapter, a development framework is presented to guide the development of widely acceptable cloud applications, following standardized open source solutions. This framework, originally developed for a robotic environment, can be extended to support other cloud environments. The study presents

L.A. Rocha (✉)
Department of Computer Engineering and Industrial Automation (DCA)
at the School of Electrical and Computer Engineering (FEEC),
State University of Campinas, São Paulo, Brazil
e-mail: l089278@dac.unicamp.br

Z. Mahmood and S. Saeed (eds.), *Software Engineering Frameworks for the Cloud Computing Paradigm*, Computer Communications and Networks,
DOI 10.1007/978-1-4471-5031-2_13,

aspects related to multi-scheduling of virtual machines and suggests how virtualized applications can be developed with different methodologies, such as dynamic IP, Web service with SOAP communication, MapReduce approach, and OCCI-based infrastructure.

Keywords Cloud computing • Hybrid cloud • OCCI • OpenID • Cloud framework • MapReduce • Virtualization

13.1 Introduction

The development of distributed cloud architectures deals with issues of scalability, elasticity over demand, broad network access, usage measurement, security aspects such as authorization and authentication, and many other concepts related to multi-tenant services in order to serve a high number of concurrent users over the Internet. The nature of a distributed cloud has implications about how the offered services are organized over different administrative domains. In order to extend the Service-Level Agreement (SLA) to thousands of users, the support architecture must have interfaces compatible with other cloud providers.

This work presents a cloud framework directed to the requirements of portability, respecting the Open Grid Forum (OGF) and Open Cloud Computing Interface (OCCI) patterns [1]. The framework has kernel components that guide the extension of the whole system. Also contemplated are the methodology, architecture, and wrapper of open source APIs, such as OpenID [2], to allow aggregation of other cloud services to the system. We discuss how other cloud technologies model their own structures. Our goal is to illustrate mechanisms to integrate private and public clouds in a hybrid model.

The above-mentioned concepts have been used to develop a real cloud laboratory offering different Linux operating systems as services. Unlike Amazon EC2 [3] or Windows Azure [4] cloud environments, in this cloud architecture, Linux systems can be used to interact with robotic resources accessible only inside the laboratory. In addition, this architecture allows the inclusion by the user of compatible virtual machines into the system. This system is unique in that it deals with network issues only during the period reserved for robotic experiments. The framework also supports multiple scheduling approaches, that is, multi-scheduling.

This framework was designed according to the Layered Design Pattern, a well-defined standard where lower levels provide services to higher ones. Each level is defined in such a way as to allow development independently from the others, according to interfaces compatible with open patterns such as OCCI.

SSL and X.509 digital certificates guarantee the security of Internet access from outside the institution. The main goal of this security infrastructure is to reduce the effort required to keep the system reliable in different physical infrastructures. Scientific applications can benefit from this approach: For example, grid computing middleware such as Globus Toolkit [5] can be virtualized in VMs of the infrastructure,

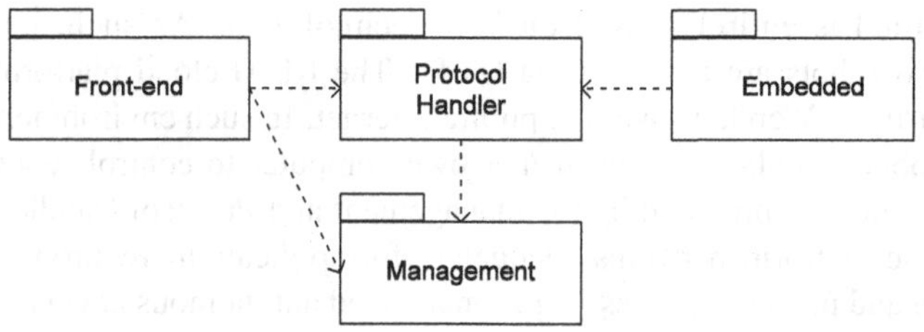

Fig. 13.1 Main packages of the REALcloud platform

reducing the complexity of developing secure intensive computational facilities for massive amounts of data. In robotics, virtualization in cloud is an alternative to keep collaborations between students and to promote robust integration of geographically distant robotic resources.

13.2 Framework for Distributed Cloud Applications

Distributed frameworks must offer sensible SLA and provide high-quality services to concurrent users. In this section, we describe an approach in robotics to develop frameworks associated with scheduling techniques of virtual resources in the design of cloud infrastructures. Extended versions of this work were reported in [6] and [7].

Networked robotics is a trend that favors the distribution of robotic applications across a set of processors located inside and outside robots. The motivation for networked robotics is the availability of network technologies allowing robots to take part in comprehensive networking environments aggregating processors, environmental sensors, mobile and stationary robots, and wireless gadgets, among other networked devices. Many software platforms have been proposed to simplify the development of networked robotic applications, offering a set of services to the applications such as access control, federated authentication, and resource protection. REALcloud is one such cloud platform for networked robotics. Its architecture has four main software packages, as shown in Fig. 13.1.

The embedded package consists of HTTP microservers capable of running on robots' onboard processors with limited processing power. Microservers have an HTTP (Hypertext Transfer Protocol) interface aggregating basic robot operations (move, turn, sense, etc.). The Protocol Handler package intercepts all HTTP requests targeted to the robots and performs functions such as security checks, HTTP proxying, and network address translations. The front-end package offers APIs (Application Programming Interfaces) and Web components for manipulating the robots. APIs are supplied in several programming languages, such as C++, Java, Python, C#, Matlab, and LabView. The management package offers a wide range of services related to users, resources, domains, and federations. An important service is the access service where authenticated users start an access session for the resources they previously reserved.

REALcloud is entirely based on Web technologies. As such, management services and robots are accessed via HTTP. The REALcloud platform has been used primarily in Web labs over the public Internet. In such environments the user develops robotic applications in his/her own computer to control robots over the network. Security is provided by the management and Protocol Handler packages. Although the platform performs adequately for applications requiring small data transferring and processing rates (e.g., sonar-based autonomous navigation), bottlenecks may degrade applications requiring efficient communication and high processing power. Slow Internet connections and HTTP inspections introduce a delay in the control that impairs performance of distributed robotic applications. The processing power of the user's computer also causes delays in control, mainly when control actions are computed via CPU intensive algorithms such as those based on computer vision and computational intelligence techniques.

In order to avoid the delays introduced by slow Internet connections and by limitations of the user's computer, an environment has been developed where user's applications run on servers directly connected to the resources manipulated by the application. The servers can provide resource sharing with much more computer power than the user's processor. Virtualization is the key technology for achieving the desired performance. In addition, applications can take advantage of specialized hardware installed on the servers such as GPUs (Graphics Processing Units) and FPGA (Field-Programmable Gate Array) specialized boards (e.g., for stereo vision processing).

In the case of the networked robotic platform, virtualization helps bringing applications closer to the robots they operate, avoiding long network delays and providing the processing power required by applications. A user can own his/her own VMs with the proper operating system plus the network robotic software necessary for developing and running the applications. This software includes the client side of REALcloud platform, robotic frameworks, APIs, and simulators. Isolation assures that applications running on different VMs do not interfere with each other. This solution requires one or more servers installed in the robotics lab, an inexpensive resource nowadays.

In order to take advantage of virtualization, an architecture must be designed to offer a virtualized environment where the distributed robotic applications will run. In this architecture, resource protection issues must be addressed in order to prevent unauthorized access to robots and other devices by the applications running on VMs. Processor allocation and VM networking sharing are important to assure an adequate distribution of processing power to applications. REALcloud offers the cloud platform as a service in a private (and small) cloud computing infrastructure. Both the client and server sides of the platform are deployed inside VMs. At the server side (management and Protocol Handler packages of Fig. 13.1), virtualization favors software distribution to the members of a federation as all the platform software comes installed and configured in a VM image compatible with a chosen virtualization solution. Each federated domain must deploy instances of this VM to manage and protect the robotic resources.

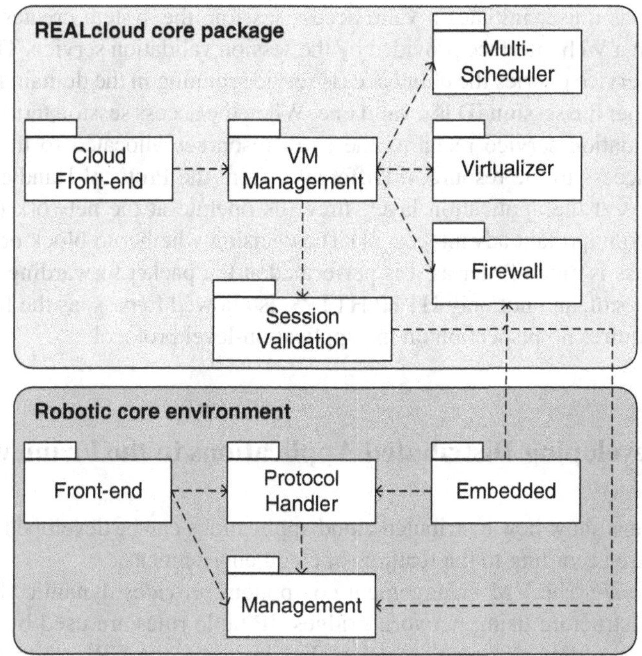

Fig. 13.2 Architecture of the REALcloud framework

At the client side, user's applications running inside VMs access the robotic resources with low communication latency and appropriate computing power. The processors where the VMs run and the robotic resources are connected to the same network or to networks a few hops apart. In order to speed up the interaction with robotic resources, applications running inside VMs access the robotic resources without HTTP inspection by the Protocol Handler package.

The REALcloud environment is built around two Web services (Fig. 13.2): *VM management service* that allows users and administrators to manage VMs and *session validation service* that allows applications running on VMs to access the robotic resources.

The VM management service controls the VM's life cycle. It allows configuring, initiating, reconfiguring, stopping, and destroying VMs. This service relies on command line interfaces supported by the chosen virtualization solution. Once a VM is created, the service configures the VM host's firewall in order to allow access to the VM from outside networks. Access is provided by the NAT (network address translation) and the port forwarding network functions. The session validation service is responsible for assigning privileges to the VMs belonging to users holding valid access sessions. It gives the same protection as provided by the Protocol Handler package (still necessary for accessing resources from the outside networks).

As soon as a user initiates a valid access session, the system creates a session identifier on a Web interface provided by the session validation service. The session validation service queries the cloud access service running in the domain in order to check whether the session ID is a valid one. When the access session terminates, the session validation service reclaims the extra resources allocated to the VM and blocks its access to the resources. Differently from the Protocol Handler package that operates at the application layer, firewalls operate at the network (IP) layer, bringing two important advantages: (1) The decision whether to block or allow the traffic to pass is much faster as it is performed at the packet forwarding level, and (2) any protocol, and not only HTTP/HTTPS, is allowed to pass, as the forwarding decision requires no inspection on the application-level protocol.

13.3 Developing Distributed Applications in the Framework

The next steps show how distributed cloud applications can be developed inside the infrastructure according to the features of cloud environments:

Dynamic IP: The VM management component provides dynamic IPs offered by the infrastructure using network bridges. IP table rules are used by the cloud application to establish communication. For instance, the URL "https://staticIP:clientVMPort/," with the same static IP, can be shared by many VMs through network bridges between the server host and the users' VMs. As shown in Fig. 13.3, the following script illustrates how the server host can be configured for this purpose.

Web Services: They are an efficient approach to the development of cloud services. The VM management component can be used to register the Web services provided by the cloud. Services are linked in a REST (Representational State Transfer) approach; that is, each cloud service has a URL accessible by the Internet. Web service methods are available by WSDL interfaces. Remote clients can have access to the Web service functionalities by querying the offered methods in this Web interface. Composition of services can be achieved by the combination of Web services. The communication channel can use SOAP (Simple Object Access Protocol) and can be encrypted by the Axis 2 toolkit [8]. As shown in Fig. 13.4, the following code fragment illustrates how a cloud application can be deployed in the cloud using Axis 2 Web services:

MapReduce Approach: Cloud applications can also be developed according to a MapReduce approach, using pre-configured VMs of the SaaS model. Ready-to-go jobs are another approach to develop distributed cloud applications. Web services can be combined when users' applications are submitted by querying the methods declared in the WSDL interface of the required service.

MapReduce is a programming model geared to the parallel processing of large amounts of data, splitting jobs into a set of independent tasks [9, 10]. It is widely used in searching mechanisms such as Google, Yahoo!, Facebook, Amazon AWS, and Last.fm. The model is noted for its simplicity. A cluster approach is used to distribute and perform the parallel processing of data in multiple cluster nodes,

```
# Syntax: cloud-NAT.sh <PRIVATE_IP_VM> <VM_PORT>
PRIVATE_IP_VM=$1
VM_PORT=$2

# Block access to internal network without losing other entries
iptables -A FORWARD -d $PRIVATE_IP_PROTECTED_RESOURCE -j DROP
iptables -A OUTPUT -d $PRIVATE_IP_PROTECTED_RESOURCE -j DROP
iptables -A OUTPUT -s $PRIVATE_IP_VM -j DROP

#Enable usage of iptables with layer 2 (bridge and MAC)
iptables -A FORWARD -m physdev --physdev-is-bridged -j ACCEPT

#Open network access to external and internal network
iptables -A INPUT -p tcp --dport $VM_PORT -j ACCEPT

#Bridge 0 (private network): Forwarding data from the public port
#to the internal network
iptables -t nat -A PREROUTING -i br0 -p tcp -m tcp --dport $VM_PORT -j
DNAT --to-destination $PRIVATE_IP_VM:9100

#Enable forwarding from the private network bridge
iptables -A FORWARD -p tcp -i br0 --dport $VM_PORT -d $PRIVATE_IP_VM
-j ACCEPT

#After forwarding, guarantee that the data return
iptables -t nat -A POSTROUTING -o br0 -j MASQUERADE
```

Fig. 13.3 Script for establishment of network bridges

known as worker nodes. The master nodes split the entry data into a set of independent parts (chunks) and distribute them to the worker nodes. A worker node performs a further split, if necessary, in a tree model. Each worker node processes a slice of the main job and forwards its result to the master node. Reduction tasks join the results of one or more worker nodes.

Frameworks to process customized data simplify the development of distributed cloud applications. Hadoop [10] is an example of a framework following the MapReduce model. Hadoop is devoted to homogeneous clusters, and the master node manages the slave nodes with similar configurations. The entry file must be stored in the Hadoop File System (HDFS). This file is split in parts of 64 MB (chunks) by default but can be replicated to reduce fault tolerance. Each chunk is processed by a mapping task that generates a list of <key-value> pairs. The lists are grouped in buckets based on the keys. When each task is processed, reduction tasks are applied to the lists according to the keys. Figure 13.5 is based on [11] and illustrates this model where master and slave nodes can run on cloud VMs.

```
public String getCloudApplicationID(
    String staticIP, String cloudVMPort, String method) {
    String result = "1";
    try {
            CloudStub stub = new CloudStub(
            "https://" + staticIP + ":" + clientVMPort +
            ":/axis2/services/CloudApplicationID");
            CloudStub.GetCloudApplicationID service =
                  new CloudStub.GetCloudApplicationID();
            service.setVirtualMachine(staticIP,cloudVMPort);
            service.setOperation(method);
            CloudStub.GetCloudApplicationIDResponse response =
                  stub.getCloudApplicationID(service);
            result = response.get_return();
    } catch (AxisFault e) {
            result = "Fail in SOAP Axis communication: " +
            e.getMessage();
    } catch (RemoteException e) {
            result = "Remote exception: " + e.getMessage(); }
    return result;
}//end getCloudApplicationID
```

Fig. 13.4 Example of function for Axis 2 Web service

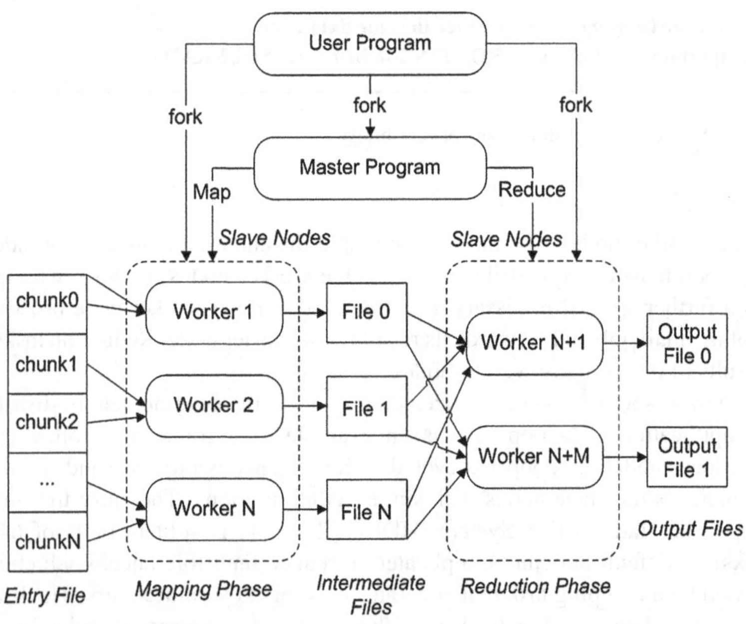

Fig. 13.5 MapReduce for cloud applications in the SaaS model

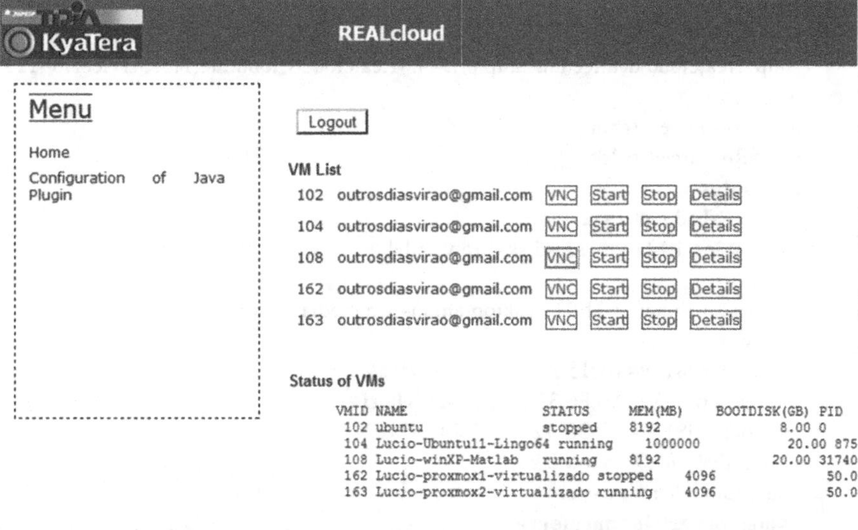

Fig. 13.6 Web client application based on OCCI specifications

Open Cloud Computing Interface (*OCCI*)-*Based Infrastructure*: OCCI is a set of specifications maintained by the Open Grid Forum (OGF) to define interfaces to deliver cloud resources. OCCI is a RESTful protocol and API for management tasks acting as a service front-end to a provider's internal management framework. The standards are described in three documents: OCCI Core [12] describes the formal definition of the OCCI Core Model; extensions in this API will be discoverable and visible to an OCCI client at run-time. OCCI Infrastructure [13] defines the model to extend the IaaS and describes resource types, their attributes, and actions over them. OCCI HTTP Rendering [14] defines the mechanism to access the OCCI Core Model in a RESTful approach using the HTTP protocol.

As an example, the REALcloud infrastructure offers a set of Web services for the development of new cloud applications and HTTP syntax for the dynamic discovery of the available users' virtual machines. "https://cloudStaticIP:cloudPort/Realcloud/resources.jsp?action=<VNC|START|STOP|DETAILS>&resourceName=VM_ID" is the URL to interact with the set of actions of the user virtual machine. HTTP queries are used to start a VNC session between the client Web browser and the cloud environment. The other actions are to start, stop, and query details about each virtual machine of the authenticated user. Figure 13.6 shows the Web client interface; a RESTful approach with HTTP queries is also available. This option is important to acquire management information about all virtual machines in the cloud environment. As shown in Fig. 13.7, the URL "https://cloudStaticIP:cloudPort/CloudInterface?id=VM_ID" returns the OCCI-based XML data.

```
- <category>
  - <scheme>
      http://realcloud.dca.fee.unicamp.br:9443/Realcloud/CloudInterfaceService?id=123
    </scheme>
    <term>resource</term>
    <title>Resource</title>
  - <attributes>
      <name>hadoop01</name>
      <ide0>local:123/vm-123-disk-1.raw</ide0>
    - <ide2>
        local:iso/ubuntu-11.04-desktop-amd64.iso,media=cdrom
      </ide2>
      <vlan0>rtl8139=4A:15:FF:9F:14:F3</vlan0>
      <vlan1>rtl8139=A6:F6:33:B9:EE:42</vlan1>
      <vlan2>rtl8139=2E:CC:12:E8:11:14</vlan2>
      <bootdisk>ide0</bootdisk>
      <ostype>other</ostype>
      <memory>2048</memory>
      <sockets>2</sockets>
      <summary>[cloud@dca.fee.unicamp.br]</summary>
      <entity_type>VM</entity_type>
    </attributes>
  </category>
```


Fig. 13.7 OCCI-based document obtained in the RESTful HTTP query

Multi-scheduler Infrastructure: The multi-scheduling approach employs different scheduling algorithms to distribute cloud resources according to resource features such as CPU availability, RAM usage, and storage capacity. Many cloud solutions use multi-scheduling approaches to optimize usage of their shared resources [15].

Eucalyptus [16] employs an allocation resource process dispatched by the cloud provider, which ends when the requested VM is instantiated in a network node. When an allocation request is placed, the CLC (cloud controller) component determines which CC (Cluster Controller) component will be able to instantiate the VM. This is done by querying for cloud resources and selecting the first CC component that has available resources.

Nimbus [17] manages its resources by means of the Workspace Resource Manager component. It gives the cloud developer control over manageable node groups using the libvirt library [18], jointly with the Workspace Pilot component, which receives user jobs and performs scheduling with additional schedulers, such as Condor [19].

REALcloud uses a multi-scheduling approach similar to OpenNebula [20], as shown in Fig. 13.8: an embedded default scheduler with a rank algorithm to distribute its VMs according to VM requirements and the servers' performance. The pseudo-code below shows the algorithm for resource allocation. The parameters used for entry requests are host, CPU and RAM availability, and type of hypervisor.

```
Algorithm for Resource Allocation in REALcloud
Required: Input: requirements, rank, hostList
Ensured: Output: selectedHost
  while (hostList.hasElements) do
    if host.satisfies(requirements) then
      candidates.new(host)
    endif
  endwhile
  sort = sort(candidates,rank)
  selectedHost = sort(1)
```

Fig. 13.8 Algorithm for resource allocation in REALcloud

The rank function sorts hosts according to their availability and the users' requirements to instantiate VMs. New scheduling algorithms can be implemented based on this policy.

Identity Management with OpenID: Public cloud services of authentication and authorization can be aggregated into private clouds in a model known as hybrid cloud, a combination of public and private cloud models.

This approach is useful to avoid keeping large databases in the internal infrastructure; that is, valid users in trusted domains can be authenticated in the private cloud. However, authorization must be managed by the internal private infrastructure. This approach can be used in the cloud front-end package. Figure 13.9 shows the basic authentication mechanism with OpenID. OpenID is a passive protocol that uses HTTP forwarding between users' applications and the identity provider. Requests to access the authentication service are based on HTTP protocol. Users must first register themselves in an identity provider with OpenID support, which in turn uses the user account to generate a unique URL in the Web. The URL is used by the client's application as an argument to discover the authentication service; that is, authentication is a service provided by the identity provider. This URL is used by the client application to query the identity provider that keeps the user's account. In the following step, users not previously authenticated must provide their credentials (typically, user ID and password) to the authentication service of the identity provider, identified by URL. OpenID also has mechanisms to delegate rules between peers of the same circle of trust.

At step 1, a user with a registered identity in an OpenID provider (Google account, for instance), but not previously registered in this domain, wants to access resources in a cloud Web site having an OpenID authentication service. In step 2, the user enters the OpenID URL that he/she received from the identity provider. In step 3, the OpenID service of the cloud Web site redirects the user's browser to the authentication service of its identity provider. In step 4, two options are available: If the user has been previously authenticated in the identity provider, the browser is redirected to the validation service of the cloud Web site. If the user has not been previously authenticated, the identity provider queries about credentials (user ID and password) to proceed with browser redirecting. In step 5, the identity provider

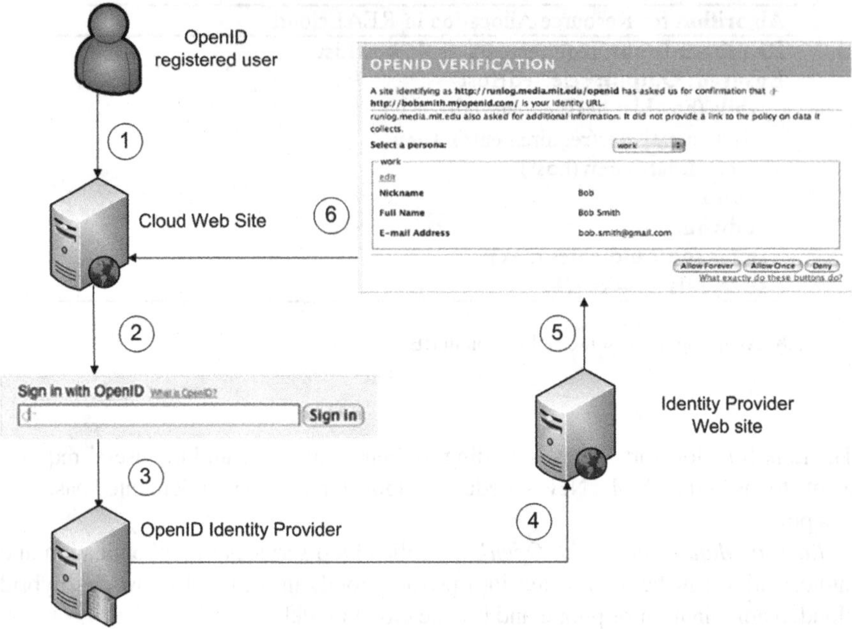

Fig. 13.9 Basic authentication with OpenID

Web site uses a verification service to validate the URL address that queries about authentication with OpenID. This step is necessary for security reasons to avoid phishing attacks (untrusted URL address). Another reason is that many sites want to have additional information about newer users, such as user name, alternative e-mail, and telephone number. In step 6, the identity provider redirects the user to the cloud resource URL.

13.4 Overview of Cloud Distributed Environments

The complete hybrid cloud environment was developed to support many concurrent users by simplifying the usage of virtual machines inside and outside the infrastructure while keeping the requirements of availability, reliability, network performance, and security of the whole system. This section describes the architecture, APIs, and methodology to develop distributed applications in this environment.

Figure 13.10 shows the main components of a generic cloud computing environment. According to this model, more specific environments can be implanted by specializing each component. There is no clear rule requiring the use of all components, but more complete environments should recognize their main parts in this model. A description of each one follows.

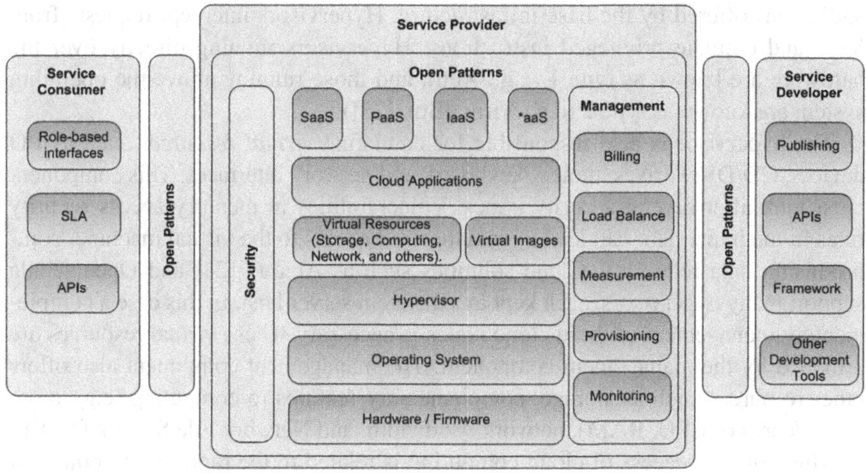

Fig. 13.10 Overview of the main components of cloud computing environments (Based on [21])

13.4.1 Service Provider

This component contains the main elements that make this environment functional. The versatility of the *service provider* component is supported by many open source solutions, mainly to increase the possibility of linkage with other cloud interfaces, extending and developing other compliant components without commercial restrictions, and reducing the usage of closed patterns. The bottom level of this core model defines the *hardware/firmware* component. Distinct environments are highly dependent on the base infrastructure. Server architecture (e.g., x86 or x64) and the availability of virtualization in hardware (e.g., CPUs with registers to support virtualization) can have a direct impact on the performance of the whole cloud system. The hardware includes physical servers, routers, switches, storage devices, backup drivers, and firewalls. Each communication device in this base network is offered by the datacenter provider.

Selecting the *operating system* is important because the type of virtualization will depend on it. Proprietary operating systems are regulated by commercial licenses, increasing implantation costs in future security updates and/or software expansion. Open source solutions bring the advantage of cost reduction, but the type of management service must use APIs compatible with the type of virtualization solution. Finally, the provider must consider the need of dedicated servers. For example, cloud solutions such as Xen XCP [22] use dedicated hosts to offer their services.

The *hypervisor* is the software layer between the hardware and the operating system and is responsible for offering shared resources to large numbers of concurrent virtual machines (VM). The hypervisor runs in supervisor mode and manages the scheduling of resources (CPU cycles, memory slices, disk storage, network linkage, and so on) offered by the base infrastructure. Hypervisors intercept requests from VMs and emulate privileged instructions. Hypervisors running directly over the hardware are known as type 1 (e.g., Xen), and those running above the operating system are known as type 2 (e.g., VirtualBox [23]).

The hypervisor is also responsible for emulating *virtual resources* such as I/O devices, CD/DVD drives, mouse, keyboard, and network interfaces. This component must look after several security issues. Vulnerabilities in memory access security rules in the hypervisor can lead to unauthorized access to the virtual machine, compromising data reliability. Cloud solutions such as Abiquo [24] and OpenNebula support many hypervisors, each kept in a different server host. In this case a complementary management of these cloud nodes is necessary. These virtual resources are provided by the management component. The management component also offers other resources such as storage, complementary features to computing (e.g., more cycles/cores of CPU, RAM), network bandwidth, and Network File System (NFS).

Much of the success of cloud computing is related to the rapid development of virtualization techniques, accomplished by technical advancements and cost reduction in computational hardware. *Virtual machines* (VMs) are an example of the success of this theme. Many VMs can be instantiated in the same server host, helping reduce the number of physical servers by means of a more efficient usage of resources, a technique known as server consolidation. A complete operating system can be installed inside a VM, which in turn can be distributed or migrate to another server host. Migration is possible if the destination server host has a compatible virtualization interface. The format of different VMs can be converted to other formats if the virtualization toolkit provides this feature, contributing to distribute "ready-to-use" systems to distinct cloud providers. In addition, many cloud providers, such as Amazon EC3 and GoGrid [25], and cloud solutions, such as Eucalyptus, OpenNebula, and Abiquo, provide templates of pre-configured VMs for their environments.

Cloud applications are inherently distributed applications with interfaces to interact with the services provided by the cloud. The main consideration in their design is that these applications have to be supplied by the cloud environment, whether using virtualized services or any other technology with Internet access such as HTTP or SOAP. Distributed cloud applications are different from conventional applications with remote access, mainly because the environment has the features of [26]:

Elasticity: Shared resources should be provided to cloud applications on demand, that is, as soon as the cloud applications need them, but only for the period of usage. The cloud management system should reallocate non-used resources when the applications no longer need them.

High access level to computational resources: Cloud applications should be accessible by a gamut of different remote devices: laptops and desktops, mobile phones, smart phones, tablets, and so on.

Multi-tenant behavior: The same cloud application can be used by multiple users (tenants). This model is valuable because multiple client applications can share the same remote application. A single instance of the software runs on the server, providing services to many concurrent client applications.

Transparency: Cloud applications are offered independently from their physical location, and although users need not care about where their applications run inside the cloud, this information should be given by the cloud provider. Legal restrictions in some countries do not allow some particular contents to be provided in their geographical location and/or jurisdiction.

Pay-per-use model: Billing is proportional to the usage of computational resources, similarly to traditional bills of electricity, water, and natural gas.

Scalability: Consumption of shared computational resources or the increase of cloud applications and users should not degrade the performance of other concurrent cloud applications in the same domain. This issue is a consequence of the elasticity model.

Different models to provide service are described in the literature:

PaaS (*Platform as a Service*): Users can develop their own applications with toolkits provided by the cloud platform. Communication services are also available, for example, Web services, storage, and programming languages. Examples are Ning [27] and Microsoft Windows Azure Platform [4].

SaaS (*Software as a Service*): The cloud provider enables usage of exclusive user applications and/or applications provided by the cloud environment, such as enterprise e-mails, discussion groups, Web site toolkits, and workflow applications. Examples are Salesforce [28] and Google Apps [29].

IaaS (*Infrastructure as a Service*): Computational resources such as storage, high-performance computing (HPC), high network bandwidth, logical servers, and a set of other resources and devices are provided by the infrastructure. Examples are Amazon AWS and FlexiScale [30].

**aaS* (*Everything as a Service*): Any services and/or application available in a cloud model such as a combination of the previously cited models.

13.4.2 Security

The main issues about security can be grouped according to their importance to the software-level (cloud applications) and to the hardware-level infrastructure. These issues should be addressed by each element in the service provider component.

Software-level security deals with the role of the communication protocol in the privacy, integrity, and authentication in interactions with cloud applications [31].

Privacy exists when only sender and receiver are able to understand the communication. If someone eavesdrops on the communication channel, its contents should not be understood by the third party.

Integrity is guaranteed when the receiver can be sure that he/she acquired the message exactly as sent by the other party.

Authentication is relevant because it increases the security access level to cloud services. Over the Internet, the HTTPS protocol, session cookies, and X.509 certificates are options to guarantee the end-to-end privacy between cloud services and their users.

Communication with SSL uses a secure channel to forward data between the server and the client application. An authenticated channel can be built using digital signatures and a public key infrastructure. In addition, the cloud management system should be able to provide tools to manage the authentication of its users to ensure confidentiality, as well as authorization techniques (e.g., role-based access control – RBAC) to differentiate the access to services [32, 33]. If the software is provided by or developed in the cloud, the platform needs to keep policies to ensure that no harmful software, such as worms, trojans, or viruses, can propagate in the system.

Security for infrastructure deals with the guarantee that access to cloud resources is protected against external malicious users. Generally this can be achieved by firewall rules between the public link access and the private cloud network (e.g., using IP table rules). Resource availability should be managed with techniques of fail tolerance, load balance, patch management, monitoring, backup redundancy, and others. However, this whole set of techniques will only be effective if clear rules are kept to control personal access to physical hosts.

13.4.3 Service Consumer

Cloud users have access to cloud services by interfaces compatible with the cloud environment. *Role-based interfaces* allow different interactions with the cloud services according to the role that each specific user plays in the environment. For example, authenticated users must be able to log into the system, instantiate/stop VMs, perform status queries, and so on, but administrative functions such as creating and removing VMs should be restricted to them. This same issue is seen in collaborative applications such as Google Docs [34] and Picasa [35], where the RBAC roles are applied to users.

Service-Level Agreements (*SLAs*) should be regulated by the law of the country. In scenarios where agility to accommodate unpredictable consumption is important, SLAs are critical to define the relationship between the cloud service provider and its consumers. A more detailed report of this issue can be found in [36].

Application Programming Interfaces (*APIs*) on the side of the service consumer must also abide by the rules when interacting with remote services. APIs simplify the development of new services, but the cloud provider must keep its APIs up to date to avoid security risks.

13.4.4 Management

Billing follows the pay-per-use model, in which the price charged is proportional to resource consumption. OpenQRM [37] is an open source example of architecture that allows billing in the private cloud and supports EC2 standards for APIs. It also supports virtualization techniques such as KVM [38] and Xen, as well as management of hosts, virtual machines, and deployments. Virtualized images of Ubuntu, Debian, and CentOS are supplied as templates. However, in many other private cloud solutions, the billing component is not necessary.

Load balance deals with how the infrastructure supports requests and how its resources are maintained to achieve high performance and better utilization.

The *measurement* component establishes metrics to perform several management tasks.

Provisioning deals with policies to offer resources to many concurrent users. Again, policies must take into account availability, scalability when more resources need to be provided by other domains, and resource scheduling. It is common for each cloud solution to implement its own solutions to monitoring, but this task can be carried out with open source middlewares, such as Nagios [39], an open source tool allowing extensions by plug-ins. For instance, the NRPE (Nagios Remote Plugin Executor) monitors the number of users logged in the system, CPU consumption, memory used by each virtual machine, and number of active processes in the server hosts [40].

13.4.5 Service Developer

Publishing describes how services are provided and how they can be accessed, either internally or over the Internet. For example, access to virtual machines can be provided by a specific URL and/or via VNC protocol. In addition, applications can show their methods in WSDL language, and communication can be done via the HTTP or SOAP protocols. Many providers offer their own sets of *APIs* (e.g., Google App Engine) to interact with their public services according to the PaaS model. Also provided are exclusive *frameworks*, for example, Microsoft Azure with .NET framework, and *other development tools*, for example, datasheets, corporate e-mail, workflows, and other tools in Salesforce.com.

13.5 Final Considerations

It is important that the development of cloud applications be guided by frameworks to avoid a mix of unrelated structures. The main features of cloud domains need to be considered jointly with the needs of the institution. Furthermore, open standards contribute to simplifying the integration with other domains and extending the portability of applications.

Related issues in the development of cloud applications are about collaborative applications such as Google Docs, storage in cloud with Dropbox, and Google Drive. Such applications are highly dependent on network performance between the client user and the service provider. In addition, cache routines in the client application guarantee data integrity.

Many other security features aim to increase the reliability of data exchange. Synchronization protocols are an example – the timestamp needs to be valid in both sides. Network data encryption with AES 256 bit and SSL connection are extra protection offered by some providers.

Portability is another issue to be considered. Customizing the cloud service according to the client device features is another challenge, for example, for Web connection with mobile devices.

Much research has been done on how to provide inter-cloud communication and establish federations [41]. Cloud computing is emerging as a new paradigm to offer services in the Web, one that can lead to new business opportunities, but the difficult issue of security remains open. This is because in a cloud numerous applications are available as services, many of which have their own access control systems. Furthermore, applications that support service compositions across distinct domains require authentication mechanisms that take into account this collaborative nature.

Acknowledgments The author thanks Marcos Favero Florence de Barros for his language editing services.

References

1. Open Cloud Computing Interface (OCCI): Available at: http://occi-wg.org/about (2012)
2. OpenID Foundation Website: Available at: http://opened.net (2012)
3. Amazon AWS. Amazon Elastic Compute Cloud (Amazon EC2): Available at: http://aws.amazon.com/ec2 (2012)
4. Windows Azure: Microsoft's Cloud Platform: Available at: http://www.microsoft.com/windowsazure (2012)
5. Globus Toolkit: Welcome to the Globus Toolkit Homepage. Available at: http://www.globus.org/toolkit (2012)
6. Rocha, L.A., Olivi, L., Feliciano, G., Paolieri, F., Rodrigues, D., Cardozo, E., Guimarães, E.: A cloud computing environment for supporting networked robotics applications, DASC. In: IEEE Ninth International Conference on Dependable, Autonomic and Secure Computing, pp. 1110–1116. Sydney, Australia (2011)
7. Rocha, L.A., Feliciano, G., Olivi, L., Cardozo, E., Guimarães, E.: A bio-inspired approach to provisioning of virtual resources in federated clouds, DASC. In: IEEE Ninth International Conference on Dependable, Autonomic and Secure Computing, pp. 598–604, Sydney, Australia (2011)
8. Apache Axis2: Available at: http://axis.apache.org/axis2 (2012)
9. Shankar, R., Narendra, G.: MapReduce programming with Apache Hadoop – process massive data sets in parallel on large clusters. Javaworld. Available online at: http://www.javaworld.com/javaworld/jw-09-2008/jw-09-hadoop.html (2008)
10. Yahoo! Developer Network: MapReduce: Available at: http://developer.yahoo.com/hadoop/tutorial/ (2012)
11. Dean, J., Ghemawat, S.: Mapreduce: simplified data processing on large clusters. Commun. ACM **51**, 107–113 (2008)
12. GFD.183 – OCCI Core (v1.1): Available at: http://www.ogf.org/documents/GFD-183.pdf (2011)
13. GFD.184 – OCCI Infrastructure (v1.1): Available at: http://www.ogf.org/documents/GFD-184.pdf (2011)

14. GFD.185 – OCCI HTTP Rendering (v1.1): Available at: http://ogf.org/documents/GFD-185.pdf (2011)
15. Gonçalves, G.E., Endo, P.T., Cordeiro, T.D., Palhares, A.V.A., Sadok, D., Kelner, J., Melander, B., Mangs, J.: Resource allocation in clouds: concepts, tools and research challenges. In: Mini-curso– SBRC. Campo Grande, MS, Brazil (2011)
16. Johnson, D., Murari, K., Raju, M., Suseendran, R.B., Girikumar, Y.: Eucalyptus Beginner's Guide – UEC Edition – Ubuntu Server 10.04 – Lucid Lynx. CSS Corp. Available online at: http://cssoss.files.wordpress.com/2010/06/book_eucalyptus_beginners_guide_uec_edition1.pdf (2010)
17. Nimbus Project: Available at: http://www.nimbusproject.org/ (2012)
18. Libvirt – virtualization API: Available at: http://www.libvirt.org (2012)
19. Condor High Throughput Computing: Available at: http://research.cs.wisc.edu/condor/ (2012)
20. OpenNebula Project Leads: Opennebula. Available at: http://opennebula.org(2012)
21. Amrhein, D., et al.: Cloud Computing Use Cases White Paper Version 4.0. Technical Report (2010)
22. XenServer: Available at: http://www.citrix.com (2012)
23. VirtualBox: Available at: http://www.virtualbox.org (2012)
24. Abiquo: Architecture Overview: Available at: http://community.abiquo.com (2012)
25. GoGrid: Available at: http://www.gogrid.com (2012)
26. Martins, A.: Fundamentos de Computação Nuvem para Governos – Amãpytuna – Computaç ão em Nuvem: serviços livres para a sociedade do conhecimento, chapter 2, pp. 47–65. ISBN: 978-85-7631-241-3. Alexandre de Gusmão Foundation (2010)
27. Ning: Available at: http://www.ning.com (2010)
28. Salesforce: Available at: http://salesforce.com (2012)
29. Google Apps for Business: Available at: http://www.google.com/a/ (2012)
30. FlexiScale public cloud: Available at: http://www.flexiant.com/products/flexiscale (2012)
31. The Globus Toolkit 4 Programmer's Tutorial: Fundamental Security Concepts. The three pillars of the secure communication. Available at: http://gdp.globus.org/gt4-tutorial/singlehtml/progtutorial_0.2.1.html (2005)
32. Ramachandran, M.: Component-Based Development for Cloud Computing Architectures. Cloud Computing for Enterprises Architectures, Computer Communications and Networks. Springer, London (2011)
33. Ahmed, K.E.U., Alexandrov, V.: Identity and Access Management in Cloud Computing. Cloud Computing for Enterprises Architectures, Computer Communications and Networks. Springer, London (2011)
34. Google docs: Available at: http://docs.google.com (2012)
35. Picasa Web Albums: free photo sharing from Google: Available at: http://picasaweb.google.com (2012)
36. Buck, K., Hanf, D.: Cloud SLA Considerations for the Government Consumer. Systems Engineering at MITRE. Cloud Computing Series. The MITRE Corporation. Available online at: http://www.mitre.org/work/tech_papers/2010/10_2902/cloud_sla_considerations_government.pdf (2012)
37. OpenQRM: Available at: http://www.openqrm-enterprise.com/ (2012)
38. Kernel-based Virtual Machine: Available at: http://www.linuxkvm.org/page/Main_Page (2012)
39. Nagios – The Industry Standard in IT Infrastructure Monitoring: Available at: http://www.nagios.org (2012)
40. Chaves, S.A., Uriarte, R.B., Westphall, C.B.: Implantando e Monitorando uma Nuvem Privada. In: VIII WCGA, Brazilian Symposium on Computer Networks and Distributed Systems, SBRC. Gramado, RS, Brazil (2010)
41. Buyya, R., Ranjan, R., Calheiros, R.N.: Modeling and simulation of scalable cloud computing environments and the CloudSim toolkit: challenges and opportunities, high performance computing & simulation. In: HPCS '09. International Conference, Leipzig (2009)

Part IV
Performance of Cloud Based Software Applications

Chapter 14
Efficient Practices and Frameworks for Cloud-Based Application Development

Anil Kumar Muppalla, N. Pramod, and K.G. Srinivasa

Abstract As cloud computing continues to burgeon throughout the technology sphere, it becomes essential to understand the significance of this emerging technology. By its nature, it offers an organization a great deal of agility and cost savings. Cloud technologies are being applied and leveraged in different applications fueling growth in the number of Infrastructure-as-a-Service (IaaS) and Platform-as-a-Service (PaaS) vendors. The business delivery models of cloud computing have raised interests across the IT industry as the resources are offered as utilities and on demand. From a developer perspective, it is important to grasp the nuances of cloud-based application development to improve the development process. This chapter discusses best practices in relation to some of the celebrated cloud features. Furthermore, most common and well-known features of cloud frameworks are presented to aid the developer's choice. Lastly, comparative cloud-based architectural discussion on developing and deploying a Web application using industry popular frameworks is presented. Although, cloud computing as a service/development paradigm addresses several well-known issues like scalability and availability, there are several concerns with respect to security and privacy of data which has opened doors for research opportunities. Some plausible research directions are also identified.

Keywords Scalability • Cloud computing • Azure • App engine • Storage • Frameworks • Application development

---

A.K. Muppalla • N. Pramod • K.G. Srinivasa (✉)
High Performance Computing Laboratory, Department of Computer Science and Engineering, M S Ramaiah Institute of Technology, Bangalore, India
e-mail: anil.kumar.848@gmail.com; npramod05@gmail.com; srinivasa.kg@gmail.com

Z. Mahmood and S. Saeed (eds.), *Software Engineering Frameworks for the Cloud Computing Paradigm*, Computer Communications and Networks,
DOI 10.1007/978-1-4471-5031-2_14,

14.1 Introduction

Prior to 2007, there was a need for any large technology corporation to maintain infrastructure to fulfill the needs of the company and its clients [1]. With the emergence of cloud computing, the situation has changed. There seems to be wide acceptance in the prospect of buying infrastructure usage rather than the hardware itself with immediate cost benefits. The on-demand delivery of hardware, software, and storage as a service is termed as *cloud computing*. The union of data center hardware, software, and storage is what we will call a *cloud*. An application based on such clouds is taken as a *cloud application*. This paradigm has revolutionized the service industry with increasing support from Microsoft [2], Google [3], and IBM [4]. Three striking aspects of cloud computing are [5]:

- The impression of infinite cloud resources available on demand, thereby dismissing the need for users to plan far ahead for provisioning.
- The on-demand commitment of resources by cloud, thereby allowing companies to start small and request resources as and when the need arises.
- The pay-per-use model has encouraged ability to pay for use of computing resources on a short-term basis as needed and release them as needed.

Efforts to conceptualize cloud computing dates back to, at least, 1998 [6]. However, the adoption and promotion of cloud computing has been slow until 2007 [1]. The background of early industrial adoptions of cloud computing coincides with that of service computing [7]. Service computing [8] received worldwide support from leading companies like IBM and Microsoft [9]. The widespread adoption of cloud computing is driven by stable and mature development of technologies and computing resources. Success stories of Web services have complemented the popularity service computing, although a Web service is one such technology to fulfill the need for service orientation [7]. Many distributed computing techniques for cloud computing have been mature [10–12]. Decoupling the parts of the application environment allows for scalability on different levels; these parts are further provided to the developers as services. Based on the type of the service provided, cloud computing can be classified as Infrastructure as a Service (IaaS), Platform as a Service (PaaS), and Software as a Service (SaaS) [13].

Developers reap several benefits developing their application on a cloud-based programming environment provided through a PaaS provider, such as automatic scaling and load balancing, as well as integration with other services (email and authentication). Such provisions alleviate much of the overhead of developing cloud applications. Furthermore, integration of their applications with other services on-demand increases the likelihood of usage of these applications, thereby driving the need to develop cloud-based applications. This in turn makes the cloud application development a less complicated task, accelerates the deployment time, and minimizes the logic faults in the application, for example, deployment of a distributed computing environment such as Hadoop [14, 26] on the cloud which provides its application developers with a programming environment, that is, MapReduce

Table 14.1 Comparison between traditional and cloud-based application

Traditional applications	Cloud-based applications
Each application is deployed and maintained as a bundle in a common environment	With diverse environment capabilities of the cloud, the application is deployed and maintained as modules, scattered across environments
Run-time infrastructure is structured and controlled, giving rise to maintenance overhead	Run-time infrastructure is unstructured and managed by cloud fabric, with computing capabilities changing
Business functionality is realized by using "controller" components that calls methods (functions) of business components	Service orchestration is used to realize business functionality—invoke one or many business services
Support for multi-tenancy is typically not required	Multi-tenancy support is assumed
User base is assumed at design time, and scalability is addressed at run-time by procuring necessary hardware	User base need not be known, potential to scale up and down rapidly
Enhancements and upgrades require downtime	No downtime required for enhancements and upgrades
Components interact with non-SOA contracts like RMI and CORBA	Standard SOA service-based interaction between components is assumed like SOAP and REST
Deployment requires traditional tools (application server admin console, ANT, etc.)	Along with traditional tools, requires knowledge and utilization of vendor-specific cloud APIs
Application is tested in controlled environment (Unit/integration/system)	Application (integration) is tested on the cloud to ensure seamless orchestration between services on one or many clouds
Security is enforced by application architecture (LDAP lookup based authentication/authorization)	Security is built into the service contracts (WS-Security, SAML, etc.)

framework for the cloud. As such, cloud software environments facilitate the process of cloud application development.

Cloud computing brings this whole new way of thinking about architecture and design, since we don't control the infrastructure directly hence one step less in the design process. The application is supported to scale horizontally, be very cost effective in operation as you can scale up and scale down and obtain granular control over CPU expense. As several platforms such as Force.com are rich and provide the boilerplate code, developing applications on it becomes a much higher-level activity. The gap between domain experts who conceptualize the product and developers who code it significantly narrows down. The adoption of cloud computing has improved the development process of several applications and services.

The differences between cloud-based application and traditional application are presented in Table 14.1. There is no significant change in the development process of a cloud application; since the division of the application development environment into infrastructure, platform, and software has significantly helped in overcoming some common challenges of traditional software development, it has led to accelerated development and deployment, ensuring shorter release cycles. The cloud application development enforces an agile form of development. Some advantages are:

- Short release cycles means processes used for developing these applications are agile/scrum based.
- Heavy stress on acceptance as well as unit tests.
- Traditional task management practices and timesheet processes are not applicable.
- No formal workflow processes for reviews.

14.2 Design Patterns for Key Issues of Cloud Application Development

14.2.1 Scalability

This is defined as the ability of the system to handle growing amount of work in a reliable manner [15]. Scalability in cloud perspective can be addressed by considering the following:

14.2.1.1 Load Sharing

It is the logical spreading of requests across similar components for handling those requests, from a cloud development point of view, and distribution of requests, which are mainly HTTP but can be any application protocol, across all the instances using an efficient configured load-balancing algorithm. This is a scaling-out approach. Several load-balancing facilities are provided across development platforms; the task of the developer would be to tie the application to these APIs.

14.2.1.2 Partitioning

Intelligent load distribution across many components by routing an individual request to a data-specific component, efficiency, and performance is dramatically increased in an application's delivery architecture while enabling this facility. Instead of having identical instances, each instance or pool of instances, as shown in Fig. 14.1, is marked as the *owner*. This enables the developers to configure the development environment to handle type-specific request. The concept of *application switching* and *load balancing* achieve individual importance as the former is used to route a particular request which can be then load balanced across a pool of resources. It's a subtle distinction but an important one when architecting not only efficient and fast but resilient and reliable delivery networks.

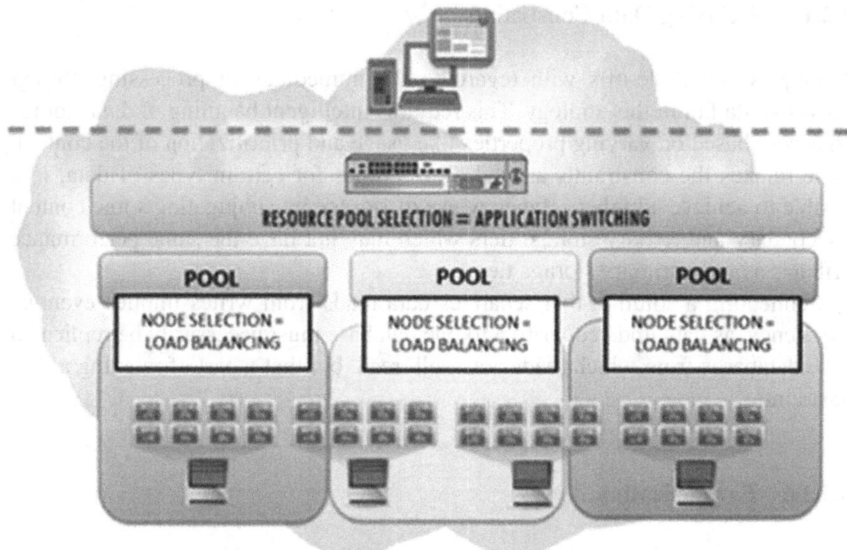

Fig. 14.1 Grouping instances into task-specific pools [16]

14.2.1.3 Vertical Partitioning

It is a partitioning using different processing units while routing application requests that we separate by function that is associated with a URI. Content wise, partitioning is the most common implementation strategy. Consider an example of creating resource pools based on the Content-Type HTTP header: content in pool *content servers* and images in pool *image servers*. This provides for greater optimization of the Web/application based on the usage pattern and the content type. In a distributed environment, architects leverage say cloud-based storage for static content while maintaining dynamic content (and its associated data stores) on premise. This hybrid strategy is regarded to have successful acceptance across the cloud community.

14.2.1.4 Horizontal Partitioning

Through partitioning, persistence-based load balancing is accomplished, as well as the handling of object caching. This also describes the way in which you might direct requests received from specific users to designated instances that are specifically designed to handle their unique needs or requirements, for example, separation of *privilege* users from *free* users based on some partitioning key, which is cookie information.

14.2.1.5 Relaxing Data Constraints

Techniques and trade-offs with regard to the immediacy of processing/storing/access to data fall in this strategy. This requires intelligent handling of data storage and access based on varying properties like usage and prioritization of the content. If one relaxes the constraints around access times for certain types of data, it is possible to achieve a higher-efficiency use of storage by subjugating some content to secondary and tertiary storage tiers which may not have the same performance attributes as your primary storage tier.

Architecting a solution that separates data reads from writes implies eventual consistency, as data updated/written to one database must necessarily be replicated to the databases from which reads are, well, read, but that's part of relaxing a data constraint.

14.2.1.6 Parallelization

This refers to working on the same task in parallel on multiple processing units employing tools and methods like MapReduce and SPDY. If the actual task can be performed by multiple processing units, then an application delivery controller could certainly be configured to recognize that a specific URL should be essentially sent to some other proxy/solution that performs the actual distribution. We can observe that the processing model here deviates sharply from the popular *request-reply* paradigm.

14.2.1.7 Going Stateless

Application state maintenance can often hinder any scalability efforts, which normally involves persistence, and persistence means storing your data in some central location, and central data store is difficult to scale. Adopting RESTful nature (without being limited to HTTP) is a viable choice.

14.2.2 Elasticity

Dynamic resource utilization is a central concept in cloud computing. Application design must allow resources to be reserved and freed as needed. The aspects that drive the need to automate elasticity are as follows: (1) applications have to monitor themselves or have to be monitored externally, (2) application resources have to be provisioned based on this information, and (3) applications have to cope with addition and removal of resources. In order to fully benefit from the dynamicity of an elastic infrastructure, the management process to scale out an application has to be automated [17]. This way, the number of used resources can be aligned to changing workload quickly. If pay-per-use pricing models are available, the resource number directly affects the running cost of the application. Manual resource scaling would not respect this.

Requests received by an application are a good measure of workload and therefore shall be used as a basis for scaling decisions. An elastic load balancer automatically determines the amount of required resources based on numbers of requests and provisions the needed resources accordingly using the elastic infrastructure's API. Number of requests in unit time is observed from the components, and required number of resources (this is crucial design element) is computed by the load balancer and provisioned on the elastic infrastructure using its API. It significantly affects the effectiveness of the scaling decisions. It should be carefully selected during the design of the application using capacity planning techniques. Also, such behavior needs to be real time.

If the application can handle asynchronous requests, another layer of optimization can be implemented since there is a possibility of fluctuation in resource costs or cloud elasticity. The tasks can be delayed based on the availability of the resources. Some non-business-critical or time-critical workload, such as report generation, can be moved to times when resources of the private cloud are less utilized. An *elastic queue* is used to distribute requests among application components. Based on the number and type of messages it contains, the elastic queue determines the number of computing nodes to be provisioned. The elastic queue can contain different message types that are handled by different components. To speed this process up, individual images for application components are stored in the image database of the elastic infrastructure. Additionally, the elastic queue can respect environmental information, such as the overall infrastructure or resource price. This is used to delay less critical messages by reducing the number of handling compute nodes and to prioritize the business-critical functionality if the overall infrastructure utilization is high.

14.2.3 Availability

The use of commodity hardware to build the cloud has an advantage to reduce costs but also reduces the availability of resources. Therefore, cloud applications have to be designed to cope with failing resources to guarantee the required availability. Sometimes, (high) availability is only expressed regarding the possibility to start new compute nodes. To guarantee high availability under such conditions, the application architecture needs to be adjusted to enable redundancy and fault-tolerant structures. The application architecture is altered to include redundant compute nodes performing the same functionality. High available communication between these nodes is assured, for example, by a messaging system. Additionally, compute nodes are monitored and replaced in case of failure.

In a setting where high available compute nodes are used, the decoupling of components can also increase the performance and enable elasticity. As in every setup where messaging is used, the compute nodes need to consider the delivery assurances made by the messaging systems. Business-critical components of an application should be available at all times even during update. During an update, the elasticity of cloud aids in provision of additional compute nodes that contain the new application or middleware versions additionally to the old versions, consequently the shutdown of old compute nodes. One such method is providing images for compute nodes with the new software version that is created and tested. Hence, a graceful transition from the old to new application versions is executed. If different versions must not be handling requests at the same time, the transition is imminent. This is handled by instantiating both application versions independently. The switch can then be made by reconfiguring the access component, such as a load balancer. However, in some cases this can result in a minimal downtime during the transition [17].

14.2.4 Multi-tenancy

Any party that uses an application is termed a *tenant*. Sometimes a tenant can be a single user of an entire organization. Many of the cloud properties, such as elasticity and pay-per-use pricing models, can only be achieved by leveraging economies of scale. Cloud providers therefore have to target large markets and share resources between customers to utilize resources effectively. Hardware virtualization has been the first to foray into resource sharing through *Infrastructure-as-a-Service* delivery model. There is need for additional architectural modifications to support sharing of higher-level application components. When application is provided to multiple customers (multi-tenacity), deployment of componentized applications can be optimized by sharing individual component instances whenever possible. This is especially feasible for application components that are configured equally for all tenants, for example, currency converters. If tenants can share common resources, then underlying resources can be utilized in more efficient ways. This requires the configuring for multi-tenacity. The tenant's individual application instances access the same application component (pool). Therefore, the run-time cost per tenant can be reduced, because the utilization of the underlying infrastructure is increased and the shared component can be scaled for all tenants. If the configuration is equivalent for all tenants, a *single instance* can be used. Sometimes, tenants are not allowed to share critical components with other users. In this case, a *multiple instance component* must be used.

Additional use case wherein an application is instantiated to support multi-tenacity but some of its components cannot be shared may be due to laws prohibiting the same. So, tenants may require integration of individually developed application components into the provided application. Deploy individual component implementations and configurations for each tenant. This arrangement allows tenants to adjust components very freely. Portions of an application, on which tenants have a versatile behavior, can be realized in such a fashion. However, the application of this pattern hinders resource sharing between tenants.

14.2.5 High Performance

A load-balancing algorithm coupled with the MapReduce programming paradigm serves the purpose of processing large volumes of data. MapReduce is a parallel programming model that is supported by some capacity-on-demand type of clouds such as Google's BigTable, Hadoop, and Sector [18]. Load balancing is helpful in spreading the load equally across the free nodes when a node is loaded above its threshold level. Though load balancing is not so significant in execution of a MapReduce algorithm, it becomes essential when handling large files for processing and when availability of hardware resources is critical. Hadoop MapReduce has wide industry acceptance also being the top programming model implemented.

An efficient load-balancing technique can sometimes make all the difference in obtaining maximum throughput. The arrangement is considered balanced if for each data node, the ratio of used space at the node to the total capacity of node (known as the *utilization of the node*) differs from the ratio of used space at the cluster to the total capacity of the cluster (*utilization of the cluster*) by no more than the threshold value [17]. In view of hyper-utilization the module moves blocks from the data nodes that are being utilized a lot to the poorly used ones in an iterative fashion. In this implementation, nodes are classified as *high*, *average*, and *low* depending upon the utilization rating of each node. In a cloud environment, the MapReduce structure increases the efficiency of throughput for large data sets. In contrast, you wouldn't necessarily see such an increase in throughput in a non-cloud system. Therefore, consider a combination of MapReduce-style parallel processing and load balancing when planning to process a large amount of data on your cloud system.

14.2.6 Handling Failure

Unlike the traditional applications which are entirely dependent on the availability of the underlying infrastructure, cloud applications can be designed to withstand even big infrastructure outages. With the goal that each application has minimal or no common points of failure, the components must be deployed across redundant cloud components. These components must make no assumptions about the underlying infrastructure; that is, it must be able to adapt to changes in the infrastructure without downtime.

Designing for failure also comes with fair share or challenges such as large data processing which requires frequent movement of large volumes of data causing inertia. By building simple services composed of a single host, rather than multiple dependent hosts, one can create replicated service instances that can survive host failures. For example, if we had an application that consisted of business logic component 1, 2, 3, each of which had to be live on a separate host, we could compose service group (1, 2, 3), (1, 2, 3)… or we could create component pools (1, 1, …), (2, 2, …), (3, 4, …). While the composition (1, 2, 3), a single machine failure would result in the loss of a whole system group. By decomposing resources into independent pools, a single host failure only results in the loss of a single host's worth of functionality.

Another practice is to ensure short response time ensured by noting if the request returns a transient error or doesn't return within a small time, a retry is triggered to another instance of the service. If you don't fail fast and retry, distributed systems, especially those that are process or thread-based, can lock up as resources are consumed waiting on slow or dead services.

Thus, separating business logic into small stateless services that can be organized in simple homogeneous pools is much more efficient. The pool of stateless recording services allows upstream services to retry failed requests on other instances of the recording service. In addition, the size of the recording server pool can easily be scaled up and down in real time based on load.

14.3 Analysis of Storage as a New Form of Service

As technology continues to mature, several previously coupled components have broken out to exist independently. One such component is storage, still part of the infrastructure in principle, which has open doors for targeting specific business areas. To understand the application of storage as a service on its own, several delivery metrics need to be discussed along with established best practices [27], with support of the general architecture in Fig. 14.2.

14.3.1 Access

One problem with Web service APIs is that they require integration with an application to take advantage of the cloud storage. Most providers implement multiple access methods, but Web service APIs are common. Many of the APIs are implemented based on REST principles, which imply an object-based scheme developed on top of HTTP (using HTTP as a transport). REST APIs are stateless and therefore simple and efficient to provide. Therefore, common access methods are also used with cloud storage to provide immediate integration. For example, file-based protocols such as NFS/Common Internet File System (CIFS) or FTP (File Transfer Protocol) are used, as are block-based protocols such as iSCSI (Internet Small Computer System Interface).

14.3.2 Performance

Performance issues of storage systems range from small transactional accuracy to large data movement, but the ability to move data between a user and a remote cloud storage provider represents the largest challenge from a cloud storage perspective.

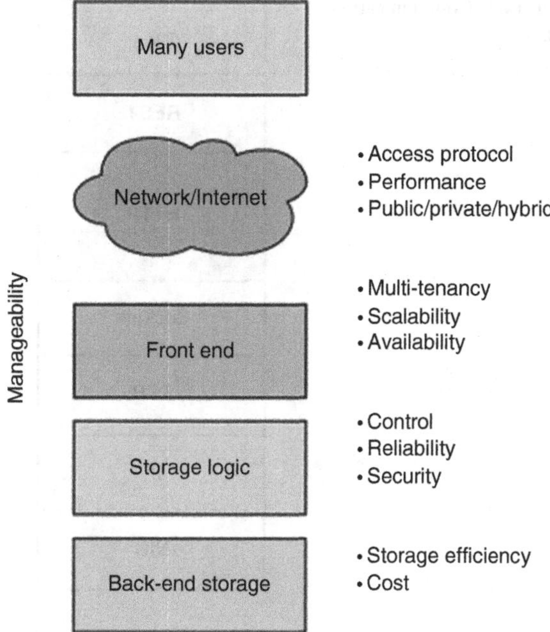

Fig. 14.2 General architecture of storage service [17]

The problem is TCP, as it controls the flow of data based on packet acknowledgments from the peer endpoint. Packet loss and late arrival enable congestion control as a useful feature but also limits performance as these are more network-intensive tasks. TCP is ideal for moving small amounts of data through the global Internet but is less suitable for larger data movement, with increasing RTT (round-trip time). This problem is solved by removing TCP from the equation. A new protocol called the *Fast and Secure Protocol* (FASP) was developed to accelerate bulk data movement in the face of large RTT and severe packet loss. The key is the use of the UDP, which is the partner transport protocol to TCP. UDP permits the host to manage congestion, pushing this aspect into the application layer protocol of FASP, as shown in Fig. 14.3.

14.3.3 Availability

Once a cloud storage provider has a user's data, he/she must be able to provide that data back to the user upon request. Given the network outages, user errors, and other circumstances, reliability and availability can prove to be a major hurdle. There are some interesting and novel schemes to address availability, such as information dispersal (Information Dispersal Algorithm (IDA)), to enable greater availability of data in the face of physical failures and network outages. IDA is an algorithm that

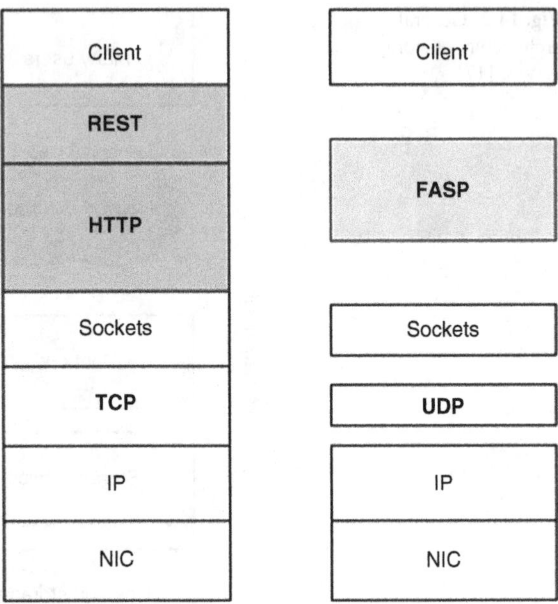

Fig. 14.3 Communication stack

allows data to be sliced with Reed-Solomon codes for purposes of data reconstruction in the face of missing data. Furthermore, IDA allows you to configure the number of data slices, such that a given data object could be carved into four slices with one tolerated failure or 20 slices with eight tolerated failures. Similar to RAID, IDA permits the reconstruction of data from a subset of the original data, with some amount of overhead for error codes (dependent on the number of tolerated failures). The downside of IDA is that it is processing intensive without hardware acceleration. Replication is another useful technique and is implemented by a variety of cloud storage providers. Although replication introduces a large amount of overhead (100 %), contrast to very low overhead by IDA, it is simple and efficient to provide.

14.3.4 Control

A customer's ability to control and manage how his or her data is stored has always motivated several storage providers. Although replication is a common method to ensure redundancy and hence availability, it also requires more than idea storage space. Reduced Redundancy Storage (RRS) is one such method that ensures to provide users with a means of minimizing overall storage costs. Data is replicated within the vendor's infrastructure, but with RRS, the data is replicated fewer times with the possibility for data loss. This is ideal for data that can be recreated or that has copies that exist elsewhere.

14.3.5 Efficiency

Storage efficiency is an important characteristic of cloud storage infrastructures, particularly with respect overall cost. This characteristic speaks more to the efficient use of the available resources over their cost. To make a storage system more efficient, more data must be stored. A common solution is data reduction, whereby the source data is reduced to require less physical space. Two means to achieve this include *compression*—the reduction of data through encoding the data using a different representation—and *de-duplication*, the removal of any identical copies of data that may exist. Although both methods are useful, compression involves processing (re-encoding the data into and out of the infrastructure), where de-duplication involves calculating signatures of data to search for duplicates.

14.4 Frameworks

Developers can use the cloud to deploy and run applications and to store data. On-premises applications can still use cloud-based resources. For example, an application located on an on-premises server, a rich client that runs on a desktop computer, or one that runs on a mobile device can use storage that is located on the cloud. Cloud application development is aided significantly with the provision of frameworks and development environments which the developers can leverage to produce applications guided by useful abstractions. These frameworks have proven to reduce the development time, therefore receiving wide acceptance. The period from 2007 to 2011 has witnessed exponential growth in adoption of cloud frameworks with Amazon kicking off this trend and recently several others perfecting it. This section provides important features of three such frameworks from industry leaders like Amazon, Google, and Microsoft.

14.4.1 Windows Azure

The Windows Azure platform by Microsoft Corporation provides hardware abstraction through virtualization. Every application that is deployed to Windows Azure runs on one or more virtual machines (VMs) [19]. The applications behave as though they were on a dedicated computer, although they might share physical resources such as disk space, network I/O, or CPU cores with other VMs on the same physical host; this is the abstraction that is possible with decoupling infrastructure from the application. A key benefit of an abstraction layer above the physical hardware is portability and scalability. Virtualization of a service allows it to be moved to any number of physical hosts in the data center. By combining virtualization technologies, commodity hardware, multi-tenancy, and aggregation of demand,

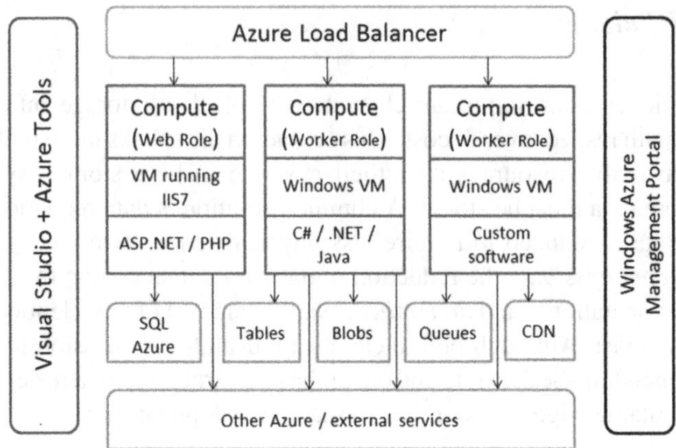

Fig. 14.4 Azure architecture [20]

Azure has become one of the most coveted platforms. These generate higher data center utilization (i.e., more useful work-per-dollar hardware cost) and, subsequently, savings that are passed along to you. Figure 14.4 presents the high-level architecture of Azure, which encapsulates the above-discussed features.

14.4.1.1 Salient Features of Azure

Here are some salient features of Windows Azure:

- Supports all major .NET technologies and provides wide language support across Java, PHP, and Python [24, 25]
- Windows Azure Compute:
  - Computing instances run Windows OS and applications (CPU + RAM + HDD)
  - Web role: Internet information services machine for hosting Web applications and WCF services
  - Worker role: long-running computations
- Azure data storage services:
  - Azure table storage: distributed highly scalable cloud database (stress entries with properties)
  - Azure queue storage: message queue service
  - Azure blobs/drives: blob/file storage, NTFS volumes
- SQL Azure: SQL server in the cloud with highly available and scalable relational database
- Azure Business Analytics: create reports with tables, charts, maps, etc.
- Azure Caching: distributed, in-memory, application cache

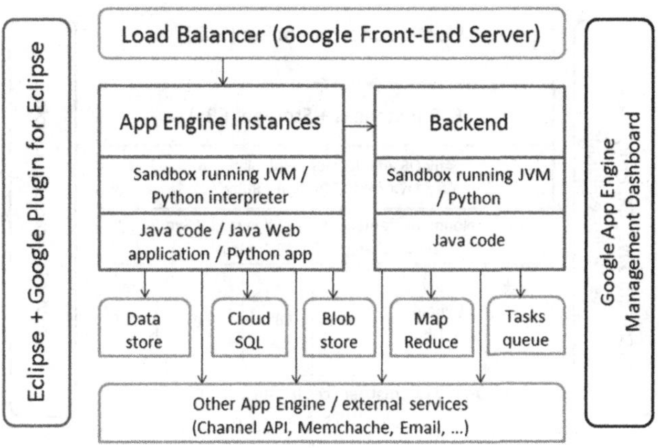

Fig. 14.5 Google App Engine architecture [20]

14.4.2 Google App Engine

Google App Engine is a Platform-as-a-Service (PaaS) cloud-computing delivery model for developing and hosting Web applications in Google-managed data centers. Applications are sandboxed and run across multiple servers [21]. App Engine offers automatic scaling for Web applications—as the number of requests increases for an application, App Engine automatically allocates more resources for the Web application to handle the additional demand [22]. Figure 14.5 represents the high-level architecture of Google App Engine outlining the structure to aid application development.

14.4.2.1 Salient Features of App Engine

- Leading Java and Python public cloud service
- App Engine instances:
  - Hosting the applications
  - Fully managed sandboxes (not VMs)
  - Provide CPU + RAM + storage + language run-time
- App Engine Backend:
  - Higher computing resources
  - Used for background processing
- App Engine data stores:
  - NoSQL schema less object database
  - Support transacts and a query engine (GQL)

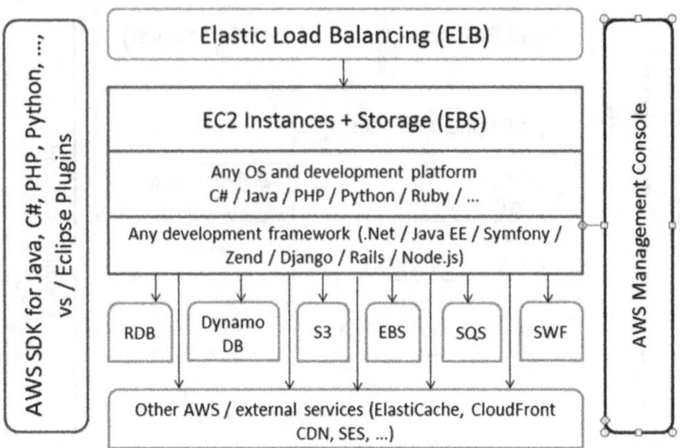

Fig. 14.6 AWS architecture [20]

- Cloud SQL: managed MySQL in App Engine
- Cloud Storage: store files as blobs and files with REST API
- MapReduce API: highly scalable parallel computing API for heavy computing tasks (based on Hadoop)
- Channel API: push notification for JavaScript applications
- Task Queues: execution of background services
- Memchache: distributed in-memory data cache

14.4.3 Amazon Web Services (AWS)

This is a collection of remote computing services (also called Web services) which constitute the cloud-computing platform provided by Amazon. Figure 14.6 represents the aggregation of wide range of features that support cloud application development on Amazon framework.

14.4.3.1 Salient Features of AWS

- Amazon Elastic Compute Cloud (Amazon EC2):
  - Virtual machines on-demand running Windows/Linux/other OS
  - Geographically distributed
  - Elastic IP addresses: a user can programmatically map an Elastic IP address to any virtual machine instance without a network administrator's help and without having to wait for DNS to propagate the new binding
- Amazon Elastic Block Store (Amazon EBS):
  - Virtual HDD volumes
  - Used with EC2 to keep the OS file system

- Amazon Simple Storage Service (Amazon S3):
  - Host binary data (images, videos, files, etc.)
  - REST API for access via Web
- Amazon DynamoDB/SimpleDB:
  - Managed NoSql cloud database
  - Highly scalable and fault tolerant
- Amazon Relational Database Service (RDS):
  - Managed MySQL and Oracle databases
  - Scalability, automated backup, replication
- Other services:
  - SQS: message queue
  - CloudFront: content delivery network
  - ElastiCache: caching
  - Route 53: Cloud DNS
  - SES: email

14.5 Comparison of AWS and Windows Azure: Applications Development

While deploying an initial Web application on the cloud, care is taken to leverage the niche technologies provided by the environment. This section performs a comparative analysis of the above-mentioned features in building a Web application on Amazon Web Services against Windows Azure.

14.5.1 Local Application Development Setup

Apache is an application server with development in PHP and storage in MySQL database. Figure 14.7 depicts the primary setup.

14.5.2 Migrating to the Cloud

AWS: In AWS, this means an Amazon EC2 Instance, an Elastic IP, and backups to the Amazon S3 storage service.

Windows Azure: In Windows Azure, the counterpart to EC2 is Windows Azure Compute. Specify a role (hosting container) and number of VM instances.

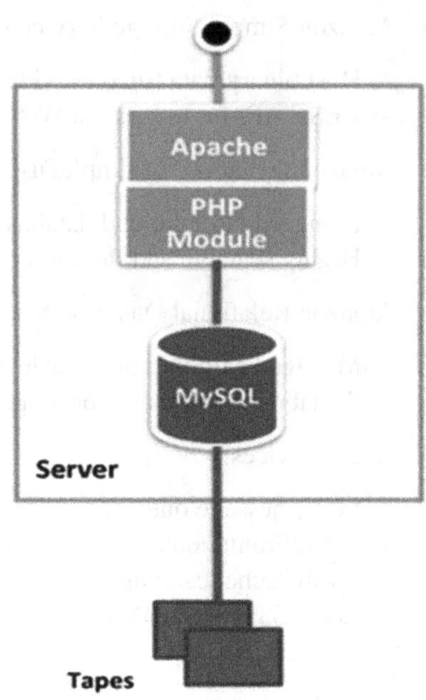

Fig. 14.7 Local application setup [23]

Choose a worker role (the right container for running Apache) and one VM instance. Upload metadata and an application package, from which Windows Azure Compute, Windows Server VM instance is created. An input endpoint is defined which provides accessibility to the Web site. Backups are made to the Windows Azure Storage service in the form of blobs or data tables.

14.5.3 Design for Failure

Keep application logs and static data outside of the VM server by using a cloud storage service. Make use of database snapshots, which can be mapped to look like drive volumes as in Figs. 14.8 and 14.9.

AWS: The logs and static data are kept in the Amazon S3 storage service. Root and data snapshot drive volumes are made available to the VM server using the Amazon Elastic Block Service (EBS).

Windows Azure: Logs and static data are written to the Windows Azure Storage service in the form of blobs or tables. For snapshots, a blob can be mapped as a drive volume using the Windows Azure Drive service. As for the root volume of the VM, this is created from the Windows Azure Compute deployment just as in the previous configuration.

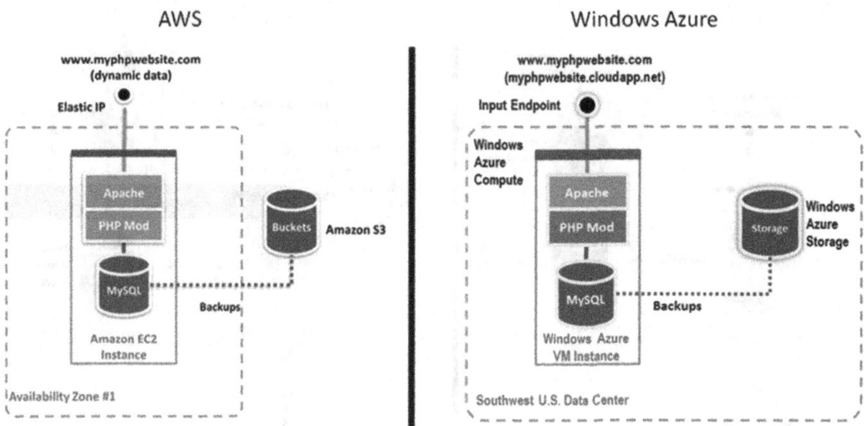

Fig. 14.8 Application deployment in AWS and Azure [23]

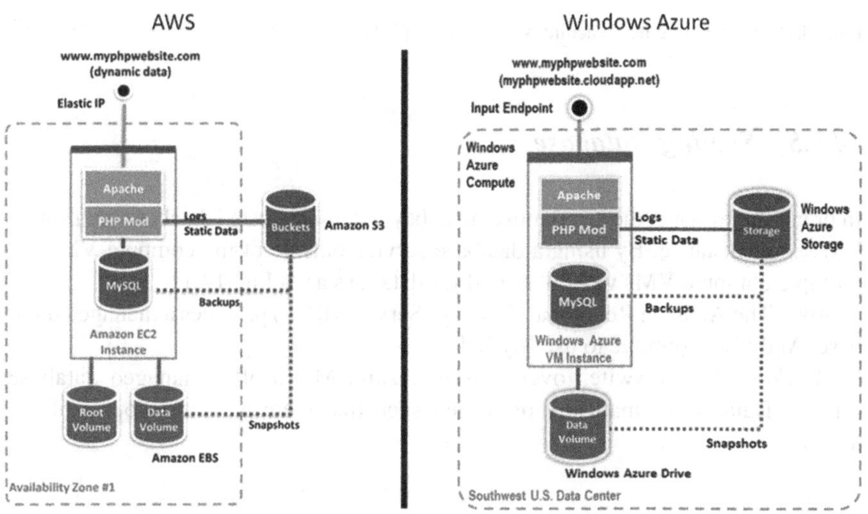

Fig. 14.9 Updated figure—design for failure [23]

14.5.4 Content Caching

Take advantage of edge caching of static content. Use content distribution network to serve up content such as images and video based on user location as in Fig. 14.10.

AWS: Amazon CloudFront is the content distribution network.

Windows Azure: The Windows Azure Content Delivery Network (CDN) can serve up blob content using a network of 24+ edge servers around the world.

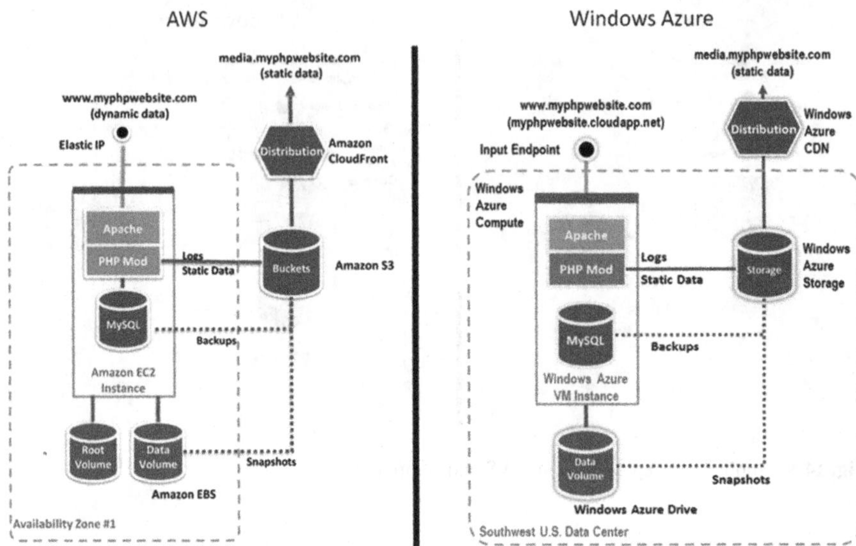

Fig. 14.10 Updated figure—caching static content [23]

14.5.5 *Scaling Database*

In preparing to scale, the setup must move beyond a self-hosted database on a single VM server instance. By using a database service outside of the compute VM, use multiple compute VMs without regard for data loss as in Fig. 14.11.

AWS: The Amazon Relational Database Service (RDS) provides a managed database. Andy can continue to use MySQL.

Windows Azure: Switch over to SQL Azure, Microsoft's managed database service. Data is automatically replicated such that there are three copies of the database.

14.5.6 *Scaling Compute*

With a scalable data, scale the compute tier, which is accomplished by running multiple instances as in Fig. 14.12.

AWS: Multiple instances of EC2 through the use of an Auto-Scaling Group. Load-balancing Web traffic to the instances by adding an Elastic Load Balancer (ELB).

Windows Azure: The input endpoint comes with a load balancer. The worker role is a scale group—its instances can be expanded or reduced, interactively or programmatically. The only change that needs to be made is to increase the worker roles instance count; a change can be made in the Windows Azure management portal.

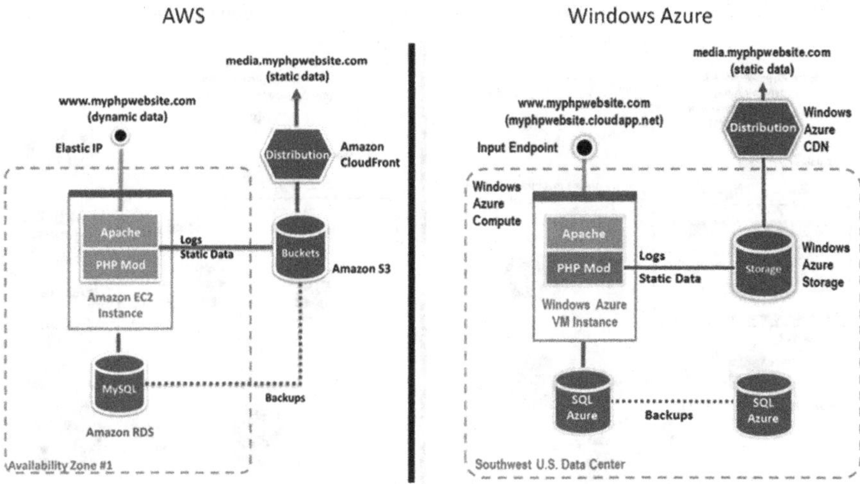

Fig. 14.11 Updated figure—database service [23]

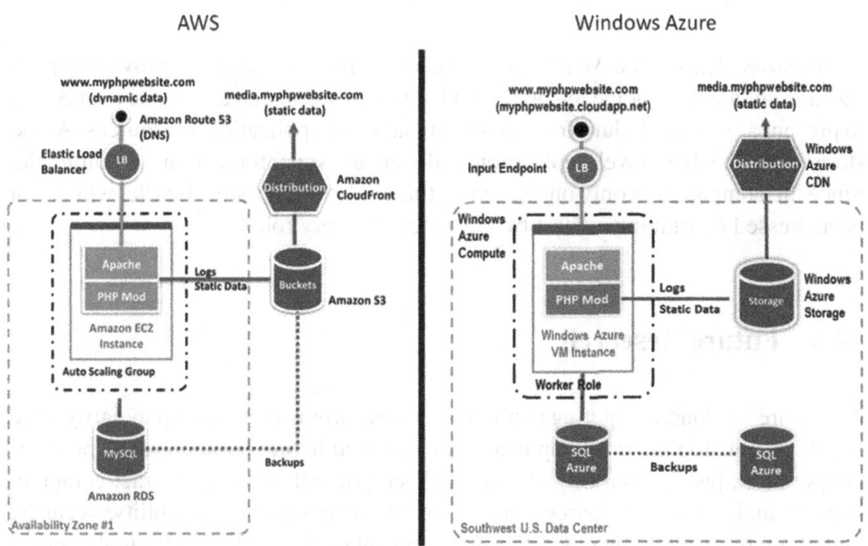

Fig. 14.12 Updated deployment—compute elasticity [23]

14.5.7 *Failover*

To keep the service up and running in the face of failures, one must take advantage of failover infrastructure as in Fig. 14.13.

AWS: The primary Amazon RDS database domain has a standby slave domain. The solution can survive the failure of either domain.

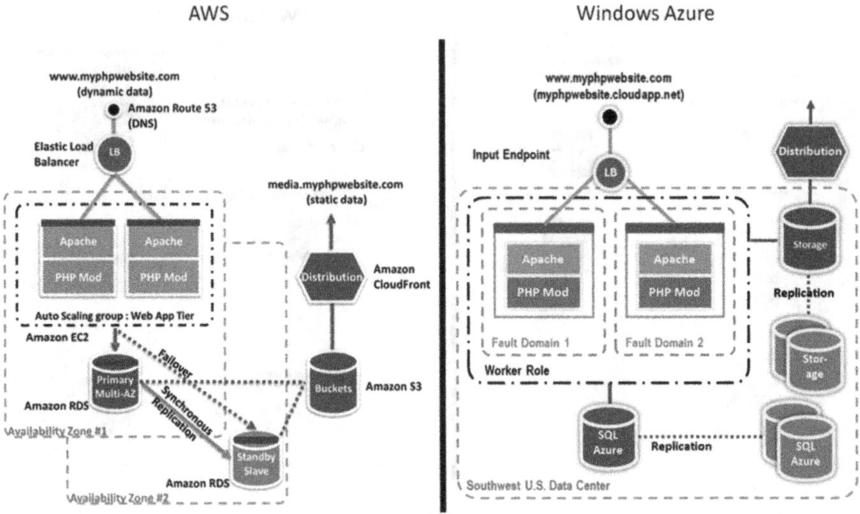

Fig. 14.13 Updated deployment—fault tolerant [23]

Windows Azure: The Windows Azure infrastructure has been providing *fault domains* all along. Storage, database, and compute are spread across the data center to prevent any single failure from taking out all of an application's resources. At the storage and database level, replication, failover, and synchronization are automatic. Since the compute was only one instance, this could be a possible hurdle, which can be addressed by running at least two instances in every role.

14.6 Future Research

The future of cloud computing continues to show promise and gain popularity. One should be able to *plug in* an application to the cloud in order to receive the power it needs to run, just like a utility. As an architect, you will manage abstract compute, storage, and network resources instead of physical servers. Scalability, security, high availability, fault tolerance, testability, and elasticity will be configurable properties of the application architecture and will be an automated and intrinsic part of the platform on which they are built.

However, we are not there yet. Today, you can build applications in the cloud with some of these qualities by implementing the best practices highlighted in this chapter. Best practices in cloud-computing architectures will continue to evolve, and as researchers, we should focus not only on enhancing the cloud but also on building tools, technologies, and processes that will make it easier for developers and architects to plug in applications to the cloud easily.

The challenge of transitioning from your local development environment seems to bother every developer; it is difficult to transition from doing stuff locally and trying it out to working in the cloud. The maturity of IDEs that can handle cloud environment is still a work in progress as well. The more seamless the transition from the local test environments to cloud-based environments, the more productive the development cycles will be. Another challenge is data security; as the application will be hosted on third-party infrastructure, the safety of the data is always at risk. There is a greater need to address this necessity both at the application level and infrastructure level.

14.7 Conclusion

Cloud-based application development process has its share of advantages and disadvantages, but many of the inherent issues are alleviated by following the basic design patterns and frameworks described in this chapter.

We can enumerate the reasons to choose either of the frameworks mentioned, clearly because the type of application that needs to be developed requires that right kind of environment. Reasons to use GAE (Google App Engine) are:

- You don't need to pay until you see a visible need to scale.
- Google services like Gmail and Calendar plug in are very easy.
- Good choice if Python or Java is used as a language.
- Locally tested app runs as is on GAE.
- Allows running multiple versions of on the same data store.

Reasons to use Azure are:

- Better suited for SOA (Service-Oriented Architecture)-based applications
- Application staging feature helps during deployment
- Two storage solutions—SQL Azure (relational) and Azure Storage (non-relational)
- Best suitable for .NET-based applications

Reasons to use Amazon Web Services are:

- Have footprint across several Linux distributions and also Windows support, while Azure allows Windows only
- Have support for myriad language platforms like C#, PHP, ASP.NET, Python, and Ruby
- Provide off-the-shelf load balancing, varying storage sizes to instances, and install custom software

While making the choice of a platform, several reasons, as listed above, need to be considered to aid in the efficient cloud application development.

References

1. Cloud computing: http://en.wikipedia.org/wiki/Cloud_computing (2008)
2. Nytimes: Software via the Internet: Microsoft in 'cloud' computing Microsoft Corporation. http://www.nytimes.com/2007/09/03/technology/03cloud.html (2007)
3. Baker, S.: Google and the wisdom of clouds. http://www.businessweek.com/magazine/content/07_52/b4064048925836.htm (2007)
4. Big blue goes for the big win: http://www.businessweek.com/magazine/content/08_10/b4074063309405.htm (2009)
5. Armbrust, M., Fox, A., Griffith, R.: A view of cloud computing. Commun. ACM **53**(4), 50–58 (2010)
6. Chellappa, R.: Cloud computing: emerging paradigm for computing. In: INFORMS 1997, Dallas, TX (1997)
7. Benatallah, B., Dijkman, R.M., Dumas, M., Maamer, Z.: Service-composition: concepts, techniques, tools and trends. In: Z. Stojanovic, A. Dahanayake (eds) Service-Oriented Software System Engineering: Challenges and Practices, pp. 48–66. Idea Group, Hershey (2005)
8. Stevens, M.: Service-oriented architecture introduction. http://www.developer.com/services/article.php/1010451 (2009)
9. Service orientation and its role in your connected systems strategy. Microsoft Corporation. http://msdn.microsoft.com/en-us/library/ms954826.aspx (2004)
10. Buyya, R.: Economic-based distributed resource management and scheduling for grid computing. Ph.D. thesis, Chapter 2. Monash University, Melbourne (2002)
11. Dell cloud computing solutions: http://www.dell.com/cloudcomputing (2008)
12. Foster, I., Kesselman, C., Tuecke, S.: The anatomy of the grid: enabling scalable virtual organization. Int. J. High Perform. Comput. Appl. **15**(3), 200–222 (2001)
13. Buyya, R., Ranjan, R., Calheiros, R.N.: Modeling and simulation of scalable cloud computing environments and the Cloudsim toolkit: challenges and opportunities in high performance computing\& simulation. In: HPCS'09. International Conference (2009)
14. Hadoop: http://hadoop.apache.org/ (2007)
15. Bondi, A.B.: Characteristics of scalability and their impact on performance. In: Proceedings of the 2nd International Workshop on Software and Performance, Ottawa, ON, Canada, ISBN 1-58113-195-X, pp. 195–203 (2000)
16. Lu, W., Jackson, J., Barga, R.: Azureblast: a case study of developing science applications on the cloud. In: Proceedings of the 19th ACM International Symposium on High Performance Distributed Computing. ACM, New York (2010)
17. Fehling, C., Leymann, F., Mietzner, R., Schupeck, W.: A Collection of Patterns for Cloud Types, Cloud Service Models, and Cloud-Based Application Architectures in Institute Architecture of Application Systems (IAAS) Report, Daimler A G (2011)
18. Load balancing and MapReduce: http://www.ibm.com/developerworks/cloud/library/cl-mapreduce (2011)
19. Chappell, D., Windows Azure and ISVs, Technical report, Microsoft: http://www.microsoft.com/windowsazure/whitepapers (2009)
20. Svetin Nakov: Cloud for Developers Azure vs Google App Engine vs Amazon vs Appharbor, slideshare.com (2012)
21. Google: Python Runtime Environment, Google App Engine, Google Code, code.google.com (2011)
22. Sanderson, D.: Programming Google App Engine: Build and Run Scalable Web Apps on Google's Infrastructure. O'Reilly Media, Sebastopol (2009). ISBN 978-0-596-52272-8
23. David: Comparative study of AWS and Azure. http://davidpallmann.blogspot.in/2011_03_01_archive.html (2011). Accessed 23 Aug 2012
24. Microsoft Documentation: http://msdn.microsoft.com
25. User Blogs, Microsoft Documentation: http://blogs.msdn.com

26. Olston, C., Reed, B., Srivastava, U., Kumar, R., Tomkins, A.: Pig latin: a not-so-foreign language for data processing. In: SIGMOD'08: Proceedings of the 2008 ACM SIGMOD International Conference on Management of Data, pp. 1099–1110. ACM, New York (2008)
27. Talasila, S., Pavan, K.I.: A generalized cloud storage architecture with backup technology for any cloud providers. Int. J. Comput. Appl. **2**(2), 256–263 (2012)

Chapter 15
A Methodology for Identifying the Relationships Between Performance Factors for Cloud Computing Applications

Luis Eduardo Bautista Villalpando, Alain April, and Alain Abran

Abstract Cloud Computing is an emerging technology for processing and storing large amounts of data. One of its most important challenges is to deliver good performance to its end users. Sometimes, anomalies affect a part of the Cloud infrastructure, resulting in degradation in Cloud performance. These anomalies can be identified by performance concepts of Cloud Computing based on software engineering quality models. This work presents these Cloud Computing concepts that are directly related to the measurement of performance from a quantitative viewpoint. One of the challenges in defining such concepts has been to determine what type of relationship exists between the various base measurements that define the performance concepts in a Cloud environment. For example, what is the extent of the relationship between CPU processing time and amount of information to process by a Cloud Computing application? This work uses the Taguchi method for the design of experiments to present a methodology for identifying the relationships between the various configuration parameters (base measures) that affect the quality of Cloud Computing applications' performance. This chapter is based on a proposed performance measurement framework for Cloud Computing systems, which integrates software quality concepts from ISO 25010 and other international standards.

L.E.B. Villalpando (✉)
Department of Electronic Systems, Autonomous University of Aguascalientes,
Av. Universidad 940, Ciudad Universitaria, Aguascalientes, Mexico
e-mail: lebautis@correo.uaa.mx

Department of Software Engineering and Information Technology,
ETS – University of Quebec, 1100 Notre-Dame St, Montreal, Canada

A. April • A. Abran
Department of Software Engineering and Information Technology,
ETS – University of Quebec, 1100 Notre-Dame St, Montreal, Canada

Z. Mahmood and S. Saeed (eds.), *Software Engineering Frameworks for the Cloud Computing Paradigm*, Computer Communications and Networks,
DOI 10.1007/978-1-4471-5031-2_15, © Springer-Verlag London 2013

Keywords Cloud Computing • Measurement • Performance • Taguchi method • ISO 25010 • Maintenance • Hadoop • MapReduce

15.1 Introduction

Cloud Computing (CC) is an emerging technology aimed at processing and storing large amounts of data. It is an Internet-based technology in which a number of distributed computers work together to efficiently process such quantities of information while at the same time rapidly processing query results for users. Some CC users prefer not to own physical infrastructure, but instead rent Cloud infrastructure, or a Cloud platform or software, from a third-party provider. These infrastructure application options delivered as a service are known as Cloud Services [1].

One of the most important challenges in delivering Cloud Services is to ensure that they are fault tolerant, as failures and anomalies can degrade these services and impact their quality, and even their availability. According to Coulouris [2], a failure occurs in a distributed system (DS), like a CC system (CCS), when a process or a communication channel departs from what is considered to be its normal or desired behavior. An anomaly is different, in that it slows down a part of a CCS without making it fail completely, impacting the performance of tasks within nodes, and, consequently, of the system itself.

According to the ISO SC38 Study Group on Cloud Computing [3], service models for CC are categorized as Infrastructure as a Service (IaaS), Platform as a Service (PaaS), and Software as a Service (SaaS). The model that relates the most to the software engineering community is the SaaS model. Software engineers focus on software components, and customers use an IT provider's applications running on a Cloud infrastructure to process information according to their processing and storage requirements. One of the main characteristics of this type of service is that customers do not manage or control the underlying Cloud infrastructure (including network, servers, operating systems, and storage), except for limited user-specific application configuration settings.

Consequently, a performance measurement model (PMMo) for CCS, and more specifically for Cloud Computing applications (CCA), should propose a means to identify and quantify "normal application behavior," which can serve as a baseline for detecting and predicting possible anomalies in the software (i.e., jobs in a Cloud environment) that may impact Cloud application performance. To achieve this goal, methods are needed to collect the necessary base measures specific to CCA performance, and analysis models must be designed to analyze and evaluate the relationships that exist among these measures.

The ISO International Vocabulary of Metrology (VIM) [4] and ISO 15939 document the consensus that exists on the following definitions:

- A measurement method is a generic description of a logical organization of operations used in measurement.

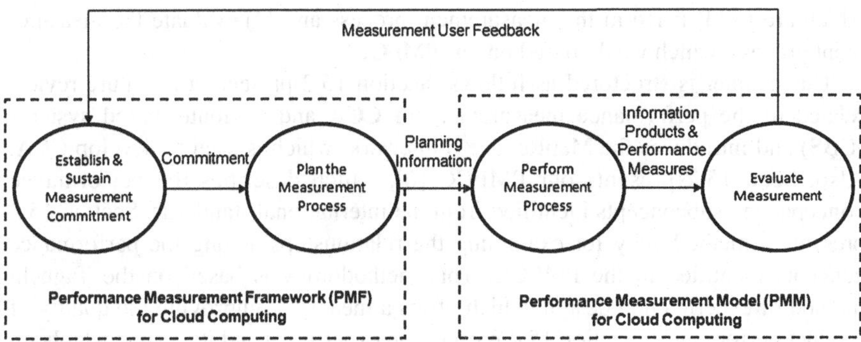

Fig. 15.1 Sequence of activities in a measurement process (Adapted from the ISO 15939 measurement process model [5])

- An analysis model is an algorithm or calculation combining one or more measures obtained from a measurement method to produce evaluations or estimates relevant to the information needed for decision making.

The purpose of a measurement process, as described in ISO 15939 [5], is to collect, analyze, and report data relating to the products developed and processes implemented in an organizational unit, both to support effective management of the process and to objectively demonstrate the quality of the products.

ISO 15939 [5] defines four sequential activities in a measurement process: establish and sustain measurement commitment, plan the measurement process, perform the measurement process, and evaluate the measurement. These activities are performed in an iterative cycle that allows for continuous feedback and improvement of the measurement process, as shown in Fig. 15.1.

The first two activities recommended by the ISO 15939 measurement process, which are to (1) establish measurement commitment and (2) plan the measurement process, were addressed in the work, "Design of a Performance Measurement Framework for Cloud Computing" (PMFCC) [6]. In this work, the basis for the measurement of Cloud Computing concepts that are directly related to performance is defined. The PMFCC identifies terms associated with the quality concept of performance, which have been identified from international standards such as ISO 25010 and those of the European Cooperation on Space Standardization. The PMFCC proposes a combination of base measures to determine the derived measures of a specific concept that contributes to performance analysis.

One of the main challenges in designing the PMFCC has been to determine what type of relationship exists between the various base measures. For example, what is the extent of the relationship between *CPU processing time* and *amount of information to process*? In this present work, we propose the use of a methodology based on the Taguchi method to determine how closely the performance parameters (base measures) involved in the performance analysis process are related. In addition, we address the other activities recommended by the ISO 15939 measurement process, which are to (3) perform the measurement process and (4) evaluate the measurement process, which we do based on our PMFCC.

This chapter is structured as follows. Section 15.2 presents a literature review related to the performance measurement of CCA and computer-based systems (CBS) and introduces the MapReduce framework, which is used to develop CCA. Also, Sect. 15.2 presents our PMFCC [6], which describes the performance concepts and subconcepts identified from the international standards. Section 15.3 presents a methodology for examining the relationships among the performance concepts identified in the PMFCC. This methodology is based on the Taguchi method of experimental design, which offers a means for improving the quality of product performance. Section 15.4 presents an experiment and its results which are based on the methodology introduced previously. Finally, Sect. 15.5 presents a summary of this chapter and suggests future work in this area of study.

15.2 Literature Review

15.2.1 Performance Measurement Approaches

The measurement of CBS performance has been investigated in the computer science literature from the following viewpoints: load balancing, network intrusion detection, and host state maintenance. For example, Burgess [7] defines system performance as "normal behavior" and proposes that this behavior can only be determined by learning about past events and by modeling future behavior using statistics from the past and observing present behavior. According to Burgess, modern computing systems are complex. They are composed of many interacting subsystems, which make their collective behavior intricate, and this behavior influences the performance of the whole system.

Some authors have attempted to predict the performance of complex systems (i.e., computer clusters) by simulating cluster behavior in a virtual environment. Rao [8], for example, estimates the variation of cluster performance through changes in task size as well as the time taken to solve a particular problem. He has also built a predictive model using regression analysis to investigate the behavior of the system and predict the performance of the cluster.

Other published approaches have focused on the reliability aspects of large, high-performance CBS to measure system performance. Smith [9] observes that failure occurrence has an impact on both system performance and operational costs. He proposes an automatic mechanism for anomaly detection aimed at identifying the root causes of anomalies and faults. Smith [9] has also developed an automatic anomaly detection framework designed to process massive volumes of data using a technique based on pattern recognition. In a case study, Smith identifies health-related variables, which are then used for anomaly detection. Each of these variables is related to a system characteristic (such as user utilization, CPU idle time, memory utilization, I/O volume operations). Once the measurement data have been collected, he proposes clustering categories, where an outlier detector identifies the nodes that potentially have anomalies. Finally, a list of those possible anomalies is sent to a system administrator who has the expertise to quickly confirm whether or not an anomaly exists.

15.2.2 Performance Analysis in Cloud Computing Applications

Researchers have analyzed the performance of CCA from various viewpoints. For example, Jackson [10] analyzes high-performance computing applications on the Amazon Web Services' Cloud. The purpose of his work was to examine the performance of existing CC infrastructures and create a mechanism to quantitatively evaluate them. The work is focused on the performance of Amazon EC2, as representative of the current mainstream of commercial CC services, and its applicability to Cloud-based environments for scientific computing. To do so, Jackson quantitatively examines the performance of a set of benchmarks designed to represent a typical High-Performance Computing (HPC) workload running on the Amazon EC2 platform. Timing results from different application benchmarks are used to compute the Sustained System Performance (SSP) metric to measure the performance delivered by the workload of a computing system. According to the National Energy Research Scientific Computing Center (NERSC) [11], SSP provides a process for evaluating system performance across any time frame and can be applied to any set of systems, any workload, and/or benchmark suite and for any time period. The SSP measures *time to solution* across different application areas and can be used to evaluate absolute performance and performance relative to cost (in dollars, energy, or other value propositions). The results show a strong correlation between the percentage of time an application spends communicating and its overall performance on EC2. The more communication there is, the worse the performance becomes. Jackson also concludes that the communication pattern of an application can have a significant impact on performance.

Other researchers focus on applications in virtualized Cloud environments. For instance, Mei [12] studies performance measurement and analysis of network I/O applications (network-intensive applications) in a virtualized Cloud. The aim of his work is to understand the performance impact of co-locating applications in a virtualized Cloud, in terms of throughput performance and resource-sharing effectiveness. Mei addresses issues related to managing idle instances, which are processes running in an operating system (OS) that are executing idle loops. Results show that when two identical I/O applications are running together, schedulers can approximately guarantee that each has its fair share of CPU slicing, network bandwidth consumption, and resulting throughput. They also show that the duration of performance degradation experienced is related to machine capacity, workload level in the running domain, and number of new virtual machine (VM) instances to start up.

Although these works present interesting methods for performance measurement of CCA, their approach is from an infrastructure standpoint and does not consider

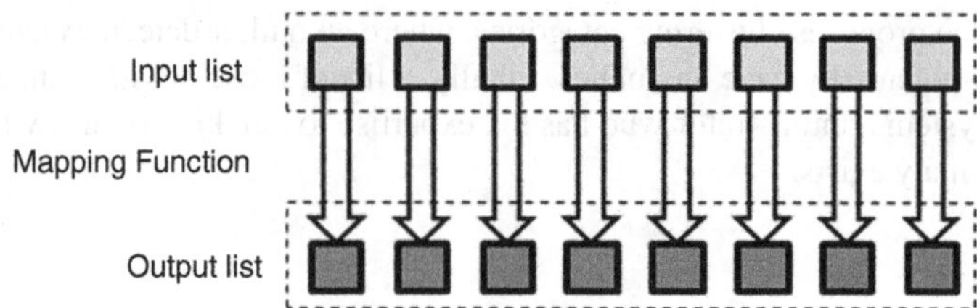

Fig. 15.2 The mapping phase, in which an output list is created

CCA performance factors from a software engineering perspective. Consequently, we focus next on the performance evaluation of CCA, which we have developed through frameworks for data-intensive processing like Hadoop MapReduce, and by integrating software quality concepts from ISO 25010 and frameworks for CCS performance measurement.

15.2.3 Hadoop MapReduce

Hadoop is the Apache Software Foundation's top-level project and encompasses the various Hadoop subprojects. The Hadoop project provides and supports the development of open-source software that supplies a framework for the development of highly scalable distributed computing applications designed to handle processing details, leaving developers free to focus on application logic [13]. Hadoop is divided into several subprojects that fall under the umbrella of infrastructures for distributed computing. One of these subprojects is MapReduce, which is a programming model with an associated implementation, both developed by Google for processing and generating large datasets.

According to Dean [14], programs written in this functional style are automatically parallelized and executed on a large cluster of commodity machines. Authors like Lin [15] point out that today the issue of tackling large amounts of data is addressed by a divide-and-conquer approach, the basic idea being to partition a large problem into smaller subproblems. Those subproblems can be handled in parallel by different workers, for example, threads in a processor core, cores in a multicore processor, multiple processors in a machine, or many machines in a cluster. In this way, the intermediate results of each individual worker are then combined to yield the final output.

The Hadoop MapReduce model results are obtained in two main stages: (1) the Map stage and (2) the Reduce stage. In the Map stage, also called the mapping phase, data elements from a list of such elements are inputted, one at time, to a function called Mapper, which transforms each element individually into an output data element. Figure 15.2 presents the components of the Map stage process.

The Reduce stage, also called the reducing phase, aggregates values. In this stage, a reducer function receives input values iteratively from an input list.

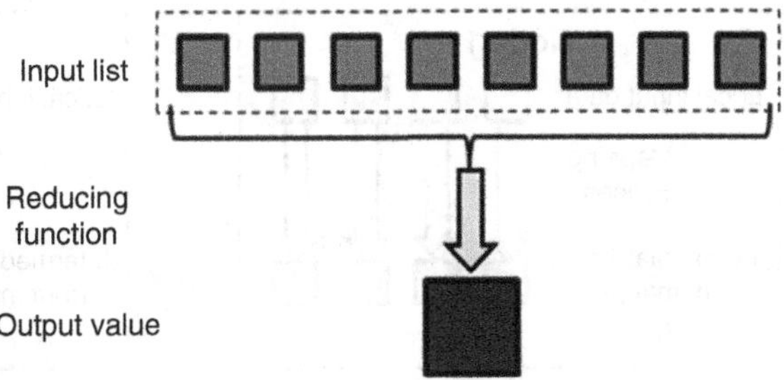

Fig. 15.3 The components of the reducing phase

This function combines these values, returning a single output value. The Reduce stage is often used to produce "summary" data, turning a large volume of data into a smaller summary of itself. Figure 15.3 presents the components of the Reduce stage.

MapReduce inputs typically come from input files stored in a Hadoop Distributed File System (HDFS) cluster. These files are distributed across all the commodity computers that are running HDFS nodes (nodes being computers that are running the HDFS). Commodity computers are computer systems manufactured by multiple vendors, incorporating components based on open standards.

According to Yahoo! [16], when a mapping phase begins, any mapper (node) can process any input file or part of an input file. In this way, each mapper loads a set of local files to be able to process them.

When a mapping phase has been completed, an intermediate pair of values (consisting of a key and a value) must be exchanged between machines, so that all values with the same key are sent to a single reducer. Like Map tasks, Reduce tasks are spread across the same nodes in the cluster and do not exchange information with one another, nor are they aware of one another's existence. Thus, all data transfer is handled by the Hadoop MapReduce platform itself, guided implicitly by the various keys associated with the values. Figure 15.4 shows a high-level dataflow into the MapReduce tasks.

Dean [14] explains that Map invocations are distributed across multiple machines by automatically partitioning the input data into a set of splits, M, and so, when a user application calls on the MapReduce application, a sequence of actions (Fig. 15.5) occurs in a MapReduce cluster. These actions are presented below, in the form of direct quotations from Dean's work:

1. The MapReduce library in the user program first splits the input files into M pieces, typically 16 megabytes to 64 megabytes (MB) per piece. It then starts up many copies of the program on a cluster of machines.
2. One of the copies is special – the master. The rest are workers that are assigned work by the master. There are M Map tasks and R Reduce tasks to assign. The master picks idle workers and assigns each one a Map task or a Reduce task.
3. A worker who is assigned a Map task reads the content of the corresponding input split. It parses key/value pairs out of the input data and passes each pair to the user-defined Map function. The intermediate key/value pairs produced by the Map function are buffered in memory.

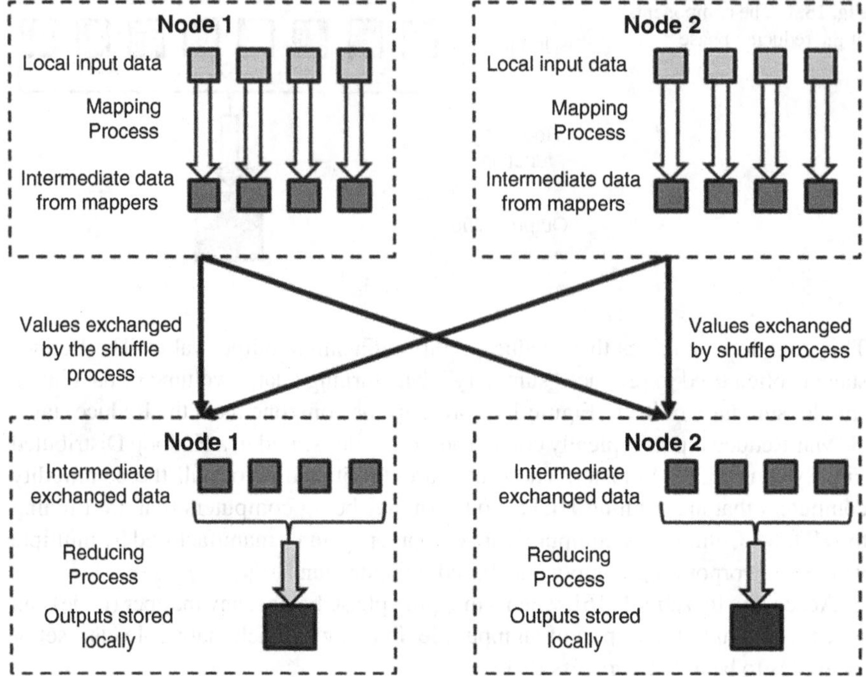

Fig. 15.4 High-level data flow into the MapReduce stages

4. Periodically, the buffered pairs are written to a local disk, partitioned into R regions by the partitioning function. The locations of these buffered pairs on the local disk are passed back to the master, who is responsible for forwarding these locations to the reduce workers.
5. When a reduce worker is notified by the master about these locations, it uses remote procedure calls to read the buffered data from the local disks of the map workers. When a reduce worker has read all the intermediate data, it sorts them by the intermediate keys, so that all occurrences of the same key are grouped together. The sorting is needed because typically many different keys map to the same Reduce task. If the amount of intermediate data is too large to fit in memory, an external sort is used.
6. The reduce worker iterates over the sorted intermediate data, and, for each unique intermediate key encountered, it passes the key and the corresponding set of intermediate values to the user's Reduce function. The output of the Reduce function is appended to a final output file for its reduce partition.
7. When all Map tasks and Reduce tasks have been completed, the master wakes up the user program. At this point, the MapReduce call in the user program returns back to the user code.

Figure 15.5 presents a summary of the actions that occur during a MapReduce application execution.

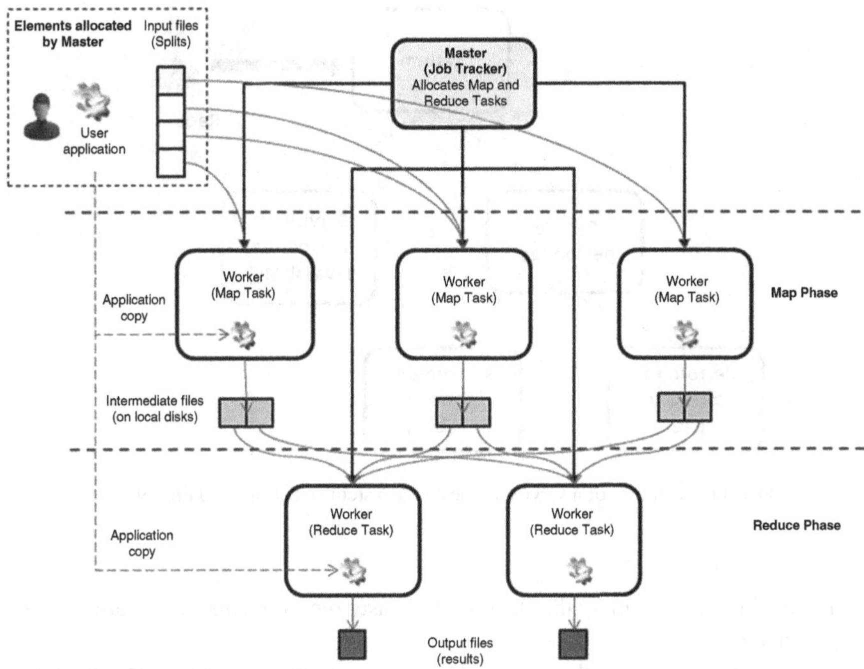

Fig. 15.5 Summary of actions occurring during a MapReduce application execution

15.2.4 ISO 25030 Performance Concepts as System Requirements

The ISO 25030 standard [17] defines quality requirements and states that systems have a variety of stakeholders who may have an interest in the system throughout its life cycle. Stakeholders include end users, organizations, developers, and maintainers, who have a legitimate interest in the system. Stakeholders have different needs and expectations of the system, and these may change during the system's life cycle. Stakeholder needs can be either explicitly stated or only implied, and sometimes they are unclear. Performance requirements need to be established and should be expressed, in order to ensure that a specific system will be able to perform an efficient and reliable service under stated conditions. ISO 19759 – Guide to the Software Engineering Body of Knowledge (SWEBOK) [18] defines a requirement as a property that must be exhibited in order to solve real-world problems.

According to ISO 25030, stakeholders' needs and expectations can be identified through requirements and can be transformed into technical views of system requirements through a design process that can be used to realize the intended system. Technical views of user requirements are often called system requirements. These should state which characteristics the system is to have, and be

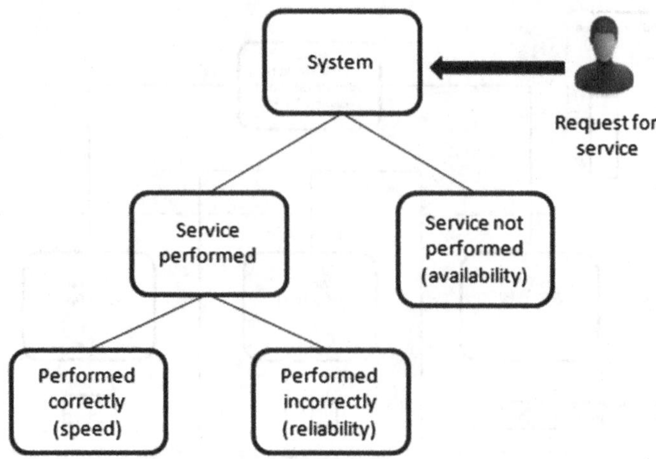

Fig. 15.6 Possible outcomes of a service request to a system, according to Jain [19]

verifiable, in order to satisfy the stakeholder's user requirements, which are defined as perceived needs.

ISO 25030 mentions that a system consists of a number of interacting elements that can be defined and categorized in different ways, and system requirements can, for example, include requirements for software, computer hardware, and mechanical systems. Section 15.2.5 indentifies the system requirements that are involved in the analysis of CCA performance.

15.2.5 Jain's System Performance Concepts and Subconcepts

A well-known perspective for system performance measurement was proposed by Jain [19], who maintains that a performance study must first establish a set of performance criteria (or characteristics) to help to carry out the system measurement process. He notes that system performance is typically measured using three subconcepts if it is performing a service correctly, (1) responsiveness, (2) productivity, and (3) utilization, and proposes a measurement process for each. In addition, Jain notes that there are several possible outcomes for each service request made to a system, which can be classified into three categories. The system may (1) perform the service correctly, (2) perform the service incorrectly, or (3) refuse to perform the service altogether. Moreover, he defines three subconcepts associated with each of these possible outcomes which affect system performance: (1) speed, (2) reliability, and (3) availability. Figure 15.6 presents the possible outcomes of a service request to a system and the subconcepts associated with them.

15.2.6 ISO 25010 Performance Concepts and Subconcepts

There are several software engineering standards on system and software quality models, such as ISO 25010 [20], which is a revision of the ISO 9126-1 [21] software quality model. The ISO 25010 standard defines software product and computer system quality from two distinct perspectives: (1) a quality in use model and (2) a product quality model:

1. The quality in use model is composed of five characteristics that relate to the outcome of an interaction when a product is used in a particular context of use. This quality model is applicable to the entire range of use of the human-computer system, including both systems and software.
2. The product quality model is composed of eight characteristics that relate to the static properties of software and the dynamic properties of the computer system.

This product quality model is applicable to both systems and software. According to ISO 25010, the properties of both determine the quality of the product in a particular context, based on user requirements. For example, performance efficiency and reliability can be specific concerns of users who specialize in areas of content delivery, management, or maintenance. The performance efficiency concept proposed in ISO 25010 has three subconcepts, (1) time behavior, (2) resource utilization, and (3) capacity, while the reliability concept has four subconcepts: (1) maturity, (2) availability, (3) fault tolerance, and (4) recoverability. In this research, we have selected performance efficiency and reliability as concepts for determining the performance of CCA.

Based on the performance perspectives presented by Jain and the product quality characteristics defined by ISO 25010, we propose the following definition of CCA performance measurement: "*The performance of a Cloud Computing application is determined by analysis of the characteristics involved in performing an efficient and reliable service that meets requirements under stated conditions and within the maximum limits of the system parameters.*"

Although at first sight this definition may seem complex, it only includes the subconcepts necessary to carry out CCA performance analysis. Furthermore, from the literature review, a number of subconcepts have been identified that could be directly related to the concept of performance, such as:

- *Performance efficiency*: The amount of resources used under stated conditions. Resources can include software products, the software and hardware configuration of the system, and materials.
- *Time behavior*: The degree to which the response and processing times and the throughput rates of a product or system, when performing its functions, meet requirements.
- *Capacity*: The degree to which the maximum limits of a product or system parameter meet requirements.
- *Resource utilization*: The degree to which the amounts and types of resources used by a product or system when performing its functions meet requirements.

- *Reliability*: The degree to which a system, product, or component performs specified functions under specified conditions for a specified period of time.
- *Maturity*: The degree to which a system meets needs for reliability under normal operation.
- *Availability*: The degree to which a system, product, or component is operational and accessible when required for use.
- *Fault tolerance*: The degree to which a system, product, or component operates as intended, in spite of the presence of hardware or software faults.
- *Recoverability*: The degree to which a product or system can recover data directly affected in the event of an interruption or a failure and be restored to the desired state.

15.2.7 Relationship Between Performance Measurement Concepts and Subconcepts

Now that the performance measurement concepts and subconcepts have been introduced, a relationship model will be helpful to show the relationship between the performance concepts proposed by ISO 25010 and the performance measurement perspective presented by Jain. In addition, this model shows the logical sequence in which the concepts and subconcepts appear when a performance issue arises in a CCS (see Fig. 15.7).

In Fig. 15.7, system performance is determined by two main subconcepts: (1) performance efficiency and (2) reliability. We have seen that when a CCS receives a service request, there are three possible outcomes (the service is performed correctly, the service is performed incorrectly, or the service cannot be performed). The outcome will determine the subconcepts that will be applied for performance measurement. For example, suppose that the CCS performs a service correctly, but, during its execution, the service failed and was later reinstated. Although the service was ultimately performed successfully, it is clear that the system availability (part of the reliability subconcept) was compromised, and this affected CCS performance.

The foundation for the PMFCC [6] was the above relationship model (Fig. 15.7). This performance measurement framework defines the base measures related to the performance concepts that represent the system attributes and which can be measured to assess whether or not the CCA satisfies the stated requirements from a quantitative viewpoint. These terms are grouped into collection functions, which are responsible for conducting the measurement process using a combination of base measures through a data collector. They are associated with the corresponding ISO 25010 quality derived measures, as presented in Table 15.1.

The base measures presented in Table 15.1 are categorized as collection functions in the PMFCC (see Fig. 15.8). These functions were designed to be interconnected through an intermediate service (IS) that shares intermediate results from common base measures, reducing the number of operations in the measurement process at the time of calculation.

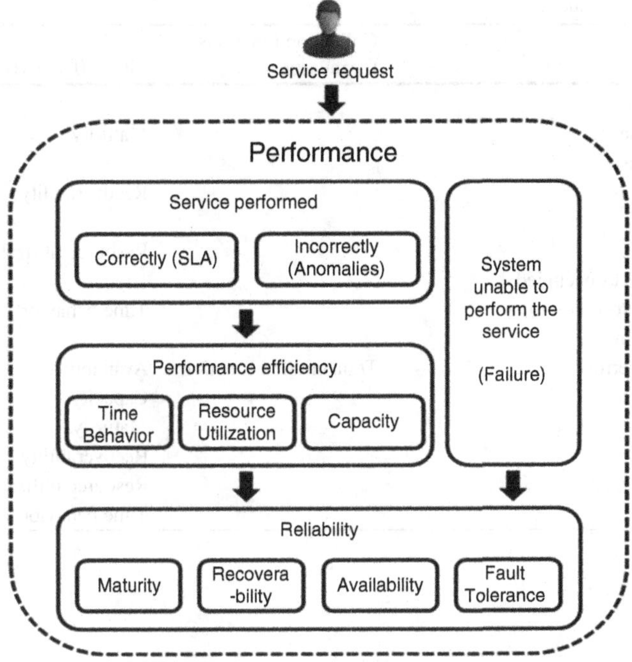

Fig. 15.7 Model of the relationships between performance concepts and subconcepts

Table 15.1 Functions associated with Cloud Computing performance concepts

Base measures	Collection functions for measures	ISO 25010 derived measures
Failures avoided	Failure function	Maturity
Failures detected		Resource utilization
Failures predicted		Fault tolerance
Failures resolved		
Breakdowns	Fault function	Maturity
Faults corrected		
Faults detected		Maturity
Faults predicted		
Tasks entered into recovery	Task function	Availability
Tasks executed		Capacity
Tasks passed		Maturity
Tasks restarted		Fault tolerance
Tasks restored		Resource utilization
Tasks successfully restored		Time behavior
Continuous resource utilization time	Time function	Availability
Downtime		
Maximum response time		Capacity

(continued)

Table 15.1 (continued)

Base measures	Collection functions for measures	ISO 25010 derived measures
Observation time		
Operation time		Maturity
Recovery time		
Repair time		Recoverability
Response time		
Task time		Resource utilization
Time I/O devices occupied		
Transmission response time		Time behavior
Turnaround time		
Transmission errors	Transmission function	Availability
		Capacity
Transmission capacity		Maturity
		Recoverability
Transmission ratio		Resource utilization
		Time behavior

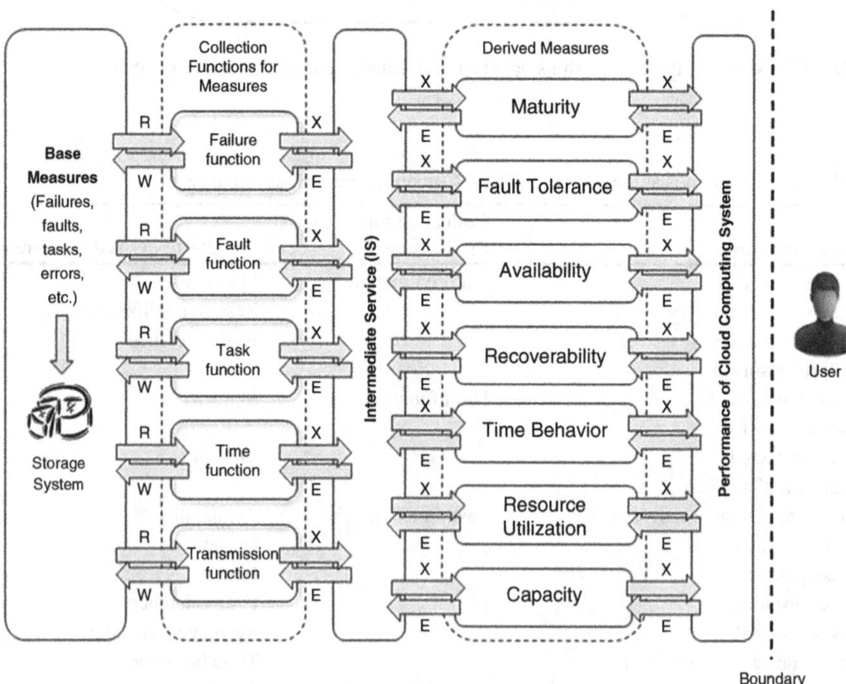

Fig. 15.8 Performance measurement framework for Cloud Computing

How can we measure the CCA availability concept (presented in Table 15.1) using the PMFCC, for example? To start with, we need three collection functions: (1) the time function, (2) the task function, and (3) the transmission function. The time function can use several different measurements, such as CPU utilization by the user, job duration, and response time. These base measures are obtained using a data collector and then inputted to a time function that calculates a derived measure of the time concept. The IS combines the results of each function to determine a derived measure of the availability that contributes to CC performance, as defined in the framework.

15.3 A Methodology to Analyze Relationships Across Performance Factors

15.3.1 Definition of the Problem

To be able to design the proposed collection functions (presented in Fig. 15.8), we need to determine how the various base measures are related and to what degree. These relationships enable us to determine the influence each of them has in the resulting derived measures. The PMFCC [6] shows many of the relationships that exist between the base measures which have a major influence on the collection functions. However, in CCA and more specifically in the Hadoop MapReduce applications, there are over a 100 base measures (including system measures) which could contribute to the analysis of CCA performance. A selection of these measures has to be included in the collection functions so that the respective derived measures can be obtained, and from there an indication of the performance of the applications. One key design problem is to establish which base measures are interrelated and how much they contribute to each of the collection functions.

In traditional statistical methods, 30 or more observations (or data points) are typically needed for each variable, in order to gain meaningful insight and analyze the results. In addition, only a few independent variables are necessary to carry out experiments to uncover potential relationships, and this must be performed under certain predetermined and controlled test conditions. However, this approach is not appropriate here, owing to the large number of variables involved and the time and effort required, which is more than we have allowed for in this research for such experiments. Consequently, we have to resort to an analysis method that is suited to our specific problem and in our study area.

A possible candidate to solve this problem is Taguchi's experimental design method, which investigates how different variables affect the mean and variance of a process performance characteristic and helps in determining how well the process is functioning. This method proposes a limited number of experiments but is more efficient than a factorial design in its ability to identify relationships and dependencies. We present the method in the next section.

15.3.2 Taguchi's Method of Experimental Design

Taguchi's *Quality Engineering Handbook* [22] describes the Taguchi method of experimental design, which was developed by Dr. Genichi Taguchi, a researcher at the Electronic Control Laboratory in Japan. This method combines industrial and statistical experience and offers a means for improving the quality of manufactured products. It is based on a "robust design" concept, according to which a well-designed product should cause no problem when used under specified conditions.

According to Cheikhi [23], Taguchi's two-phase quality strategy is the following:

- Phase 1: The online phase, which focuses on the techniques and methods used to control quality during the production of the product.
- Phase 2: The offline phase, which focuses on taking those techniques and methods into account before manufacturing the product, that is, during the design phase, the development phase, etc.

One of the most important activities in the offline phase of the strategy is parameter design. This is where the parameters are determined that make it possible to satisfy the set quality objectives (often called the *objective function*) through the use of experimental designs under set conditions. If the product does not work properly (does not fulfill the objective function), then the design constants (also called *parameters*) need to be adjusted so that it will perform better. Cheikhi explains that this activity includes five (5) steps, which are required to determine the parameters that satisfy the quality objectives. These five steps are the following:

1. Definition of the objective of the study, that is, identification of the quality characteristics to be observed in the output (results expected).
2. Identification of the study factors and their interactions, as well as the levels at which they will be set. There are two different types of factors: (1) *control factors*, factors that can be easily managed or adjusted, and (2) *noise factors*, factors that are difficult to control or manage.
3. Selection of the appropriate orthogonal arrays (OAs) for the study, based on the number of factors, and their levels and interactions. The OA shows the various experiments that will need to be conducted in order to verify the effect of the factors studied on the quality characteristic to be observed in the output.
4. Preparation and performance of the resulting OA experiments, including preparation of the data sheets for each OA experiment according to the combination of the levels and factors for the experiment. For each experiment, a number of trials are conducted and the quality characteristics of the output are observed.
5. Analysis and interpretation of the experimental results to determine the optimum settings for the control factors, and the influence of those factors on the quality characteristics observed in the output.

According to Taguchi's *Quality Engineering Handbook* [22], the OA organizes the parameters affecting the process and the levels at which they should vary. Taguchi's method tests pairs of combinations, instead of having to test all possible

Table 15.2 Taguchi's orthogonal array L4

No. of experiments (*L*)	P1	P2	P3
1	1	1	1
2	1	2	2
3	2	1	2
4	2	2	1

combinations (as in a factorial experimental design). With this approach, we can determine which factors affect product quality the most in a minimum number of experiments.

Taguchi's OA can be created manually or they can be derived from deterministic algorithms. They are selected by the number of parameters (variables) and the number of levels (states). An OA is represented by Ln and Pn, where Ln corresponds to the number of experiments to be conducted and Pn corresponds to the number of parameters to be analyzed. Table 15.2 presents an example of Taguchi OA L4, meaning that four experiments are conducted to analyze three parameters.

An OA cell contains the factor levels (1 and 2), which determine the type of parameter values for each experiment. Once the experimental design has been determined and the trials have been carried out, the performance characteristic measurements from each trial can be used to analyze the relative effect of the various parameters.

Taguchi's method is based on the use of the signal-to-noise ratio (SNR). The SNR is a measurement scale that has been used in the communications industry for nearly a century for determining the extent of the relationship between quality factors in a measurement model [22]. The SNR approach involves the analysis of data for variability in which an input-to-output relationship is studied in the measurement system. Thus, to determine the effect each parameter has on the output, the SNR is calculated by the follow formula:

$$\mathrm{SN}_i = 10\log\frac{\bar{y}_i^2}{s_i^2} \tag{15.1}$$

where

$$\bar{y}_i = \frac{1}{N_i}\sum_{u=1}^{N_i} y_{i,u}$$

$$s_i^2 = \frac{1}{N_i - 1}\sum_{u=1}^{N_i}\left(y_{i,u} - \bar{y}_i\right)$$

i = experiment number
u = trial number
N_i = *number of trials for experiment i*

Table 15.3 Rank for SNR values

Level	P1	P2	P3
1	$SN_{1,1}$	$SN_{2,1}$	$SN_{3,1}$
2	$SN_{1,2}$	$SN_{2,2}$	$SN_{3,2}$
3	$SN_{1,3}$	$SN_{2,3}$	$SN_{3,3}$
Range	R_{P1}	R_{P2}	R_{P3}
Rank	–	–	–

To minimize the performance characteristic (objective function), the following definition of the SNR should be calculated:

$$SN_i = -10\log\left(\sum_{u=1}^{Ni}\frac{y_u^2}{N_i}\right) \quad (15.2)$$

To maximize the performance characteristic (objective function), the following definition of the SNR should be calculated:

$$SN_i = -10\log\left[\frac{1}{N_i}\sum_{u=1}^{N_i}\frac{1}{y_u^2}\right] \quad (15.3)$$

Once the SNR values have been calculated for each factor and level, they are tabulated as shown in Table 3, and then the range *R* (R = high SN–low SN) of the SNR for each parameter is calculated and entered on Table 15.3.

According to Taguchi's method, the larger the *R* value for a parameter, the greater its effect on the process.

15.4 Experiment

15.4.1 Experimental Setup

All the experiments were conducted on a DELL Studio Workstation XPS 9100 with Intel Core i7 12-core X980 processor at 3.3 GHz, 24-GB DDR3 RAM, Seagate 1.5 TB 7200 RPM SATA 3 GB/s disk, and 1-Gbps network connection. We used a Linux CentOS 5.8 64-bit distribution and Xen 3.3 as the hypervisor. This physical machine hosts five virtual machines (VM), each with a dual-core Intel i7 configuration, 4-GB RAM, 10-GB virtual storage, and a virtual network interface type. In addition, each VM executes the Apache Hadoop distribution version 0.22.0, which includes the Hadoop Distributed File System (HDFS) and MapReduce framework libraries. One of these VM is the master node, which executes NameNode (HDFS) and JobTracker (MapReduce), and the rest of the VM are slave nodes running DataNodes (HDFS) and JobTrackers (MapReduce). Figure 15.9 presents the cluster configuration for the set of experiments.

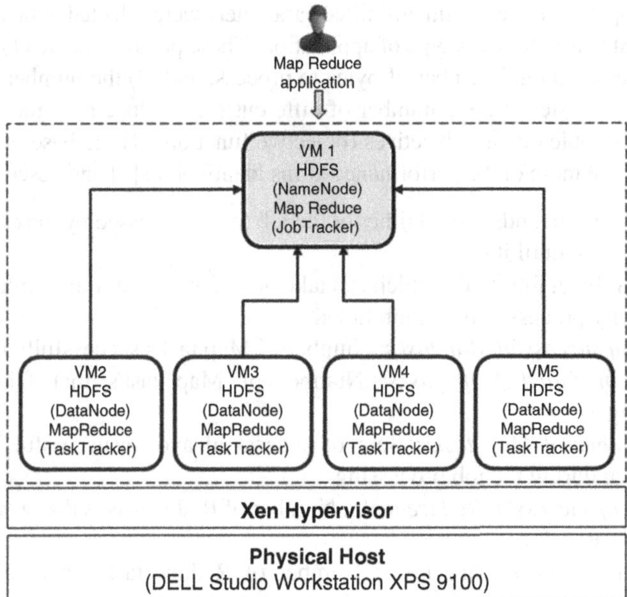

Fig. 15.9 Cluster configuration for the experiments

The Apache Hadoop distribution includes a set of applications for testing the performance of a cluster. According to Hadoop [13], these applications can test various cluster characteristics, such as network transfer, storage reliability, and cluster availability. Four applications were selected to obtain performance measures from the Hadoop cluster. For example, *CPU utilization time* is a measure that varies according to values given to configuration parameters, such as the number of files to process and the amount of information to process. The viewpoint taken for the selection of the above applications is that it is possible to use the same types of parameters to configure each cluster machine.

Below is a brief description of the applications used in the experiments:

1. TestDFSIO. This is a MapReduce application that reads and writes the HDFS test. It executes tasks to test the HDFS to discover performance bottlenecks in the network; to test the hardware, the OS, and the Hadoop setup of the cluster machines (particularly the NameNode and the DataNodes); and to determine how fast the cluster is in terms of I/O.
2. TeraSort. The goal of this application is to sort large amounts of data as fast as possible. It is a benchmark application that combines HDFS testing as well as testing the MapReduce layers of a Hadoop cluster.
3. MapRed Reliability. This is a program that tests the reliability of the MapReduce framework by injecting faults/failures into the Map and Reduce stages.
4. MapRedTest. This application loops a small job a number of times. This puts the focus on the MapReduce layer and its impact on the HDFS layer.

To develop the set of experiments, three parameters were selected, which can be set with different values for each type of application. These parameters are (1) number of files to process, (2) total number of bytes to process, and (3) the number of tasks to execute in the cluster. Also, a number of different MapReduce base measures were selected as possible quality objectives (objective function). These base measures are related to one or more of the performance terms identified in [6] and described below:

- *Job duration* (seconds): Total time for the job to be processed by the cluster, from its submission until it ends.
- *Job status*: Final job status, which can take one of the two nominal values: (1) job successfully processed or (2) job failed.
- *Number of successful Map tasks*: Number of Map tasks successfully processed.
- *Number of failed Map tasks*: Number of Map tasks that failed during processing.
- *Total number of Map tasks*: Sum of successful and unsuccessful Map tasks undertaken during the job processing.
- *Numbers of successful Reduce tasks*: Number of Reduce tasks that were successfully processed.
- *Number of failed Reduce tasks*: Number of Reduce tasks that failed during processing.
- *Total number of Reduce tasks*: Sum of successful and unsuccessful Reduce tasks undertaken during the job processing.
- *Number of combined tasks*: Tasks that run at times when a Map task is finished and intermediate result values need to be ordered to be processed by Reduce more efficiently. This is the total number of combined tasks when the Map tasks have ended and Reduce tasks begin.
- *Spilled records*: Number of records spilled to disk in all Map and Reduce tasks in the job.
- *Number of bytes read by the job*: Total number of bytes read by the Map and Reduce stages during job processing.
- *Number of bytes written by the job*: Total number of bytes written by the Map and Reduce stages during job processing.
- *Amount of physical memory used by the job* (in number of bytes): How much of the Random Access Memory (RAM) is being used in the cluster by the submitted job during its execution.
- *Amount of virtual memory used by the job* (in number of bytes): How much of the virtual memory (space on disk storage) is being used in the cluster by the submitted job during its execution.
- *CPU time per execution* (seconds). Time taken by the CPU (cluster) to process a MapReduce job (application).

15.4.2 Definition of Factors and Quality Objective

In a virtualized Cloud environment, Cloud providers implement clustering by slicing each physical machine into multiple virtual machines (VM) interconnected through virtual interfaces. Therefore, a virtual cluster with the features mentioned above was established to obtain representative results.

Fifty experiments were performed to test the Hadoop virtual cluster, varying the following parameters: number of files, bytes to process, and tasks to perform, which are parameters that can be modified in each application.

In each experiment, four different applications were executed, and performance results were recorded for their analysis. In this way, the set of experiments investigates the effect of the following variables (or control factors, according to Taguchi's terminology) on the output dependent variable:

- Number of files to be processed by the cluster
- Total number of bytes to be processed by the cluster
- Number of tasks into which to divide the job application

According to Taguchi, quality is often referred to as conformance to the operating specifications of a system. To him, the quality objective (or dependent variable) determines the ideal function of the output that the system should show. In our experiment, the observed dependent variable is the following:

- CPU processing time per execution (seconds)

15.4.3 Experiment Development

According to the Hadoop documentation [13], the number of files and the amount of data to be processed by a Hadoop cluster will be determined by the number of processors (cores) available and their storage capacity. Also, the number of tasks to be processed by the cluster will be determined by the total number of processing units (cores) in the cluster. Based on the above premises and the configuration of our cluster, we have chosen two levels for each parameter in the experiment. We determine the different levels of each factor in the following way:

- Number of files to process:
  - Small set of files: Fewer than 10,000 files for level 1
  - Large set of files: 10,000 files or more for level 2
- Number of bytes to process: Determined by the storage capacity of the cluster:
  - Fewer than 10,000 MB to process for level 1 (a small amount of data to process)
  - 10,000 or more MB to process for level 2 (large amount of data to process)
- Number of tasks to create: According to the MapReduce framework [13], the number of tasks to be created to process a job will be determined by the number of processing units (cores) in the cluster and by the number of input files to process. Since our cluster has a total of ten cores, we decided to perform tests with:
  - Fewer than ten tasks for level 1
  - Ten or more tasks for level 2

Table 15.4 Factors and levels

Factor number	Factor name	Level 1	Level 2
1	Number of files to process	<10,000	≥10,000
2	Number of MB to process	<10,000	≥10,000
3	Number of tasks to create	<10	≥10

Table 15.5 Matrix of experiments

No. of experiments (*L*)	Number of files	Number of bytes (MB)	Number of tasks
1	<10,000	<10,000	<10
2	<10,000	≥10,000	≥10
3	≥10,000	<10,000	≥10
4	≥10,000	≥10,000	<10

Table 15.6 Trials, experiments, and resulting values

Trial	Experiment	Number of files	MB to process	Number of tasks	CPU time (s)
1	1	10	3	1	0.39
1	2	10	10,000	10	406.09
1	3	10,000	450	10	3.50
1	4	10,000	10,000	2	0.82
2	1	100	33	2	6.29
2	2	100	1,000	100	442.73
2	3	96,000	29	42	283.35
2	4	10,000,000	10,000,000	4	292.16
3	1	100	300	1	3.79
3	2	1,000	10,000	1,000	615.76
3	3	1,000,000	3,300	10	141.60
3	4	10,000,000	50,000	2	78.73

Table 15.4 presents a summary of the factors, levels, and values for this experiment.

Using Taguchi's experimental design method, selection of the appropriate OA is determined by the number of factors and levels to be examined. The resulting OA for this case study is L4 (presented in Table 15.2). The assignment of the various factors and values of this OA is shown in Table 15.5.

Table 15.5 shows the set of experiments to be carried out with different values for each parameter selected. For example, experiment no. 2 involves fewer than 10,000 files, the number of bytes to be processed is greater than or equal to 10,000 MB, and the number of tasks is greater than or equal to 10.

A total of 50 experiments were carried out by varying the parameter values. However, only 12 experiments met the requirements presented in Table 15.5. This set of 12 experiments was divided into three groups of four experiments each (called *trials*). The values and results of each experiment are presented in Table 15.6.

Taguchi's method defined the SNR used to measure robustness, which is the transformed form of the performance quality characteristic (output value) used to analyze the results. Since the objective of this experiment is to minimize the quality

Table 15.7 SNR results

Experiment	Number of files	MB to process	Number of tasks	CPU time trial 1	CPU time trial 2	CPU time trial 3	SNR
1	<10,000	<10,000	<10	0.39	6.29	3.79	0.0235
2	<10,000	≥10,000	≥10	406.09	442.73	615.76	1.2712
3	≥10,000	<10,000	≥10	3.50	283.35	141.60	−0.1497
4	≥10,000	≥10,000	<10	0.82	292.16	78.73	−0.4666

Table 15.8 Factor effect on the output objective

	Number of files	MB to process	Number of tasks
Average SNR at level 1	0.6473	−0.0631	−0.2216
Average SNR at level 2	−0.3082	0.4023	0.5607
Factor effect (difference)	0.9555	0.4654	0.7823
Rank	**1**	**3**	**2**

characteristic of the output (CPU time used per job execution), the SNR for the "the smaller the better" quality characteristic is given by formula 2, that is, (15.2)

The SNR result for each experiment is shown in Table 15.7.

According to Taguchi's method, the factor effect is equal to the difference between the highest average SNR and the lowest average SNR for each factor. This means that the larger the factor effect for a parameter, the larger the effect the variable has on the process or, in other words, the more significant the effect of the factor. Table 15.8 shows the factor effect for each variable studied in the experiment.

15.4.4 Analysis and Interpretation of Results

Based on the results in Table 15.8, we can observe the following:

- *Number of files* is the factor that has the most influence on the quality objective (CPU time) of the output observed, at 0.9555.
- *Number of tasks* is the second most influential factor, at 0.7823.
- *Number of MB to process* is the least influential factor in this case study, at 0.4654.

Figure 15.10 presents a graphical representation of the factor results and their levels.

To represent the optimal condition of the levels, also called the *optimal solution of the levels*, an analysis of SNR values is necessary in this experiment. Whether the aim is to minimize or maximize the quality characteristic (CPU time), it is always necessary to maximize the SNR parameter values. Consequently, the optimum level of a specific factor will be the highest value of its SNR. It can be seen that the optimum level for each factor is represented by the highest point in the graph (as presented in Fig. 15.10), that is, L1, L2, and L2, respectively.

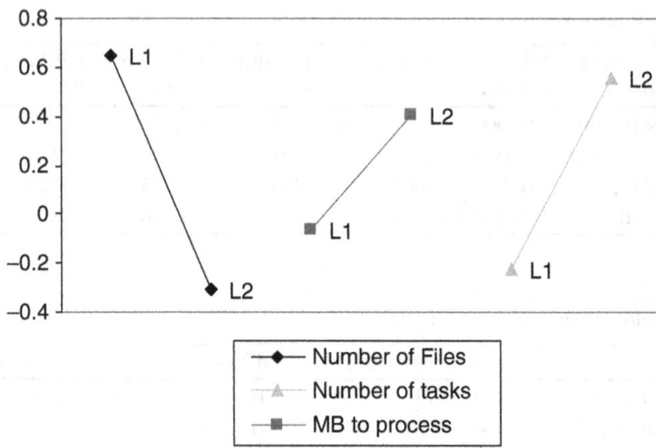

Fig. 15.10 Graphical representation of factors and their SNR levels

Using findings presented in Tables 15.5 and 15.8 and in Fig. 15.10, we can conclude that the optimum levels for the factors in this experiment based on our experimental configuration cluster are as follows:

- Number of files to process: The optimum level is fewer than 10,000 files (level 1).
- Total number of bytes to process: The optimum level is equal to 10,000 MB or more (level 2).
- Number of tasks to be created to divide the job: The optimum level is greater than or equal to 10 tasks or more per job (level 2).

15.5 Statistical Data Analysis

The analysis of variance (ANOVA) is a statistical technique usually used in the design and analysis of experiments. According to Trivedi [24], the purpose of applying the ANOVA technique to an experimental situation is to compare the effect of several factors applied simultaneously to the response variable (quality characteristic). It allows the effects of the controllable factors to be separated from those of uncontrolled variations. Table 15.9 presents the results of this analysis of the experimental factors.

As can be seen in the contribution column of Table 15.9, these results can be interpreted as follows (represented graphically in Fig. 15.11):

- *Number of files* is the factor that has the most influence (52 % of the contribution) on the processing time in this case study.
- *Number of tasks* is the factor that has the second greatest influence (35 % of the contribution) on the processing time.
- *Total number of bytes to process* is the factor with the least influence (12 % of the contribution) on the processing time in the cluster.

Table 15.9 Analysis of variance (ANOVA)

Factors	Degrees of freedom	Sum of squares (SS)	Variance (MS)	Contribution (%)	Variance ration (F)
No. of files	1	0.9130	0.9130	52	4
Total no. of bytes to process	1	0.2166	0.2166	12	
No. of tasks	1	0.6120	0.6120	35	3
Error	0	0.0000	0.0000		
Total	3	1.7416			
Error estimate	1	0.2166			

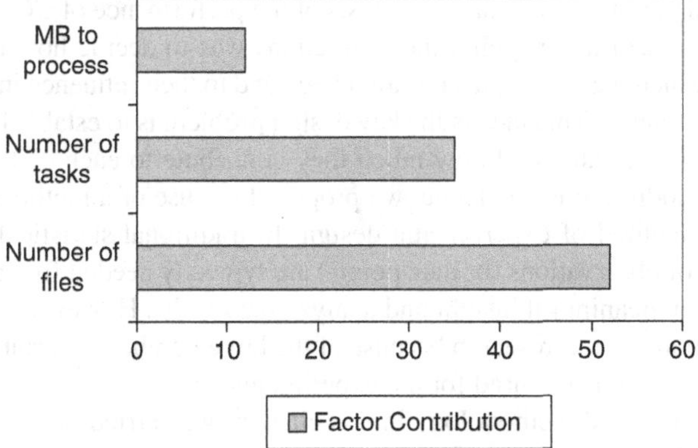

Fig. 15.11 Percentage contribution of factors

In addition, based on the column related to the variance ratio F shown in Table 15.9, we can conclude that:

- The factors *number of files* and *number of tasks* have the most dominant effect on the output variable, respectively.
- According to Taguchi's method, the minor factor contribution is taken as the error estimate. So, the *total number of bytes to process* factor is taken as the error estimate, since it corresponds to the smallest sum of squares.

The results of this case study show, based on both the graphical and statistical data analyses of the SNR, that the number of files to process by a MapReduce application in our cluster has the most influence, followed by the number of tasks into which to divide the job, and, finally, the number of bytes to process.

To summarize, when an application is developed in the MapReduce framework to be executed in this cluster, the factors mentioned above must be taken into account in order to improve the performance of the application and, more specifically, the output variable, which is CPU processing time.

15.6 Summary

Cloud Computing is an emerging technology designed to process very large amounts of data in a more efficient way, and one of its most important challenges is to deliver good performance to its end users. In this chapter, a methodology is proposed for determining the relationships among the CCA performance parameters. This methodology is based on the performance measurement framework for Cloud Computing systems [6], which defines a number of terms which are necessary to measure the performance of CCS using software quality concepts. The terminology and vocabulary associated with the proposed performance framework are aligned with many different international standards, such as ISO 25010, 9126, 19759, and 25030. In addition, the PMFCC defines several collection functions which are required to obtain derived measures and enable analysis of the performance of CCA. One of the challenges we faced in designing these functions was to decide how to determine the extent to which the base measures are related and to their influence in the analysis of CCA performance. This means the key design problem is to establish which base measures are interrelated and how much they contribute to each of the collection functions. To address this challenge, we proposed the use of a methodology based on Taguchi's method of experimental design. In traditional statistical methods, a large number of observations (or data points) are typically needed for each variable, in order to gain meaningful insight and analyze the results. However, this approach is not appropriate for our research because of the large number of variables involved and the time and effort required for the experiments.

Using the proposed methodology in this chapter, we carried out experiments to analyze the relationship between the configuration parameters of several Hadoop applications and their performance quality measures based on CPU processing time. We found that when an application is developed in the MapReduce programming model to be executed in our cluster, the number of files to process has the most influence, followed by the number of tasks into which to divide the job and, finally, the number of bytes to process. Thus, the factors mentioned above must be taken into account in order to improve the performance of the application and, more specifically, the performance of the output variable, which is CPU processing time. In conclusion, we found that there is a strong relationship between the number of files to be processed by a MapReduce application and the time required by the CPU to process a job.

Our next research activity will be to reproduce this experiment in a production environment, in order to verify these "trial group" results with greater validity. In addition, this early research work will serve as a basis for determining the most important relationships between the performance concepts defined in [6] and enable us to propose a robust model for CCA performance analysis.

Further research is needed on the design of measurement models and mechanisms to analyze the performance of a real Cloud Computing application, which could contribute to validating our proposed methodology. Such evaluation work will include performance concepts related to software, hardware, and networking.

These concepts will be mapped to the collection functions identified in the PMF previously developed to improve it. Therefore, we expect that it will be possible to propose a robust model in future research to analyze Hadoop cluster behavior in a real Cloud Computing environment, in order to enable the detection of possible anomalies that affect CCS and CCA performance.

References

1. Jin, H., Ibrahim, S., Bell, T., Qi, L., Cao, H., Wu, S., Shi, X.: Tools and technologies for building clouds. In: Antonopoulos, N., Gillam, L. (eds.) Cloud Computing: Principles, Systems and Applications. Computer Communications and Networks, pp. 3–20. Springer, London (2010)
2. Coulouris, G., Dollimore, J., Kindberg, T.: Distributed Systems Concepts and Design, 4th edn. Addison-Wesley/Pearson Education, Edinburgh (2005). ISBN 0-321-26354-5
3. ISO/IEC JTC 1 SC38: Study Group Report on Cloud Computing. International Organization for Standardization, Geneva (2011)
4. ISO/IEC Guide 99–12: International Vocabulary of Metrology – Basic and General Concepts and Associated Terms, VIM. International Organization for Standardization, Geneva (2007)
5. ISO/IEC 15939: Systems and Software Engineering – Measurement Process. International Organization for Standardization, Geneva (2007)
6. Bautista, L., Abran, A., April, A.: Design of a performance measurement framework for Cloud Computing. J. Softw. Eng. Appl. **5**(2), 69–75 (2012)
7. Burgess, M., Haugerud, H., Straumsnes, S.: Measuring system normality. ACM Trans. Comput. Syst. **20**(2), 125–160 (May 2002)
8. Rao, A., Upadhyay, R., Shah, N., Arlekar, S., Ragho-thamma, J., Rao, S.: Cluster performance forecasting using predictive modeling for virtual Beowulf clusters. In: Garg, V., Wattenhofer, R., Kothapalli, K. (eds.) ICDCN 2009. LNCS 5408, pp. 456–461. Springer, Berlin/Heidelberg (2009)
9. Smith, D., Guan, Q., Fu, S.: An anomaly detection framework for autonomic management of compute cloud systems. In: 2010 I.E. 34th Annual IEEE Computer Software and Applications Conference Workshops (COMPSACW), pp. 376–381. Seoul, South Korea (2010)
10. Jackson, K.R., Ramakrishnan, L., Muriki, K., Canon, S., Cholia, S., Shalf, J., Wasserman, H.J., Wright, N.J.: Performance analysis of high performance computing applications on the Amazon Web Services Cloud. In: 2010 I.E. Second International Conference on Proceeding of Cloud Computing Technology and Science (CloudCom), Indianapolis, Indiana, USA, November 2010, pp. 159–168. doi:10.1109/CloudCom.2010.69
11. Kramer, W., Shalf, J., Strohmaier, E.: The NERSC Sustained System Performance (SSP) Metric. Technical report. Lawrence Berkeley National Laboratory, Berkeley. Technical Information Center Oak Ridge Tennessee, Corporate Author: Lawrence Berkeley National Lab, Berkeley, CA. http://www.ntis.gov/search/product.aspx?ABBR=DE2006861982 (2005)
12. Mei, Y., Liu, L., Pu, X., Sivathanu, S.: Performance measurements and analysis of network I/O applications in Virtualized Cloud. In: Proceedings of the 2010 I.E. 3rd International Conference on Cloud Computing (CLOUD '10), Washington, DC. pp. 59–66 (2010). doi:10.1109/CLOUD.2010.74
13. Hadoop Apache Foundation: http://hadoop.apache.org/ (2010)
14. Dean, J., Ghemawat, S.: MapReduce: simplified data processing on large clusters. Commun. ACM **51**(1), 107–113 (2004)
15. Lin, J., Dyer, C.: Data-Intensive Text Processing with MapReduce. Manuscript of a book in the Morgan & Claypool Synthesis Lectures on Human Language Technologies, University of Maryland, College Park (2010)
16. Yahoo! Inc.: Managing a Hadoop Cluster. http://developer.yahoo.com/hadoop/tutorial/module7.html#configs (2010)

17. ISO/IEC 25030:2006(E): Software Engineering – Software Product Quality Requirements and Evaluation (SQuaRE) – Quality Requirements. International Organization for Standardization, Geneva (2006)
18. ISO/IEC 19759: Software Engineering – Guide to the Software Engineering Body of Knowledge (SWEBOK). International Organization for Standardization, Geneva (2005)
19. Jain, R.: The Art of Computer Systems Performance Analysis: Techniques for Experimental Design, Measurement, Simulation, and Modeling. Wiley-Interscience, New York (1991). ISBN 0471503361
20. ISO/IEC 25010:2010(E): Systems and Software Engineering – Systems and Software Product Quality Requirements and Evaluation (SQuaRE) – System and Software Quality Models. International Organization for Standardization, Geneva (2010)
21. ISO/IEC 9126–1:2001(E): Software Engineering – Product Quality – Part 1: Quality Model. International Organization for Standardization, Geneva (2001)
22. Taguchi, G., Chowdhury, S., Wu, Y.: Taguchi's Quality Engineering Handbook. Wiley, Hoboken (2005)
23. Cheikhi, L., Abran, A.: Investigation of the relationships between the software quality models of ISO 9126 Standard: An empirical study using the Taguchi method. Softw. Qual. Prof. **14**(2), 22–34 (2012)
24. Trivedi, K.S.: Probability and Statistics with Reliability, Queuing and Computer Science Applications, 2nd edn. Wiley, New York, (2002). ISBN 0471333417

Index

Z. Mahmood and S. Saeed (eds.), *Software Engineering Frameworks for the Cloud Computing Paradigm*, Computer Communications and Networks,
DOI 10.1007/978-1-4471-5031-2, © Springer-Verlag London 2013

Printed in the United States
By Bookmasters

Printed in the United States
By Bookmasters